Lecture Notes in Information Systems and Organisation

Volume 38

Lecture Notes in Information Systems and Organization—LNISO—is a series of scientific books that explore the current scenario of information systems, in particular IS and organization. The focus on the relationship between IT, IS and organization is the common thread of this collection, which aspires to provide scholars across the world with a point of reference and comparison in the study and research of information systems and organization. LNISO is the publication forum for the community of scholars investigating behavioral and design aspects of IS and organization. The series offers an integrated publication platform for high-quality conferences, symposia and workshops in this field. Materials are published upon a strictly controlled double blind peer review evaluation made by selected reviewers.

LNISO is abstracted/indexed in Scopus

More information about this series at http://www.springer.com/series/11237

Rocco Agrifoglio · Rita Lamboglia ·
Daniela Mancini · Francesca Ricciardi
Editors

Digital Business Transformation

Organizing, Managing and Controlling
in the Information Age

 Springer

Editors
Rocco Agrifoglio
Department of Business and Economics
Parthenope University of Naples
Naples, Italy

Rita Lamboglia
Department of Business and Economics
Parthenope University of Naples
Naples, Italy

Daniela Mancini
Faculty of Law
University of Teramo
Teramo, Italy

Francesca Ricciardi
Department of Management
University of Turin
Turin, Italy

ISSN 2195-4968   ISSN 2195-4976 (electronic)
Lecture Notes in Information Systems and Organisation
ISBN 978-3-030-47354-9   ISBN 978-3-030-47355-6 (eBook)
https://doi.org/10.1007/978-3-030-47355-6

This Springer imprint is published by the registered company Springer Nature Switzerland AG
The registered company address is: Gewerbestrasse 11, 6330 Cham, Switzerland

Introduction

Abstract This chapter introduces the theme of digital business transformation, which is an emerging research topic in the fields of information systems, organization, accounting, and management studies. This volume contains a collection of 21 research papers focusing on the relationships between technologies, processes, and firms with peculiar reference to the areas of organizing, managing, and controlling. It is divided into four parts, each of which is briefly described in what follows. This book provides critical insights into emerging topics of digital business transformation and offers a plurality of views that make this book particularly relevant for users, companies, scientists, and governments.

Keywords Digital transformation · Digital business model ·
Business administration process · Industry 4.0 · Smart organizations ·
Collaborative networked organizations

This book explores a range of emerging topics and critical linkages between information technology and digital business transformation and encourages debate and opens new avenues of inquiry in the fields of information systems, organization, accounting, and management studies.

The recent surge of interest in "digital transformation" is changing the business landscape and posing several both organizational and sectoral challenges [1]. The digital transformation of business is a change associated with the application of digital technology in all aspects of business and enables organizations to create new products, services and find more efficient ways of doing business. It concerns the changes digital technologies can bring about on some or all segments within an organization or on entire business models within a specific industry [1]. An interesting example of digital transformation (at different levels of analysis) is the music industry where the advent of the Internet, and related software developments, caused a deep shift in the mechanics of music distribution. Within music industry, first the CDs were replaced by downloads music, such as MP3 and MP4 files, and then streaming services of total recorded music were grown globally [2]. This means that technology transformation has caused deep changes on ways of music distribution, so influencing business strategies, organizational structures, and processes—even before the services provided—of music companies and the growth of a new sector, well known as "Artist and Label Services".

The digital transformation is happening within and across organizations of all types, in every industry, so resulting as a disruptive innovation enabling to break down barriers between things, people, and organizations, as well as to create more adaptive processes. In the information age, it is imperative for organizations to develop IT-related capabilities that allow leveraging the potential from digital technologies. Due to the pervasive effects of such transformation on processes, firms, and industries, both scholars and practitioners are interested in better understanding the key mechanisms behind digital business transformation emergence and evolution. The relevance of the phenomenon was also proved by a MIT Sloan Management Review Research Report [3] that points out how the 78% of corporate leaders and managers across various industries consider digital transformation achievement a critical asset for organizational performance. According to Berman [4], the digital transformation enables organizations to achieve various advantages in terms of (i) creating new business models; (ii) improving operational processes; and (iii) enhancing customer experiences. More recent research on the topic has revealed further advantages deriving from digital transformation in terms of key impacts, such as value creation, competitive advantage, and improved relationships, and transformed areas, such as employees, culture, and infrastructure (see Morakanyane, Grace and O'Reilly [5] for a systematic literature review).

Scholars and managers are looking for possible organizational and management solutions that allow easier management of the changes deriving from digital transformation [6]. It is no coincidence that several initiatives were conducted for exploring new digital technologies and for exploiting their benefits within all industries [76]. As Hess and colleagues pointed out, "integrating and exploiting new digital technologies is one of the biggest challenges that companies currently face. No sector or organization is immune to the effects of digital transformation. The market-changing potential of digital technologies is often wider than products, business processes, sales channels or supply chains -entire business models are being reshaped and frequently overturned" [1, p. 123].

The existing managerial literature agrees that organizations should establish management practices to handle the complex transformations triggered by digitalization [e.g., 1, 3]. In this regard, it is critical to formulate a digital transformation strategy that takes into account different options and elements enable to obtain advantages of digital transformation endeavors and to avoid the risk that such process does not meet the company needs. Consistent with previous research on the alignment between business strategies and IT strategies [8], it is critical that business leaders formulate and execute digital transformation strategies that focus on "the transformation of products, processes, and organizational aspects owing to new technologies" [3, p. 339]. Existing research on digital transformation issue has sought to consolidate IT strategies and business strategies into a comprehensive "digital business strategy" [8] that stresses the effects of digital technologies for firms [7, 9].

Furthermore, another research has investigated digitalization processes through controlling perspective [e.g., 10, 11, 12]. Like other business areas, digital transformation has also caused changes on transactional processes in the back-office activities. Digitalization is rapidly changing a company's value chain, so involving the various dimensions, such as the controlling that cannot avoid such impact. It is no coincidence that chief financial officers (CFOs) argue that ICT's standardization and automation are currently rated as most important challenges in the next years [12]. With reference to the effects of digital transformation on controlling, Schäffer and Weber [11] identified various challenges that will shape the work of controllers who are increasingly engaged in managing external and internal data with the help of efficient tools, such as the big data.

This volume contains a collection of research papers focusing on the relationships between technologies (e.g., digital platforms, AI, blockchain, etc.), processes (e.g., decision making, co-creation, financial, compliance, etc.), and organizations (e.g., smart organizations, digital ecosystems, Industry 4.0, collaborative networked organizations, etc.) with peculiar reference to the areas of organizing, managing, and controlling. It also provides critical insights into emerging topics of digital business transformation and offers a plurality of views that make this book particularly relevant for users, companies, scientists, and governments.

The volume is divided into four parts, each one focused on a specific theme such as (i) "Digitization and Business Model Transformation", (ii) "Digitization, Accounting, Controlling, and Reporting" (iii) "ICT, Organizational Processes, and New Ways to Work and Interact via Internet", and (iv) "Digital Ecosystems for Business Innovation and Digital Transformation". The content of the book is based on a selection of the best papers (original double-blind peer-reviewed contributions) presented at the annual conference of the Italian Chapter of AIS which took place in Napoli, Italy, in September 2019.

Digitization and Business Model Transformation

The first part of the book includes papers that analyze the impact that digital technologies produce on business models transformation.

In the era of digital transformation, companies are seeking new opportunities to reshaping their business model and to transform their operations, in the order of greater customer interaction and collaboration and to gain competitive advantage through differentiation strategies. Recent studies show how companies with a cohesive plan for integrating the digital and physical components of operations can successfully transform their business models and are able to optimize all elements of the value chain satisfying the need of their stakeholders.

Businesses aiming to generate new stakeholders value propositions by transforming their operating models need to develop also new capabilities. Foremost among capabilities is that companies must constantly explore the best new ways to capture revenue, structure enterprise activities, and stake a position in new or existing industries. Another key competency is finding new ways to engage customers and communities. This requires interaction with stakeholders across every phase of business activity—not just sales, marketing and service, but also product design, supply chain management, human resources, IT, and finance. Engaging with customers at every point where value is created is what differentiates a customer-centered business from one that simply targets customers well. Stakeholders interaction in all these areas often leads to open collaboration that accelerates innovation using online communities.

As summarized below, the papers presented in this part of the book consider the impacts that the application of digital transformation produces in different business model's elements: financial, marketing, and administrative performance; portfolio management strategies; process and decision management; security risk and vulnerability in IT governance; decision-making practices; strategic decision; and competition.

Chapter "Impact of Artificial Intelligence on Firm Performance: Exploring the Mediating Effect of Process-Oriented Dynamic Capabilities" of Serge-Lopez Wamba-Taguimdje, Samuel Fosso Wamba, Jean Robert Kala Kamdjoug, and Chris Emmanuel Tchatchouang Wanko develops a research framework to integrate in a more inclusive and comprehensive approach the capabilities of artificial intelligence (AI) into organizations. The study is based on an in-depth review of 150 case studies and highlights the added value of AI capabilities in terms of financial, marketing, and administrative performance. The analysis also reveals that companies improve their performance when they use capabilities of AI to reconfigure their dynamic process-driven capabilities.

Chapter "Artificial Intelligence and Ethics in Portfolio Management" of Elena Beccalli, Viktor Elliot, and Francesco Virili aims to explore ethical dilemmas connected to the use of AI in portfolio management strategies and their managerial implications. To exploring these dilemmas, authors examine empirical evidence drawn from MDOTM, an innovative and successful young enterprise developing AI-driven investment strategies for financial market. The analysis reveals some simple managerial implications: Traditional economic incentives do not work to appropriately prevent ethical issues with AI programmers in financial portfolio management. Furthermore, AI-based investing is particularly crucial not only for the role and accountability of machine learning in decision making, but also for the fact that there is no specific regulation for AI in Europe.

Chapter "Putting Decision Mining into Context: A Literature Study" of Sam Leewis, Koen Smit, and Martijn Zoet conducts a literature analysis on the current state of decision mining, with the scope to discover the research gaps and where decision mining can be improved. The findings of the research show that the concepts used in the decision mining field and related fields are ambiguous and show overlap. Future research directions could increase the quality and maturity of decision mining research, by focusing more on decision mining research, a change is needed from a business process decision mining approach to a decision focused approach.

Chapter "Cloud Sourcing and Paradigm Shift in IT Governance: Evidence from the Financial Sector" by Niloofar Kazemargi and Paolo Spagnoletti conducts an exploratory case study in to large companies in the financial sector in order to demonstrate how security risk and vulnerabilities in digital resources in cloud reshape IT governance process and practices. The study shows that cloud adoption alters the locus and scope of IT governance which consequently compels organizations to rethink their control mechanisms to mitigate security risks.

Chapter "Data-Imagined Decision Making in Organizations: Do Visualization Tools Run in the Family?" of Angela Locoro and Aurelio Ravarini proposes an exploratory analysis of decision-making model and data visualization characteristics, in order to extract a set of common aspects of decision making and to configure a set of connections between them and data visualization tools features. Authors demonstrate how these connections may serve to improve the current decision routines in the enterprises.

The chapter of Niloofar Kazemargi and Paolo Spagnoletti entitled "IT Investment Decisions in Industry 4.0: Evidences from SMEs" focuses on a propensity of SMEs in IT investment in an industry 4.0 context. In order to achieve this scope, authors analyze the responses of 1889 Italian SMEs to government policies designed to facilitate SMEs in adopting technologies for Industry 4.0. The study contributes to the literature highlighting the importance of IT investments strategic decision in Industry 4.0.

Chapter "Creating a New Innovation Orientation Through Idea Competitions" of Hanne Westh Nicolajsen and Ada Scupola conducts an in-depth case study of the implementation of an idea competition in a consulting company. Based on 27 interviews with company managers as well as users and users of the idea competition, the case shows how the implementation of the idea competition in the company has changed the innovation orientation of the company along several dimensions including creativity and empowerment, innovation infrastructure, innovation influence, and innovation intention.

Digitization, Accounting, Controlling, and Reporting

The second part of the book collects papers that analyze the link between digital technologies and business administration processes. Even if those kinds of technologies have been studied in several business areas, as commercial function, marketing, organization, and human resources management, little investigations are developed in accounting, control, and reporting fields. Researcher asks for more enquiries to help companies to face several questions regarding business administration: Why they have to implement or to not implement digital technologies to manage administrative and control processes considering opportunities and challenges; How they can implement digital technologies to better manage administrative processes in terms of cost savings, efficiency, quality, etc.; What are the impacts of those technologies on accuracy and effectiveness of accounting and reporting; and so on.

This part includes paper discussing implications of blockchain and electronic invoice.

Chapter "Accounting Information Systems: The Scope of Blockchain Accounting" of Iacopo Ennio Inghirami develops some reflections and considerations around the impacts of blockchain technology on accounting and accounting information systems and gaps in current research. The author, underlining that currently research works mainly focused on a technical view of blockchain, calls for investigation on accounting implications of this type of technology. Finally, the relevance of a distributed ledger and condition for the adoption are highlighted.

Chapter "Understanding Blockchain Adoption in Italian Firms" of Adele Caldarelli, Luca Ferri, Gianluca Ginesti, and Rosanna Spanò investigates factors affecting people intention to use blockchain adopting a quantitative analysis on 267 Italian information systems practitioners and entrepreneurs and the Unified Theory of Acceptance and Use of Technology (UTAUT). Findings show that the intention to use blockchain technologies, particularly in accounting practices, is positively affected by performance expectancy and social influence blockchain, conversely experience has a negative effect.

Chapter "Improving Invoice Allocation in Accounting—An Account Recommender Case Study Applying Machine Learning" of Markus Esswein, Joerg H. Mayer, Diana Sedneva, Daniel Pagels, and Jean-Paul Albers focuses on the use of machine learning in classifying and codifying invoices to recommend the most effective and accurate general ledger account. This paper highlights two very relevant needs of companies, which are approaching to digital finance transformation, and answers to two important calls for research: (a) understanding opportunities and challenges of digitization considering the implementation of different kinds of technologies at different type of accounting processes; (b) comprehending how digital technologies could be implemented to ameliorate processes. The article designs an algorithm based on machine learning, able to automatically classify invoices without an order, and defines a guideline to help companies in the implementation phase.

Finally, the contribution "Performance-Based Funding in the Italian Higher Education: A Critical Analysis" of Alberto Ezza, Nicoletta Fadda, Gianfranco Pischedda, and Ludovico Marinò is a theoretical paper, which aims at critically analyzing the funding mechanisms of Italian Higher Education System. The paper highlights criticalities of the funding systems and the related effects that influence the strategic choices and consequent actions taken by universities to achieve a higher level of performance and, so, more funds.

People, Organizations, and New Ways of Working in the Information Age

The third part of the book analyzes the effects of digital transformation on users' attitudes and behaviors, organizational processes, and structures, as well as on the new ways to organize work inside and across organizations. The relationships between digital transformation, people, and organizations are an emerging topic in managerial literature and information systems (IS) research. While the effects of digital transformation on business models and on industrial changes are well noted in the managerial literature—and business management in particular—less attention has been given to organization's capability to manage such constant (or disruptive) revolution. It is interesting to note how managers design organizational processes and new of working inside and across organizations—respect than traditional work—in order to manage digital transformation.

The third part of this book collects various contributions on topic that are illustrated below.

Chapter "Organizational Impacts on Sustainability of Industry 4.0: A Systematic Literature Review from Empirical Case Studies" of Emanuele Gabriel Margherita and Alessio Maria Braccini focuses on the organizational impacts on sustainability of Industry 4.0. Authors conducted a systematic literature review of empirical case studies from Industry 4.0 context in order to understanding the organizational impacts on sustainability that was measured through three dimensions, such as economic, social, and environment. Findings have shown that the economic dimension is prominent in the literature, while little attention has been paid on organizational impacts on social and environmental dimensions.

The chapter of Giovanna Morelli, Cesare Pozzi, and Antonia R. Guerrieri entitled "Industry 4.0 and the Global Digitalised Production. Structural Changes in Manufacturing" investigates the impact of Industry 4.0 on the Italian SMEs operating in the manufacturing sector and the effects of technology on work and organizations with respect to SMEs and networks. Authors remarked that Industry 4.0 could be an effective driving force for networking SMEs, despite the employees in manufacturing sector were reduced.

The chapter of Claudia Dossena and Francesca Mochi entitled "Managing Online Communities and E-WOM: Prosumers' Characteristics and Behaviors in the Food Service Sector" investigates the prosumers' use of social media in choosing a restaurant and reviewing it online. It aims to understand if prosumers' characteristics influence the social media's perception and usage in terms of information, writing feedbacks, and trust online reviews. Findings have shown that social media usage—gathering information and experience reviewing—depending on how many times they go to the restaurant. Moreover, findings have also shown that prosumers that have an "explorative" behavior (i.e., trying new restaurants) use social media respect than prosumers with a "loyal" behavior (i.e., staying by a familiar restaurant).

The chapter of Ronald Van den Heuvel, Rogier Van de Wetering, Rik Bos, and Jos Trienekens entitled "Identification of IT-Needs to Cope with Dynamism in Collaborative Networked Organizations—A Case Study" focuses on the need for IT systems to overcome (or to react) to the network dynamics that a collaborative networked organization encounters. Using via a systematic literature review, authors developed a framework to gather results in the case study—15 interviews over 12 organizations that participate in the CNOs. This chapter provides insight into the IT needs used to cope with the dynamics a CNO encounters.

The chapter of Haruka Ikegami and Junichi Iijima entitled "Unwrapping Efforts and Difficulties of Enterprises for Digital Transformation" aims to investigate the efforts and difficulties of enterprises when digital transformation occurs. Such research identified three key topics that enterprises should consider for digital transformation, such as (1) customer experience, (2) strategic intent, and (3) ecosystem.

Finally, the chapter of Mina Haghshenas and Thomas Østerlie entitled "Coordinating Innovation in Digital Infrastructure: The Case of Transforming Offshore Project Delivery" investigates how digital innovation influences project delivery in the offshore construction industry. Based on a case study, such research emphasizes how digital innovation unfolds within the confines of existing industrial, organizational, and technological structures. It is also shown that digital innovation network dynamics emerge through the interplay between generativity and installed base.

Digital Ecosystems for Business Innovation and Digital Transformation

The fourth part of the book analyzes the research topic of digital ecosystems, with peculiar reference to business innovation and digital transformation inside and across organizations. Digital ecosystem is a critical and current topic in managerial literature and IS research. It is a dynamic integration of people, processes, companies, and data aimed at enabling organizations to drive transformation and improve business outcomes. It should be noted that when digital transformation occurs, organizations with limited resources and competencies look at outside their industry boundaries to seek new ways of supporting their business through cooperative and interactive relationships with partners. In this regard, organizations and business processes need to be integrated through a digital ecosystem strategy, as well as new systems and tools should be embraced for delivering value to stakeholders through increased flow of data and shared insights.

The fourth part of this book collects various contributions on topic that are illustrated below.

The chapter of Claudia Dossena and Francesca Mochi entitled "Organizational Capabilities for Social Media Management: How Restaurant Managers Approach to the Digital Ecosystem" is an explorative research on how restaurant managers approach to (an manage) the digital ecosystem, as well on the organizational competences required to effectively manage the digital ecosystem. Findings of the explorative research have shown that restaurant managers' and owners' approach to digital ecosystems in a variety of ways (i.e., via Web, social media, and restaurant website), as well as they identified various organizational competences required to effectively manage the digital ecosystem.

The chapter of Giovanni Vaia, William DeLone, Daria Arkhipova, and Anna Moretti entitled "Achieving Trust, Relational Governance and Innovation in Information Technology Outsourcing Through Digital Collaboration" focuses on the theme of information technology outsourcing. In particular, it aims to explore how the adoption of a digital collaboration tool influenced trust and the effectiveness of relational governance in an IT outsourcing relationship. Using a case study qualitative research method, they have shown that digital collaboration can affect trust before and during the engagement phase of the IT outsourcing process.

The chapter of Roberta Cuel and Gabriella Maria Cangelosi entitled "In Vino Veritas? Blockchain Preliminary Effects on Italian Wine SMEs" focuses on the topic of the adoption of blockchain in the Italian wine industry. This research aims to explore the effects of blockchain on the complex inter-organizational supply chain systems SMEs are engaged in. Results of a pilot study have enabled to identify the advantages or drawbacks managers perceive during the experimentation of blockchain in the wine industry.

Finally, the chapter of Nunzio Casalino, Tommaso Saso, Barbara Borin, Enrica Massella, and Flavia Lancioni entitled "Digital Competences for Civil Servants and Digital Ecosystems for More Effective Working Processes in Public Organizations" focuses on the adoption of digital technologies in the European public sector. It presents the preliminary results of a research that aims at analyzing the adoption of digital technologies in the European public sector, with peculiar reference to the motivations leading adoption, the kind of technologies adopted, and the value chain's activities where the new technologies investments are focused.

Rocco Agrifoglio
rocco.agrifoglio@uniparthenope.it
Rita Lamboglia
rita.lamboglia@uniparthenope.it
Daniela Mancini
dmancini@unite.it
Francesca Ricciardi
francesca.ricciardi@unito.it

References

1. Hess, T., Matt, C., Benlian, A., & Wiesböck, F. (2016). Options for formulating a digital transformation strategy. *MIS Quarterly Executive, 15*(2), 123–139.
2. Günther, P. (2016). *Transformation of the recorded music industry to the digital age: A review of technology-driven changes in the EU copyright framework focusing on their effect on digital music markets.* Hanken School of Economics.
3. Fitzgerald, M., Kruschwitz, N., Bonnet, D., & Welch, M. (2014). Embracing digital technology: A new strategic imperative. *MIT Sloan Management Review, 55*(2), 1.
4. Berman, S. J., (2012). Digital transformation: Opportunities to create new business models. *Strategy & Leadership, 40*(2), 16–24.
5. Morakanyane, R., Grace, A. A., & O'Reilly, P. (2017, June). Conceptualizing digital transformation in business organizations: A systematic review of literature. In *Bled eConference* (p. 21).
6. Nambisan, S., Wright, M., Feldman, M., & Western, C. (2019). The digital transformation of innovation and entrepreneurship: Progress, challenges and key themes. *Research Policy, 48*(8).
7. Matt, C., Hess, T., & Benlian, A. (2015). Digital transformation strategies. *Business & Information Systems Engineering, 57*(5), 339–343.
8. Henderson, J. C., & Venkatraman, N. (1993). Strategic alignment: leveraging information technology for transforming organizations. *IBM Systems Journal, 32*(1):4–16.
9. Bharadwaj, A., El Sawy, O. A., Pavlou, P. A., Venkatraman, N. (2013). Digital business strategy: Toward a next generation of insights. *MIS Quarterly, 37*(2):471–482.
10. Parviainen, P., Tihinen, M., Kääriäinen, J., & Teppola, S. (2017). Tackling the digitalization challenge: how to benefit from digitalization in practice. *International Journal of Information Systems and Project Management, 5*(1), 63–77.
11. Schäffer, U., & Weber, J. (2019). Digitalization will radically change controlling as we know it. In *Behavioral controlling* (pp. 159–168). Wiesbaden: Springer Gabler.
12. Kamphake, A. G. (2020). Digitalization in controlling. In *Digitization in controlling* (pp. 3–25). Wiesbaden: Springer Gabler.

Contents

**People, Organizations, and New Ways of Working
in the Information Age**

**Digital Ecosystems for Business Innovation and Digital
Transformation**

Digitization and Business Model Transformation

Impact of Artificial Intelligence on Firm Performance: Exploring the Mediating Effect of Process-Oriented Dynamic Capabilities

Serge-Lopez Wamba-Taguimdje, Samuel Fosso Wamba,
Jean Robert Kala Kamdjoug, and Chris Emmanuel Tchatchouang Wanko

Abstract Organizations still dependent on information technology innovation have already adopted the in AI subfields and techniques to adapt or disrupt the market while improvement their performance. Other research has examined the relationship between computing capabilities and organizational performance, with a mediating effect on dynamic process-driven capabilities. We extend this flow of literature and examine the same relationship by taking into account the capabilities of artificial intelligence (AI). Our conceptual framework is based on the paradox of productivity, resource-based view and dynamic capabilities. We relied on an in-depth review of 150 case studies collected on websites related to the integration of AI into organizations. Our study highlights the added value of AI capabilities, in terms of organizational performance, with a focus on improving organizational performance (financial, marketing, and administrative). Our analyses also show that companies improve their performance when they use capabilities of AI to reconfigure their dynamic process-oriented capabilities.

Keywords Capabilities of AI · Process-Oriented Dynamic Capabilities · Firm Performance

S.-L. Wamba-Taguimdje (✉) · J. R. K. Kamdjoug · C. E. T. Wanko
Catholic University of Central Africa, GRIAGES, BP 11,628, Yaoundé, Cameroon
e-mail: lopezserge501@gmail.com

J. R. K. Kamdjoug
e-mail: jrkala@gmail.com

C. E. T. Wanko
e-mail: chrisemmanuelt@gmail.com

S. F. Wamba
Toulouse Business School, Midi-Pyérées, France
e-mail: s.fosso-wamba@tbs-education.fr
URL: http://www.fossowambasamuel.com

R. Agrifoglio et al. (eds.), *Digital Business Transformation*, Lecture Notes in Information Systems and Organisation 38, https://doi.org/10.1007/978-3-030-47355-6_1

1 Introduction

The year 1974 saw the advent of the first expert systems; the most famous being MYCIN [1, 2] designed to assist in the diagnosis and treatment of bacterial blood diseases. At the middle of the twentieth Century, McCulloch and Pitts worked on artificial neurons simulating the laws of logic [3]. Turing carried out research on a universal machine that is theoretically able to solve all problems by manipulating symbols [4, 5], and this was the starting point of investigations on an artificial system that might be as good as a human mind. In line with the fast-paced sophistication of technologies, Garry Kasparov, a world chess champion, was beaten in 1996 by the Deep Blue software of IBM [6, 7]. In 1967, the first program of chess with satisfactory performances was created by Greenblatt to beat a player. This significant event demonstrates that AI performs better than men in specific areas, and the proven efficiency of expert systems leads to increased sales of hardware using this system [8]. AI begins to democratize to appear in large companies such as Google, Amazon, IBM.

The digital revolution has produced its effects and is translating the modern world into data. Data is no longer confined to data centers. With sensors of any kind, any object, or environment of objects, becomes capable of measuring and producing data. The impact of the industrial and digital revolutions has undoubtedly had a financial impact on virtually every aspect of our society, life, business and employment. In fact, digital transformation is changing business models and organizational culture. It has an impact on its functioning, its organization, its teams, but more generally on its governance [6, 7]. Thus, those who are at the end of the digital transition see a new turning point: the one of intelligent transition. In the same way as digital technology transformation, which has had a transversal impact on organization, will involve all the functions of organizations during its operationalization [9, 10]. The major advances in AI are based on three main factors: technological, economic and human [9, 10]. Despite its relatively low level of integration, AI helps to modify organizational processes, improve process and organizational performance, improve cost reduction and track activities through its informational, automational and transformational effects [9, 11]. With an average fundraising of $22 million per company, the total amount raised by AI start-ups reached a record $10 billion. With a contribution of $15.7 trillion to the global economy in 2030, AI is positioning itself as a catalyst for organizational growth [11]. According to analysts TRACTICA and GARTNER, the potential market for AI is expected to reach $11.1 billion by 2024, up from $200 million in 2015 [12, 13]. The AI is expected to generate nearly $90 billion in profits by 2025, compared to just over $11.3 billion this year [12, 13]. The exponential growth in the power of processing processes, combined with an unprecedented increase in available data, has made AI extremely attractive to organizations. Its deployment requires significant investments in infrastructure, training, integration and maintenance, in addition to an increase in IT budgets, particularly for hardware and data storage including the cloud [14].

Our study proposes to analyze the effects of AI capabilities on improving performance at the organizational level and their intermediate effects process-oriented dynamic capabilities (PDCs) within organizations. Do AI capabilities influence organizational performance? What is the mediating impact of dynamic process-driven capabilities on the relationship between AI capabilities and organizational performance? We will first develop and justify our hypotheses based on a research model that will be tested. But before then, we will describe our method of data collection and techniques as well as the tools used for analysis. Recommendations will be formulated following discussion of results.

2 Literature Review

Information technology (IT) has become ubiquitous in professional activities, leading to profound transformation at the organizational level and affecting all core processes and operations [15]. When integrated with the ecosystem of businesses, ITs can produce a significant impact, especially on the relationship between the company and its customers, prospects, and partners. They also play a key role in the way companies' processes and operations will evolve. Artificial intelligence (AI) remains the most spectacular IT, as it has gone through an unequaled development over the last decades [10, 15]. Since 1977, one of the main lines of research in information systems has focused on the issue of IT evaluation. Studying the relationship between IT and organizational performance is a permanent concern, although it has evolved over the years. Today, IA has experienced unprecedented innovations, thus giving rise to more scientific studies aiming to analyze their influence on organizational performance through several theoretical models and foundations: Paradox Productivity, Process-Oriented Perspective, Resource-Based View theory, and Dynamic Capabilities.

2.1 Paradox Productivity

This theory stems from a well-known statement by R. Solow: *"The age of the computer has arrived everywhere, except in productivity statistics"*. For this author, the technological evolution experienced during the last decades coincided with a significant slowdown in the rate of productivity growth in organizations [16]. Analyzing the relationship between IT equipment rate and productivity through the estimation of Cobb-Douglas traditional production functions, they were able to demonstrate that organizations with higher IT equipment/infrastructure ratios have an apparent productivity of higher work, and that organizations using more intensely IT users are not penalized in relation to others in terms of productivity [15, 17]. Yet, the measured productivity growth has halved over the last decade. Systems using artificial intelligence match or surpass human performance in a growing number of areas. As they take advantage of rapid advances in other technologies, they potentially serve as catalysts that can significantly increase the productivity and performance of organizations [15, 17].

2.2 Process-Oriented Perspective

Identifying the potential impact/influence of IT requires a "process-oriented" model that accurately measures input (IT investment) and output (the outcome) while making it possible to explicitly explain the use of IT by organizations. For this purpose, Soh and Markus proposed a model that describes the relationship between IT and its organizational impacts in the form of a value-creating process [18]. It is composed of three types of processes, namely (i) the conversion process that turns IT investment into assets, (ii) the usage process that deploys, mobilizes and overpowers IT assets at the organizational level, and the competitive process that turns the use of IT into organizational performance [19]. The link between IT, organizational processes and organizational performance has lured the interest of other scholars, as they take into account the effect of the competitive environment. Thus, organizational processes consist of two categories: business processes and management processes. Each category is subdivided into an automation, information and transformational process [20].

2.3 Resource-Based View Theory

The organizations have resources (human resources, business resources and technological resources) which are valuable, rare, difficult to imitate, imperfectly substitutable and non-transferable, a subset of which enables them to establish a competitive position, competitive and privileged advantage, a source of superior performance, provided that they are protected against imitation and substitution [21, 22]. Bharadwaj [22] highlights the concept of information technology capacity, defined as the ability to mobilize IT-based resources in combination with other resources and capabilities. "IT capacity" is built on tangible resources, human resources and intangible resources [21, 22]. He demonstrated that IT capacity is positively associated with organizational performance.

2.4 Dynamic Capabilities

Dynamic capacity is conceptualized as "the potential of the organization to reconfigure, integrate and coordinate internal and external skills to deal with rapid turbulence in commercial environments" [23, 24]. To create, upgrade or transform organizational capabilities, the organization will use specific processes that implement and express dynamic capabilities. Organizational capacity is defined as the ability of the organization to carry out its productive activities efficiently and effectively by deploying, combining and coordinating its resources and skills through different value-creating processes, according to previously defined objectives [23, 24]. Individual skills determine, direct and support the dynamic capabilities of the organization [19]. They can be seen as a link between organizational resources and performance, such as a converter that turns resources into improved performance because of its valuable features. They can effectively use competitive combinations of resources to improve performance at the organizational and process level [23, 24].

3 Conceptual Model and Hypotheses

The previous theoretical models allowed us to highlight different constructs: artificial intelligence capabilities, intelligence management capacity, the expertise of the personnel in artificial intelligence, the flexibility of the infrastructure of artificial intelligence, process-level performance improvement, automationnal effect, informational effect, transformational effect, process-driven dynamic capabilities, organizational performance improvement, financial performance, marketing performance and administrative performance.

AI Capabilities (AICAP): are the organization's ability to create a set of organizational, personal and artificial intelligence resources for creating and capturing business value. Thus, artificial intelligence capabilities refer to an organization's ability to combine IT, AI techniques/technologies resources to quickly adapt to changing environments and maintain competitive advantage [15, 19, 22]. Based on previous research, we consider three types of artificial intelligence resources in our study: AI Management Capability, AI personal Expertise, and AI infrastructure Flexibility.

AI Management Capability (AIMC): It is the ability of an organization and its staff to administer or to model intelligent behavior in a computer or technology to create added value for the organization's sustainability. AI management capability potential is peculiar to strategic planning, strengthening relationships within and between companies, investment decision-making, coordination and control [19, 25].

AI personal Expertise (AIPE): It is defined as the professional skills and knowledge of AI-related technologies, business functions and relational (or interpersonal) domains required by the organization's staff for modeling and/or using intelligent behavior in a computer or technology to accomplish the tasks assigned to it [19, 25].

AI infrastructure Flexibility (AIIF): It refers to the composition of all technological assets (software, hardware and data, etc.), systems and their components, network and telecommunication installations and applications that are necessary for the implementation of an AI system capable of performing tasks [26, 27] The flexibility of deploying AI infrastructure for organizational operations allows the organization's staff to rapidly support various system components, and adapt to changing business conditions and business strategies, such as economic pressures, strategic alliances, acquisitions, global partnerships or mergers [26].

Process-Oriented Dynamic Capabilities (PDCs): they refer to the ability of a company to improve these organizational processes in order to reduce costs and optimize business intelligence. By integrating PDCs, the company should see the efficiency of these operational processes grow, increase its knowledge management and better align its resources with the company's vision [19].

The main objective of AI adoption by an organization is to solve a problem either at the process level or at the level of dynamic process-oriented capabilities. The, we can identify four IA capabilities: (1) modify organizational processes to improve integration, cost reduction, business intelligence, avoid ecosystem and business line hazards; (2) increase and optimize the effectiveness of business processes; (3) promote and improve the acquisition, assimilation of internal and external knowledge; (4) configuration/reconfiguration of resources, strategies and processes to align themselves with the organization's vision [9, 11, 15]. These AI capabilities positively associated with organizational performance improvement and process-oriented dynamic capabilities have been demonstrated in several IT-based industry sectors [19, 28, 29]. Therefore, we can enounce this hypothesis:

H1 *AI capability has a significant positive effect on process-oriented dynamic capabilities.*

In social sciences, an organization is a social group of interacting individuals with a collective purpose, but whose preferences, information, interests and knowledge may diverge. Then, an organization may be the result of regulated actions: a company, a public administration, a trade union, a political party, an association. Productivity paradox theory considers organizational performance in productivity sense. In this vein, it aims to measure the degree to which one or more factors of production (material factors consumed or intangible factors implemented) contribute to the variation in the final result of a transformation process [15, 17, 30–32].

Organizational Performance (PERF) represents the ability of the organization to achieve financial/market/administrative performance that allows it to maintain its position in competitive environments [19, 20, 33–35].

Financial Performance (FP): ability of the firm to attain financial gains. Profitability, cost cutting, labor savings and budget reductions [19, 20, 33–35].

Marketing Performance (MP): organizational direction to create value for the company's customers. Improved customer satisfaction, reduced prices, new products and services, combination of products and services, buyback rate, retention of new customers, number of new products/services launched [19, 20, 33–35].

Administrative Performance (AP): the firm's renewed control over resources, enhanced coordination among and within organizations. It is also viewed as an enhanced co-ordination among department's and management's control over firm's resources [19, 20, 33–35].

H2 *AI capability has a significant positive effect on performance improvement at the organizational level.*

H3 *Process-oriented dynamic capabilities have a significant positive effect on organizational performance.*

In nowadays literature, the examination of the effects of process-oriented dynamic capabilities, on how it improves organizational performance, has been limited to specific processes or technologies. In fact, these studies provided limited information on the role of process-oriented dynamic capability improvements as a mediator between the effects of IT capabilities on organizational performance improvements [19, 24, 29, 36–38]. We also argue in this study that process-oriented dynamic capabilities will mediate the relationship between AI capability and organizational performance (H4).

4 Research Methodology

We used a quantitative approach based on a number of case studies of organizations that adopted AI. Basically, a case study is the in-depth study of a particular situation rather than a broad statistical survey [39–41]. This method is used to refine a very large search field into an easily documentable subject. The research design of case studies is also useful for testing whether scientific theories and models work in the real world [39–41]. This method of study is particularly useful for testing theoretical models by using them in real-life situations [41–44]. A case study usually has several parts, including: (i) the context that answers the questions 'who', on which domain does the client work? What is his story? What are the members of the organization (the remarks on which are reported in the case study). This part highlights the capabilities of AI; (ii) the problem, which in this case is the challenge faced by the customer and solved through this provider. Here we see how the capabilities of AI come into play [45]; the answer provided, which is the solution provided to the client and which always take the view of the customer into account, as well as the angle by which the profit and the added value granted thanks to the supplier's intervention. This part highlights the benefits of AI at the level of PIOL and PDCs; and (iv) the results achieved, which are the concrete and tangible results achieved by the client, that is, quantified data, quantifiable, measurable and striking facts (e.g., in order to increase the turnover, attract more customers each month, ensure more efficient security measures). All figures/elements that prove that the action of the provider has been beneficial to the customer will have to be highlighted. PIOL is usually found in this part, which often includes the PDCs. It should be noted that all the cases studies considered here derived from several industrial sectors.

In this digital age, case studies are more easily collated and available for all kinds of analysis. Moreover, it is regularly observed that the primary data collected at a high price are often poorly or not sufficiently exploited, which is a kind of waste of resources. Therefore, the evaluator should also think about secondary data [46,

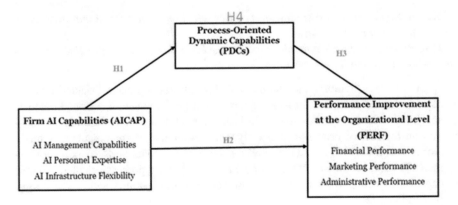

Fig. 1 Conceptual model

47]. These case studies provide verifiable facts, such as the contact details of the organizations, the personal contacts of the members involved in the AI integration process in their organizations, and excerpts from their interviews. The successful adoption of AI explained in these case studies and in the literature, allows us to support and consolidate the research elements at first. Second, allows us to propose and develop an in-depth analysis of each research proposal. So, we examined 150 archived cases that had adopted AI, all of which were drawn from the website of a leading vendor of AI techniques and technologies (Appendix).

For each identified case, the first author ensured the elements to be used to build the search pattern were available. Such elements included: AI management capabilities, AI personnel expertise, AI infrastructure flexibility, Process-Oriented Dynamic Capabilities, financial performance, marketing performance, and administrative performance (Fig. 1). Then, two investigators took on the data coding process and used a scale with values ranging from 1 to 4. The value 1 is assigned when the construct is not mentioned in the case. Value 2 corresponded to the lowest value, 4 the highest value and 3 the average value when a given construct is mentioned in the case study. The two (02) readers codified the case studies in a progressive manner. Before assigning a score to a construct, the reader performs an evaluation process. Subjective character is therefore not so much in the difficulty of measuring the quantities that describe an object, but rather in the overall perception of the case studies [48–50]. We started from the premise that subjectivity could influence the process of coding constructs [50, 51]. The overall process is done in three steps. First, the choice of case studies on the websites of AI solution providers was unanimously made by both readers. Second, each participant performed latent coding (transforming qualitative data into quantitative data). During this phase, it was to collect all the evidence for each score assigned to a construct in each case study. Third, both researchers provided the scores for each case study. All case studies that were incompatible in terms of scores for both readers were simply eliminated to avoid any subjectivity.

This was to ensure, first, that our codification process is universal and neutral. And secondly, what does not depend on a reader and is valid for both [52, 53].

Table 1 gives examples of the scores that we assigned to a few individuals in our sample. And Table 2 presents some of the results obtained after case coding. The link to each case study included in this study can be found in Appendix.

We consider that the AI capabilities of an organization correspond to the sum of AI management capabilities, AI personal expertise and AI infrastructure flexibility. The performance Improvement at organizational level is considered as the sum of administrative, marketing and financial performance. The missing value of

Table 1 Sample item ratings from the cases studies

Cases no.	Sample expects	Item rated	Assigned score
79	*"By mid-2018, TINE had saved 50% on its IT costs compared to its previous on-premises solution. The company has begun to drive faster development cycles since migrating to AWS and expects to increase its software development and delivery speed by 60%"*	Financial performance	4
19	*"Happy employees. The team likes the Slack integration for approving expenses, and they like the mobile app, which lets them just take a picture and submit immediately. People get paid back faster, which they appreciated"*	Process-oriented dynamics capabilities	3
79	*"We knew that we had collected and would continue collecting data that could be used for good, and we started with one simple question when evaluating the evolution of our organization and the technology we use: what benefits the farmer? We wanted to develop the next generation of tools for farmers to enable data analysis and decision making that could lead to happier cows and better quality milk, says Volden"*	AI management capabilities	3
1	*"Hani Nehaid, ADNOC's Geoscience Team Leader, and his team were considering using AI to augment and accelerate the thin section description process"*	Administrative performance	2
5	*"Coca-Cola Amatil gained 1.3% market share in the Assai Pacific region within five months"*	Financial performance	4

Table 2 Sample extract from the dataset

Case no.	AIMC	AIPE	AIIF	PDCs	FP	MP	AP	AICAP	PERF
1	4	3	3	4	4	2	2	10	8
2	4	4	4	2	3	4	4	12	11
3	4	3	4	3	4	4	2.5	11	10.5
4	4	1.5	3	3	3	3	3.5	8.5	9.5
5	3	2	3	4	4	4	3	8	11
6	4	3	3	3	3	4	4	10	11
7	3	3	3	3	3	4	3	9	10
8	4	3	4	3	4	2	2	11	8
9	4	3	3	4	3	4	1	10	8
10	4	2	2	1	3	3	2	8	8

AIMC AI management capabilities, *AIPE* AI personnel expertise, *AIIF* AI infrastructure flexibility, *PDCs* Process-oriented dynamic capabilities, *FP* Financial performance, *MP* Marketing performance, *AP* Administrative performance, *AICAP* Capabilities of AI, *PERF* Performance improvement at organizational level

construct is labelled as 1. The hypotheses are tested employing [54, 55]. Bootstrapping Procedure and for testing meditated effects. The computations were performed utilizing SMARTPLS software. This method allows us to generalize problems that were previously almost impossible to solve, such as the ability to simultaneously process several sets of explanatory and explained observed variables, the ability to analyze the relationships between unobservable theoretical variables and to take into account measurement errors, and the ability to confirm [56, 57]. The study of variability in factor analysis results (eigenvalues, eigenvectors) or variance estimation in complex surveys are carefully treated. To avoid underestimating variability (i.e., confidence intervals that tend to be too small or have insufficient coverage), we used a sample of 150 archived case studies such as Seddon and Calvert [58] and Bhattacharya and Seddon [59].

5 Results

From Fig. 2, we can see that all our proposed hypotheses are supported. More precisely, we can see that AICAP has a significant positive effect on PDCs ($\beta = 0.292, p < 0.001$) (H1 is supported). Also, AICAP has a direct significant positive effect on PERF ($\beta = 0.370, p < 0.001$) (H2 is supported), and PDCs have a positive significant effect on PERF ($\beta = 0.221, p < 0.01$) (H3 is supported). Moreover, the R2 of PERF is about 23, 30% and the one of PDCs is about 8.5%. Finally, as we can notice from Table 3, PDCs mediate the relationship between AICAP and PERF ($\beta = 0.065, p < 0.05$) (H4 is supported).

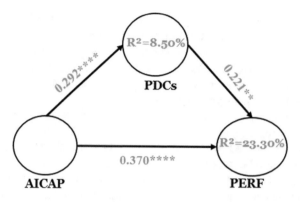

Fig. 2 Structural equation modeling estimation

Table 3 Meditated effects

	Original sample (O)	Sample mean (M)	Standard deviation (STDEV)	T statistics (|O/STDEV|)	P values
AICAP → PDCs → PERF	0.065	0.065	0.026	2.468	0.014

The careful analysis of our results shows that 39.25% (Table 4) of our sample uses what we have called generic AI, the term AI here referring to several types or parts of AI that are used for example to perform analysis, for automation of tasks, decision support or for redesigning a company's processes by integrating digital transformation. This trend may be justified by the fact that, in general, firms do not

Table 4 Classification of case studies according to AI technology used

Types of AI	Total	Percentage
AI	73	39.25
Machine learning	49	26.34
Deep learning	8	4.30
Cognitive	25	13.44
Cognitive cyber security	6	3.23
Natural language processing	15	8.06
Robotic personal assistant	2	1.08
Pattern/visual recognition	3	1.61
Chatbots	2	1.08
Neural networks	1	0.54
Virtual companion	2	1.08
Total	186[a]	100

[a]There is repetition of AI type: some cases have multiple types of AI

need a single solution or type of AI but a combination of these to make a greater benefit. This result is important in practice and for business leaders and providers of AI solutions. Indeed, in view of this result, the suppliers of AI solutions should put a particular emphasis on solutions that integrate a set of technology rather than providing a single type of technology to businesses. Business leaders should explore the benefits of using multi-type AI solutions.

Our study also reveals a propensity for companies to use Machine Learning. 26.34% of our sample reports on its use in companies. This attraction for machine learning can be explained by the fact that this type of technology reduces human intervention in the processes to a minimum. Moreover, with this technology, the system becomes more and more intelligent because it learns itself with use. Thus, the more machine learning is used, the more efficient the system becomes the more accurate and efficient the results and the less man intervention are needed to make it work.

6 Discussion

Contrary to previous studies that examined the influence and the impact of IT on specific business processes only, the conceptual framework proposed in this paper examines the cumulative effects of AI capabilities on improving process-oriented dynamic capabilities and the mediation effect of these between AICAP and organizational performance improvement. Furthermore, most of the previous research on AI has been limited to either financial measures, marketing measures or administrative measures as a key indicator of organizational performance, our research also applies to administrative and marketing performance to highlight the direct and indirect influence of AI on organizational performance. Therefore, the results of this research are new in terms of satisfying the need for leaders and managers to capture, control and understand the direct and indirect benefits of AI capabilities in their organizations. Our study also reveals that process-oriented dynamic capabilities contribute significantly to improving organizational performance (marketing performance, financial performance and administrative performance). This means that organizations must use AI to modify their business processes so that they can adapt to the ever-changing environment.

Our study has several theoretical implications for AICAP research to be considered in future research. First, it is one of the first studies to assess the direct impact of AICAP on firm performance and dynamic process-driven capabilities, and to assess the mediating effect of PDCs on the relationship between AICAP and PERF. Also, our study contributes to the research stream on business value of IT by confirming the importance of investing into complementary assets (e.g., dynamic process-driven capabilities). The result is in line with those obtained by [29, 60] in their studies on the influence of IT capabilities on business performance.

In addition to the theoretical implications, our study has several managerial implications. Firstly, the results suggest in particular that companies with improved PDCs will generate better performance and achieve a competitive advantage [19]. Secondly, our results show that the use reconfiguration of PDCs by companies in order to benefit from the advantages of AI allows them to improve their performance, the profitability of their investments in AI and thus have a competitive advantage. Our analyses are consistent with proposals by [14] suggesting to managers who invest in AI to develop capabilities to redefine their processes. Managers can therefore confidently discuss the role played by AI in implementing business strategies and improving business performance as suggested [61, 62].

7 Conclusion

We adopted a methodology based on secondary case studies to conduct this research. The choice of this approach is justified by the benefits it offers to the type of research based on secondary data (case studies). The quantitative approach allowed us to study the causal links between the different variables of the conceptual research model, to test the hypotheses/proposals constructed. The case studies collected were analysed qualitatively to highlight the elements related to each variable. Then, a coding process was applied to them in order to transform them into quantitative data on the basis of a four (04) level scale. The concept of AI consists in developing computer programs capable of reproducing and performing tasks achieved by human beings, and which require learning, organization, memory and reasoning. AI is the next computer and Cultural Revolution for businesses. In the continuity of their digital transition, companies are now preparing for the intelligent transition, which integrates both the Internet of Things and artificial intelligence. AI is obviously a business topic, and it is important for IT to be a support, or even a pilot of this new business model. The research framework adopted in our work integrates a more inclusive and comprehensive approach to better account for the intangible benefits of AI in organizations. In our study, we were able to appreciate the indirect effect that process-oriented dynamic capabilities have on AI capabilities. It is also apparent that firm's AI capabilities have a direct and significant influence on the firm's organizational performance. Our results show that firm's AI capabilities have a mediating effect on process-oriented dynamic capabilities, and that PERF is not the only indicator to examine the effects of AI capabilities, as we also have process-oriented dynamic capabilities. This indicates that organizations gain AI performance when using these features to reconfigure their process-oriented dynamic capabilities.

Appendix

Available upon request. Contact one of the authors to access the list of case studies, and the links.

References

1. Hopfield, J. J. (1984). Neurons with graded response have collective computational properties like those of two-state neurons. *Proceedings of the National Academy of Sciences, 81*(10), 3088–3092.
2. Shortliffe, E. H. (1974). *MYCIN: A rule-based computer program for advising physicians regarding antimicrobial therapy selection.* Stanford University California Department of Computer Science.
3. McCulloch, W. S., & Pitts, W. (1943). A logical calculus of the ideas immanent in nervous activity. *The Bulletin of Mathematical Biophysics, 5*(4), 115–133.
4. Turing, A. M. (1950). Can a machine think. *The world of Mathematics, 59*(236), 433–460.
5. Turing, A. M. (1937). On computable numbers, with an application to the Entscheidungs problem. *Proceedings of the London Mathematical Society, 2*(1), 230–265.
6. Aghion, P., Jones, B. F., & Jones, C. I. (2017). *Artificial intelligence and economic growth* (No. w23928). National Bureau of Economic Research.
7. Agrawal, A., Gans, J., & Goldfarb, A. (2018). The economics of artificial intelligence. *McKinsey Quarterly.*
8. Greenblatt, R. D., Eastlake, D. E., & Crocker, S. D. (1988). The Greenblatt chess program. In *Computer chess compendium* (pp 56–66). Springer.
9. von Krogh, G. (2018). artificial intelligence in organizations: New opportunities for phenomenon-based theorizing. *Academy of Management Discoveries.*
10. Russell, S. J., & Norvig, P. (2016). *Artificial intelligence: A modern approach.* Malaysia: Pearson Education Limited.
11. PWC. (2019). Sizing the prize: Exploiting the AI revolution, what's the real value of AI for your business and how can you capitalise? In *PwC's Global Artificial Intelligence Study.* Cited 2019, 31 Mar 2019. Available from: https://www.pwc.com/gx/en/issues/data-and-analytics/publicati ons/artificial-intelligence-study.html.
12. Scanner, V. (2019). *Artificial intelligence market report and data.* Cited 2019, 02 Aug 2019; Venture Scanner is your analyst and technology powered research firm. Gain deep insights with our carefully crafted executive summaries. Analyze our extensive data on startups, investors, and exits to complete your research. Available from: https://www.venturescanner.com/artifi cial-intelligence.
13. Microsoft. (2019). *Les 5 chiffres à absolument connaître sur l'IA.* Cited 2019, 02 Aug 2019. Available from: https://experiences.microsoft.fr/business/intelligence-artificielle-ia-business/ ia-chiffres-cles/.
14. Françoise Mercadal-Delasalles, K. V. (2017). *Les enjeux de mise en œuvre opérationnelle de l'intelligence artificielle dans les grandes entreprises* (Vol. 36). CIGREF, réussir le numérique ed. CIGREF, ed. l.i.a.d.l.g. entreprises. CIGREF, réussir le numérique.
15. Brynjolfsson, E., Rock, D., & Syverson, C. (2018). Artificial intelligence and the modern productivity paradox: A clash of expectations and statistics. In *The economics of artificial intelligence: An agenda.* University of Chicago Press.
16. Triplett, J. E. (1999). The Solow productivity paradox: What do computers do to productivity? *The Canadian Journal of Economics/Revue Canadienne d'Economique, 32*(2), 309–334.
17. Brynjolfsson, E. (1993). The productivity paradox of information technology: Review and assessment. *Communications of the ACM, 36*(12), 66–77.
18. Soh, C., & Markus, M. L. (1995). How IT creates business value: A process theory synthesis. In *ICIS 1995 Proceedings* (p 4).
19. Kim, G., et al. (2011). IT capabilities, process-oriented dynamic capabilities, and firm financial performance. *Journal of the Association for Information Systems, 12*(7), 487.
20. Mooney, J. G., Gurbaxani, V., & Kraemer, K. L. (1996). A process oriented framework for assessing the business value of information technology. *CM SIGMIS Database: The DATABASE for Advances in Information Systems, 27*(2), 68–81.
21. Peteraf, M. A., & Barney, J. B. (2003). Unraveling the resource-based tangle. *Managerial and decision economics., 24*(4), 309–323.

22. Bharadwaj, A. S. (2000). A resource-based perspective on information technology capability and firm performance: An empirical investigation. *Management Information Systems Quarterly, 24*(1), 169–196.
23. Teece, D. J., Pisano, G., & Shuen, A. (1997). Dynamic capabilities and strategic management. *Strategic Management Journal, 18*(7), 509–533.
24. Eriksson, T. (2014). Processes, antecedents and outcomes of dynamic capabilities. *Scandinavian Journal of Management, 30*(1), 65–82.
25. Hamet, P., & Tremblay, J. (2017). Artificial intelligence in medicine. *Metabolism, 69,* S36–S40.
26. Jorfi, S., Nor, K. M., & Najjar, L. (2011). The relationships between IT flexibility, IT-business strategic alignment, and IT capability. *International Journal of Managing Information Technology, 3*(1), 16–31.
27. Terry Anthony Byrd, D. E. T. (2000). Measuring the flexibility of information technology infrastructure: Exploratory analysis of a construct. *Journal of Management Information Systems, 17*(1), 167–208.
28. Tallon, P., & Kraemer, K.L. (1999). *A process-oriented assessment of the alignment of information systems and business strategy: Implications for IT business value.* Unpublished Ph.D. Dissertation (UC Irvine).
29. Wamba, S. F., et al. (2017). Big data analytics and firm performance: Effects of dynamic capabilities. *Journal of Business Research, 70,* 356–365.
30. David, P. A. (1989). The dynamo and the computer: An historical perspective on the modern productivity paradox. *The American Economic Review, 80*(2), 355–361.
31. Pilat, D. (2004). Le paradoxe de la productivité: l'apport des micro-données. *Revue Économique de l'OCDE, 38*(1), 41–73.
32. Wachter, R. M., & Howell, M. D. (2018). Resolving the productivity paradox of health information technology: A time for optimism. *JAMA, 320*(1), 25–26.
33. Dehning, B., Richardson, V. J., & Zmud, R. W. (2007). The financial performance effects of IT-based supply chain management systems in manufacturing firms. *Journal of Operations Management., 25*(4), 806–824.
34. Delen, D., Kuzey, C., & Uyar, A. (2013). Measuring firm performance using financial ratios: A decision tree approach. *Expert Systems with Applications., 40*(10), 3970–3983.
35. Ittner, C. D., et al. (2003). Performance implications of strategic performance measurement in financial services firms. *Accounting, Organizations and Society, 28*(7–8), 715–741.
36. Benner, M. J. (2009). Dynamic or static capabilities? Process management practices and response to technological change. *Journal of Product Innovation Management., 26*(5), 473–486.
37. Dosi, G., Nelson, R., & Winter, S. (2001). *The nature and dynamics of organizational capabilities.* OUP Oxford.
38. Teece, D. J. (2007). Explicating dynamic capabilities: The nature and microfoundations of (sustainable) enterprise performance. *Strategic Management Journal., 28*(13), 1319–1350.
39. Breslow, N. E., & Day, N. E. (1980). *Statistical methods in cancer research. Vol. 1. The analysis of case-control studies* (Vol. 1). Distributed for IARC by WHO, Geneva, Switzerland.
40. Merriam, S. B. (1998). *Qualitative research and case study applications in education. Revised and expanded from "Case Study Research in Education".* ERIC.
41. Rowley, J. (2002). Using case studies in research. *Management Research News, 25*(1), 16–27.
42. Siggelkow, N. (2007). Persuasion with case studies. *Academy of Management Journal, 50*(1), 20–24.
43. George, A. L., et al. (2005). *Case studies and theory development in the social sciences.* MIT Press.
44. Walsham, G. (1995). Interpretive case studies in IS research: Nature and method. *European Journal of Information Systems, 4*(2), 74–81.
45. Kelly, J. E. III, & Hamm, S. (2013). *Smart machines: IBM's Watson and the era of cognitive computing.* Columbia University Press.
46. Noël, J. G. (2009). *Isabelle Gaboury, Ph.D. Josée Guignard Noël, M.Sc. Éric Forgues, Ph.D. Louise Bouchard, Ph.D.*

47. Center, A. H., et al. (2008). *Public relations practices: Managerial case studies and problems.* Pearson Prentice Hall.
48. Madill, A., Jordan, A., & Shirley, C. (2000). Objectivity and reliability in qualitative analysis: Realist, contextualist and radical constructionist epistemologies. *British Journal of Psychology, 91*(1), 1–20.
49. Kracauer, S. J. (1952). The challenge of qualitative content analysis. *Public Opinion Quarterly,* 631–642.
50. Grbich, C. (2012). *Qualitative data analysis: An introduction* (2nd edn). London: Sage Publications.
51. Mauthner, N. S., & Doucet, A. J. S. (2003). Reflexive accounts and accounts of reflexivity in qualitative data analysis. *Sociology, 37*(3), 413–431.
52. Ratner, C. (2002, September). Subjectivity and objectivity in qualitative methodology. In *Forum Qualitative Sozialforschung/Forum: Qualitative Social Research, 3*(3).
53. Nonaka, I., & Toyama, R. (2005). The theory of the knowledge-creating firm: Subjectivity, objectivity and synthesis. *Industrial and Corporate Change., 14*(3), 419–436.
54. Lockwood, C. M., & MacKinnon, D. P. (1998, March) Bootstrapping the standard error of the mediated effect. In *Proceedings of the 23rd Annual Meeting of SAS Users Group International* (pp 997–1002). Citeseer.
55. Bollen, K. A., & Stine, R. A. (1992). Bootstrapping goodness-of-fit measures in structural equation models. *Sociological Methods and Research., 21*(2), 205–229.
56. Balambo, M. A., & Baz, J. (2014). De l'intérêt de l'analyse des modèles des équations structurelles par la méthode PLS dans les recherches sur les relations inter organisationnelles: Le cas des recherches en Logistique. In *7ème Edition du colloque international LOGISTIQUA.*
57. Chin, W. W. (1998). The partial least squares approach to structural equation modeling. *Modern Methods for Business Research, 295*(2), 295–336.
58. Seddon, P. B., Calvert, C., & Yang, S. J. M. Q. (2010). A multi-project model of key factors affecting organizational benefits from enterprise systems. *Management Information Systems Quarterly, 34*(2), 305–328.
59. Bhattacharya, P. J., Seddon, P. B., & Scheepers, R. (2010, December). Enabling strategic transformations with enterprise systems: Beyond operational efficiency. In *ICIS* (p 55).
60. Kala Kamdjoug, J. R., Nguegang Tewamba, H. J., & Fosso Wamba, S. (2018). IT capabilities, firm performance and the mediating role of ISRM: A case study from a developing country. *Business Process Management Journal.*
61. Balint, B., Forman, C., & Slaughter, S. (2010). Process standardization, task variability, and internal performance in IT business services outsourcing. *Working paper.* http://www.devsmith.umd.edu/doit/events/pdfs….
62. Guest, D. (2014). Employee engagement: A sceptical analysis. *Journal of Organizational Effectiveness: People and Performance, 1*(2), 141–156.

Artificial Intelligence and Ethics in Portfolio Management

Elena Beccalli, Viktor Elliot, and Francesco Virili

Abstract This work in progress aims to explore ethical dilemmas connected to the use of Artificial Intelligence (AI) in financial portfolio management, and their managerial implications. In old school quantitative investing, portfolio allocation decisions are typically based on a well-defined investment strategy. Financial portfolio managers devise and apply investment strategies to maximize expected returns for customers' portfolios. The introduction of AI-enhanced algorithms enables smart machines to automatically revise and update investment strategies, learning from the past. AI itself might produce significant effects on the gains and losses of the portfolio management strategies, raising ethical dilemmas connected with human versus machine responsibility, accountability, and risk. From the managerial point of view, a new dimension of performance measuring, competence evaluation and incentive allocation is required for managing AI software developers in this area. To explore such dilemmas, empirical evidence is drawn here from MDOTM, an innovative and successful young enterprise developing AI-driven investment strategies for financial markets.

Keywords Artificial intelligence · Agency theory · Finance

E. Beccalli
Universita' Cattolica del Sacro Cuore, Milan, Italy
e-mail: elena.beccalli@unicatt.it

V. Elliot
University of Gothenburg, Gothenburg, Sweden
e-mail: viktor.elliot@gu.se

F. Virili (✉)
University of Sassari, Sassari, Italy
e-mail: fvirili@uniss.it

R. Agrifoglio et al. (eds.), *Digital Business Transformation*, Lecture Notes in Information Systems and Organisation 38, https://doi.org/10.1007/978-3-030-47355-6_2

1 Introduction

There is clearly an ethical imperative implicit in the growing influence of automation in market behavior. The ethical dimension of market automation is therefore worthy of serious study. —Hurlburt et al. [19]

Discussions of ethics in financial markets and financial services generally focus on professional responsibilities of money managers, brokers, investment advisors, and traders, who are bound by the codes of ethics of their respective professions as well as by governmental regulation and exchange rules. In the new age, however, the intermediaries are automated agents in a global automated mechanism (not members of any profession). —Davis et al. [9]

The two quotes are illustrative of the new dimension that automation and artificial intelligence (AI) brings to financial investment. Compared to old school quantitative financial investing, where the human had to invent and create the investment strategy (see e.g. Ou and Penman [27]; Holthausen and Larcker [18]),[1] with AI the machine continuously adapts the investment strategy on the basis of market conditions and evolving performances; humans only focus on developing the right machine (i.e. to devise and eventually improve the machine learning process). Because of this change in the role of developers in financial modelling—rather than building a strategy, the coders develop a machine that will eventually come up with its own strategy—their work is not primarily evaluated in terms of performance (yield), but in terms of the robustness/persistence/consistency of the training process of the AI.

The ultimate goal in AI-based tech investing is to develop strategies that will adapt over time. But, who is accountable if the machine learning process eventually leads the investment strategy to bad performances? As reported below, the AI developer might face a trade-off between short term and long term portfolio performance, raising issues on how to understand, evaluate and control the ethical and technical correctness of the programmer's job and its contribution to value production.

For the purpose of this paper we build on agency theory to discuss and analyse the incentive conflicts that may arise among managers and AI developers when they work together to teach machines how to make investments. In particular, via the agency theory framework, we focus on how the ethical issues traditionally associated with investment practice can be adapted to take into account the peculiarities of AI-programming, so that we discuss ethical machine investments.

The rest of the paper is organized as follows. Section 2 provides the theoretical framework based on agency theory in the context of machine ethics. Section 3 describes the methodology used to collect and analyse the empirical evidence on the case of a AI-investment company. Preliminary results are discussed in Sect. 4. Section 5 concludes.

---

[1] These studies develop quantitative trading strategies based on statistical models designed to predict the sign of subsequent excess returns from accounting ratios.

2   Theoretical Framework

In the 2015 article entitled "The Irrelevance of Ethics", MacIntyre [22] argues that acquiring the moral virtues would undermine someone's capacity to be a good trader in the financial system. Yet, ethics is far from being irrelevant in finance. Accordingly, Rocchi et al. [30] explain the challenge at the heart of MacIntyre's [22] claims can be crystallized in the question, "under which conditions, if any, can a person be an effective trader and simultaneously live a worthy human life?" They conclude that there are realistic possibilities of integrity and growth in moral virtue for those who work in the financial sector, at least for those operating in a work environment minimally permissive toward virtue, provided they possess characters of integrity and genuine aptitude for the skills and attitudes required in their professional tasks.

Following on, a recent stream of literature focuses on unethical managerial decisions. At sociological level, de Bruin [9] argues that a key element of the global financial crisis of 2007–2008 was a failure of epistemic (i.e. knowledge-based) virtue, whilst Borg and Hooker [6] argue that this is fundamentally not an epistemic but a moral issue and change in the financial sector is best promoted by reconceiving of the relationship between financial institutions and the societies they serve. At organizational level, Rafeld et al. [29] investigate three major collusive rogue traders in banking (at National Australia Bank, JPMorgan with its London Whale) and the interest reference rate manipulation/LIBOR scandal. There have been instances of unauthorized acting in concert between traders, their supervisors and/or firms' decision makers and executives. They explore organizational misbehaviour theory through a descriptive model of organizational/structural, individual and group forces. Their model draws conclusions on how banks can set up behavioural risk management and internal control frameworks to mitigate potential collusive rogue trading. Azim and Kluvers [4], with a focus on corruption within organisations, explore the successful management of corruption by the Grameen Bank, a leading microfinance institute that operates in Bangladesh. Their study explores the impact of the anti-corruption structures, policies and processes implemented by Grameen Bank.

In what follows, we introduce machine ethics after which we discuss how the broader agency theory concepts can be linked to the field of machine ethics and used as a template to analyse how firms are creating different forms of incentive structures to promote ethics in AI-based investment algorithms.

2.1   AI and Machine Ethics

Artificial intelligence is an Information Systems area with antique roots in decades of interdisciplinary research. Being addressed to emulation of human beings, AI has been concerned with moral aspects since the very beginning, but in recent years moral issues are becoming of crucial importance in many different application fields [36]. In particular, AI "designers have both ethical and legal responsibilities to provide such justification for decisions that could result in death, financial loss, or denial of parole" [25].

The emerging field of machine ethics is concerned with giving machines ethical principles, or finding procedures for solving the ethical dilemmas that machines may encounter. This means enabling machines to function in an ethically responsible manner. Machine ethics links to autonomy, because by providing an ethical framework for machines we effectively allow them to operate autonomously without human intervention. There is an abundance of tasks that we would like to distribute to machines (because the jobs are dangerous, unpleasant, shortage of humans, or simply because the machine can do a better job), but no one would feel comfortable to give machines autonomy without ethical safeguards [3].

Machine ethics in investment is intrinsically linked to the algorithms that develop, suggest, or perform new investment strategies. According to Hill [16, p. 47] an algorithm is a mathematical construct with "a finite, abstract, effective, compound control structure, imperatively given, accomplishing a given purpose under given provisions." Still as argued by Mittelstadt et al. [24], it makes little sense to consider the ethics of algorithms independent of how they are implemented and executed in computer programs, software and information systems. The authors introduce a framework for diagnosing the ethical challenges related to the use of algorithms.

The diagnostic framework is based on algorithms that (i) are used to turn data into evidence for a given outcome, (ii) have an outcome which trigger and motivate an action that may not be ethically neutral, and (iii) are complex and (semi-)autonomous, complicating the apportionment of accountability and/or responsibility for the effects of the actions driven by algorithms. The first three (darker grey) are considered epistemic concerns meaning that they question the quality of evidence provided by the algorithm, whereas the following two (lighter gray) are normative concerns, i.e. used to evaluate the actions taken by the algorithms. Because all five concerns are associated with potential failures that may involve multiple actors, the question of who should be held responsible and/or accountable for failures is pertinent and, therefore, the final (white) overarching concern is traceability.

Algorithms are ethically challenging because of the scale of analysis and complexity of decision-making. In addition, the uncertainty and opacity of the work being done by algorithms and its impact is also increasingly problematic. Algorithms have traditionally required decision-making rules and weights to be individually defined and programmed 'by hand'. While still true, AI-based algorithms increasingly rely on learning capacities [35], meaning that such rules and weights are no longer necessary. In the next sub-sections, we frame the machine ethics issue into agency theory to analyze how firms are creating different forms of incentive structures to promote ethics in AI-based investment algorithms.

2.2 The Agency Problem

Berle and Means' (1932) seminal study [5] on the problems associated with dispersed shareholders that cannot perfectly observe the actions of opportunistic managers was the starting point of extensive theoretical and empirical work on agency theory (see, Jensen and Meckling [20], Ross [31], Holmstrom [17], Fama [11], Eisenhardt [10] and Shapiro [32] for important contributions and reviews). Agency theory (widely applied to a multitude of academic fields as explained in Panda and Leepsa [28]) appears particularly relevant in the investigation of financial investment.

One such stream of research are the studies that apply agency theory to the relation between investors and investment advisors (e.g., Golec [14], Ottaviani [26], Das and Sudaram [8], Cuoco and Kaniel [7], Mitchell and Smetters [23], Tan and Lee [34]). The majority of these studies focus on identifying models for the optimal incentive contract that minimize agency costs. In this setup, the investor is the principal and the investment advisor is the agent.

Building on Eisenhardt's [10], Tan and Lee [34] elaborate on three problems arising when a principal delegates to an agent: goals, risks, and information.

Goal asymmetry (GA) arise when the principal believes that the agent has different goals from the principal. GA may lead to opportunistic behaviour either if the agent have de facto different goals from the principal (as was common during the global financial crisis, when poorly designed incentive systems encouraged investment advisors to disregard risk in favour of bonuses), or when the agent fails to understand the principal's goal/s.

Risk asymmetry (RA) stems from the principals' beliefs that the agent has different risk preferences and, alas, will take decisions that are more or less risky than what the principal would have preferred. This is based on risk-sharing between the principal and the agent, but they differ in risk attitudes. In standard economic setting the investor is risk averse, whereas the investment advisor is risk neutral. In addition, moral hazard may enter if the agent shares the upside, but not the downside, risk. Because financial products are credence goods (i.e. have qualities that cannot be observed by the consumer after purchase, which makes it difficult to assess their utility), RA might arise even if the risk preferences between the principal and the agent are aligned. Especially, if the customer cannot accurately predict the expected return.

Information asymmetry (IA) arises when one party has information that the other party desires but does not have. In line with Eisenhardt [10], the principal can rely on "information systems" as monitoring tools to evaluate and verify the behaviour of the agent (see also, Aggarwal and Mazumdar [1]).

In our case on an asset management company selling investment strategies based on AI, we rely on the three asymmetries listed above to analyse how the principal agency relationship plays out in a specific organizational setting in which the role of the principal is played by the top management of the company and the agents are the developers of the company.

2.3   Agency Theory in Complex and Uncertain Settings

As crystalized by Grandori [15, p. 169], for very complex activities and subject to strong uncertainty, the agency relationship is in crisis since neither a greater transfer of risk(to address risk asymmetry) nor the intensification of control (to address goal and information asymmetries) are efficient. Therefore, the theory of the agency predicts that in such conditions agency contracts will tend to be replaced by contracts of an associative nature and by a sharing of ownership rights by the actors, that is by a re-unification of the figures of the principal and of the agent and by the formation of groups of peers [12, 13].

These implications are valid in the hypothesis of particular utility functions and objectives that need to be realigned because they tend to be opposed (the hypothesis of the effort as a cost). However, situations may arise where the management of agency relations is simpler because the motivation of the agents is intrinsic to the job and less instrumental than that assumed in the prevalent models of agency theory. In addition, there are also other mechanisms for aligning objectives in addition to incentives, in particular cultural and value-related mechanisms.

In our case, both the risk sharing mechanisms and the cultural and value-related mechanisms appears to be relevant and actually used to deal with the accountability and ethical issues raised by the introduction of AI.

3   Methodology

The study presented here considers how a young and innovative company is evolving and applying digital technology (machine learning and other mechanisms commonly linked to AI) to the traditional field of financial investments. The case firm is MDOTM, a start-up that develops AI-driven investment strategies for global financial markets. We chose the firm because of our interest in machine ethics and especially linked to finance. MDOTM are considered as one of the innovation leaders in terms of applying AI to financial investing and has been selected twice by Google for its entrepreneurship programmes in Silicon Valley (Blackbox, focusing on business acceleration and scale-ups) and Zurich (focusing on the business applications of AI and machine learning).

At present we have done four formal interviews as presented in Table 1. The fourth interview was purposefully a site visit in order to experience some of the things that were mentioned during the previous interviews. During all interviews diligent notes were taken, and these notes were transcribed directly after the interview. While the empirical material is still somewhat limited there is a persistency in some of the arguments that implies an emergent saturation (at least in terms of the CEO and COO).

This paper is still an early draft version and we are developing the methods linked to data collection and data analysis with respect to our conceptual model.

Table 1 Scheduling of the field work

Date	Informant designation	Researchers present	Time in interview (min)
May-2018	CEO and COO	EB	120
June-2018	CEO and COO	EB	120
03/06-2019	CEO, COO and analyst	EB, FV, VE	120
14/06-2019	CEO, CTO, COO, analysts and researchers	EB, FV	60

Because this is an area with limited previous research, an exploratory and qualitative approach is chosen. The exploratory purpose of the study motivates a search for emergent generalizations rather than the testing of established patterns [21]. In line with Suddaby [33] we rely on an abductive approach where matching, rather than testable hypothesis or propositions, guides us in moving back and forth between framework, data sources and analysis. In the words of, Alvesson and Sandberg [2, p. 266]) "sometimes empirical findings play a major role in the formulation of a study, such as in cases when one (re)formulates the research task quite late in the process", a point that well describes this study. In particular, while the starting-point of our study was machine ethics more broadly, the moving back and forth between data and theory helped us identify agency theory as a promising theoretical lens to further our understanding of the empirical scenery. To some extent that paper has moved from exploring machine ethics in finance to testing the relevance of traditional agency theoretical arguments in an entrepreneurial and complex setting.

4 Preliminary Evidence on the MDOTM Case

4.1 Background of the Firm

MDOTM develops AI-driven investment strategies for global financial markets. It has a B2B model and its clients are exclusively institutional investors (banks). Its technology leverages large-scale financial data and the latest break-throughs in artificial intelligence and advanced statistical modeling to develop automated investment strategies. To date, MDOTM has over $50 million running on their algorithms. To date, MDOTM has 15 employees (expected 20 by the end of 2019) and over $50 million running on their algorithms.

MDOTM was founded in Milan (with a foothold in London) in late 2015 by longtime friends Tommaso Migliore (CEO), who graduated in Finance, and Federico Mazzorin (CTO), who has a Master's degree in Physics.

The MDOTM leadership team guides developers (especially with a background in physics) in their RandD efforts and, on the other side, manages the relationships with existing clients and prospects. Research mainly focuses on themes that are widely debated in academia and aims, through a trial-and-error process, at finding areas of inefficiency in standard financial modeling. Building on new approaches to tackle those inefficiencies, investment strategies are developed and brought to market.

MDOTM competitors are both status quo incumbent and other research start-ups. Its distinctive feature is the development of investment strategies using a systematic approach through AI.

MDOTM is a start-up able to do better than big incumbents for two reasons. Most big asset companies failed when creating their own internal group of developers because of the incentives of developers, who are too far away from the final outcome. Also, start-up can grant stock options at the team level, and this creates strong incentives for the developers. Incumbents, especially when big in size, tend not to valorize developers.

4.2 The Regulation of the AI-Fintech Industry in Europe

Fintech is still not regulated in Europe (few exceptions, among which the "regulatory sandbox" in the UK), whereas banks and insurance companies are heavily regulated.

Discussion on two possible regulatory approaches: rules-based (preferred by Germany) or principles-based (preferred by the UK). However, there is no specific regulation for AI in Europe.

4.3 New Challenges from AI

AI brings new challenges in the investment industry. Firstly, in a human-driven investment approach the individual trader needs to deliver performance over the short-term, whilst in an AI tech-investing approach the team of developers (not the individual developer) needs to provide stable algorithms. The team (with, possibly, several different developers working on the algorithm over time) will make the machine work in the long run. This determines managerial challenges because the CEO job changes due to AI. On the one hand, MDOTM CEO needs to test the team of developers in terms of persistence over 3–5 years ahead. On the other hand, he needs to avoid cheating of developers. This is why it is essential to develop a system of incentives (short-term and long-term). For the future, the main concern of MDOTM CEO is that his employees link the performance to the results of the machine in the short run: if developers focus just on the performance and develop new algorithms, the challenge is that developers push hard on the performance in the short-term of the algorithms rather than on their persistency. Intellectual property protection. The issues are those of potential reverse engineering of the algorithms and data protection.

Secondly, accountability for developers is probably one of the most important challenges for AI tech-investing. There is a clear gap between the work of developers and their impact on the output of the investment strategy they are working on. The decisions of the development team are not immediately visible in the outcomes of the investments as the shift towards AI means development work does not add or modify specific parameters to an algorithm but rather intervenes on how to set up the learning process of the machine. It becomes extremely difficult to identify ex-post specific tweaks that led to certain results.

AI algorithms are designed to evolve over time and adapt to new market conditions. Hence, their efficacy might be stressed and/or put into question years after their development and in a modified market context, dramatically widening the time frame for evaluation of developers' work. A remedy to the gaps that arise is the correct use of incentives for developers (see next section) that need to be long-term, and team-based.

Building Up Right Incentives for Algorithm Developers in AI Companies
Developers should be at the center of the company, notwithstanding the nature of their job, that, especially as projects grow bigger, becomes more and more limited in scope. At the same time an AI company is culturally centered around the research and coding processes. This allows for a developer's role that is culturally central in the company, that however does not have to rely too much on any individual's work.

The company must develop the right incentive scheme to align the developers to the goals of the management.

Incentives should not be at the individual developer level, but at the team level so that all developers contribute to the same algorithm to ensure its statistical robustness. This helps to tackle the gaps in accountability that arise from working with AI because it incentivizes a peer review-like approach from the rest of the research team that has an economic incentive to contribute to the robustness of the models.

MDOTM actually changed its incentive scheme over time from an individual- to a team-oriented approach, and now developers' incentives are based on the company revenues. Trial-and-error process. Their first incentive scheme was based on individual performance and induced developers to keep developing new strategies rather than optimizing the existing ones resulting in strategies providing only short-term results (i.e. not significant over time). Following on, the CEO introduced a new incentive scheme based on the performance (revenues) of the company. The developers' salary is made of three components: fixed, variable and stock options.

MDOTM developed a program of M.Sc. dissertations' supervision by developers, to promote the change in role of developers (i.e. developers experiencing a new role and point of view detecting inconsistencies and "shortcuts" in the students' work).

AI and Challenges for the Relationship with the Asset Managers
The trust of the asset manager builds on facts to be evaluated in the medium-term (not in the short-term as in the other tech-investing firms): different horizon on trust.

In AI-based strategies, the distinctive feature is that the company does not sell just performance but persistence.

For MDOTM asset managers are partners. MDOTM develops an AI investment strategy, the asset managers do the execution.

As in any other firm providing investment strategies, MDOTM's CEO needs to manage the emotions of clients (CEOs and top managers but still with emotional biases). The distinctive feature of MDOTM, following from AI, is that it sells the ability of a machine to learn from the past and to adapt.

MDOTM pays attention to the selection of clients in each country/distribution channel, in order to preserve the goal of the clients to protect their position. This has an effect on the pricing (fees composed by a flat fee plus a performance fee).

AI and Challenges for Ethical Issues

A central question is whether in AI-based investing companies should introduce rules of conducts for developers.

As AI is so complex, values are more effective than rules. Especially for the developers, to share company's values is more effective than to establish rules of conduct.

MDOTM requires its developers to sign the company's values rather than rules of conduct. Their list of values is:

- Think big and innovate
- We are one team, we respect and help each other
- Communication is a must
- Be the best and lead by example
- Be courageous, don't be afraid to be scared
- Always strive to improve yourself
- We never quit
- Passion for winning.

The enforcement of the values occurs via "lead by examples". In short, values for developers' discipline, and incentives for alignment.

5 Expected Results and Implications

The collection and analysis of preliminary evidence briefly reported here, together with the selection of the latest developments of agency theory as theoretical framework, are encouraging, suggesting to proceed with further research development. After completing a theory-driven, in-depth semi-structured interview guide, further stages of data collection and analysis of the MDOTM case, and triangulation with further similar cases, are expected to shed light on this innovative and challenging area of investigation.

Handling ethical issues in AI-based investing is particularly crucial not only for the role and accountability of machine learning in decision making, but also for the fact that there is no specific regulation for AI in Europe. This contrasts with the heavy regulation of the finance industry in general, making the AI-based investing particularly interesting to investigate from an ethical perspective.

From the theoretical point of view, a closer understanding of alternative ways of handling the principal-agent relationships in complex and uncertain settings is expected to contribute to an important contemporary area of theoretical development and debate. The managerial implications are straightforward: traditional economic incentives do not work to appropriately prevent ethical issues with AI programmers in financial portfolio management. The expected theoretical developments would represent a basis for devising and designing new value-based incentive systems in forthcoming organizations.

Acknowledgements We wish to thank Nien-hê Hsieh for his contribution in the initial phase of the interviews. We also acknowledge the helpful comments by reviewer and participants at ITAIS and MCIS conference (Naples 2019), and at AEDBF Conference (Milan 2019). This research was supported by the Italian Ministry of Education (MIUR): "Dipartimenti di Eccellenza" Program (2018–2022)—Department of Economics and Business—University of Sassari.

References

1. Aggarwal, P., & Mazumdar, T. (2008). Decision delegation: A conceptualization and empirical investigation. *Psychology and Marketing, 25*(1), 71–93.
2. Alvesson, M., & Sandberg, J. (2011). Generating research questions through problematization. *Academy of Management Review, 36*(2), 247–271.
3. Anderson, M., & Anderson, S. L. (Eds.). (2011). *Machine ethics.* Cambridge University Press.
4. Azim, M. I., & Kluvers, R. (2019). Resisting Corruption in Grameen Bank. *Journal of Business Ethics, 156,* 591–604. https://doi.org/10.1007/s10551-017-3613-4.
5. Berle, A., & Means, G. (1932). *The modern corporation and private property.* New York, NY: Macmillan.
6. Borg, E., & Hooker, B. (2019). Epistemic virtues versus ethical values in the financial services sector. *Journal of Business Ethics, 155,* 17–27. https://doi.org/10.1007/s10551-017-3547-x.
7. Cuoco, D., & Kaniel, R. (2011). Equilibrium prices in the presence of delegated portfolio management. *Journal of Financial Economics, 101*(2), 264–296.
8. Das, S. R., & Sundaram, R. K. (2002). Fee speech: Signaling, risk-sharing, and the impact of fee structures on investor welfare. *Review of Fin. Studies, 15*(5), 1465–1497.
9. Davis, M., Kumiega, A., & Van Vliet, B. (2013). Ethics, finance, and automation: A preliminary survey of problems in high frequency trading. *Science and Engineering Ethics, 19*(3), 851–874.
10. Eisenhardt, K. M. (1989). Agency theory: An assessment and review. *Academy of Management Review, 14*(1), 57–74.
11. Fama, E. (1980). Agency problems and the theory of the firm. *Journal of Political Economy, 88*(2), 288–307.
12. Fama, E. F., & Jensen, M. C. (1983). Agency problems and residual claims. *The Journal of Law and Economics, 26*(2), 327–349.
13. Fama, E. F., & Jensen, M. C. (1983). Separation of ownership and control. *The Journal of Law and Economics, 26*(2), 301–325.
14. Golec, J. H. (1992). Empirical tests of a principal-agent model of the investor-investment advisor relationship. *Journal of Financial and Quantit. Analysis, 27*(1), 81–95.
15. Grandori, A. (1999). *Organizzazione e comportamento economico.* Il Mulino.
16. Hill, R. K. (2015). What an algorithm is. *Philosophy and Technology, 29*(1), 35–59.
17. Holmstrom, B. (1979). Moral hazard and observability. *Bell Journal of Economics, 10*(1), 74–91.
18. Holthausen, R. W., & Larcker, D. F. (1992). The prediction of stock returns using financial statement. *Journal of Accounting and Economics, 15*(2–3), 373–411.
19. Hurlburt, G. F., Miller, K. W., & Voas, J. M. (2009). An ethical analysis of automation, risk, and the financial crises of 2008. *IT Professional, 11*(1), 14–19.

20. Jensen, M., & Meckling, W. (1976). Theory of the firm: Managerial behavior, agency costs, and ownership structure. *Journal of Financial Economics, 3*(4), 305–360.
21. Kvale, S., & Brinkmann, S. (2014). *Den kvalitativa forskningsintervjun (the qualitative research interview)*. Lund: Studentlitteratur. (in Swedish).
22. MacIntyre, A. C. (2015). The irrelevance of ethics. In A. Bielskis & K. Knight (Eds.), *Virtue and economy* (pp. 7–21). Farnham VT: Ashgate.
23. Mitchell, O. S., & Smetters, K. (Eds.). (2013). *The market for retirement financial advice*. OUP Oxford.
24. Mittelstadt, B. D., Allo, P., Taddeo, M., Wachter, S., & Floridi, L. (2016). The ethics of algorithms: Mapping the debate. *Big Data and Society, 3*(2), 1–21.
25. Monroe, D. (2018). AI explain yourself. *Communications of the ACM, 61*(11), 11–13.
26. Ottaviani, M. (2000). *The economics of advice*. University College London, Mimeo.
27. Ou, J. A., & Penman, S. H. (1989). Financial statement analysis and the prediction of stock returns. *Journal of Accounting and Economics, 4*(1), 295–329.
28. Panda, B., & Leepsa, N. M. (2017). Agency theory: Review of theory and evidence on problems and perspectives. *Indian Journal of Corporate Governance, 10*(1), 74–95.
29. Rafeld, H., Fritz, S. G., & Posch, P. N. (2019). Whale watching on the trading floor: Unravelling collusive rogue trading in banks. *Journal of Business Ethics*, 1–25.
30. Rocchi, M., Pelletier, L., & Desmarais, P. (2017). The validity of the interpersonal behaviors questionnaire (IBQ) in sport. *Measurement in Physical Education and Exercise Science, 21*(1), 15–25.
31. Ross, S. A. (1973). The economic theory of agency: The principal's problem. *The American Economic Review, 63*(2), 134–139.
32. Shapiro, S. P. (2005). Agency theory. *Annual Review of Sociology, 31,* 263–284.
33. Suddaby, R. (2006). What grounded theory is not. *Academy of Management Journal, 49,* 633–642.
34. Tan, J. C. K., & Lee, R. (2015). An agency theory scale for financial services. *Journal of Services Marketing, 29*(5), 393–405.
35. Tutt, A. (2016). *An FDA for algorithms*. SSRN scholarly paper no. id 2747994.
36. Vardi, M. Y. (2016). The moral imperative of artificial intelligence. *Communications of the ACM, 59*(5), 5.

Putting Decision Mining into Context: A Literature Study

Sam Leewis, Koen Smit, and Martijn Zoet

Abstract The value of a decision can be increased through analyzing the decision logic, and the outcomes. The more often a decision is taken, the more data becomes available about the results. More available data results into smarter decisions and increases the value the decision has for an organization. The research field addressing this problem is Decision mining. By conducting a literature study on the current state of Decision mining, we aim to discover the research gaps and where Decision mining can be improved upon. Our findings show that the concepts used in the Decision mining field and related fields are ambiguous and show overlap. Future research directions are discovered to increase the quality and maturity of Decision mining research. This could be achieved by focusing more on Decision mining research, a change is needed from a business process Decision mining approach to a decision focused approach.

Keywords Decision mining · Data mining · Process mining · Business intelligence

1 Introduction

Decisions in the modern world are often made in fast-changing, sometimes unexpected, situations [1]. Such situations require the selection of the right decision maker and supplying them with the necessary data. Decision mining solves this problem by estimating data quality and interpretation of their semantics and relevance, the actual meaning, and unit of measurement [1]. The second major advantage is the classification of decisions which allow the discovery of correspondence between decision

S. Leewis (✉) · K. Smit
HU University of Applied Sciences Utrecht, Utrecht, The Netherlands
e-mail: Sam.Leewis@hu.nl

K. Smit
e-mail: Koen.Smit@hu.nl

M. Zoet
Zuyd University of Applied Sciences, Sittard, The Netherlands
e-mail: Martijn.Zoet@zuyd.nl

© The Editor(s) (if applicable) and The Author(s), under exclusive license to Springer
Nature Switzerland AG 2020
R. Agrifoglio et al. (eds.), *Digital Business Transformation*, Lecture Notes in Information
Systems and Organisation 38, https://doi.org/10.1007/978-3-030-47355-6_3

makers and their roles through the development of decision models and (semi) automatic decision analysis techniques [1]. Decision mining can be segmented into three types: Discovery, Conformance checking, and Improvement (similar as in Process mining research [2]. An often-used definition of Decision mining, and also referred to as decision point analysis, is *"aims at the detection of data dependencies that affect the routing of a case"* [3]. This focus leaves out other decision elements embedded in decision trees, database tables etc., such as business rules, business decision tables, or executable analytic models. Therefore, we define Decision mining as *"the method of extracting and analyzing decision logs with the aim to extract information from such decision logs for the creation of business rules, to check compliance to business rules and regulations, and to present performance information"*. The system supporting and improving decision making is known as a Decision Support System (DSS). DSSs is *"the area of the information systems (IS) discipline that is focused on supporting and improving managerial decision making"* [4]. The current DSSs give insufficient insight into how decisions are executed, this is especially the case for executing multiple decisions at once (a group of decisions), thereby lacking the transparency [5, 6]. Methods of Data mining are used in Decision mining and DSSs for the following purposes: finding associative rules between decisions and the factors affecting them, user clustering using decision trees and neural networks, recognition of common users' features or interests [7–9].

To the knowledge of the authors, little research exists on the topic of Decision mining, especially that of a comprehensive literature study. Furthermore, to the knowledge of the authors, no research exists where the concepts of Decision mining, Data mining and Process mining are compared. The Decision mining field and its related fields lack the use of unambiguous concepts. Conducting a literature study on the Decision mining field and its related fields creates a clear overview of which concepts and definitions are used and if any overlap between these concepts exists. This research will focus on more than just the business process aspect when considering mining decisions compared to previous research [3, 10]. To do so, we aim to answer the following research question: *"What is the current state of the Decision mining research field?"*

The remainder of the paper is structured as follows: First, the research method that was utilized to collect and review the literature for the theoretical review. This is followed by the results of the literature review depicting Decision mining and its context, resulting in the conceptual framework. Finally, we discuss the conclusions of our research and provide a discussion about this research and the results, which is followed by possible future research directions.

2　Research Method

The goal of this study is to evaluate the current state of Decision mining and to discover possible future research directions. To achieve this, a conceptual framework is created to evaluate the current state and to identify possible future directions [11].

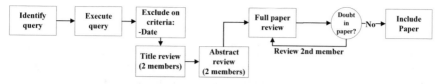

Fig. 1 Review protocol

Edmondson and Mcmanus [12] differentiate three archetypes of different levels of maturity: Nascent (e.g. Decision Mining), Intermediate (e.g. Process Mining), and Mature (e.g. Data Mining). The quality of research can be quantified with the H-index, created by Hirsch [13], where Decision mining has a H-index of 54, Process mining has a H-index of 116, and Data mining has a H-index of 305. With the rather immature state, "Nascent" [12], of the Decision mining research field and the low level of quality research (H-index of 54) a type of literature study is needed which utilizes existing empirical and conceptual studies for the creation of a conceptual framework together with possible future research directions. Therefore, a theoretical review is selected as the literature review method. Paré, Trudel, Jaana, and Kitsiou [11] state that a theoretical review draws on existing empirical and conceptual studies providing context for the identification, description, transformation into a higher theoretical structure for concepts, constructs, and their relations. The primary artefact of this type of literature study is the development of a conceptual framework with a set of research propositions [14, 15]. The contribution and value of the theoretical review lies in its ability to the development of novel conceptualizations or extend any current ones by the identification of knowledge gaps between the current knowledge and future directions [15]. To ensure quality, rigor, and transparency, the theoretical review was commenced by setting up a literature review protocol, as shown in Fig. 1. Google Scholar was used as main search database due to the fact that it has a higher coverage compared to other search engines or individual database searches [16–20].

2.1 Identify Query

Webster and Watson [15] state that Information Science is an interdisciplinary field and is based on research from other disciplines and therefore reviewing inside the IS field is not enough. To identify all concepts, constructs, and their relations concerning Decision mining, a wide range of search queries are used in order to achieve this. A difference is made between primary search queries focused on the research question (Decision Mining) and secondary search queries (Process Mining, Data Mining, Business Intelligence, Decision Management, Business Process Management, Decision Support Systems, Business Process Model and Notation, Decision Model and Notation) providing context for the primary search queries. The relations between the search queries are elaborated further in the result section.

2.2   Exclusion Criteria

Commonly used exclusion criteria for literature reviews are Date, Number of Citations, and High impact journals. Because of the low maturity and low H-index of the research field, no citation criterion is used during this study. The common use of the high impact factor journal inclusion and exclusion criterion [21–23] is not used for this specific study. The difference between maturity in research fields and the low research quality (H-index 54) is that the high impact factor journals do not publish relevant articles on Decision mining. The dissimilarity between search queries related to maturity and research quality is of that large a difference that the inclusion or exclusion based on a high impact factor source would exclude a large number of sources from the immature and lower research quality search queries. This review protocol includes only the Date criterion and is defined as everything between January 2000 and December 2018. The focus of this study lies on the current state of Decision mining and by implementing a date threshold the actual current state can be quantified in a date. Furthermore, Levy and Ellis [24] point out that by using a review protocol, the actual moment a literature review is completed becomes much clearer. An example of an element of a review protocol is a date range this clarifies which papers with the specific dates are included [25].

2.3   Paper Review

Two reviewers (R1 and R2) are involved during the abstract and paper review. R1 is a PhD-candidate with six years of practical and research experience in the field of Decision Management; R2 is a lecturer and researcher with seven years of practical and research experience in the field of Decision Management. The reviewers include or exclude the papers based on the title and based on abstract, see Fig. 3. When the two reviewers include the same paper based on the title, the paper is reviewed based on the abstract. If the situation occurs that a paper was marked with one included and one excluded, the two reviewers discuss the reviewing of the title. The same process of reviewing also applies to the abstract review. R1 decides during the review of the full paper on the relevancy of the paper. When any doubt on the relevancy exists by R1, R2 decides if the paper is excluded or included.

3   Search Results

The executed search query resulted in 810 potential useable articles, see Fig. 2. Duplicates and non-English papers were excluded, resulting in 74 papers being left out. After title reviews 656 papers were excluded, 80 papers were included. Reviewing the abstracts resulted in the exclusion of 24 papers, resulting in 56 papers that were

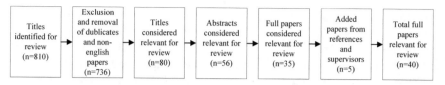

Fig. 2 Search results

included. After reviewing the full papers, 35 papers remained. Based on references and feedback from the supervisors 5 articles were included.

4 Results

The review process resulted in a longlist of papers distributed over the primary and secondary research queries. The identified concepts and their relationships are the pillars of the conceptual framework and this paper. The concepts and the relationships to each other are shown as a metamodel in Fig. 3. The following sections will create context to capture the current state of Decision mining.

4.1 Business Intelligence, Business Process Management and Decision Management

Business intelligence (BI) is described as a set of models and analysis methodologies that utilizes the available data to generate information and knowledge for the support of decision-making processes [26–28]. BI can be divided into four phases [29]: (1) identification of information needs, (2) information acquisition, (3) information analysis, and (4) storage and information utilization. Focusing more on information and data, BI can be defined as a subset of the two (information and data). Where data are facts or recorded measures of certain phenomena, information is structured

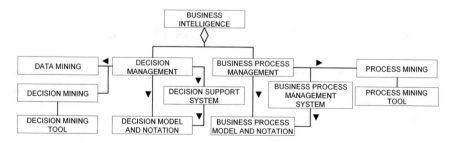

Fig. 3 Search query metamodel

data for the support of the decision-making process or to define any relationships between two facts [27]. Business process management (BPM) [30] and Decision management (DM) are examples of approaches utilizing available data to generate information and knowledge for the support of decision-making processes.

BPM is "*a collaboration of concepts, methods, and techniques to support the design, administration, configuration, enactment, and analysis of business processes*" [30]. The base of BPM is the explicit representation of business process containing activities with the execution constraints between these activities. After defining the business processes, they can be analyzed, improved, and enacted [30]. The industry standard for defining a business process is the Business Process Model and Notation (BPMN) [31].

DM is "*the practice of managing smart, agile decisions*" [32]. Decisions are amongst an organization most important assets [33] Therefore, adequately managing these decisions is vital. A decision is "*A conclusion that a business arrives at through business logic and which the business is interested in managing*" [34] and business logic is "*a collection of business rules, business decision tables, or executable analytic models to make individual business decisions*" [35]. Modelling the decisions and business logic to make them explicit for further analysis is an aspect of DM. Decision Model and Notation (DMN) [34] is used as an industry standard for the modelling of decisions.

4.2 Decision Support Systems

The first decision support systems (DSS) were developed for the support of decision makers by analyzing data using predefined models [36]. Due to recent advancements in technology and market demand, the DSSs are improved to serve future needs, implementing, i.e., analytical tools [37]. The current DSSs lack the transparency into how decisions are executed, especially for a group of decisions [5, 6]. DSSs play a major role in IS. Looking at the importance of DSS research, 12% of the articles published in IS journals are focused on DSSs [38] and citation-based analysis were DSSs is one of the three core subfields of IS [39].

4.3 Decision Mining, Process Mining, and Data Mining

The literature review showed that research published in the fields of Data mining, Process mining, and Decision mining have an overlap in used concepts The following meta models [40] are used to ground the literature of the Data mining, Process mining, and Decision mining fields.

Fig. 4 Data mining
literature relations

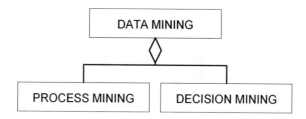

The Data mining field is consentient in its direction, the literature showed, on the other hand, no specifications towards Process mining and Decision mining, identifying these fields as an aggregation of Data mining focused on sequence (Process mining) and derivations (Decision mining), as shown in Fig. 4 [41–44].

The Process mining field is comparable to the Data mining field as it is consentient in its direction. Process mining utilizes Data mining techniques for mining of events from event logs for process discovery, conformance checking, and process improvement, as shown in Fig. 5 [2]. The Process mining field identifies Decision mining as a case perspective focus in Process mining, also known as decision point analysis, as shown in Fig. 5 [2, 3].

The Decision mining field has two main influences 1) Decision mining focused on mining Decision Points from business processes (decision-annotated) [3] and (2) a Decision mining approach where more implicit data involved in the decision-making process (decision-aware) is taken into account [10, 45]. Both directions have overlap and are a type of Decision mining with a Process mining focus and the utilization of Data mining techniques, as shown in Fig. 6.

Data Mining is defined as *"the automated or convenient extraction of patterns representing knowledge implicitly stored or captured in large databases, data warehouses, the Web, other massive information repositories, or data streams"* [41].

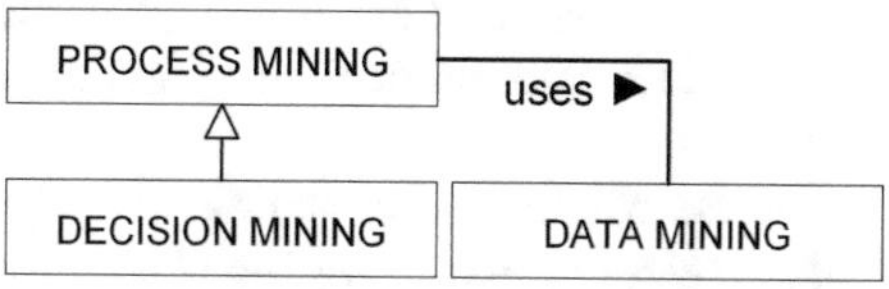

Fig. 5 Process mining
literature relations

PROCESS MINING

uses ▶

DECISION MINING

DATA MINING

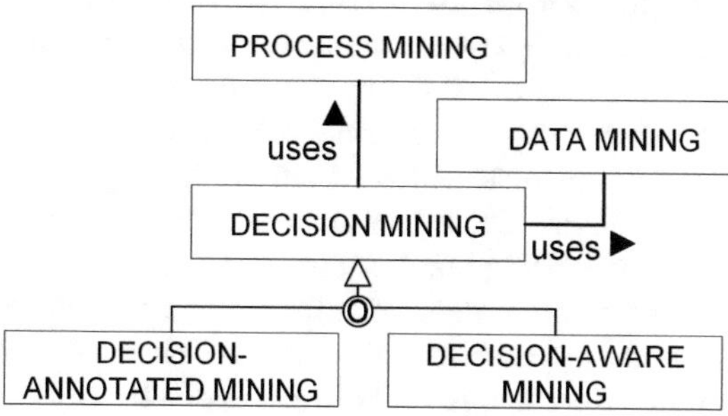

Fig. 6 Decision mining
literature relations

PROCESS MINING

uses

DATA MINING

DECISION MINING

uses ▶

DECISION-
ANNOTATED MINING

DECISION-AWARE
MINING

Therefore, the term Data mining is a misnomer, as the goal of Data mining is the extraction of patterns of aggregations from large volumes of data, not the extraction of said data [41]. Data mining utilizes techniques for finding data patterns, these patterns enables accurate and fast decision making or provide new insights [42]. Data patterns could contain a specific sequence (processes), or a specific derivation (decisions). An example where Data mining can be performed is whether a specified class of customers will buy a combination of products, a business can utilize this data by predicting whether to increase the price on one of the articles or include an article in a sale, also known as a basket analysis [46]. Prediction, together with description, make up for the two Data mining categories [43]: (1) Predictive Data mining, which utilizes variables of existing data to predict any unknown or future values of other variables of value and (2) Descriptive Data mining, focusses on the discovery of patterns non trivially describing data which in turn can be interpreted by interested parties. Predictive and descriptive Data mining can be achieved by utilizing Data mining algorithms for the following Data mining classifications [43]: (1) Classification, a classification which discovers a predictive learning function that generalizes the known structure for the application of new data items. (2) Regression, a classification where a predictive learning function models the data, for the estimation of relations between data items. (3) Clustering, a classification where a descriptive task identifies a set of categories or clusters for the description of data. (4) Summarization, a classification where a descriptive task provides a compact representation of the data. (5) Dependency Modelling, a classification which searches for relations between multiple variables. (6) Change and Deviation Detection, a classification where changes or unusual records are discovered. The algorithms that are widely used for Data mining are C4.5 [47], k-means algorithm [48], Support vector machines [49], the Apriori algorithm [50], and CART [51], for a more extensive list see the work of Wu et al. [52]. The Data mining algorithms look for structural descriptions, these descriptions can become rather complex and are typically expressed as a set of rules or a decision tree. Rules and decision trees are easier understood by people and explain what has been learned, thereby serving as a base for future predictions [42]. Besides Data mining being in a mature state, major issues can be identified [41].

Process Mining is defined as *"the discovery, monitoring and improvement of real processes by extracting knowledge from event logs readily available in today's information systems"* [2], i.e., the mining of sequencing patterns. This technique is frequently used in BPM [30, 53]. Process Mining can be considered a twofold, on one side an analysis technique for Data mining and on the other side a technique for process modelling. The three types of Process mining are [2]; (1) process discovery, (2) conformance checking, and (3) process improvement. Process Discovery constructs a representation of an organization's business process and any major variations. Event logs are used as input to set up the process models [2] and serve as the starting point of Process mining [54]. Information systems utilized by organizations store detailed information about the specific sequence of activities performed by these information systems during the execution of a process [53]. The events in the event logs symbolize each one activity which in turn is part of a business process. Detailed information on events is stored in these event logs concerning: e.g. finishing time of an activity. The algorithms that are widely used for process discovery include Alpha Miner, Heuristic Miner, Trace Clustering, and Fuzzy Miner [54, 55]. During conformance checking, the discovered and created process model is analyzed and it is checked on any discrepancy between the event logs and the process model [2, 56]. The main purpose of conformance checking is to identify any problem areas which can be improved by utilizing this knowledge. The modification of the process model to comply with the event logs is done during process improvement. Process improvement aims to extend or improve the process model using information from the event logs about the actual process [2]. Two improvement types exists (1) repair, the modification of the process model to better reflect the actual process [57], and (2) extension, adding a new perspective after cross-referencing this with the event log [2]. In relation to the three types of Process mining, four perspectives are characterized [2] control-flow, organizational, case, and time. The four perspectives are all related to each other. The control-flow perspective focuses on the ordering of activities. The organizational perspective focuses on resource information hidden in the event logs e.g. involved actors, and their relations. The case perspective focuses on case properties e.g. characterization of a case by the process path. The time perspective focuses on the time and frequency on events e.g. prediction of processing time utilizing timestamps.

An often-used definition of Decision mining, and also referred to as decision point analysis, is *"aims at the detection of data dependencies that affect the routing of a case"* [3], i.e., the mining of derivation patterns. One of the major tasks of Decision mining is the estimation of data quality and interpretation of their semantics, interpretation of data whether it is relevant, the actual meaning, and unit of measurement [1]. The second major task is the classification of decisions which allow the discovery of correspondence between decision makers and their roles through the development of decision models and (semi) automatic decision analysis techniques [1]. The work of Rozinat and van der Aalst [3] assumes the mining of decisions as the mining of decision points from a business process. This method is comparable to the three types of Process mining [2]: discovery, conformance checking, and improvement. This approach uses a version of the C4.5 algorithm [47] for the construction of decision trees which allow the analysis of the choice in the decision points of a process.

Rozinat and van der Aalst [3] proposes the use of Petri Nets [58] for this approach, thereby being able to determine the specific points where a choice is made and which branches are followed. After the identification of a decision point, the authors try to determine if certain cases with certain properties follow each a specific route. However, this approach has many limitations. For example, this approach cannot deal with event logs containing deviating behavior and with more complex control-flow constructs [59]. Many variations on the decision point analysis variant of Decision mining have been published, mostly focusing on refining the way to retrieve the decision information [60–62].

Another approach of Decision mining is the focus on implicit knowledge of the decision maker. The actions of the decision maker and the identification of the decision-making strategy, and determining what data and information is used, how this is used, and what knowledge is employed by the decision maker for the choice between two alternatives [63]. The implicit knowledge is captured using the Decision Model and Notation standard (DMN) [34], together with the clear intention to use it in the context of business processes using Business Process Model and Notation (BPMN) [31]. Hybrids also surfaced such as Product Data Model (PDM) [64]. Showing the influence that context plays on decision making is an important task because [1]: (1) finds and models typical scenarios of interactions between users, (2) discover reoccurring situations within large volumes of raw data, and (3) cluster decision makers, allowing the reduction of supported user models and increasing data presentation. The current Decision mining technique has a limited applicability and is only usable for workflows that uses representations in Petri Nets. This current approach utilizes control flow-based discovery techniques which lack in-depth analysis of the specific action that is performed. Future Decision mining techniques should be driven by the construction of a decision model than by a control flow containing decision points [10, 65]. The Data mining techniques used for Decision mining, which do focus on temporal aspects, often leave out the importance of decisions being the driver of the analyzed result. More can be gained to know which attributes are important to a decision. Furthermore, it is paramount to understand the importance of the decision-making process. The use of Data mining techniques can be improved by implementing decision models [10].

Organizations using algorithms in decision-making processes have to adhere to European legislation which stipulates that automated decision making, without the interaction of a person, is in principle not allowed. However, an exception is made for automated decision making based on a legal basis, provided that it provides for appropriate measures to protect the rights and freedoms and legitimate interests of the data subject [66]. Therefore, the importance of transparent algorithms is clear. Another example of mandatory transparency is the safety critical systems in autonomous cars [67] which need to adhere to the ISO 26262 standard [68].

Furthermore, by reviewing the literature on Data mining, Process mining, and Decision mining, the segregation of these concepts seems incorrect. Reviewing the focus of each concept Data mining is data pattern focused, Process mining is event log focused, and Decision mining can be depicted into two directions, calling it a decision point analysis focused on annotating decisions, or focused on being decision-aware. Therefore, Data mining seems a more general concept where Process mining and Decision mining are included as a type of Data mining, as shown in Fig. 4.

5   Conceptual Framework

The conceptual framework depicts Decision mining and its related concepts, as shown with annotations[x] in Fig. 7, and is the result of the theoretical review. *Data mining*[1], *Process mining*[2], and *Decision mining*[3] are identified as elements of BI, were BI is described as a set of models and analysis methodologies that utilizes the available

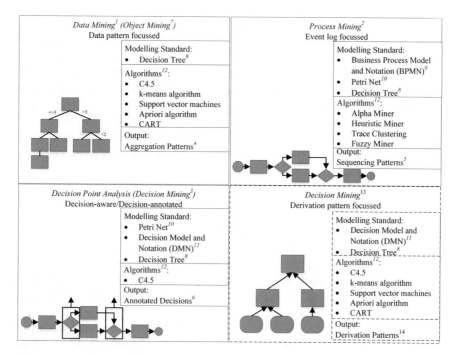

Fig. 7 Conceptual framework

data to generate information and knowledge for the support of decision-making processes [26–28]. Data mining is the mining of *aggregation patterns*[4], Process mining is the mining of *sequencing patterns*[5], and Decision point analysis is utilizing *annotated decisions*[6], thereby utilizing data to generate information and knowledge for the support of decision-making processes. Additionally, reviewing the literature of the context of Decision mining showed that Data mining is not the mining of data, a so-called misnomer [41]. Changing this to *Object mining*[7] would be more appropriate. Specifying and designing focused on data, processes, or decisions each has its standards, where *decision trees*[8] are widely used, and for the more specific models (processes and decisions) *BPMN*[9] [31], *Petri Nets*[10] [69], and *DMN*[11] [34] are used. Each mining technology uses each their own set of *algorithms*[12] to identify patterns based on statistical analysis.

6 Conclusion

The goal of this research is to review the current state of Decision mining. To do so, the following research question was addressed: *"What is the current state of the Decision mining research field?"* In order to answer this question, we conducted a theoretical review consisting of 810 papers which were cut down to a total of 40 papers which were deemed relevant in covering the topic of Decision mining. This study depicted the term Decision mining and where Decision mining falls under (BI, BPM, and DM) or is directly related to (Data mining/Object mining and Process mining). The theoretical review resulted into a conceptual framework were all the discovered concepts were depicted. The conceptual framework revealed several gaps in the existing research. Therefore, several research directions could be considered for researchers to target and extend this scarcely covered topic. Additionally, the conceptual framework revealed the inconsistency in the involved research fields covering the same subjects and using the same concepts but not using a clear definition, or the same name.

7 Discussion and Future Research

The theoretical review resulted into a conceptual framework were all the discovered concepts are depicted. The conceptual framework revealed several gaps in the existing research Therefore, several research directions could be considered for researchers to target.

The main future research focus should be directed to improve the level of research maturity of the Decision mining research field. Therefore, the level of maturity should mature out of the "Nascent" phase using the classification of research domain maturity of Edmondson and Mcmanus [12]. Other authors support the notion of a more direct focus for improving the maturity of the Decision mining research field [10, 65].

In relation to the previous research focus, the current research on *Decision mining*[3] is focused on the perspective from a business process point of view, and a more standalone viewpoint is needed where *Decision mining*[13] is focusing on the decision viewpoint with *derivation patterns*[14] as output, as shown in Fig. 7. The two main Decision mining influences lack the capacity to deal with event logs containing deviating behavior and dealing with more complex control-flow constructs [59] and lacks a holistic overview of the decision model [10]. Recent research focusses on a more holistic discovery of decisions [70], which still has a business process point of view with event logs as its data input. Additionally, with the focus on the viewpoint shift, the data input for Decision mining should shift from an event log to a decision log [10], as shown in Fig. 8. Supporting the previous notion the following Decision mining definition is created to cover the new research directions: *"the method of extracting and analysing decision logs with the aim to extract information from such decision logs for the creation of business rules, to check compliance to business rules and regulations, and to present performance information"*.

The third focus for future research is conducting research on algorithms in the Decision mining field. Current Decision mining algorithm research is focused on the assumption that the algorithms in ProM [3] are the best fit for mining decisions. Future research should focus on creating an overview of useable algorithms for Decision mining, and if needed, create a new algorithm if existing algorithms lack the capacity for mining decisions. Recent technologies as Reinforcement learning

Fig. 8 Decision mining activities

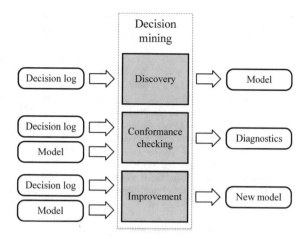

[71, 72] and Deep learning [73, 74] algorithms could create added value for Decision mining. Lastly, the previous mentioned future research should be focused on the elements centered around the activities of Decision mining: Discovery, Conformance checking, and Improvement, as shown in Fig. 8.

References

1. Smirnov, A., Pashkin, M., Levashova, T., Kashevnik, A., Shilov, N. (2009). Context-driven decision mining. In *Encyclopedia of data warehousing and mining* (pp. 320–327). Information Science Reference, Hershey, NY.
2. van der Aalst, W. M. P.: *Process mining: Discovery, conformance and enhancement of business processes.* Springer Science & Business Media (2011).
3. Rozinat, A., van der Aalst, W. M. P.: Decision mining in ProM. In: Dustdar, S., Fiadeiro, J. L., & Sheth, A. P. (Eds.), *Business process management: 4th international conference, BPM 2006, Vienna, Austria,* 5–7 September 2006. Proceedings (pp. 420–425). Heidelberg, Berlin: Springer. https://doi.org/10.1007/11841760_33.
4. Arnott, D., & Pervan, G. (2005). A critical analysis of decision support systems research. *Journal of Information Technology, 20,* 67–87.
5. Horita, F. E. A., de Albuquerque, J. P., Marchezini, V., & Mendiondo, E. M. (2017). Bridging the gap between decision-making and emerging big data sources: An application of a model-based framework to disaster management in Brazil. *Decision Support Systems, 97,* 12–22. https://doi.org/10.1016/j.dss.2017.03.001.
6. Mohemad, R., Hamdan, A. R., Othman, Z. A., & Noor, N. M. M. (2010). Decision support systems (DSS) in construction tendering processes. *International Journal of Computer Science Issues, 7,* 35–45. https://doi.org/10.1109/ICSSSM.2008.4598482.
7. Chiang, W. Y. K., Zhang, D., & Zhou, L. (2006). Predicting and explaining patronage behavior toward web and traditional stores using neural networks: A comparative analysis with logistic regression. *Decision Support Systems, 41,* 514–531. https://doi.org/10.1016/j.dss.2004.08.016.
8. Li, X.-B. (2005). A scalable decision tree system and its application in pattern recognition and intrusion detection. *Decision Support Systems, 41,* 112–130. https://doi.org/10.1016/j.dss.2004.06.016.

9. Thomassey, S., & Fiordaliso, A. (2006). A hybrid sales forecasting system based on clustering and decision trees. *Decision Support Systems, 42,* 408–421. https://doi.org/10.1016/j.dss.2005.01.008.

10. De Smedt, J., Vanden Broucke, S. K. L. M., Obregon, J., Kim, A., Jung, J. Y., Vanthienen, J. (2017). Decision mining in a broader context: An overview of the current landscape and future directions. In *Lecture notes in business information processing* (pp. 197–207). Springer International Publishing. https://doi.org/10.1007/978-3-319-58457-7_15.

11. Paré, G., Trudel, M. C., Jaana, M., & Kitsiou, S. (2015). Synthesizing information systems knowledge: a typology of literature reviews. *Information & Management, 52,* 183–199. https://doi.org/10.1016/j.im.2014.08.008.

12. Edmondson, A. C., & Mcmanus, S. E. (2007). Methodological fit in management field research. *Academy of Management Review, 32,* 1155–1179.

13. Hirsch, J. E. (2010). An index to quantify an individual's scientific research output that takes into account the effect of multiple coauthorship. *Scientometrics, 85,* 741–754. https://doi.org/10.1007/s11192-010-0193-9.

14. Baumeister, R. F., & Leary, M. R. (1997). Writing narrative literature reviews. *Review of General Psychology, 1,* 311–320. https://doi.org/10.1037/1089-2680.1.3.311.

15. Webster, J., Watson, R. T. (2002). Analyzing the past to prepare for the future: Writing a literature review. *MIS Quarterly, 26,* xiii–xxiii. https://doi.org/10.1.1.104.6570.

16. Harzing, A. -W., Alakangas, S. (2016). Google scholar, scopus and the web of science: A longitudinal and cross-disciplinary comparison. *Scientometrics 106,* 787–804 (2016). https://doi.org/10.1007/s11192-015-1798-9.

17. Wildgaard, L. (2015). A comparison of 17 author-level bibliometric indicators for researchers in astronomy, environmental science, philosophy and public health in web of science and google scholar. *Scientometrics, 104,* 873–906. https://doi.org/10.1007/s11192-015-1608-4.

18. Franceschet, M. (2010). A comparison of bibliometric indicators for computer science scholars and journals on Web of Science and Google Scholar. *Scientometrics, 83,* 243–258. https://doi.org/10.1007/s11192-009-0021-2.

19. Amara, N., & Landry, R. (2012). Counting citations in the field of business and management: Why use Google scholar rather than the web of science. *Scientometrics, 93,* 553–581. https://doi.org/10.1007/s11192-012-0729-2.

20. Gehanno, J.-F., Rollin, L., & Darmoni, S. (2013). Is the coverage of google scholar enough to be used alone for systematic reviews. *BMC medical informatics and decision making, 13,* 7. https://doi.org/10.1186/1472-6947-13-7.

21. Parmesan, C., & Yohe, G. (2003). A globally coherent fingerprint of climate change impacts across natural systems. *Nature, 421,* 37–42. https://doi.org/10.1038/nature01286.

22. Lek, M., Karczewski, K. J., Minikel, E. V., Samocha, K. E., Banks, E., Fennell, T., et al. (2016). Analysis of protein-coding genetic variation in 60,706 humans. *Nature, 536,* 285–291. https://doi.org/10.1038/nature19057.

23. Cardinale, B. J., Duffy, J. E., Gonzalez, A., Hooper, D. U., Perrings, C., Venail, P., et al. (2012). Biodiversity loss and its impact on humanity. *Nature, 486,* 59–67. https://doi.org/10.1038/nature11148.

24. Levy, Y., Ellis, T.J. (2006). A systems approach to conduct an effective literature review in support of information systems research. *Informing Science 9,* 181–211. https://doi.org/10.28945/479.

25. Okoli, C. (2015). A guide to conducting a standalone systematic literature review. *Communications of the Association for Information Systems, 37,* 879–910. https://doi.org/10.2139/ssrn.1954824.

26. Vercellis, C.: *Business intelligence: Data mining and optimization for decision making.* New York: Wiley.

27. Zikmund, W., Babin, B., Carr, J., Griffin, M. (2009). *Business research methods.* South-Western.

28. Chen, H., Chiang, R. H. L., Storey, V. C.: Business intelligence and analytics: From big data to big impact. *MIS Quarterly,* 1165–1188. https://doi.org/10.2307/41703503.

29. Loennqvist, A., & Pirttim, V. (2006). The measurement of business intelligence. *Information Systems Management, 23,* 32–40. https://doi.org/10.1080/07366980903446611.
30. Weske, M. (2012). *Business process management.* Berlin: Springer. https://doi.org/10.1007/978-3-642-28616-2.
31. Object Management Group (OMG) (2011) Business process model and notation (BPMN) Version 2.0. *Business, 50,* 508. https://doi.org/10.1007/s11576-008-0096-z.
32. Von Halle, B., & Goldberg, L. (2009). *The decision model: A business logic framework linking business and technology.* New York, NY: Taylor and Francis Group, LLC.
33. Blenko, M.W., Mankins, M.C., Rogers, P.: The Decision-Driven Organization. Harv. Bus. Rev. 10 (2010).
34. Object Management Group. (2016). *Decision model and notation.*
35. Object Management Group. (2016). *ArchiMate® 3.0 specification.*
36. Shim, J., Merrill, W., Courtney, J., Power, D., Sharda, R., & Carlsson, C. (2002). Past, present and future of decision support system. *Decision Support Systems, 33,* 111–126.
37. Chugh, R., & Grandhi, S. (2013). Why Business Intelligence? Significance of business intelligence tools and integrating BI governance with corporate governance. *International Journal of Entrepreneurship and Innovation, 4,* 1–14. https://doi.org/10.4018/ijeei.2013040101.
38. Arnott, D., & Pervan, G. (2014). A critical analysis of decision support systems research revisited: The rise of design science. *Journal of Information Technology, 29,* 269–293. https://doi.org/10.1057/jit.2014.16.
39. Taylor, Dillon, & Wingen, Van. (2010). Focus and diversity in information systems research: Meeting the dual demands of a healthy applied discipline. *MIS Quarterly, 34,* 647. https://doi.org/10.2307/25750699.
40. van de Weerd, I., Brinkkemper, S. (2008). Meta-modeling for situational analysis and design methods. In: Handbook of research on modern systems analysis and design technologies and applications (vol. 35).
41. Han, J., Kamber, M., Pei, J. (2011). *Data mining: Concepts and techniques.* Morgan Kaufmann Publishers, Burlington, MA. https://doi.org/10.1016/B978-0-12-381479-1.00001-0.
42. Witten, I. H., Frank, E., Hall, M. A., & Pal, C. (2016). *Data mining: Practical machine learning tools and techniques.* Burlington, MA: Morgan Kaufmann Publishers.
43. Kantardzic, M. (2011). *Data mining : Concepts, models, methods, and algorithms.* Wiley Online Library.
44. Rokach, L., Maimon, O. (2015). *Data mining with decision trees: Theory and application.*
45. Petrusel, R., Vanderfeesten, I., Dolean, C. C., Mican, D. (2011). Making decision process knowledge explicit using the decision data model. In: Business Information Systems, 340.
46. Berry, M. J. A., Linoff, G. S. (2004). *Data mining techniques: for marketing, sales, and customer support.* New York: Wiley.
47. Ross, Q. J. (1993). *C4.5: Programs for machine learn.* Morgan Kaufmann Publishers.
48. Lloyd, S. P. (1982). Least squares quantization in PCM. *IEEE transactions on information theory, 28,* 129–137. https://doi.org/10.1109/TIT.1982.1056489.
49. Vapnik, V. N. (1995). *The nature of statistical learning theory.* New York: Springer.
50. Agrawal, R., Srikant, R. (1994). Fast algorithms for mining association rules in large databases. In *Proceedings of the 20th International Conference on Very Large Data Bases* (pp. 487–499). Morgan Kaufmann Publishers Inc., San Francisco, CA, USA.
51. Breiman, L., Friedman, J. H., Olshen, R. A., & Stone, C. J. (1984). Classification and regression trees. *Chapman & Hall/CRC.* https://doi.org/10.1201/9781315139470.
52. Wu, X., Kumar, V., Ross, Q. J., Ghosh, J., Yang, Q., Motoda, H., et al. (2008). Top 10 algorithms in data mining. In: *Knowledge and information systems* (pp. 1–37). https://doi.org/10.1007/s10115-007-0114-2.
53. Dumas, M., La Rosa, M., Mendling, J., & Reijers, H. A. (2018). *Fundamentals of business process management.* Berlin: Springer.
54. van der Aalst, W. M. P., Adriansyah, A., De Medeiros, A. K. A., Arcieri, F., Baier, T., Blickle, T., et al. (2012). *Process mining manifesto. Lecture notes in business information processing.* 99 LNBIP (pp. 169–194). https://doi.org/10.1007/978-3-642-28108-2_19.

55. Rojas, E., Munoz-Gama, J., Sepúlveda, M., Capurro, D. (2016). Process mining in healthcare: A literature review. *Journal of Biomedical Informatics, 61*, 224–236. https://doi.org/10.1016/j.jbi.2016.04.007.
56. Rozinat, A., & van der Aalst, W. M. P. (2008). Conformance checking of processes based on monitoring real behavior. *Information Systems, 33*, 64–95. https://doi.org/10.1016/j.is.2007.07.001.
57. Rovani, M., Maggi, F. M., de Leoni, M., & van der Aalst, W. M. P. (2015). Declarative process mining in healthcare. *Expert Systems with Applications, 42*, 9236–9251. https://doi.org/10.1016/j.eswa.2015.07.040.
58. Petri, C. A. (1966). Communication with Automata. *Application Data Research, 15*, 357–62. https://doi.org/AD0630125.
59. de Leoni, M., van der Aalst, W. M. P. (2013). Data-aware process mining: Discovering decisions in processes using alignments. In: *Proceedings of the 28th Annual ACM Symposium on Applied Computing* (pp. 1454–1461). dl.acm.org.
60. Kim, A., Obregon, J., Jung, J.-Y. (2014). Constructing decision trees from process logs for performer recommendation. In *International Conference on Business Process Management* (pp. 224–236) (2014). https://doi.org/10.1007/978-3-319-06257-0_18.
61. Mannhardt, F., de Leoni, M., Reijers, H. A., van der Aalst, W. M. P.: Decision mining revisited-discovering overlapping rules. In *International Conference on Advanced Information Systems Engineering* (pp. 377–392).
62. de Leoni, M., Dumas, M., Garçka-Bañuelos, L.: Discovering branching conditions from business process execution logs. In *International Conference on Fundamental Approaches to Software Engineering* (pp. 114–129). Berlin: Springer. https://doi.org/10.1007/978-3-642-370 57-1.
63. Petrusel, R. (2010). *Decision mining and modeling in a virtual collaborative decision environment*. Rijeka: In-Tech.
64. Vanderfeesten, I., Reijers, H. A., van der Aalst, W. M. P. (2008). Product based workflow support: A recommendation service for dynamic workflow execution. In *Proceedings of 20th International Conference on Advance Information System Engineering* (pp. 571–574). https://doi.org/10.1007/978-3-540-69534-9_42.
65. Sarno, R., Sari, P. L. I., Ginardi, H., Sunaryono, D., Mukhlash, I. (2013). Decision mining for multi choice workflow patterns. In *Proceeding—2013 International Conference on Computer, Control, Informatics and Its Applications. Recent Challenges Computer, Control Informatics, IC3INA* (pp. 337–342). https://doi.org/10.1109/IC3INA.2013.6819197.
66. European Union. (2016). *General data protection regulation. Official Journal of European Union, L119*, 1–88 (2016).
67. Borg, M., Englund, C., Durán, B. (2017). Traceability and deep learning—safety-critical systems with traces ending in deep neural networks. In: Grand challenges of traceability: The next ten years (pp. 48–49). https://arxiv.org/abs/1710.03129.
68. ISO. (2018). ISO 26262-2:2018.
69. Petri, C. A. (1962). Kommunikation mit Automaten.
70. De Smedt, J., Hasić, F., vanden Broucke, S. K. L. M., Vanthienen, J. (2017). Towards a holistic discovery of decisions in process-aware information systems. In *International Conference on Business Processing Management* (pp. 183–199). https://doi.org/10.1007/978-3-319-65000-5_11.
71. Silver, D., Schrittwieser, J., Simonyan, K., Antonoglou, I., Huang, A., Guez, A., et al. (2017). Mastering the game of go without human knowledge. *Nature, 550*, 354.
72. Sutton, R. S., & Barto, A. G. (2018). *Reinforcement learning: An introduction*. Cambridge: MIT Press.
73. De Fauw, J., Ledsam, J. R., Romera-Paredes, B., Nikolov, S., Tomasev, N., Blackwell, S., et al. (2018). Clinically applicable deep learning for diagnosis and referral in retinal disease. *Nature Medicine*. https://doi.org/10.1038/s41591-018-0107-6.
74. Lecun, Y., Bengio, Y., & Hinton, G. (2015). Deep learning. *Nature, 521*, 436–444. https://doi.org/10.1038/nature14539.

Cloud Sourcing and Paradigm Shift in IT Governance: Evidence from the Financial Sector

Niloofar Kazemargi and **Paolo Spagnoletti**

Abstract In the digital age, organizations are increasingly shifting their applications, services and infrastructures to the cloud to enhance business agility and reduce IT-related costs. However, in moving applications and data to cloud resources organizations face new risks of privacy violations. To manage this risk, organizations need to be fully aware of threats and vulnerabilities affecting their digital re-sources in cloud. Although some previous studies have focused on the emerging challenges of cloud adoption to governance and control, we know little regarding the paradigm shifts in IT governance processes and practices. To address this gap, we conducted an exploratory case study in two large companies in the financial sector. Our findings show that cloud adoption alters the locus and scope of IT governance which consequently compels organizations to rethink their control mechanisms to mitigate security risks. Our findings contribute to the literature on IT governance and IT outsourcing, and support IT executives and decision makers in mitigating the risks of cloud adoption.

Keywords Cloud sourcing · IT governance · Information security

1 Introduction

Cloud computing technologies enable organizations to remotely access scalable digital resources such as applications, platforms and infrastructures [30]. The potential benefits of cloud-based services for organizations are cost convenience, business agility and scalability of resources [28] that have led to a growing trend in adopting cloud-based solutions in recent years [31]. However, many organizations are today concerned with the security and privacy implications of cloud sourcing.

N. Kazemargi (✉)
Department of Business and Management, Luiss Guido Carli, Rome, Italy
e-mail: Nkazemargi@luiss.it

P. Spagnoletti
Department of Information Systems, University of Agder, Kristiansand, Norway

© The Editor(s) (if applicable) and The Author(s), under exclusive license to Springer Nature Switzerland AG 2020
R. Agrifoglio et al. (eds.), *Digital Business Transformation*, Lecture Notes in Information Systems and Organisation 38, https://doi.org/10.1007/978-3-030-47355-6_4

47

These security concerns significantly influence sourcing decisions and outcomes [6–16, 42].

The recent survey by the Society for Information Management (SIM)—mainly based on US organizations—shows an increase in the adoption of cloud-based solutions especially Software-as-a-Service, following a decrease in hardware and software investment. At the same time, the study shows that cybersecurity and privacy are the main concerns for organizations and IT leaders. The security concerns among organizations result in higher IT expenditure on security, in particular investment on the cybersecurity skills development of the workforce [9]. One of the reasons is that cloud adoption poses security challenges to organizations [19]. Security threats in the cloud environment, such as unauthorized access to sensitive data, can lead to significant financial consequences and reputation damage for client firms. The financial consequences of data breaches cost a company around $3.86M in 2018, as reported by Forbes. The number of companies that have been victims of data breaches is increasing; this compels organizations to reconsider security threats and their governance efforts to mitigate security risks while reaping the benefits of cloud solutions. For instance, not only are organizations investing in technology development (e.g. encryption algorithms), but also national/international bodies are developing standards and regulations (e.g. Convention on Cybercrime, ISO/NP 23485 NIST and GDPR) to mitigate the security and privacy risks of cloud.

Existing studies focus on the relationship between information security and sourcing decisions [e.g. 6, 8]. Despite these efforts, considering the peculiar characteristics of cloud technologies, it is still unclear how organizations govern cloud-based services to mitigate security risk and promote desirable outcomes. Our study addresses this gap. We aim to answer how cloud sourcing reshapes IT governance in order to ensure the security and privacy of data while enabling organizations to enjoy the benefits offered by cloud computing (e.g. agility and cost reduction). To address this gap, we conducted an exploratory case study of two large companies in the financial sector. We elected to study large companies operating with relatively sensitive data that have recently adopted cloud services. Our analysis investigates how cloud sourcing induces paradigm shifts in IT governance processes and practices. Our findings show that cloud adoption alters the locus and scope of IT governance which consequently compels organizations to rethink their control mechanisms to mitigate security risks in order to grant desirable IT outcomes. Our findings contribute to the literature on IT governance and IT outsourcing, and support IT executives and decision makers in mitigating the risks of cloud adoption.

The paper is organized as follows; first, we present related literature at the intersection of IT out-sourcing and IT governance. Then, we present our research design and the findings of our study on the security implications of cloud sourcing decisions. Finally, we present the discussion, and theoretical and managerial implications.

2 Relevant Literature

2.1 IT Outsourcing

Organizations outsource IT resources, which otherwise would be costly to develop in-house, to service providers. The main benefits of outsourcing resources to cloud service providers, besides cost convenience, are business agility and scalability of resources [28]. Organizations can access three service levels offered by service providers [30]: Infrastructure as a Service (IaaS), Platform as a Service (PaaS) and Software as a Service (SaaS). The pay-per-use and on-demand characteristics of cloud computing cause many organizations to change the way they store, save and back-up business data and applications. Based on the service environment, there are different cloud delivery models: (1) public cloud as a shared service environment with no (or little) control over data; (2) private cloud as a contract-based cloud with a higher level of control over data; (3) hybrid cloud in which consumers can use public cloud for scalability and cost convenience as well as private cloud for storing sensitive data [30].

In the IS field, IT outsourcing has been studied extensively, covering mainly the drivers and associated risks of IT outsourcing (ITO) [14–21]. Lacity et al. [23] develop a theoretical framework by looking at factors that influence IT outsourcing decisions and ITO outcomes. Although ITO has a broad scope, in this section we focus on the security aspects that influence cloud sourcing decisions and cloud sourcing outcomes respectively (see Fig. 1).

As for cloud sourcing decisions, two elements act as barriers to these: lack of full control over data and IT infrastructure [8–25, 41], and emerging new security vulnerabilities characterized by cloud service levels and deployment models [1, 2,

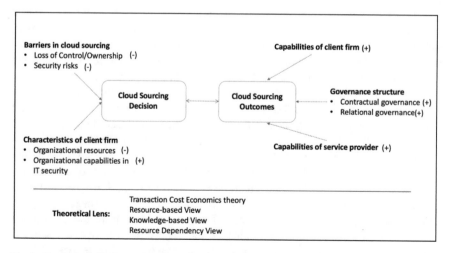

Fig. 1 Review of cloud sourcing literature

42]. Moreover, previous research has suggested a set of factors such as business context, the level of sensitivity of data, and the nature of business processes, that influence organizational decisions related to what resources can be moved to cloud [25–27, 29]. For instance, banking, aerospace and healthcare sectors are more reluctant to adopt cloud solutions due to their high level of data sensitivity. Moreover, it is essential to consider internal IT skills, organizational capabilities and size of the organization before moving to cloud [8–16, 39]. For example, small-sized organizations have different intentions and lower security expectations in cloud sourcing than large enterprises [42], thus, we observed a different trend of cloud sourcing by small- and medium-sized enterprises (SMEs) with higher organizational flexibility than large organizations.

Moreover, Fig. 1 illustrates three elements that reinforce the security outcomes of cloud sourcing from the literature. The first element is the capabilities of the client firm: the higher its internal IT skills, the more an organization is able to identify and take proper security measures [36, 41]. Second, previous research highlights that desirable security outcomes in cloud sourcing may be promoted by the ability and power to negotiate terms and conditions of contracts with service providers [1–3, 27]. Although establishing relationships with service providers may support higher quality and availability of the services, not all organizations can develop and leverage inter-organizational relationships effectively [6, 8]. This is mainly because only a few firms, which have dominant power and control over infrastructures, offer cloud resources. Third, the level of security of the client's firm partially depends also on the capabilities of cloud providers in identifying and reacting to cyber-threats [26, 42].

From a theoretical perspective, the literature on IT outsourcing is vast and mainly incorporates transactional views that are used as a framework to explain make or buy decisions [22]. Transaction Cost Economics theory examines whether to make or buy assets from an external vendor considering transaction costs [51, 52]. Cloud-based solutions are based on multi-tenancy and standard solutions which allow cloud providers to maximize economies of scale, and offer services lower than on-premises investment, and further based on a pay-per-use model. However, new security issues and risks in cloud-based solutions [1, 2] cause managerial concerns. To address these security concerns and mitigate cloud computing risks, client firms need new competences and skills to determine what the risks are and to identify a set of security measures. One way is to negotiate and customize service level agreements (SLAs) which, on the one hand, augment security through the increased liability of cloud providers, on the other hand, increase transaction costs for the client firm [27].

However, as argued by [22], the concept of IT outsourcing is beyond make or buy decisions. Firms need to retain control over strategic assets as a source of competitive advantage. The IT strategic assets could be data, software, platforms or hardware. Thus, firms typically opt to outsource non-core IT activities [40], and instead insource strategic activities. Given the importance of data as an asset, firms prefer to retain control and governance over their sensitive data and critical business processes. Hence, organizations have a low propensity to shift sensitive data or core business processes to cloud. This is because leakage of data and knowledge to competitors puts the client firm in a challenging position [8–36, 39].

Based on Resource-Based theory and Knowledge-Based view, firms outsource to access specific resources and knowledge in order to sustain their competitive position [5]. Cloud sourcing provides client firms with access to cloud computing resources such as applications (SaaS); platforms (PaaS); infrastructures (IaaS), which otherwise are expensive for a single firm to develop in-house. In addition, Resource-Based theory explains the decision on service levels (SaaS, PaaS or IaaS), depending on organizational IT skills and expertise level. The successful adoption of IaaS and PaaS solutions relies on the client firm's IT capabilities to maintain and upgrade the systems, while SaaS requires less effort and expertise from the client firm [39].

From a Resource Dependency View [34], handing over control of IT resources to cloud providers increases the client firm's dependency on the cloud provider. Therefore, capabilities, skills and investments of cloud providers in business continuity, disaster recovery, data security and privacy directly influence the IT security outcomes of the client firm [26, 42].

2.2 IT Governance

IT governance is a prominent topic in the literature by focusing on how organizations govern their IT activities and IT assets [33–45, 50]. IT governance is defined as decision rights and responsibilities related to IT in order to ensure the proper outcomes of IT use in an organization [50]. The outcomes of IT use in organizations refer to the alignment of IT strategy with business strategy, management of risks, and finally organizational performance [48, 53]. Tiwana et al. [46] outline three dimensions of IT governance as follows: (1) the locus of IT artifacts to be governed, e.g. software and hardware, (2) the scope of governance which use IT artifacts and grant the desirable IT outcomes within the organization, and (3) IT governance mechanisms to ensure alignment use of IT with organizational strategies.

However, the main streams of IT governance focus on well-defined physical IT artifacts. Despite the usefulness of IT governance, existing practices and processes are not sufficient for emerging digital technologies and digitalization. Tilson et al. [44] mention that digital technologies are changing the locus of IT artifacts and the scope of governance, and consequently IT governance mechanisms.

As for the locus of IT artifacts, as highlighted by Tallon et al. [43], the main focus of the IT governance literature was mainly on the physical facets of IT artifacts, including IT infrastructure, hardware, networks and software. While the IT governance literature is very valuable, recently studies have been investigating the governance of the non-physical facets of IT artifacts, such as data and information [43, 46].

Regarding the scope of governance, traditionally IT experts were mainly accountable for the outcomes of IT use. With the development of IT and its growing use, the scope of governance has been broadened and now includes the use of IT across functions and business units. In particular, considering IT outsourcing and digital technologies, the scope of governance has spanned the inter-organizational level [15].

Moreover, IT governance mechanisms can be in the form of (1) structural practices such as formal assignments for responsibilities regarding the control and management of IT artifacts and the locus of decision making; (2) procedure practices such as controlling IT investment and allocation of resources, and control points; and (3) relational practices such as establishing and maintaining intra and inter organizational relationships to learn and share knowledge [33, 43].

While numerous studies focus on how security threats influence IT outsourcing decisions and outcomes, a better understanding of how cloud sourcing challenges and induces a paradigm shift in IT governance is needed. Thus, in this study we aim to explore how cloud sourcing alters the locus, scope and mechanisms of IT governance and how organizations manage and control cloud solutions, aligning IT assets with organizational strategy in the short- and long-term, and mitigating associated risks [7]. We first describe our research methodology and then present our findings.

3   Research Method

We used an inductive case study to investigate how cloud sourcing has reshaped IT governance by focusing on security and privacy risks. The case study methodology provides a tool to examine a complex phenomenon [10] and allows a rich description and an in-depth understanding of cases [12, 54].

In our empirical analysis, we refer to two cases which are large, for-profit companies operating in the financial sector. The two cases match our research settings and fulfill the relevancy criteria for this study: (1) both companies have adopted cloud-based solutions during the last years, (2) both have strategic commitment to cloud adoption, (3) both show a propensity for more cloud adoption in the future, and (4) in the industrial sector, confidentiality and privacy are critical for IT security. The two selected cases are reported in Table 1 where real names have been anonymized for confidentiality reasons.

The semi-structured interview was used as one of the sources of data collection to obtain information from various informants experiencing the phenomenon [10, 13]. Interviews were conducted with informants from different areas such as security, IT infrastructure and legal departments. Data were collected from September 2018 till June 2019. The interviews ranged from 45 to 90 min. We have also been given access to archival documentation provided by both companies.

In parallel, we have collected and analyzed an extensive amount of data from different sources and in different formats. The data has been collected from participation in roundtables/forums with companies adopting cloud computing, reports by organizational, national and international bodies, direct conversations with informants and decision makers—see Table 2. This empirical data along with other

Table 1 Companies' profiles and their cloud sourcing strategy

Company	Background	Cloud adoption
Alfa	>130,000 employees >€600 million annual profit	In 2012, adopted IaaS in private cloud In 2015, adopted SaaS for mailing system and PaaS for non-critical business processes. All critical business processes are developed and implemented internally and on-premises Recently, Alfa has also considered moving some critical data and assets to cloud
Beta	>96,000 employees >€7000 million annual profit	In 2010–2011, adopted IaaS in private cloud Beta manages and controls all infrastructures internally Private cloud is the main cloud delivery model In 2016, the company established a separate office under its information systems department dedicated to cloud services and cloud strategy. There is a shift from IaaS to PaaS adoption, and toward public cloud

Table 2 Sources of evidence

Source of evidence	Description	Total number
Direct observation	Roundtables and forums, informal conversation with informants and decision makers on the topic of cloud adoption and security	6
Interviews	Semi-structured interviews with informants from different fields of work: Security, IT infrastructure and legal departments	5
Archival records	Organizational websites and press, strategy documents, meeting presentations	30
Documentation	Newspapers, specialist magazines, national and international reports, protocols and recommendations	50
Articles	Specialist and academic articles	60

secondary collected data enabled us to triangulate and increase the reliability from various data sources [18]. We used NVivo to arrange and analyze the collected data—see Table 3.

4 Case Analysis and Findings

In this section we describe and analyze the cloud sourcing strategy and then focus on the security practices of the two cases.

Through the development of cloud computing technology, by adopting cloud services, the two cases sought to create and deliver business values through cost reduction and agility. The potential for cost reduction is mainly in the procurement

Table 3 Sample of data table

Sample codes	Selected quotes
Business strategy alignment to create and deliver business values/cost reduction/agility etc.	*"[…] we need to adopt different IT solutions with higher speed, and lower cost which enable us to be more flexible"* *"To have a standard and complete solution, the timeframe shifts from several months to a few hours"*
IT security challenges Sensitivity of data/compliance with regulations/shift from physical threats to logical cyber threats etc.	*"A recommendation is published to provide guidelines and practices of different companies"* *"When it comes to contact, they [cloud providers] don't want any audit from cloud users"*
Shifts in IT governance practices To evaluate and select providers/significant effort dedicated to SLAs etc.	*"It is wrong to think that security is all done by the cloud provider"* *"We see security is different at different layers"*

and maintenance phases of sourcing new IT components. As one manager expressed it: *"Before [adoption of cloud services] it was a long procedure […] we needed to prepare bids, go through procurement phase, then install, implement, test, modify and finally use the system […] All procurement, operations like installation, upgrades and maintenance were costly …."*. Cloud sourcing enables the companies to shorten the time to market, temporal dimension of agility. As one informant explained: *"To have a standard and complete solution, the timeframe shifts from several months to a few hours. At the beginning, it was various steps like manual configuration, server procurement, and so on"*. Furthermore, the two companies have started their cloud outsourcing as infrastructure-as-a-service and eventually have moved to platform-as-a-service level. This initiative set the ground for more standard solutions and developing new applications and services—the flexibility dimension of agility. As one informant summarized: *"[…] we need to adopt different IT solutions with higher speed, and lower cost which enable us to be more flexible."*

While the companies show a propensity to increasingly adopt cloud services in future, especially for flexibility, speed and innovation, some challenges in cloud outsourcing were recognized. The main challenge was related to IT security. In particular, we realized a number of key challenges related to data confidentiality and privacy. First, the major IT security concern was related to cyber security in cloud outsourcing. Regarding the sensitivity of data in the financial sector, the two companies not only develop their security measures to mitigate cyber risks but also need to adhere strictly to security measures and compliance with national and international regulations in the industrial sector. For instance, some informants described the importance of national regulations in defining internal strategy toward cloud outsourcing.

Second, by adopting cloud solutions, the primary focus of IT security has shifted from physical threats (i.e. in-house security threats) to logical cyber threats. This is due to the fact that cloud service providers store and process data in dispersed systems and data centers across the globe. Moreover, the companies highlight the fact that cloud service providers may subcontract some services to third parties. This makes the control over data even more challenging. Another issue that emerged was related to the state of data. Data is not static in data centers, but rather in transit or in process from one layer to another, or from one application to another. In other words, data moves from the organizational IT infrastructure to cloud or vice versa. Therefore, those challenges induce a paradigm shift in IT security governance and new practices in the management of data and applications. While cloud service providers manage the security of outsourced applications or infrastructures, informants consistently reported the importance of internal security measures and control points. As one informant highlighted: "*It is wrong to think that security is all done by the cloud provider*". By analyzing cases, a number of security practices emerge. The security teams play a key role in mitigating security risks by developing security measures based on cloud services such as authentication, encryption algorithms, control of network traffic, etc. As explained by one informant: "*We see security is different at different layers, for instance for SaaS we use passwords and we control access. For PaaS, we mainly use encryption for communication and information exchange. And for mitigating risks in networks, we have firewalls to protect from denial of service attacks.*"

As emerged from the interviews, a best practice suggested by cloud service providers is encrypting data. Cloud service providers offer encryption services; they store encrypted files in data centers and manage and store encryption keys. Yet, interviewees consistently emphasized the need for controlling and managing encryption keys internally, which mitigates the risk of data breach. This included, for example, data breaches by third parties or any security incident by malicious attackers at the cloud providers' data centers.

Third, cloud service providers have control over infrastructure, applications and data; consequently, they play an important role in client firms' security level. Therefore, the companies emphasized the need to carefully evaluate and select providers, with the main purpose of aligning the security level of cloud providers with the organization's expected security level. For instance, the security management team of company Beta has the responsibility for evaluating and certifying cloud providers according to internal security measures. However, as stated by the interviewees, this leads to the minimum accepted security level, and more effort is still needed.

Fourth, significant effort was dedicated to SLAs in order to define terms and conditions, including disaster recovery plans of cloud providers; alignment with GDPR; compliance of subcontractors with obligations; access to data; and auditing rights. All of this allowed client firms to implicitly detail the liability of cloud providers and to expect cloud providers to fully comply with their obligations in SLAs.

Although a more comprehensive SLA would increase the security liabilities of cloud providers, the interviewed cases experienced challenges in defining terms and conditions, as well as managing SLAs with multiple cloud providers. Therefore, there is a need for common measures and cooperation among companies to determine the requirements for cloud service providers, particularly in the case of an IT security incident. Furthermore, interviewees emphasized the existing power imbalance with cloud service providers. The dominant position of cloud providers makes any negotiation challenging for client firms and constrains room for the customization of SLAs. This is because coordination and managing standard SLAs for multiple clients demand less effort. As one informant from the Beta company explained: *"When it comes to contact, they [cloud providers] don't want any audit from cloud users [...] now there is not any response from cloud providers in request of auditing data centers"*. While the Beta company experiences rigidity from cloud providers, the Alfa company has had some progress in customizing and negotiating its SLA's terms and conditions with a cloud provider. This might be due to the position and characteristics of the cloud provider and modification requests to terms and conditions. Overall, with the evolution of cloud services, more data and applications are expected to migrate to cloud. This significantly demands the need to counterbalance the power dominance by collaboration and cooperation with cloud service providers.

5   Discussion and Conclusion

In this study, we aimed at shedding light on the ways in which cloud adoption reshapes IT governance [39]. The key contribution of our study is that we demonstrate how security risks and vulnerabilities in digital resources in cloud reshape IT governance processes and practices—see Table 4.

The two companies have a propensity for adopting diverse cloud-based resources to enhance business agility and reduce costs. However, their primary concern was to ensure security of data in a cloud environment. As both companies operate in a context with relatively sensitive data, their security concerns were reflected in how they both carefully revisited their IT governance processes and practices.

First, our findings highlight the need to expand our understanding of the locus of IT governance in cloud sourcing beyond the existing focus on physical assets to consider data flow in digital resources in cloud. As shown in the two cases, the locus is shifted from on-premises IT artifacts, with well-defined physical boundaries, to cloud-based solutions geographically dispersed. To reap benefits, organizations may adopt different levels of services (such as low-level infrastructure service, middle-level software service, to top-level application services) and deployment models. Thus, the client firm needs to be careful to understand the level of control over digital resources in cloud. Moreover, findings provide evidence that the focus has been shifted to data-transported digital resources in cloud [43, 44]. Equally important is that much effort is devoted to identifying and mitigating security risks of cloud-resources as organizations neither have control over cloud resources nor over data treatment in cloud.

Second, while previous literature has focused on project and firm [44], our findings highlight the important roles of service providers and third parties [1, 28] in IT security management, rather than only client firms. Cloud sourcing leaves security responsibilities partially in the hand of the cloud providers. Therefore, the competences and maturity level of cloud providers play crucial roles in how an organization effectively prevents or responds to cyber-attacks [4]. While cloud sourcing challenges

Table 4 - Governing cloud-based services

Dimension	Selected codes
Focus • Cloud-based solutions (i.e. applications, platforms and infrastructures) • Data (bits) flows in cloud-based solutions	• Adopting diverse cloud service levels and deployment models, with different levels of control over data • Enhancing business agility and reducing IT costs by adopting cloud-based services • The focus has been shifted from physical IT artifacts to data flow in IT artifacts • Mitigating data security risks
Scope • Cloud service providers • Third parties • Regulatory parties	• Governing dyad relationships with cloud service providers • Power of cloud service providers in decision rights over services • Ensuring that subcontractors comply with obligations and regulations • Adhering to security measures and compliance in the industrial sector • Implementing national/international regulations within internal strategy
Mechanisms • Formal control mechanisms depending on service level • Informal control mechanisms • Negotiating formal processes • Relational mechanisms	• Defining procedures and assessment criteria to evaluate cloud service providers • Defining control measures according to service levels • Benchmarking of the best practices in the financial sector • Seeking recommendations from regulatory bodies • Negotiating SLAs • Establishing relationship with cloud service providers • Knowledge exchange and shared learning within business networks

control over IT artifacts through leaving some decisions to cloud providers and third parties, it is important to note that cloud providers' decisions may not necessarily be in favor of the client firm. Also, cloud providers may not disclose all information related to the reliability of services and disaster recovery plans, although it is reliability of the client firm to manage and control disaster recovery and back-up. In addition, cloud service providers may subcontract some activities to third parties. This introduces further security vulnerabilities and risks which need to be identified and managed by the client firm.

Moreover, our findings emphasize the role of regulatory bodies in developing standards and formal procedures that influence strategic decisions within organizations. By adding cloud vendors and other actors to the picture, this study highlights the scope of IT governance changes with the rise in sourcing cloud-based services. In addition, findings show the transformation of IT departments in terms of roles, skills and activities to ensure added value practices are in favor of the organization. Transforming the role of IT departments includes cloud vendor assessment and selection, managing information system policies, and ensuring security of data and privacy [1–28, 47]. In sum, given the increasing value of data, the security of data in cloud is important and demands actions from all involved actors.

Third, in cloud adoption, organizations face new security [11] such as data breaches and lack of transparency in security measures by cloud service providers. The security risks act as a barrier to cloud adoption and lack of proper IT governance practices may lead to huge financial losses, especially for large organizations [42]. Our findings show the shift in locus and scope of IT governance due to security risks results in development of new IT governance mechanisms. In the following we present efforts by organizations to redefine governance mechanisms to mitigate security risks.

Our findings illustrate that the cases have defined assessment criteria in order to evaluate cloud service providers before adopting cloud services. We show that organizational ability to develop control measures and policies to mitigate security risks is important. By defining new standards and practices such as access permissions and using authentication, organizations can prevent access to any sensitive data in public servers. This is aligned with previous literature that has investigated security practices. For example, Brender and Markov [8] and Sood [41] highlight some issues in cloud adoption such as security, disaster recovery and governance, and list a series of security practices that can be adopted by organizations to mitigate security risks.

Moreover, we notice that regulatory bodies are actively engaged in providing directions, recommendations and policy to manage security risks. Even though each organization develops internal IT security controls, the influence of external policies by regulatory bodies on internal practices has to be considered. Moreover, organizations learn to better govern digital resources in cloud through interactions and knowledge exchange within regulatory bodies and other partners in networks. For instance, the two cases interact with other organizations in order to share the best governance practices to avoid the financial consequences of data breaches.

In addition, we find that both contractual and relational governance structures are important to realize a favorable situation for client firms in terms of data security. Making a legally binding agreement reduces the risks of a partner's opportunism and provides a guideline for various situations in the future and for managing conflicts. Client organizations can enhance the security of data by including detailed rights and obligations in SLAs. The contract and agreement should detail responsibilities of the client organization and cloud providers in case of cyber-attacks and breaches of data at the data layer, or malware at the service layer. Moreover, due to the complementarity of contractual and relational governance structures [24, 35], we argue that the ability to build and strengthen relationships with cloud service providers is important for mitigating security risks by leveraging the power in negotiations.

In sum, in moving applications and data to cloud resources, organizations face new risks of privacy violation. To manage these risks, organizations need to be fully aware of threats and vulnerabilities affecting their digital resources in cloud. Our findings highlight that cloud sourcing reshapes the traditional IT governance arrangements

[39]. We argue that cloud adoption alters the locus and scope of IT governance which consequently compels organizations to rethink their control mechanisms to mitigate security risks [47]. We especially focus on the impact of cloud on security and privacy issues that must be addressed through proper IT governance practices [17, 49]. Given the financial consequences of security breaches, it is important for IT executives and decision makers to rethink their IT governance processes and practices to mitigate the risks of cloud adoption.

References

1. Ali, M., Khan, S. U., & Vasilakos, A. V. (2015). Security in cloud computing: Opportunities and challenges. *Information Sciences (Ny), 305,* 357–383. https://doi.org/10.1016/j.ins.2015. 01.025.
2. August, T., Niculescu, M. F., & Shin, H. (2014). Cloud implications on software network structure and security risks cloud implications on software network structure and security risks. *Information Systems and Research, 25,* 489–510. https://doi.org/10.1287/isre.2014.0527.
3. Baset, S. A. (2012). Cloud SLAs: present and future. *ACM SIGOPS Operating Systems Review, 46,* 57–66.
4. Baskerville, R., Spagnoletti, P., & Kim, J. (2014). Incident-centered information security: Managing a strategic balance between prevention and response. *Information & Management, 51,* 138–151. https://doi.org/10.1016/j.im.2013.11.004.
5. Barney, J. B. (1991). Firm resources and sustained competitive advantage. *Journal of Management, 17*(1), 99–120.
6. Benlian, A., & Hess, T. (2011). Opportunities and risks of software-as-a-service: Findings from a survey of IT executives. *Decision Support Systems, 52,* 232–246. https://doi.org/10.1016/j. dss.2011.07.007.
7. Bowen, P. L., Cheung, M.-Y. D., & Rohde, F. H. (2007). Enhancing IT governance practices: A model and case study of an organization's efforts. *International Journal of Accounting Information Systems, 8,* 191–221.
8. Brender, N., & Markov, I. (2013). Risk perception and risk management in cloud computing: Results from a case study of Swiss companies. *International Journal of Information Management, 33,* 726–733. https://doi.org/10.1016/j.ijinfomgt.2013.05.004.
9. David, A., Nguyen, Q., Johnson, V., Kappelman, L., Torres, R., Maurer, C. (2018). The 2017 SIM IT issues and trends study. MIS Q Executive 17. https://doi.org/10.1177/106648071351 4945.
10. Eisenhardt, K. M., & Graebner, M. E. (2007). Theory building from cases: opportunities and challenges. *Academy of Management Journal, 50,* 25–32. https://doi.org/10.1002/job.
11. European Network and Information Security Agency. (2009). *Cloud Computing Security Risk Assessment.* https://www.enisa.europa.eu/publications/cloud-computing-risk-assessment.
12. Flick, U., von Kardoff, E., & Steinke, I. (Eds.). (2004). *A companion to qualitative research.* Sage.
13. Gioia, D. A., Corley, K. G., & Hamilton, A. L. (2013). Seeking qualitative rigor in inductive research: Notes on the Gioia methodology. *Organizational Research Methods, 16,* 15–31.
14. Gonzalez, R., Gasco, J., & Llopis, J. (2006). Information systems outsourcing: A literature analysis. *Information & Management, 43,* 821–834.
15. Gregory, R. W., Kaganer, E., Henfridsson, O., Ruch, T. J. (2018). IT consumerization and the transformation of it governance. *MIS Quarterly 42,* 1225–1253. https://doi.org/10.25300/ MISQ/2018/13703.
16. Gupta, P., Seetharaman, A., & Raj, J. R. (2013). The usage and adoption of cloud computing by small and medium businesses. *International Journal of Information Management, 33,* 861–874. https://doi.org/10.1016/j.ijinfomgt.2013.07.001.

17. Hoberg, P., Wollersheim, J., Krcmar, H. (2012). The business perspective on cloud computing—a literature review of research on cloud computing. In: *AMCIS 2012 Proceedings*, Paper 5.
18. Jick, T. D. (1979). Mixing qualitative and quantitative methods: Triangulation in action. *Administrative Science Quarterly, 24*, 602–611.
19. Kaspersky Lab. (2018). *On the money: Growing IT security budgets to protect digital transformation initiatives.*
20. Kern, T., Kreijger, J., & Willcocks, L. (2002). Exploring ASP as sourcing strategy: Theoretical perspectives, propositions for practice. *Journal of Strategic Information Systems, 11,* 153–177.
21. Lacity, M. C., & Hirschheim, R. (1993). The information systems outsourcing bandwagon. *Sloan Management Review, 35,* 73.
22. Lacity, M. C., Willcocks, L. P., & Khan, S. (2011). Beyond transaction cost economics: Towards an endogenous theory of information technology outsourcing. *Journal of Strategic Information Systems, 20,* 139–157. https://doi.org/10.1016/j.jsis.2011.04.002.
23. Lacity, M. C., Khan, S., Yan, A., & Willcocks, L. P. (2010). A review of the IT outsourcing empirical literature and future research directions. *Journal of Information Technology, 25,* 395–433. https://doi.org/10.1057/jit.2010.21.
24. Lee, Y., & Cavusgil, S. T. (2006). Enhancing alliance performance: The effects of contractual-based versus relational-based governance. *Journal of Business Research, 59,* 896–905.
25. Lin, A., & Chen, N.-C. (2012). Cloud computing as an innovation: Perception, attitude, and adoption. *International Journal of Information Management, 32,* 533–540. https://doi.org/10.1016/j.ijinfomgt.2012.04.001.
26. Loske, A., Widjaja, T., Buxmann, P. (2013). Cloud computing providers' unrealistic optimism regarding IT security risks: A threat to users? *ICIS* 1–20 (2013). https://doi.org/10.5121/ijnsa.2012.4206.
27. Maher, N., Kavanagh, P., Glowatz, M. (2013). A vendor perspective on issues with security, governance and risk for Cloud Computing. In: *26th Bled eConference—eInnovations Challenges Impacts Individ. Organ. Soc. Proc.* (pp. 103–114).
28. Marston, S., Li, Z., Bandyopadhyay, S., Zhang, J., & Ghalsasi, A. (2011). Cloud computing—The business perspective. *Decision Support Systems, 51,* 176–189. https://doi.org/10.1016/j.dss.2010.12.006.
29. McLeod, A., & Dolezel, D. (2018). Cyber-analytics: Modeling factors associated with healthcare data breaches. *Decision Support Systems, 108,* 57–68. https://doi.org/10.1016/j.dss.2018.02.007.
30. Mell, P., & Grance, T. (2011). *The NIST definition of cloud computing—recommendations of the national institute of standards and technology.* Gaithersburg: U.S. Department of Commerce.
31. Oliveira, T., Thomas, M., & Espadanal, M. (2014). Assessing the determinants of cloud computing adoption: An analysis of the manufacturing and services sectors. *Information & Management, 51,* 497–510.
32. Payton, S. (2010). Fluffy logic. *Financial Management*, 22–25 (14719185).
33. Peterson, R. R. (2004). Exploring IT governance in pharmaceutical and high-tech industries: Trends, challenges and directions.
34. Pfeffer, J., Salancik, G. R. (2003). *The external control of organizations: A resource dependence perspective.* Stanford University Press (2003).
35. Poppo, L., & Zenger, T. (2002). Do formal contracts and relational governance function as substitutes or complements? *Strategic Management Journal, 23,* 707–725.
36. Ramachandran, M., & Chang, V. (2016). Towards performance evaluation of cloud service providers for cloud data security. *International Journal of Information Management, 36,* 618–625. https://doi.org/10.1016/j.ijinfomgt.2016.03.005.
37. Ramireddy, S., Chakraborty, R., Raghu, T. S., Rao, H. R. (2010). Privacy and security practices in the arena of cloud computing—a research in progress. In: *AMCIS*, p. 574 (2010).
38. Rastogi, Gloria. (2015). Hendler: security and privacy of performing data analytics in the cloud: A three-way handshake of technology, policy, and management. *Journal of Information Policy, 5,* 129. https://doi.org/10.5325/jinfopoli.5.2015.0129.

39. Schneider, S., Sunyaev, A.: Determinant factors of cloud-sourcing decisions: Reflecting on the IT outsourcing literature in the era of cloud computing. *Journal of Information Technology* *31*(1), 1–31. https://doi.org/10.1057/jit.2014.25.
40. Schwarz, A., Jayatilaka, B., Hirschheim, R., & Goles, T. (2009). A conjoint approach to understanding IT application services outsourcing. *Journal of the Association of the Information Systems, 10,* 1.
41. Sood, S. K. (2012). A combined approach to ensure data security in cloud computing. *Journal of Network and Computer Applications, 35,* 1831–1838. https://doi.org/10.1016/j.jnca.2012. 07.007.
42. Sultan, N. A. (2011). Reaching for the "cloud": How SMEs can manage. *International Journal of Information Management, 31,* 272–278. https://doi.org/10.1016/j.ijinfomgt.2010.08.001.
43. Tallon, P. P., Ramirez, R. V, Short, J. E., Tallon, P. P., Ramirez, R. V, Short, J. E. (2013). The Information artifact in IT Governance : Toward a Theory of Information governance the information artifact in IT governance : Toward a theory of information governance. *Journal of Management Information System 30.* https://doi.org/10.2753/MIS0742-1222300306.
44. Tilson, D. (2010). Digital infrastructures : The missing IS research agenda. *Information System Research,* 748–759. https://doi.org/10.1287/isre.1100.0318.
45. Tiwana, A., & Konsynski, B. (2010). Complementarities between organizational it architecture and governance structure. *Information System Research, 21,* 288–304. https://doi.org/10.1287/ isre.
46. Tiwana, A., Konsynski, B., & Venkatraman, N. (2013). Information technology and organizational governance: The IT governance cube. *Journal of Management Information System, 30,* 7–12.
47. Vithayathil, J. (2017). Will cloud computing make the Information Technology (IT) department obsolete? *Information System Journal.* https://doi.org/10.1111/isj.12151.
48. vom Brocke, J., Braccini, A. M., Sonnenberg, C., & Spagnoletti, P. (2014). Living IT infrastructures—an ontology-based approach to aligning IT infrastructure capacity and business needs. *International Journal of Accounting Information Systems, 15,* 246–274.
49. Wang, N., Liang, H., Jia, Y., Ge, S., Xue, Y., & Wang, Z. (2016). Cloud computing research in the IS discipline: A citation/co-citation analysis. *Decision Support Systems, 86,* 35–47. https:// doi.org/10.1016/j.dss.2016.03.006.
50. Weill, P., & Ross, J. W. (2004). *IT governance.* Boston: Harvard Business School Press.
51. Williamson, O. E. (1981). The modern corporation: Origins, evolution, attributes. *Journal of Economic Literature, 19,* 1537–1568.
52. Williamson, O. E. (1985). *The economic institutions of capitalism.* New York: Free Press.
53. Wilkin, C. L., & Chenhall, R. H. (2010). A review of IT governance: A taxonomy to inform accounting information systems. *Journal of Information System, 24,* 107–146.
54. Yin, R. K. (2013). *Case study research: Design and methods.* Sage publications.

Data-Imagined Decision Making in Organizations: Do Visualization Tools Run in the Family?

Angela Locoro and Aurelio Ravarini

Abstract This paper reports of an experimental crossover between two different perspectives of organizational activities: decision making and data management. Although there are ever growing contact points between the two, it is also true that in enterprises data-driven decision making often shows many room for improvements. A converging direction of these two aspects of organizational routine could be that of comparing and coupling decision making steps, activities and characteristics with data visualization properties, capabilities and enablers of information sharing and assimilation. This study goes in this direction, by proposing an exploratory analysis of decision making models and data visualization characteristics in order to extract a set of common aspects of decision making and to configure a set of connections between them and data visualization tools features. These connections may serve to investigate the strength of synergies between decision making activities and data management visualization, their effectiveness for data-driven decision making and the margin of improvements with respect to the current decision routines in enterprises. This study contributes to set the terrain for making a clearer picture of the strengths and weaknesses of data-driven decision making, to find implications for design of data visualization tools for supporting decision making activities, and to provide indications of how proactively data visualization toolboxes should run in the family at all decision levels and for each role in organizations.

Keywords Data visualization · Decision making · Data visualization features · Decision making models

A. Locoro (✉) · A. Ravarini
Università Carlo Cattaneo—LIUC, Castellanza, (VA), Italy
e-mail: alocoro@liuc.it

A. Ravarini
e-mail: aravarini@liuc.it

© The Editor(s) (if applicable) and The Author(s), under exclusive license to Springer Nature Switzerland AG 2020
R. Agrifoglio et al. (eds.), *Digital Business Transformation*, Lecture Notes in Information Systems and Organisation 38, https://doi.org/10.1007/978-3-030-47355-6_5

1 Introduction

The ability to manage data has ever been and is becoming even more essential, since the impact and the role of IT in shaping the information flows of an enterprise has become hegemonic. As a consequence, the role of decision-makers and in particular the competences they should exhibit are changing in the direction of a higher sensibility together with the ability to scrutinize and critically interpret data, either big or small. The familiarity with electronic devices as well as with software like data visualization tools is becoming strategic in configuring the latter as companions of decision-makers in the analysis, management and partial control of the informational flow of their organization, both at operational and strategic levels. For these reasons, an investigation of the commonalities, influences and reciprocity between decision making and data interpretation can be traced along the following research questions:

- What are, if any, the main aspects common to decision making models, guidelines and methodologies that rely on data availability and management?
- What are, if any, the main features of data visualization that are able to support the decision making process?
- Why and how an organization do or should adopt data visualization tools as part of their cultural assets for supporting decision making effectiveness in all its key aspects?

The paper tries to answer the first two research questions so that the third question could be rooted properly for future assessments. An outline of the paper is the following: Sect. 2 is an overview of the principal decision making models considered for the extraction of common aspects of decision making activities; Sect. 3 reports the main features of data visualization related to the content, the presentation and the processing aspects of data management; Sect. 4 accounts for a model of connections between decision making aspects and data visualization features that represent a conceptual frame of our analysis able to drive the assessment of our hypothesis about the synergies between decisions and data interpretation; Sect. 5 draws some conclusions about the work done so far.

2 Decision Making Models

A first scrutiny of salient aspects of decision making has been inspired by the analysis of well known models. Starting from the point that decision-making is a process (sequence of steps) converting available information (inputs) into decisions (outputs), many theorists and researchers, after Simon's [24], doubts about the validity of 'perfect rationality' or 'global rationality' model, and tried to figure out the 'best' way in which this process may be applied in real life. The term 'best' is reported into inverted commas because it's not possible to certify in absolute terms the superiority of a model rather than another, but it is the context or the presence of some elements (like the nature of the problem, time pressure, costs, availability of resources and decision-maker characteristics) that defines the most suitable approach. Nevertheless, we extrapolated a common set of properties from each model that recalls the need to rely on the collection, availability, management and sharing of data.

The models analyzed are the *Incremental Decision Model* [18], the *Carnegie Model*; the *Garbage Can model* [9]; the *Observe, Orient, Decide, Act Loop (The OODA Loop)* [7, 12]; the *Recognition-Primed Decision Model (RPD)* [15]; the *Analytic Hierarchy Process (AHP)* [22]; and the *Ladder of Inference* [20]. A list of the main characteristics of each model are reported in Table 1. In this table, each model is summarized into a set of characteristics, which represent the main elements involved in the decision making process: the initial conditions and constraints, the way to proceed and to simplify assumptions and conditions, the people involved (either singular or teams) and the description of the final phase before the decision.

2.1   Decision Making Properties

The decision-making models described in the previous section provide a general view of the main theories developed around the paths that decision-makers should follow in order to find out a solution at an existing problem through the consideration of some aspects like the environment, timing and even the complexity of the initial situation which has a significant impact on the final decision. From these considerations, we may derive a series of factors that are common to all of the above models and help contextualize data management tasks in support of the decision making loop that may benefit from data visualization functionalities. We identified seven of such common factors:

2.1.1   Sharing of a Common Language

This is factor concerning the concept of common knowledge and cooperation of people. Common knowledge allows individuals to share and integrate aspects of knowledge which are not common between them [13]. According to Grant's above definition, common language is a type of common knowledge.

2.1.2   Availability of a High Number of Data and Information

This factor is strictly linked with the high presence of Big Data in our everyday life, a tremendously popular topic which will increase its importance in the next years. Nevertheless, it's not said that the availability of such amount of data always represents a positive element, but only that it can be turned into an advantage if data are managed properly.

Table 1 The decision making models analyzed with their main characteristics

Decision making models	Characterizing features
Bounded rationality	Limited Rationality
	Limited cognitive power
	Selection of the 'Satisfactory Option'
	Single decision-maker
Incremental decision model	Step by step process made of small choices
	Long length in process application
	step back in case of 'decision interrupts'
	Nonprogrammed decisions
	One decision for each process (Single decision)
Carnegie model	Initial ambiguity about the goals
	Presence of limitations affecting the individual
	Group of decision-makers (Organizational Coalitions)
	Decision taken in a short-time period
	One decision for each process (Single decision)
	Selection of the 'Satisfactory Option'
Garbage can theory	High uncertainty
	Rapid changes in the environment
	Chaotic process
	Streams of events
	Group of decision-makers
	More decisions in the same process (Multiple decisions)
OODA	Step by step process
	Continuous application of the process
	Decision taken in a short-time period
	High competition presence in the environment
RPD	Experience of single person can make the difference
	Decision taken in a short-time period
	Unconscious comparison of alternatives
	Selection of the 'Satisfactory Option'
AHP	Step by step process
	Simplification of complex problems into sub-problems
	Definition of goals, criteria and sub criteria
	Judgment application
	Comparison of alternatives
Ladder of inference	Step by step process
	Freedom for decision-makers in evaluating options
	Selection of the 'Best Option' in that moment
	Cognitive Biases avoided

2.1.3 Routine Presence

This factor refers to all of the forms, rules, procedures, conventions, strategies, and technologies around which organizations are constructed and through which they operate [13]. It's quite common to find the application of this factor on a daily basis, especially when the decision requires little research or time investment. Routine concept can even be referred to decision-makers' ability to apply the same procedure in different situation, no matter what the problem is. At the end of the day, two interpretations can be derived from the 'routine presence' property: the first one is applied when a programmed decision is requested to be taken and as a consequence decision-makers behave in the same way every time a specific problem needs to be managed; the other interpretation requires the application of the same decision-making procedure without considering the different nature of the problem.

2.1.4 Knowledge Sharing

This factor describes the process of transferring knowledge (mix of know-how, experience, skills and information) from a person to another within an organization. This exchange can lead to the creation of new knowledge which can be in turn an important source for an organization to get competitive advantage [21]. People should wish to communicate and share their knowledge, otherwise the process wouldn't start. Under this point view, people have to put the sake of the company above any personal interest.

2.1.5 Lack of Clarity in Cause-Effect Relationships and Presence of Cognitive Traps

This factor is characteristic of the Garbage Can model, where problems, solutions, participants and choices flow through the organization. However, the presence of all of these elements cause uncertainty in estimating the problem and potential solution as well. Organizational decisions are not derived from a step by step process, instead they are a mix of problems and solutions acting as independent events. In such a situation the cause-and-effect relationships within the organization are difficult to be identified [9]. Moreover, the presence of cognitive traps increases the complexity of cause-and-effect relationships causing a distortion of the facts and influencing decision-makers with prejudices not necessarily conform to the reality.[1]

---

[1] For an example of cognitive information bias see https://en.wikipedia.org/wiki/List_of_cognitive_biases.

2.1.6 Identification of Opportunities Regardless of Problems

This decision-making factor describes the possibility that participants can keep identifying ideas without focusing just on a specific problem [9]. In other words, the existence of a problem requiring a solution doesn't impede to generate opportunities that are not applicable in that case but may be useful in the future.

2.1.7 Capacity of Making Predictions by Considering Available Information

This factor has been derived from the OODA loop and it explains how a decision-maker applies the model by considering the available information that he has to extract from the observation of the environment. Then orienting towards it allows to form a mental image of the circumstances. It's the orientation turning information into knowledge that makes this knowledge become a good decision. In fact, one decision should even be able to predict the next move of the opponent. The OODA loop can be applied to competitive business scenarios where knowledge of an opponent's behavioral patterns can be exploited through fast and agile anticipatory action [12].

3 Data Visualization Features

Data visualization can be defined as 'the representation and presentation of data that exploit visual perception abilities in order to amplify cognition' [14].

Data Visualization tools are software working as powerful instruments to manage, represent and show data so to get insights and facilitate the identification of trends or solve problems. They have features that correspond to the desired characteristics or attributes that can support people in the decision-making process. A list of Data Visualization features that we identify as meaningful factors for decision making are reported in Table 2. They are inherent to the presentation, the processing and the interaction with Data Visualization tools. The first three divisions have been borrowed from a foundational work on the semiology of graphics [5]. Most of these features have been defined in [2, 8, 16]. In what follows, some main features are described in more details and definitions are given for each of them.

3.1 Data Organization

Data organization refers to the syntax of data in graphic visualizations. Multidimensionality refers to the potential of data visualization tools to represent in a single picture several dimensions besides the 2-D of the Cartesian plane, by exploiting other perceptive variables such as size, color, shape, orientation, shades, and the like [23]. *Selectivity* and *associativity* are, respectively, the features that allow to filter and to

Table 2 A list of identified meaningful factors for Data Visualization affecting decision-making

Data organization	Data processing	Data communication	Ease of use
Multidimensionality	Expressiveness	Shareability	Familiarity
Order	Readability	Universality	Intuitivity
Proportionality	Extensibility	Storytelling	Usability
Selectivity	Sinteticity	Interactivity	Flexibility
Associativity	Minimalism		Adaptability
	Predictivity		
	Immediacy		
	Clarity		
	Informativity		

group data into sets and not in terms of individual data points that are of no interest in most cases. Within the data visualization tools, it's possible to distinguish (resp. aggregating) measures or dimensions. The type of aggregation applied may change every time according to the context of the view. *Order* and *proportionality* are related, respectively, to the ordinal or numerical nature of the data that are to be represented.

3.2 Data Processing

When processing data, a series of features are necessary to manipulate them in order to better interpret them for decision purposes. For example, *expressiveness* identifies how the graphical language that expresses the desired information is relevant, minimal and without noise [17]. *Readability* pertains to the good comprehension of a topic through the interpretation of charts. A readable graph is not only appealing because of the quality of the image drawn, but it mostly consents to get knowledge of the underlying meaning and structure [3]. Sinteticity allows to reproduce reality with the minimal use of informative resources [16]. In other words, a context can be represented by relying just on some resources which are anyway able to provide enough information for describing the reality.

Clarity and *informativity* refers, respectively to the 'ease of understanding and fruition of information by users' and to the 'complete representation of the reality' [16]. Indeed, the reader of the graph is the one who needs to interpret the data and be informed on the facts, but the creator of the figure is much more relevant because he is directly involved in the process and in its choices, like the selection of sources or the type of chart, the impact on the clarity of a representation and the reporting into graphs all of the necessary information for the audience so that a detection of the reality is possible. An accurate knowledge of the context analysed is what a representation aims to achieve, and the application of the so called visualization process allows it.

This process begins with raw data, so the selection of a dataset capable of helping users to detect reality is a good starting point. For instance, a design is judged effective when it can be interpreted accurately or quickly, when it has visual impact or when it can be rendered in a cost-effective manner (Mackinlay, 1986). In other words, a visualization is more effective than another one if the information expressed by one visualization are more readily perceived than the information in the other visualization. As already said human brain has not been made for translating binary code or quickly elaborating written information, so the visual representation of data seems to be the most adapt way to deal with this problem. Under this point of view, data visualizations play an important role since they allow a more efficient flow of information within the organization which is directly converted in more efficiency for the business. Thus, the better is the effectiveness of a visualization, the higher is going to be the comprehension of the context and as consequence more knowledge can be derived by users.

3.3   Data Communication

Data and charts can be easily transferred from a user to another so that anyone could make its own analysis by having them at his disposal. In this way, the communication would be facilitated by the fact that even people not being physically in the same location can exchange impressions about a graph resulting from the data visualization process. This is *shareability* of data.

The charts should be understood by the majority of people even if the audience speaks another language or has a different cultural education than the 'creator'. Data Visualization in this sense has the feature of *universality*, and it may be considered as the business's new Lingua Franca [4]. The visualization of a dataset into a chart is without any doubt a useful form of communication, comprehensible by the majority of people even if may be required a minimum level of knowledge of the context from which the chart is derived because otherwise wouldn't be possible to analyse it and the chart would be for its own sake. In fact, visualization is not the goal of the process but it is the mean through which data can be analysed. Understanding is the final objective. However, becoming fluent in communicating through data visualization is a necessary skill that should be trained so to have more opportunities in the business field.

Storytelling is the data visualization feature which permits to apply the available techniques so to improve the comprehension of reality. Making it simpler users have the possibility to use previously collected data, convert them into charts or graphs and tell a story, from the beginning until the end. An example is the representation of a fact though a storyline (e.g. the genealogical tree of a family) or a timeline reporting a sequence of temporal events (e.g. all the wars that took place in the last three centuries). The claim is 'data tell what's happening, but stories explain the reason' [6]. A tale made of charts simplifies the understanding of raw data because human mind is able to create connections based on emotions and memorize images.

Elements like color, length, width, size and shape can positively work in favour of people who would better remember a chart. Thus, users aim to tell a story from which knowledge can be extrapolated but this story brings advantages for different figures that may have interests into the company. These people are mainly stakeholders and customers. Its use may help in having an overview of the context, identifying potential trends and making decisions but the last one is referred to managers.

Interactivity permits users to navigate within the data visualization tool, manipulate data that may be useful for the visualization process and display them at various levels of detail and in various formats. A 'dialogue' between humans and machine is required so to exploit the potentiality of interactive visualizations [10]. A good design facilitates users' examination since the presentation of data is clearer and a better detection of solutions or new trends is possible.

3.4   Ease of Use

Ease of Use refers to the user friendly experience with an information tool that helps users achieve their goals (like accomplishing a task and making a decision). The ease of use has been associated with the familiarity dimension, and both have been observed influencing the attractiveness as well [19]. *Familiarity* is the feature describing the high standardization and diffusion of classical charts which are provided by every data visualization tool. In fact, users can choose among the most known presentation styles like bar, line, scatter, pie graphs and flow charts that are all easily understood by visual creators as well as consumers. They are usually adopted to solve common visualization problems even if their use is limited to specific data types and the degree of novelty is quite low [8]. *Usability* is also part of the easiness of use and is defined as 'the extent to which a product can be used by users to achieve specified goals with effectiveness, efficiency and satisfaction in a specified context of use' (ISO 9241-11 definition). In other words, this feature explains how the data visualization tools would allow to achieve well defined objectives by providing a high perception of the context and by yielding users' satisfaction.

Intuitivity refers to the organization of information in terms of context, so that it can convey all the properties of the reality of interest 'at a glance' [16]. The idea is that important concepts need to be translated into visualization and the objective in this case is to reduce the time thinking about how to use or how to read and interpret the chart. The speed with which users are able to read or interpret a visualization should be determined by the complexity of the subject and the purpose of the project, not by the ineffectiveness of design. Indeed, a clear representation of data and the familiarity with the chart selected are both important aspects allowing to get an immediate comprehension of the situation.

Flexibility and *adaptability* are the interactivity counterpart related to the effectiveness and satisfaction of users while manipulating data through visual means. The objective of evaluating visualization flexibility is to improve computer users' understanding of a dataset, otherwise the visualization would be totally useless [25], while adaptability is more related to represent charts and graphs on every kind of device, no matter if the version of the tool is specifically developed for computers or mobile devices. However, the visualization on different devices has been recently analysed and according to some studies a reduction of the clutter on the screen is the key for a better perception and comprehension of data reproduced. The problem is that on-screen clutter becomes significant in the context of mobile devices which have much smaller screens than traditional desktops [11].

4   A Preliminary Set of Connections

After having analyzed each decision-making factor and each data visualization feature in its group, we finally identified a first set of possible intersections between the two. In the following paragraphs we describe and motivate them.

4.1   Connection 1: Better Communication Between Decision-Makers

The factor 'sharing of a common language' describes how much is important the comprehension between people since they cooperate into organizational coalitions and share their know-how. In particular, the common language refers to charts and graphs which are drawn through the data visualization tools. The type of communication that should be developed in order to improve the decision-making process is the data communication. The question is: Do data communication support and improve the sharing of a common language? And how? All the features associated to data communication come into play to determine this dimension of synergy. A prominent topic in this respect is also related to the need of specific roles in organizations that are in charge of proactively mediating between data management visualizations and decision makers (e.g., storytellers, and the like).

4.2   Connection 2: More Manageability of Data Which Flow Through the Organization

Due to the increased availability of data from internal and external environment, their collection and analysis would allow decision-makers to better understand the market, find out potential trends, estimate customers' preferences and evaluate the growth of the company. If exploited, these possibilities will advantage the organization against competitors. The management of such a big amount of data requires the application of data communication as well as data organization and data processing features. All the features of data visualization are crucial in the ambit of this connection.

4.3   Connection 3: Enhancement in Picking Up the Most Adapt Option within a Set of Alternatives

The decision-making process is applied so to get a final decision which can solve an existing problem. However, it's the decision-making model that provides the guidelines for the path to follow in order to achieve the final decision. In some cases, the decision is the result of a step by step process leading to that solution, in other cases decision-makers have to pick up an option from a set of alternatives. The identified features helping this enhancement are those of data organization and data processing.

4.4   Connection 4: More Efficiency in Terms of Quality and Time

The 'Routine presence' property allows to increase the efficiency of the decision-making process. The result is translated in a better use of time and energy so that any waste of them will be avoided. Moreover, even the quality of the final decision is going to take advantage from the routine application since the higher is the familiarity of decision-makers with a context, the better will be the decision. In fact, practice makes perfect and once understood how to handle a situation, the successful approach can be fast applied with a consequent low probability of committing mistakes. The time saved can be used to focus on other tasks. The data visualization features that can help this process are data organization and ease of use.

4.5   Connection 5: Creation of a Knowledge Flow

The creation of knowledge is what data visualization tools aim to obtain. In fact, these software transform raw data into graphical representations which are consequently interpreted by decision-makers through their competences. The outcome of such interpretations is the acquired knowledge which allows to clarify eventual doubts the decision-makers may have and take a decision. Thus, it's like this new knowledge needs human competences, skills and experience to be extrapolated from graphical representations. However, competences, skills and experience can be considered as components of knowledge itself. The creation of a knowledge flow may be optimized by the data processing and data communication features of data visualization.

4.6 Connection 6: Improvement of Data Quality When Scenarios Are Full of Uncertainty

As the decision-making property 'Lack of clarity in cause-effect relationships and presence of cognitive traps' has been derived from the Garbage Can model, this model is taken as an example for this connection. Therein, participants throw problems and potential solutions into a figurative garbage can. The outcome of this decision-making process may lead to a final decision which results from the match between problems and potential solutions. Thus, it's not said that a potential solution will be paired to a problem as well as a problem may not find the correspondent solution. In such scenario the identification of cause-effect relationships is really complicated since problems and solutions are independent variables. It generates a natural disorder and decisions are taken in a context characterized by a high level of uncertainty. Moreover, the presence of cognitive traps may influence decision-makers ability in considering the reality as it is, so the choices are taken without the adequate level of perception. In a nutshell the main consequences of the Garbage Can model application are:

1. not all the problems are solved since the correspondent solution may not have been proposed by participants;
2. potential solutions might be proposed even if problems don't exist at the moment.

In this scenario, data visualization tools may support the decision process with features of information organization and ease of use.

4.7 Connection 7: Increase of Decision-Makers' Satisfaction

The satisfaction principle corresponds to the main pillar of alternatives selection in Simon's Bounded Rationality decision-making model. The result of this model application is the identification of the main problem and the consequent creation of a set of possible alternatives from which the most satisfactory ones are going to be selected. Since decision-makers can't achieve the 'maximum solution', they try to find out a course of actions that is good enough according to their minimal acceptability criteria [1]. The data visualization tool features impacting on the decision-making property in order to increase decision-makers' are potentially all of the four groups of features detected for data visualization. Also specific roles in organizations that can match the data management visualization features with decision making activities are strongly required in this scenario.

5   Conclusions

In this paper, we put together well known decision-making models and data visualization features. The goal of our study was to intersect them into a model framing data visualization for decision-making practices. This model has been introduced and described so that the first two research questions were answered and there is room to validate it with qualitative future work in order to answer to the third research question. Further assessment should be made with observational studies in enterprises that wish to share with us their decision-making models and their use of data visualization tools to support decisions at all levels and frequency. These further studies aim for example at selecting among data visualization features the most relevant ones for each connection or whether some of them may be for example considered general enough to be supportive of all of the decision-making properties.

Our last point regards the present-day trends for which our research project fits well. One of them is in line with the topics of EU calls next to come, regarding for example the impacts on the future advancements of intelligent systems, machine learning and pervasive technologies in the direction of proposing solutions for 'algorithms opaqueness, implicit biases in decision making and lack of explicability for trusting, accepting and adopting the next generation of intelligent machines on a wider scale'.[2] Our study goes in the direction of supporting decision making for the next generation of data management. Citing a bit more from the above call we discover that 'explanation could be more tightly intertwined with the decision making process itself so that decisions can be challenged, interpreted, refined and adjusted through mutual exchange, introspection [...] and active learning of both system and user, for example through dialogue or other forms of multi-modal interaction aimed at establishing mutual trust'.

References

1. Barros, G. (2010). Herbert A. Simon and the concept of rationality: Boundaries and procedures. *Brazilian Journal of Political Economy, 30*(3), 455–472.
2. Batini, C., Scannapieco, M., et al. (2016). *Data and information quality*. Cham, Switzerland: Springer, Google Scholar.
3. Bennett, C., Ryall, J., Spalteholz, L., & Gooch, A. (2007). The aesthetics of graph visualization. *Computational Aesthetics, 2007*, 57–64.
4. Berinato, S. (2016). *Good charts: The HBR guide to making smarter, more persuasive data visualizations*. Harvard Business Review Press.
5. Bertin, J. (1983). *Semiology of graphics*. University of Wisconsin Press.
6. Boje, D. M. (1991). The storytelling organization: A study of story performance in an office-supply firm. *Administrative Science Quarterly*, 106–126.
7. Brehmer, B. (2005). The dynamic OODA loop: Amalgamating Boyd's OODA loop and the cybernetic approach to command and control. In *Proceedings of the 10th International Command and Control Research Technology Symposium* (pp. 365–368).

---

[2]See for example H2020 Human centric AI EU call at https://ec.europa.eu/info/funding-tenders/opportunities/portal/screen/opportunities/topic-details/fetproact-eic-05-2019.

8. Cairo, A. (2012). *The functional art: An introduction to information graphics and visualization*. New Riders.
9. Cohen, M. D., March, J. G., Olsen, J. P., et al. (1972). A garbage can model of organizational choice. *Administrative Science Quarterly, 17*(1), 1–25.
10. Dilla, W., Janvrin, D. J., & Raschke, R. (2010). Interactive data visualization: New directions for accounting information systems research. *Journal of Information Systems, 24*(2), 1–37.
11. Gaber, M. M., Krishnaswamy, S., Gillick, B., AlTaiar, H., Nicoloudis, N., Liono, J., et al. (2013). Interactive self-adaptive clutter-aware visualisation for mobile data mining. *Journal of Computer and System Sciences, 79*(3), 369–382.
12. Galinec, D., & Macanga, D. (2012). Observe, orient, decide and act cycle and pattern-based strategy: Characteristics and complementation. In: *Central European Conference on Information and Intelligent Systems* (p. 371). Varazdin: Faculty of Organization and Informatics.
13. Grant, R. M. (1996). Toward a knowledge-based theory of the firm. *Strategic Management Journal, 17*(S2), 109–122.
14. Kirk, A. (2012). *Data visualization: A Successful Design Process*. Packt Publishing Ltd.
15. Klein, G. A. (1993). *A recognition-primed decision (RPD) model of rapid decision making*. New York: Ablex Publishing Corporation.
16. Locoro, A., Cabitza, F., Actis-Grosso, R., & Batini, C. (2017). Static and interactive infographics in daily tasks: A value-in-use and quality of interaction user study. *Computers in Human Behavior, 71*, 240–257.
17. Mackinlay, J. (1986). Automating the design of graphical presentations of relational information. *Acm Transactions on Graphics (ToG), 5*(2), 110–141.
18. Mintzberg, H. (1975). *The managers job: Folklore and fact*.
19. Quispel, A., Maes, A., & Schilperoord, J. (2016). Graph and chart aesthetics for experts and laymen in design: The role of familiarity and perceived ease of use. *Information Visualization, 15*(3), 238–252.
20. Ross, R. (1994). *The ladder of inference. The fifth discipline fieldbook: Strategies and tools for building a learning organization* (pp. 242–246).
21. Rusuli, M. S. C., Tasmin, R., & Hashim, N. (2011). *Knowledge Sharing Practice in Organization*.
22. Saaty, T. L. (2014). *Analytic heirarchy process*. Wiley.
23. Shneiderman, B. (2003). The eyes have it: A task by data type taxonomy for information visualizations. In *The craft of information visualization* (pp. 364–371). Elsevier.
24. Simon, H. A. (1990). Bounded rationality. In *Utility and probability* (pp. 15–18). Springer.
25. Wong, D. H. T., & Chee, C. M. (2015). Adaptive network data visualization design for manifold computer users. *ICIC Express Letters. Part B, Applications: An International Journal of Research and Surveys, 6*(1), 41–46.

IT Investment Decisions in Industry 4.0: Evidences from SMEs

Niloofar Kazemargi⬤ and Paolo Spagnoletti⬤

Abstract Organizational processes, production, business strategy, value creation and value delivery are undergoing significant change as a result of emerging new technologies in industry 4.0 context. This has drawn attention across many countries and not only organizations, but also stakeholders and policy makers as the fourth industrial revolution. While Industry 4.0 has been widely investigated in large enterprises, yet to date, little is known about how SMEs with limited financial resources make strategic decisions in particular about IT investment on diverse emerging technologies. To close this gap, this paper focused on the propensity of SMEs in IT investment in an industry 4.0 context. We analyze the responses of 1889 Italian SMEs to Government policies designed to facilitate SMEs in adopting technologies for Industry 4.0. This study aims to contribute to alignment literature by highlighting the importance of IT investment as a strategic decision in Industry 4.0. Moreover, the paper offers a set of practical implications.

Keywords Industry 4.0 · IT alignment · IT investment · SMEs

1 Introduction

Organizational processes, production, strategy, value creation and value delivery are undergoing significant change as result of emerging technologies. The deep impact of these technologies on business processes [12, 41] highlight the integration of IT strategy with business strategy [9, 16]. Considering the fast-changing and diverse emerging technologies, recent research emphasizes that IT alignment is a continuous process [49]. Organizations need to consecutively align their IT strategy with business strategy through investment and development their organizational IT resources and

N. Kazemargi (✉)
Department of Business and Management, Luiss Guido Carli, Rome, Italy
e-mail: Nkazemargi@luiss.it

P. Spagnoletti
Department of Information Systems, University of Agder, Grimstad, Norway

R. Agrifoglio et al. (eds.), *Digital Business Transformation*, Lecture Notes in Information Systems and Organisation 38, https://doi.org/10.1007/978-3-030-47355-6_6

infrastructures. IT investment and developing digital infrastructure enable organizations to enhance their innovation performance, however, organizations have struggled to opt and invest on the right technologies in consistent with their business objectives which may create a path dependency and constrain the future organizational capability to innovate [40]. Moreover, when an organization has invested on a specific technology and integrated it with the legacy system, adopting another technology will be complex and costly.

Despite the increasing interest in Industry 4.0, our understanding of how firms invest and align their IT strategy with business strategy in industry 4.0 is limited. In particular, while the concept of Industry 4.0 has been widely investigated in large enterprises [3], few studies focus on SMEs [34]. SMEs having limited resources and capabilities face challenges in making IT investment decisions to align its IT strategies with business strategies. Thus, in this paper, we examine the IT investments made by SMEs in Industry 4.0.

In this study we focus on Italian SMEs investments on industry 4.0. Our rationale behind our research design is that Italian government has launched a strategic plan in 2016 to accelerate technology adoption and boost the Italian production system.[1] Therefore, access to financial aids remove financial barriers to invest on industry 4.0. This provides us with a unique occasion to examine IT investments and typology of technologies on industry 4.0 across different industrial sectors and geographic dimensions.

Based on accessing to a large-scale dataset including 1889 Italian SMEs benefiting from the Italian financial incentive for Industry 4.0, the purpose of this paper is to analyze IT investment by SMEs focusing on industry 4.0. The findings illustrate the propensity of IT investments by SMEs and invested technologies. More specifically, since the financial incentive targets SMEs from all sectors, an analysis of the technologies and assets that SMEs acquired for Industry 4.0 can provide us with more detailed insights on IT alignment in SMEs.

The structure of paper is as follows. First, we present related studies on industry 4.0. Second, we present and discuss the importance of IT investment decisions in business strategy and alignment. Third, we present the results of analysis conducted on 3670 purchases by SMEs who benefit from industry 4.0 initiative. Finally, we present the discussion and theoretical and managerial implications.

---

[1]Looking at data reported on digital economy society index in 2017, although Denmark, Ireland, Sweden and Belgium are leading in digital economies in the EU, the rank of Italy is 25th among 28th EU member states. To fill this gap and support digital transformation by SMEs, thus, Italian government has launched a strategic plan for digitalization in 2016.

2   Relevant Literature

2.1   *Industry 4.0*

The German government initiative known as Industry 4.0 refers to integration of cyber and physical systems through interconnection of sensors, machines and systems to create connected and smart value chain beyond a single firm's boundaries. The businesses have undergone significant change due to embedded systems that create hybrid physical-cyber systems [38]. Following Rüßmann et al. [42], we consider industry 4.0 as combination of different technologies See Fig. 1.

Advances in technologies enhance capability of firms to generate, collect and analyze big amount of data. Capturing and processing real-time data enhance organizational capabilities in decision making and create new value creation opportunities for firms [37].

The evolving robots allow firms to reduce cost and flexibility due to automation and decentralization of decision making, for example, automated guided vehicles (AGVs).

Cloud computing technologies enable organizations to remotely access scalable digital resources: applications, platforms and infrastructures [31]. The potential benefits of cloud-based services for organizations are cost convenience, business agility

Fig. 1 Industry 4.0 as combination of different technologies. Adapted from Rüßmann et al. [42]

and scalability of resources [30], that have led to a growing trend in adopting cloud-based solutions in recent years [35], specifically for small and medium enterprises [23].

Simulating production process leverage by availability of massive real-time data can allow firms to optimize process settings in terms of time and quality.

Internet of Things (IoT) refers to a network of interconnected machines, devices and sensors with capability to communicate via standard protocols. Devices with embedded computing systems connect via the internet, and enable to collect and exchange data, and interact together. Real-time information can be captured and exchanged through embedded systems which enhances productivity and facilitates interoperability [50].

Prototyping and producing products in small batches with high level of customization is feasible by using additive manufacturing like 3-D printing. The cutting-edge technology enhances flexibility to produce customized products.

Augmented reality provides information via devices such as augmented-reality glasses for better decision making.

Integration of systems refers to platforms and data-integration networks that allow firms to access and exchange data across different processes, departments and also across supply chain.

With increased connectivity among systems and devices, firms are more dependent on management and protection systems to imitate cyberthreats. Cyber-connected systems collect huge amount of data from devices, sensors and actuators which facilitate real-time monitoring flow of materials and data along the supply chain. In adoption of cutting-edge technologies, firms need to pay particular attention on emerged vulnerabilities and security threats. As to adopting cloud, multi-tenant characteristics of cloud that contains data of multiple organizations increase the risk of direct attacks on cloud infrastructures [4]. Poorly-secured systems make firms prone to cyber security threats, especially when new IT technologies are integrated with the legacy systems [20]. Thus, firms need to ensure security in terms of: (1) accessibility of data only by authorized actors and protection of sensitive data i.e. confidentiality; (2) controlling any modification i.e. integrity (3) continuity of operations i.e. availability [2].

The combination of these technologies is extensively expanding the span of the services and products and business networks [9]. The embedded and connected sensors, microprocessors, software and systems with in physical artifacts allow organizations to expand the value of products and services [38] and more room for product differentiation. At the same time, the on-demand resources e.g. cloud computing enhance organizational scaling ability [9]. When it intertwines with availability of real time data it allows rapid mass customized production and highly customized services [41]. The expanded span of data collection (e.g. data created by embedded sensors or digital actions by individuals knowing as Big data), analysis and monitoring capabilities across value chain enable organizations to manage the whole business processes more efficiently and effectively. Moreover, the hybrid physical-cyber systems facilitate integration of organizations (vertically and/or horizontally) across the value chain. The plug-and-play concept in products and services, automation and standardized processes facilitate integration of value chain.

Furthermore, industry 4.0 enhances the flexibility through decentralized control, autonomous robots, and data-driven decision making across value chain networks [12]. Simultaneously, automation and integration of value chain across organizations enable organizations to reduce the time to market –named Smart supply chain [22]. Organizations aim to meet the needs of customers and adopt available technologies to create new value propositions. Industry 4.0 introduces a paradigm shift in the way organizations create value: offered services and products, customer interface, required resources, core competences, partner network, and capture value [12, 36].

In sum, industry 4.0 enables firms to enhance flexibility, quality and productivity and can facilitate monitoring and controlling of energy consumptions, thus, improve sustainability [13]. However, research stresses on considering the overall sustainability view since for instance some technologies such as automation and robots are expected to challenge social aspects of sustainability such as employment [7].

2.2   *IT Investment and Alignment in SMEs*

One of the dominant topics in the IS research relates to alignment of IT strategy with business strategy. The traditional view of IT alignment is limited to alignment of IT strategy at IT functional level strategy with business strategy [21]. The recent IS research highlights the peculiar characteristics of new emerging technologies and the embeddedness of digital technologies in organizational operations which influence and transform the business operations and business models of many organizations [12, 41]. Consequently, the IT strategy is not apart from business strategy anymore. Instead, it is intertwined and integrated with business strategies [9, 16]. Moreover, the changes in IT landscape and emerging new technologies require that organizations consecutively align the IT strategy with business strategy [49]. This means that organizations need to develop and change organizational IT resources and infrastructures in consistent with business strategy. In particular, organizations need to align the business resources and IT investment [33]. IT investment decisions influence organizational and innovation performance [26]. For example, Kleis et al. [25] emphasize on the link between investment on IT infrastructure and innovation. At the same time, making IT investment decisions and opting typology of IT and infrastructure create a path dependency that may constrain and influence the future capability of organizations to develop new resources, processes, and even business models [40]. Therefore, considering the complex and fast changing IT landscape, managers need to make sense [48] of IT trends and diverse emerging technologies in order to make the proper IT investment decisions [1].

As reported by Gartner, organizational IT spending is expected to increase also in 2019 [17], yet it is challenging for organizations to align IT investment decision with business strategy and adopt proper IT resources and infrastructure to create and add value. In particular, the SMEs may face difficulties in aligning and integrating IT strategies with business strategies due to several reasons. First, SMEs mainly focus on short-term strategy [32]. Second, the characteristics of SMEs lead to different IT adoption rates in comparison with large organizations [19], since SMEs usually target a niche market in order to sustain their competitive position in the market [15]. Consequently, even high-tech SMEs have adopted very specific technologies to meet the niche demands. Third, the decision of what technology to adopt in SMEs is influenced by external environmental factors such as competitive supply side [43]. Moreover, SMEs are usually characterized by limited knowledge and capabilities of managers who making strategic decisions [28], limited IS skills of workforce, lack of financial resources, and IT infrastructures [11, 45]. The lack of financial resources also acts as barriers for SMEs to use external knowledge sources or to develop internal IT skills. The uncertainty regarding the technologies and level of capability of managers in seeing long-term benefit of IT investments influence IT adoption by organizations [43]. However, Levy et al. [28] present evidence that managers of SMEs align their IS investment with business strategies: either to focus on efficiency and cost reduction or on added value strategies.

To develop new emerging technologies, SMEs require to invest on IT infrastructures, IT services, and train or hire new workforce in an industry 4.0 context. However, the lack of sufficient resources may limit SMEs capabilities to adopt new technologies. For instance, SMEs face difficulty in successful implementation of Enterprise Resource Planning software which relies on high level of IS skills [14]. Another example is decisions related to cloud service level (Software-as-a-Service, Platform-as-a-Service or Infrastructure-as-a-service) which is based on organizational IT skills and expertise level: Platform-as-a-Service or Infrastructure-as-a-Service solutions demand higher IT capabilities to maintain and upgrade the systems, while Software-as-a-Service requires less efforts and expertise from firms [44].

As evidence shows 58% of firms who are victims of cyber-attacks are small organizations [47]. Thus, in aligning IT with business strategies, IT governance [10] and investments is prerequisite in order to not only support business strategy in short and long term, but also mitigate associated risks.

3   Dataset and Data Description

The significant influence of Industry 4.0 on businesses makes it an inevitable concept in future industrial operations. For the purpose of our study, we focus on Italian SMEs investment on industry 4.0. Our rationale behind our research design is that Italian government has launched strategic plan in 2016 to accelerate technology adoption and boost the Italian production system. As the major part of Italian enterprises are SMEs, they have limited financial resources and face difficulty to access finance from banks. Thus, the Italian Government has designed a number of direct and indirect aids, among which an incentive for bank loans for SMEs investing on new assets related to industry 4.0. The new policies following the National Plan for Business 4.0 embrace two types of incentives and supports: (1) tax benefits and credits for organizations investing in new technologies, developing research projects, driving incomes from intellectual properties (IPs), or investing in training workforce in an industry 4.0 context, (2) bank loans and guarantee for organizations investing in new technologies and innovation project (Piano Nazionale Impresa 4.0 by the Italian ministry economic development).

We had access to a unique database including SMEs requests for IT investments, funded IT investments and the typology of invested technology. We analyzed the responses of SMEs to Italian Government policies designed to facilitate SMEs in adopting technologies for Industry 4.0. The original database contains 3670 accepted applications (1889 Italian SMEs) for bank loan support package out of 5130 applications made in 11 months from February 15th, 2017 to April 13th, 2018. All registered SMEs (1) operating in production sectors and (2) considered as low risk of bankruptcy/not in difficulty were eligible to apply. This incentive includes physical assets such as plant and machinery, industrial and commercial equipment, as well as, intangible assets like software and digital technologies that support industry 4.0. The loan ranges from 20.000 € and 2.000.000 € with maximum 5-year duration. For all 3670 confirmed financial aid, our database includes also the type of purchased asset/s based on Budget Law in 2017,[2] in total 42 categories.

The database, then, was merged with data extracted from AIDA[3] (Italian Digital Database of Companies) which provides detailed data on Italian companies such as size, industrial sector, region, foundation year and some financial information.

In order to further analysis of the technological investments, we initially adopt the nine pillars in Industry 4.0 following Rüßmann et al. [42]. Since not all of assets can be categorized based on the nine pillars in Industry 4.0, we identify another category named "advanced manufacturing" referring to a various set of advanced machineries, devices, equipment and systems for production processes.

4 Data Analysis and Findings

In total 5130 SMEs applied for financial aids through banks or intermediaries which 1889 of them granted for the financial incentive to purchase assets. For SMEs received loans, Table 1 illustrates the demographic characteristics.

The majority of firms are located in the north part of Italy that around 44.5% of them are small-sized: 21.9% North West and 22.49% North East (Fig. 2). The number of SMEs located in South (2.4%) is much lower than in Center of Italy (16.3%).

---

[2]Annex 6a, Annex 6b, INTERMINISTERIAL DECREE—List of Capital Goods eligible for the incentive, January 25th 2016.

[3]AIDA is the Italian provider of the Bureau Van Dijk European Database. The database contains structured information on over 1,000,000 Limited Companies operating in Italy, providing updated information such as shareholding, personal data, financial and economic information, investments and M&A etc.

Table 1 Demographic
characteristics of SMEs

Foundation year	(%)
Before 1970	4.37
1970s	12.33
1980s	21.94
1990s	23.94
2000s	24.16
2010 and After	13.26
Total	100
% Of craft companies	**36.13**
% Of startups	**0.36**
No. of employees	
Less than 10 employees	20.79
10-49 employees	62.01
50-249 employees	17.19
Total	100

Bold indicates main headings

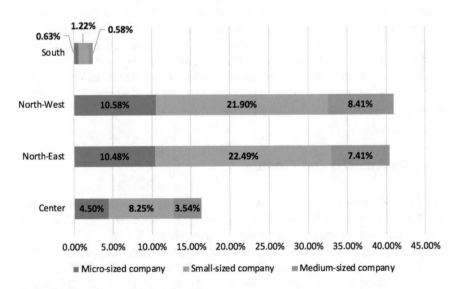

Fig. 2 Size and regional distribution of SMEs

Our findings show that around 89% of firms gained financial benefits belong to manufacturing sector. In particular, SMEs from manufacturing sector are concentrated in the following industrial subsectors:

- 33.5% manufacture of metal products (excluding machinery and equipment);
- 8.7% manufacture of machinery;

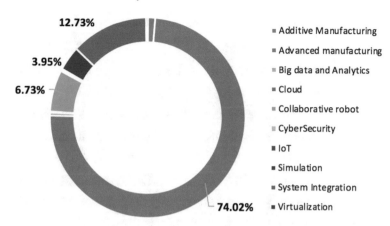

Fig. 3 Percentage of investments by technology category (purchases in 11 months period)

- 7.4% manufacture of rubber items and plastic materials.

It is important to highlight that firms operating in other industrial sectors are very few, less than 5% for each industrial sector. Thus, the companies operating in manufacturing sector may perceive the investment on new assets and technologies as an opportunity to enhance operational effectiveness and productivity.

The main results of our analysis show the distribution of technology investments on advanced technologies in context of industry 4.0. By looking at acquired assets, as shown in Fig. 3, 74% of the investments in industry 4.0 are related to advanced manufacturing. More than 12% of the firms invested on system integration. System integration allows firms to monitor and control products by data exchange, not only across different departments such as manufacturing and maintenance or inventory, but also across supply chain; with suppliers, customers and other actors. Thus, one of the main criteria to allocate financial aids emphasizes on standards and communication protocols. This not only allows infra-firm data exchange but also is fundamental for future connectivity at inter-firm and industrial level.

Although the majority of investments are on advanced manufacturing and system integration, firms have also shown the propensity to invest on collaborative robots (6.73%) and simulation technologies (3.95%).

As for cloud computing, according to findings, however, only few firms have invested in cloud computing (0.2%). Cloud-based solutions are based on multi-tenancy and standard solutions which allow cloud providers to offer services lower than in-house investment by a single firm. Pay-per-use model enables SMEs to use computing resources with very low cost by reducing significantly IT administration and maintenance costs. Thus, SMEs can access to IT resources with little invest-ment [39]. That is why although the general trend in cloud adoption is increasing

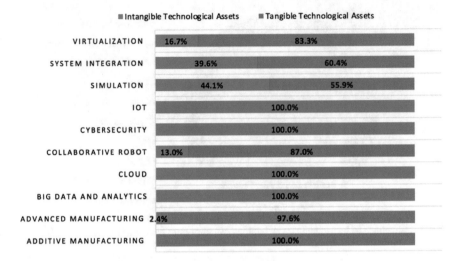

Fig. 4 Percentage of tangible and intangible investments for each technologies

specially by SMEs,[4] the findings of this study reveals that SMEs have seldom used this financial aid to invest in cloud.

Surprisingly, evidence from this analysis shows the low propensity of SMEs in investing on cybersecurity. Only few SMEs requested financial aid to invest on cyber security. This is particularly an important issue, since insufficient attention to IT security may lead to significant financial consequences and reputation damage for firms. Specially, the increased connectivity resulted from adoption of cloud resources and IoT increases the risk exposure of production and service systems [5].

For collaborative robots, SMEs purchased machines, tools and devices for un/loading, handling, weighing, sorting materials and automated lifting and collaborative robots. As for simulation technologies, major purchase orders belong to 3D modeling, simulation, experimentation and prototyping that allows organizations to test production processes and optimize process settings in terms of time and quality.

In total, SMEs invested mainly on physical assets (90%), while only few invested on digital assets such as platforms, systems and software (10%). Figure 4 shows the investments of firms in each technology based on tangible and intangible assets.

Additionally, based on detailed description on each purchase, four industrial performance objectives were identified. As shown in Fig. 5, about 74% of SMEs have invested on new assets to improve productivity of which 72% are dedicated to acquisition of tangible assets. Around 15% of the firms invested to enhance flexibility: 12.6% for physical assets. Even if results show significant investment to enhance productivity and flexibility, it is interesting to see that SMEs concern with sustainability and energy consumptions (4%). For instance, to improve sustainability,

---

[4]Europe's Digital Progress Report (EDPR) 2017, Country Profile Italy.

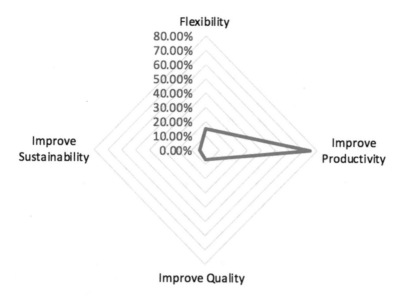

Fig. 5 Percentage of investments by performance objective

the three main asset acquisitions are related to waste tracking, recovery and treatment, and intelligent human-machine interfaces (HMI) that assist the operator in safety and efficiency of processing, maintenance and logistics operations.

The evidence revealed concern by SMEs on sustainability and energy consumptions. Although the number of purchases is not as significant as for productivity and flexibility, it sheds light on increased concerns of SMEs respect to regulations and laws related to energy consumptions and waste management.

5 Discussion and Conclusion

The ways organizations create, and capture value have undergone a significant change due to emerging new technology and the embeddedness of such technologies in business operations. Hence, as pointed out in literature, aligning organizational IT strategy with business strategy is pivotal for business [8]. Moreover, the pace and breadth of emerging new technologies induce challenges for firms in making decisions about what technology to invest and how to align IT strategy with business strategy [1].

In particular, for SMEs the challenges mainly refer to limited financial resources, IS skills and knowledge. As for the financial challenge, given that the significant contribution of Italian SMEs in economic growth, the Italian Government has introduced the National Plan for Industry 4.0 aiming at removing financial barriers and facilitating SMEs in adopting new technologies. However, SMEs face difficulty in making strategic decisions about technologies due to limited skills and knowledge, especially considering the wide range of cutting-edge technologies, the substantial influence on the organizational performance and future development capability due to path dependency [40]. For instance, having complex legacy systems makes integration of the new system challenging and influences organizational performance. Thus, SMEs need to make sense of fast pace of new technologies [48] and understand what technology to invest in order to better align IT strategy with business strategy.

The findings of this study present a detailed insight on SMEs' investments on industry 4.0 supported by the Government following the National Plan. While digital technologies are transforming business processes and business models, the findings show that SMEs mainly invest on tangible assets e.g. plant, machinery, industrial equipment. One plausible explanation for the current trend is that Italy is lagged behind in digitalization of enterprises[5] respect to the European average. Thus, we can see that SMEs that mainly operating in manufacturing industry invest to develop advanced production systems aiming at improving productivity. Our findings are aligned with previous studies that highlight SMEs have a high tendency to keep the existing business model [24], and by investing on technologies they pursue efficiency goals [27] in current business which requires less efforts to realize.

Moreover, a negligible number of firms invest on IoT, virtualization, big data and analytics. Since digital technologies have significant influence on business processes, firms need to carefully assess and adopt these technologies aligned with the overall business strategy. Thus, SMEs may need to better understand how they can reap benefits from new technologies before any investment. It is worth noting that limited resources are main barriers for SMEs to explore different technologies and access to external knowledge. While large companies have sufficient resources to allocate for exploring different technologies and innovative projects even in different markets, SMEs mainly focus on specific technologies to meet demands in specific markets. The limited IT skills and knowledge in SMEs act as a barrier in exploring new technologies and strategic IT investment by managers [11–28, 45].

In particular, we found few SMEs invest on cybersecurity which might be due to lack of awareness of managers making IT strategic decisions. Another reason for that can be the security expectation of SMEs is lower than large enterprises, since the lack of proper protection on IT infrastructure has higher financial consequences for large enterprises [46]. Large organizations may be willing to pay more for customized service level agreements to increase security measures. For SMEs, however, there is a trade-off between security and cost [18, 29]. Lack of sufficient investment on cybersecurity technologies can lead to significant financial consequences and reputation damage for firms. Considering the fact that significant number of SMEs are victims of cyber-attacks [47], proper information security strategies necessarily entail employing practices for predictable and unpredictable security threats [6]. In particular, investment on cybersecurity technologies is crucial for organizations adopting system integration since integrating information systems such-as supply chain-blurs organizational boundaries which consequently increases exposure to cyber risks [5].

---

[5] Source: Europe's Digital Progress Report 2017—Research & Innovation.

While main stream of literature has focused on benefits of industry 4.0 [12–22, 41], in this study we argue that the lack of investment on cybersecurity and adequate knowledge of impact on technologies limit associated benefits of new technologies and may lead to negative consequences.

To align IT investments with business strategy, possess IT skills and access to external knowledge play an important role for SMEs. Thus, in the following year, significant effort was dedicated by the Italian Government to operationalize digital innovation hubs and competence centers to further support SMEs in innovation investments through raising awareness and facilitating access to external knowledge such as universities and other actors. This will allow SMEs to not only explore and exploit new technologies, but at the same time be aware of security challenges, and consequently wisely invest on IT technologies in industry 4.0 context.

The paths in technology adoption by SMEs are different from large organizations [19]. While the concept of Industry 4.0 has been widely investigated in large enterprises [3], this study on Italian SMEs provides a useful insight into the actual investments on digital technologies. The findings illustrate the propensity of SMEs in embedding advanced technologies for Industry 4.0 across different industrial sectors and regions.

While the incentive by Italian government to some extent remove the financial barriers for SMEs in investing and acquiring new technologies, this study aims to contribute to alignment literature by highlighting the importance of IT investments as strategic decisions in Industry 4.0. Moreover, the implications of this paper for practice are twofold. First, the results can help policy makers understand how SMEs are likely to embed new technologies in an industry 4.0 context. Second for practitioners, the results highlight the importance of integration of IT investment in new emerging technologies with business strategy.

References

1. Adomavicius, G., Bockstedt, J. C., Gupta, A., & Kauffman, R. J. (2008). Making sense of technology trends in the information technology landscape. *MIS Quarterly, 32,* 779.
2. Anderson, J. M. (2003). Why we need a new definition of information security. *Computers & Security, 22,* 308–313.
3. Arnold, C., Kiel, D., & Voigt, K.-I. (2016). How the industrial internet of things changes business models in different manufacturing industries. *International Journal of Innovation Management, 20,* 1640015.
4. August, T., Niculescu, M. F., & Shin, H. (2014). Cloud implications on software network structure and security risks cloud implications on software network structure and security risks. *Information Systems Research, 25,* 489–510. https://doi.org/10.1287/isre.2014.0527.
5. Baskerville, R., Rowe, F., & Wolff, F.-C. (2018). Integration of information systems and cybersecurity countermeasures. *ACM SIGMIS Database Advances in Information Systems. 49,* 33–52. https://doi.org/10.1145/3184444.3184448.
6. Baskerville, R., Spagnoletti, P., & Kim, J. (2014). Incident-centered information security: Managing a strategic balance between prevention and response. *Information & Management, 51,* 138–151. https://doi.org/10.1016/j.im.2013.11.004.

7. Beier, G., Niehoff, S., Ziems, T., & Xue, B. (2017). Sustainability aspects of a digitalized industry—A comparative study from China and Germany. *International Journal of Precision Engineering and Manufacturing Green Technology, 4,* 227–234.

8. Bergeron, F., Raymond, L., & Rivard, S. (2004). Ideal patterns of strategic alignment and business performance. *Information & Management, 41,* 1003–1020.

9. Bharadwaj, A., El Sawy, O.A., Pavlou, P. A., & Venkatraman, N. (2013). Digital business strategy: toward a next generation of insights. *MIS Quarterly,* 471–482.

10. Bowen, P. L., Cheung, M.-Y. D., & Rohde, F. H. (2007). Enhancing IT governance practices: A model and case study of an organization's efforts. *International Journal of Accounting Information Systems, 8,* 191–221.

11. Bridge, S., O'Neill, K., & Cromie, S. (1998). *Understanding Enterprise.* Macmillan, London: Entrepreneurship and Small Business.

12. Burmeister, C., Lüttgens, D., & Piller, F. T. (2016). Business model innovation for Industrie 4.0: why the "Industrial Internet" mandates a new perspective on innovation. *Die Unternehmung, 70,* 124–152.

13. Dalenogare, L. S., Benitez, G. B., Ayala, N. F., & Frank, A. G. (2018). The expected contribution of Industry 4.0 technologies for industrial performance. *International Journal of Production Economics, 204,* 383–394.

14. Deep, A., Guttridge, P., Dani, S., & Burns, N. (2008). Investigating factors affecting ERP selection in made-to-order SME sector. *Journal of Manufacturing Technology Management, 19,* 430–446.

15. Fligstein, N. (1996). Markets as politics: A political-cultural approach to market institutions. *American Sociological Review,* 656–673.

16. Galliers, R. D. (2011). Further developments in information systems strategizing: unpacking the concept. In *Oxford handbook of management Information systems: Critical perspectives and new directions* (pp. 329–345). Oxford Oxford: University Press (2011).

17. Gartner Group. (2018). Gartner Says "Global IT Spending to Grow 3.2 Percent in 2019" Press Release https://www.gartner.com/en/newsroom/press-releases/2018-10-17-gartner-says-global-it-spending-to-grow-3-2-percent-in-2019.

18. Gupta, P., Seetharaman, A., & Raj, J. R. (2013). The usage and adoption of cloud computing by small and medium businesses. *International Journal of Information Management, 33,* 861–874. https://doi.org/10.1016/j.ijinfomgt.2013.07.001.

19. Harland, C. M., Caldwell, N. D., Powell, P., & Zheng, J. (2007). Barriers to supply chain information integration: SMEs adrift of eLands. *Journal of Operations Management, 25,* 1234–1254.

20. He, H., Maple, C., Watson, T., Tiwari, A., Mehnen, J., Jin, Y., & Gabrys, B. (2016). The security challenges in the IoT enabled cyber-physical systems and opportunities for evolutionary computing & other computational intelligence. In *2016 IEEE Congress on Evolutionary Computation (CEC)* (pp. 1015–1021). IEEE.

21. Henderson, J. C., & Venkatraman, H. (1999). Strategic alignment: Leveraging information technology for transforming organizations. *IBM Systems Journal, 38,* 472–484.

22. Ivanov, D., Dolgui, A., Sokolov, B., Werner, F., & Ivanova, M.: A dynamic model and an algorithm for short-term supply chain scheduling in the smart factory industry 4.0. *International Journal of Production Research, 54,* 386–402.

23. Kaufman, L. M. (2009). Data security in the world of cloud computing. *IEEE Security and Privacy, 7,* 61–64.

24. Kleindl, B. (2000). Competitive dynamics and new business models for SMEs in the virtual marketplace. *Journal of Developmental Entrepreneurship, 5,* 73.

25. Kleis, L., Chwelos, P., Ramirez, R. V., & Cockburn, I. (2012). Information technology and intangible output: The impact of IT investment on innovation productivity. *Information Systems Research, 23,* 42–59.

26. Kohli, R., Devaraj, S., & Ow, T. T. (2012). Does information technology investment influences firm's market value? The case of non-publicly traded healthcare firms. *MIS Quarterly.*

27. Levy, M., Powell, P., & Yetton, P. (2001). SMEs: aligning IS and the strategic context. *Journal of Information Technology, 16,* 133–144.
28. Levy, M., & Powell, P. (1998). SME flexibility and the role of information systems. *Small Business Economics, 11,* 183–196.
29. Maher, N., Kavanagh, P., & Glowatz, M. (2013). A vendor perspective on issues with security, governance and risk for Cloud Computing. In *26th Bled eConference—eInnovations Challenges Impacts Individuals Organizations and Social Processing* (pp. 103–114).
30. Marston, S., Li, Z., Bandyopadhyay, S., Zhang, J., & Ghalsasi, A. (2011). Cloud computing—The business perspective. *Decision Support Systems, 51,* 176–189. https://doi.org/10.1016/j.dss.2010.12.006.
31. Mell, P., & Grance, T. (2011). *The NIST definition of cloud computing—Recommendations of the national institute of standards and technology.* Gaithersburg: United States Department of Commerce.
32. Mintzberg, H. (1982). Structure et Dynamique des organisations, edited by Editions d'Organisation. *Vingt-troi. ed. Eyrolles, 434,* 978–2708119710.
33. Mithas, S., & Tafti, A., Mitchell, W. (2013). How a firm's competitive environment and digital strategic posture influence digital business strategy. *MIS Quarterly,* 511–536.
34. Moeuf, A., Pellerin, R., Lamouri, S., Tamayo-Giraldo, S., & Barbaray, R. (2018). The industrial management of SMEs in the era of Industry 4.0. *International Journal of Production Research, 56,* 1118–1136.
35. Oliveira, T., Thomas, M., & Espadanal, M. (2014). Assessing the determinants of cloud computing adoption: An analysis of the manufacturing and services sectors. *Information & Management, 51,* 497–510.
36. Osterwalder, A., Pigneur, Y., & Tucci, C. L. (2005). Clarifying business models: Origins, present, and future of the concept. *Communications of the Association for Information Systems, 16,* 1.
37. Pigni, F., Piccoli, G., & Watson, R. (2016). Digital data streams: Creating value from the real-time flow of big data. *California Management Review, 58,* 5–25.
38. Porter, M. E., & Heppelmann, J. E. (2014). How smart, connected products are transforming competition. *Harvard Business Review, 92,* 64–88.
39. Radziwon, A., Bilberg, A., Bogers, M., & Madsen, E. S. (2014). The smart factory: exploring adaptive and flexible manufacturing solutions. *Procedia Engineering, 69,* 1184–1190.
40. Reynolds, P., & Yetton, P. (2015). Aligning business and IT strategies in multi-business organizations. *Journal of Information Technology, 30,* 101–118.
41. Rudtsch, V., Gausemeier, J., Gesing, J., Mittag, T., & Peter, S. (2014). Pattern-based business model development for cyber-physical production systems. *Procedia CIRP, 25,* 313–319.
42. Rüßmann, M., Lorenz, M., Gerbert, P., Waldner, M., Justus, J., Engel, P., & Harnisch, M. (2015). *Industry 4.0: The future of productivity and growth in manufacturing industries* (Vol. 9, pp. 54–89). Boston Consulting Group.
43. Salmeron, J. L., & Bueno, S. (2006). An information technologies and information systems industry-based classification in small and medium-sized enterprises: An institutional view. *European Journal of Operational Research, 173,* 1012–1025.
44. Schneider, S., & Sunyaev, A. (2016). Determinant factors of cloud-sourcing decisions: Reflecting on the IT outsourcing literature in the era of cloud computing. *1*(31), 1–31. https://doi.org/10.1057/jit.2014.25.
45. Stokes, D. (2000). Marketing and the small firm. I: S. Carter & D. Jones Eves (Eds.), *Enterprise and small business: Principles, practice and policy.* London: Pearson Education Ltd.
46. Sultan, N. A. (2011). Reaching for the "cloud": How SMEs can manage. *International Journal of Information Management, 31,* 272–278. https://doi.org/10.1016/j.ijinfomgt.2010.08.001.
47. *Verizon 2019 data breach investigations report.* https://enterprise.verizon.com/resources/reports/2019-data-breach-investigations-report.pdf (2019).
48. Weick, K. (1979). *The social psychology of organizing.* Reading, MA: Addison-Wesley.

49. Yeow, A., Soh, C., & Hansen, R. (2018). Aligning with new digital strategy: A dynamic capabilities approach. *Journal of Strategic Information Systems, 27,* 43–58.
50. Zhang, Y., Zhang, G., Wang, J., Sun, S., Si, S., & Yang, T. (2015). Real-time information capturing and integration framework of the internet of manufacturing things. *International Journal of Computer Integrated Manufacturing, 28,* 811–822.

Creating a New Innovation Orientation Through Idea Competitions

Hanne Westh Nicolajsen◉ and Ada Scupola◉

Abstract This paper conducts an in depth case study of the implementation of an idea competition in a consulting company. Based on 27 interviews with company managers as well as employees acting as users or non users of the idea competition in the company has changed the innovation orientation of the company along several dimensions including creativity and empowerment, innovation infrastructure, innovation influence and innovation intention.

Keywords Idea competition · Innovation orientation · Culture · ICT

1 Introduction

Being innovative is highly important for most companies in order to stay competitive, also for service companies. Having a supportive innovation culture or strong innovation orientation is essential regarding how innovative a company is [1]. An innovation culture is in general described as a culture where risk- taking, empowerment and open communication among other factors are appreciated [1, 2]. Chesbrough talks about a closed and an open approach to innovation [3]. The open approach values external partnerships and inspiration whereas the closed one values control and secrecy.

In the last two decades or more the open innovation approach has received high emphasis as a way to strengthen the innovation potential. This is among other things fueled by access to the Internet and software developments such as online collaborative functionalities and lately social media that have made interaction and community building infrastructures even easier to build and access [4, 5]. Many service companies have taken advantage of these interactive tools to involve their customers in different phases of the innovation process [6–8].

H. W. Nicolajsen (✉)
IT University Copenhagen, Rued Langgaardsvej 7, 2300 Kbh S, Denmark
e-mail: hwni@itu.dk

A. Scupola
Roskilde University (Roskilde Universitet), Universitetsvej 1, 25.3, 4000 Roskilde, Denmark
e-mail: ada@ruc.dk

© The Editor(s) (if applicable) and The Author(s), under exclusive license to Springer Nature Switzerland AG 2020
R. Agrifoglio et al. (eds.), *Digital Business Transformation*, Lecture Notes in Information Systems and Organisation 38, https://doi.org/10.1007/978-3-030-47355-6_7

93

The studies investigating interactive tools for internal use such as the innovation jams in IBM [9] or organizational Wikis [10] are flourishing. Idea competitions are one category of these tools. The success of using these tools to involve external partners such as customers to come up with ideas has been widely researched (e.g. [7, 11, 12]). However we argue that there is a new and not highly researched trend of companies using such tools for internal use. It may be argued that these tools carry with them an inherent approach to innovation much in line with the open innovation paradigm due to functionalities supporting open communication, participation, empowerment etc. [13]. Therefore we investigate the following research question: How does a consulting company use an internal idea competition to influence the innovation orientation in the organization?

We analyze a case study of a consulting company's implementation of an idea competition by investigating its conceptualization and the initial attempts to change the innovation orientation in the company.

The paper is structured as follows. First we describe the theoretical grounding defining service innovation, innovation orientation and idea competitions. Then we present the research method. This is followed by the analysis, discussion and conclusions.

2 Theoretical Grounding

To frame our understanding of innovation orientation and culture we first define the concept of innovation and service innovation. Service innovation is defined by Gallouj and Weinstein as any change affecting either the technologies (methods or materials) involved in the service provision, the competencies (employees, organizational or client) or any part of what makes the final service [14]. This definition allows us to investigate and describe all sorts of innovations no matter which element or extent of change involved as long as it results in added value.

Only few researchers have worked with the concept of innovation culture, which is strictly related to innovation orientation. Brentani and Kleinschmidt define a firm's innovation culture as "involving entrepreneurship, risk taking, and openness to new ideas" [2, p. 312]. The innovation culture is considered as a subculture with a style of corporate behavior valuing new ideas, change, risk and not at least failure as a necessary part of working innovatively. Also, an innovation culture is described as one nurturing a climate of openness, informal communication, involvement, thinking out of the box and adaptive to change. Whether this "subculture" is part of the organizational culture as such or only counts for innovation departments or when innovation is planned for is unclear.

Dobni, in line with Brentani and Kleinschmidt argues that an organization's strategy and degree of innovativeness is affected by what he coins "the innovation orientation" [1]. Dobni argues that four dimensions are of importance to describe the innovation orientation of a company (see Table 1 below): the intention to be innovative, the infrastructure to support innovation, the behaviors needed to influence a market/value orientation and the environment to support implementation [1]. Dobni's overall understanding is that innovation orientation, which is part of the organizations culture, affect the competitive strategy of the company and therefore the organizations performance [1, p. 333].

According to Dobni [1] a strong innovation orientation engage behaviors such as valuing risk taking, creativity, freedom, teamwork, it instills trust and respect as well as fast decision making (p. 334) very much in line with Brentani and Kleinschmidt [2]. The innovation culture definitions presented here provide a normative stand, defining the companies as having a strong or weak innovation culture/orientation with given values of what makes a strong innovation culture. However, no considerations are made in terms of differences across the organizations with respect to for example innovation and coordination needs, resources and qualifications, leaving open questions as to whether it is positive that everybody are innovative at all times? Dobni ends up asking whether it is possible to manage strategy through designing the innovation orientation, a question in line with what we ask in this article.

Such questions point back to an old debate within the organizational culture literature as to whether culture can be managed and how it changes. Pliskin et al. state that the organizational culture literature can be divided into two streams [15]. The first one is descriptive and has the purpose of understanding and describing organizational culture. The second one, which has a normative approach, assumes that organizational culture can be managed, where Schein is a strong advocate [16]. Hatch further develops Scheins model of organizational culture and argues for a dynamic relationship [17]. She understands organizational culture as constituted by assumptions, values, artifacts and in addition symbols and the ongoing processes that link them. Hatch's understanding indicates that culture is changeable but that it is difficult to manage culture due to the dynamics in play including the interpretation processes going on. It may not be fully manageable and controlled and it makes more sense to argue that it can be designed for [18].

This understanding is in line with the studies by Doherty and Doig [19] and Doherty and Perry [20] examining how new technologies may become a catalyst in transforming espoused cultural values into reality whereas or help strengthened organizational values. These studies are however different then ours as they look at innovating a certain practice, whereas our focus is on a tool to support innovation in general.

Markus [21] argue that it is not the technology per se but rather the organizational set- up around the new IT which creates the changes. Markus [21] also argues that implementation of new systems fail if there are too big differences between the IT system and the existing organizational culture.

2.1   Online Idea Competitions

Online idea competitions allow an organization to post problems or themes online, where a group of participants may provide solutions to a given problem. These solutions may then be further elaborated by other participants or voted on online or may be moved to another community for further evaluation and development. The winning ideas are awarded some form of a prize, and the organization may implement the idea for its own gain.

According to Ebner et al. [22] and Bullinger et al. [23] the key design elements describing idea competitions are: the organizer, the timeline, incentives, problem specification, target group, composition of groups, media, evaluation criteria, idea review, idea review committee, elaborateness, context and community functionality.

Especially the element of community functionality, which is only part of Bullinger et al's framework, is essential as it makes idea competitions suitable for open communication and interaction, thus providing possibilities for collaboration and competition, which again allow for community building [23]. According to Bullinger et al. [23], low and high cooperation orientation supports high degrees of innovativeness, whereas medium cooperation orientation results in low degree of innovativeness. The importance of community functionality is further supported by a more recent study by Hutter et al. finding that the tension between competition and collaboration is what makes an online innovation community flourish [24].

3   Research Method

To investigate the research question a case study methodology was considered appropriate as we investigate a real-life phenomenon—implementing an idea competition tool - where control over the context is impossible [25]. The main data collection method was semi-structured interviews with open-ended questions. We conducted 27 interviews (Table 2). The respondents were selected on the base of their involvement in the planning, implementation and participation to the idea competition. At the beginning of the research, the informants were selected by the competence manager and the innovation director that we also interviewed. Later snowball sampling [26] was used to find respondents with different profiles. 17 of the interviews lasted about 1–1½ hours each, the other 10 were short interviews of approx. ½ hour. All interviews were tape recorded and transcribed. We asked about the purpose of the idea competition, how the tool and the organizational set-up were designed and supported as well as about the organizational and individual outcome and challenges.

Documentation review and field notes were complementary data collection methods including material about the idea competition process; schemes to submit ideas, samples of submitted ideas, the winning ideas and criteria for idea selection. The researchers also gained access to the idea competition platform for a short period

Table 1 Dimensions of innovation culture [1]

1. Innovation intention	
Innovation propensity	The degree to which the organization has a formally established—within their business model—architecture to develop and sustain innovation. This would be communicated through vision, goals, objectives, and operationalized through the business model and business processes
Organizational constituency	Considers the level to which employees are engaged in the innovation imperative and how employees think of themselves vis-á-vis their colleagues in respect to value, equity, and contributions made within the organization
2. Innovation infrastructure	
Organizational learning	The degree to which the training and the educational opportunities of employees are aligned with the innovation objectives
Creativity and empowerment	Determination of the creative capacity of employees and the amount of creativity that employees are allowed to express in their work. AIt assesses the degree of empowerment held by employees, and the ability of employees to improvise and enact at will
3. Innovation influence	
Market orientation	Market sensing and contextual awareness behaviors of employees. It considers the extent to which employees generate and disseminate knowledge on customers, competitors, the industry, as well as their understanding of the value chain or cluster in which their operate
Value orientation	The degree to which employees are focused on and involved in the process to create value for customer/clients
4. Innovation implementation	
Implementation context	The organization's ability to execute value-added ideas. It considers the ability to proactively co-align systems and processes with the changes in the competitive environment

of time to get an idea of its functionalities. The interviews are combined with the secondary material to create so-called rich descriptions [27] (Table 2).

The data analysis follows Miles and Huberman [28] instructions for analysing qualitative data and interviews. In the process of data collection, data coding [28] it became clear that the biggest issue was establishing an innovation orientation rather different from the established innovation practice in The Company. In order to analyze these attempted changes and challenges we use Dobni's [1] understanding of innovation orientation. Before we move into the analysis, we shortly present the case company.

Table 2 Interview data

Number of interviews	27
From HQ	17
From regional offices	8 (4 regional offices)
Other	1 customer 1 supplier
Duration of interviews	Normal 1–1.5 h (17) Short ca. 30 min (10)
The informants' positions	Competence manager Innovation director Innovation champion Project manager Project member IdeaExchange team members Marketing director

3.1 The Engineering Consulting Company

The Company (a pseudonym) is a large engineering consulting company with 1600 employees specializing in different fields including construction and design, infrastructure and transport, energy and climate, environment and water and IT and telecommunications. The Company is part of a leading engineering, design and consultancy group, headquartered and founded in Denmark.

4 Analysis and Results

4.1 Idea Exchange Implementation

In The Company, the main source of innovation occurs, develops and is financed through consulting projects. However, it is believed that the company's employees possess a great deal of knowledge about the internal processes that could be a source of organizational efficiency. The decision to use the idea competition platform was taken at a directors meeting about the company strategy. A group of eight "smart employees with drive" from different department in Denmark was invited to form a project group—"The innovation team". Their task was to develop a sustainable concept around the idea management platform from Nosco (the software provider) called "Idea Exchange" to crowdsource ideas from the employees. The Idea Exchange platform includes a number of community functionalities that enhance interaction and collaboration. For example, it is possible to submit one's own ideas or comment on ideas posted by others to suggest improvements or to further develop the idea. Each employee is given an amount of virtual money at the beginning of the competition, which can be invested into ideas contributed by others. At any point in time, the spot value of an idea—together with the comments that support it—is proxied by the aggregate investment positions held on it relative to all other ideas. The ideas get ranked automatically in the system according to their spot value.

The implementation of Idea Exchange is much more than implementation of the Idea Exchange platform. It is a concept including components such as: the roll out plan including invitations, follow up communication, deadlines, log ins, articles in the internal newsletter, information provided on the intranet, information screens running commercials about the Idea Exchange event and the Innovation Day, a formula for presentation of the ideas, nomination of the winning ideas and the strategic implementation of the winning ideas.

By applying the design variables from Ebner et al. [22] and Bullinger et al. [23], The Company is the organizer and the employees are the participants which participate as individuals with user name without needing to state their position in the company. The context is a call for ideas for upcoming strategy. Five strategic themes were formulated by top management along with an online format to guide the form of input desired. The activities on the online Idea Exchange lasted sixes weeks, whereas the whole idea competition event including the off line activities followed the strategic year and a little longer, as the winning ideas were turned into strategic action areas for the upcoming year. Three rounds of review process took place. After the online idea posting and trading period expired, prizes were given to the ideas with the highest spot value in each theme, a prize to the best trader and a prize to the best commentator. These prizes were symbolic such as an Ipad. The highest ranked idea within each of the five themes entered into a pool of 10 ideas to be further developed for a final evaluation along with five ideas selected through an off line evaluation process. In fact, the Innovation Team screened the rest of the ideas (approx. 100) and selected 20 promising ideas according to a number of criteria developed by the Innovation Team and communicated at the very beginning of the Idea Exchange event. These 20 selected ideas were presented to the management group who in turn selected 5 of these ideas (Wildcards) for further development together with the 5 highest ranked ideas. A number of work hours were then allocated to these 10 finalist idea "owners" and each idea owner was assigned a couple of experts to help them further develop the ideas and define the implementation needs. The Idea Exchange event culminated with the Innovation Day, where the 10 finalist ideas were presented to an audience of company employees and external people and three "winner" ideas were selected by an innovation panel for final implementation. The panel was composed by company directors and an external expert. The prizes included participation to innovation courses and implementation of the idea. The incentives to participate are both external such gifts, and internal as recognition and influence if the idea get implemented.

4.2   Changes in the Innovation Orientation

Innovation intention

According to Dobni there is a need of "a formally established architecture to develop and sustain innovation". The whole event of the Idea Competition with its anchoring in the company strategy both regarding the themes' formulation as well as the eventual implementation of the winning ideas is a way to ensure formality and business alignment in The Company.

The primary intention of the Idea Competition was getting access to many different ideas for innovation. The assumption is that all employees possess insight into The Company's internal processes and therefore might have ideas on how The Company may do better. This is in contrast to the existing innovation culture as some respondents state that having employee's ideas heard, developed and implemented is not easy. The leaders often act as "gatekeepers". The idea competition is recognized as a way to overcome this also by the employees as showed by the following statement:

> You get innovation on the agenda and it becomes more approachable, more fun and more interesting making people want to use their spare time on it. The main advantage is that it shortcuts the distance between high and low in the system, meaning ideas that normally don´t get to the management group, gets there. Project member #14

Likewise it has created a recurrent architecture supporting employee driven innovations which otherwise aren't supported as shown in the following quotes:

> ".. how to move on when you bump into a good idea – well it has become rather easy here in The Company, because you know that there are these possibilities occasionally" project leader #23

> I think many have thought about ideas before, but they would not come and tell, but now it is easy, you just go and write it. Project member #15

Regarding the level of engagement of employees—there is an intention to reach out and make it easy for all employees to participate. The focus on internal process innovation along with the possibilities to take on different roles is a way to appreciate any kind of engagement and acknowledging other roles in innovation than just providing ideas. All employees should feel invited no matter if they are used to take part in innovation or not.

> .. innovation takes place on many levels and it may take many different forms, not necessarily the one who has a good idea (..) it may also be the one sitting beside "well, what if you did this" (..) It was meant to include widely to get people participating. Innovation Team member #10

This approach is rather different as innovation in the company is acknowledged as done by a few highly innovative and resource strong employees.

> I believe it is really important to have an open forum, where you can voice all your ideas, before it was some "fiery souls" who knew the system and knew how to apply for money, now everyone can throw in an idea. Project member #19

Others are however reluctant to participate, as they are afraid of the quality level of their ideas. No resources are given to the employees to participate in the idea competition and therefore it becomes "con amore" and the more "enthusiastic rather than the crowd" as emphasized by an Innovation Team member. This is a way to limit the participation. It may constrain the number of ideas for good and bad. However, some of the employees also argue that not everybody is tuned towards innovation.

Innovation infrastructure

There are no particular qualifications needed to participate in the Idea Exchange event as promising ideas can be further developed with help of organizational experts. On the other hand, the constituency of the different roles is a way to create a learning opportunity and to create a broader innovation awareness in The Company. The employees are lured into the Idea Exchange as dealers, thus taking part in this "funny", non-risky part of the Idea Exchange event. Getting them into the Idea Exchange platform is a way to get them exposed to the innovation process, which may make them learn from the ideas of others and create awareness and confidence about what innovation can be.

> if you don't think of your self as super innovative, then you can take part by playing the game and be a good dealer. Innovation team member #15

The majority had contributed as s dealers rather than as idea contributors. Many had entered the online Idea Exchange but did not even participate as dealers. One respondent questions the ease to use the system. Many informants state that they used almost an hour the first time to understand the Idea Exchange concept. One argues it is due to too much text.

> There is too much explanation on the different categories, you need to invest too many resources to get into it, it's a pity, everybody is busy. Project member #17

Another argues that some employees refrain to participate even as dealers due to lack of overview

> I could see that it would take a long time if I wanted to get a good overview. I probably feel a little bad about putting my shares in one idea and then there are many other ideas, I haven't noticed which I would rather have supported. Project member #16

Negative learning also occurred. An employee explains that during the first idea competition he thought it was really funny and contributed with three ideas. Some of his ideas got selected for further development, but afterwards nothing happened. In the second round he prioritized only to play the game for the fun of it arguing that time constraints was crucial.

> You could say I feel I already contributed. I would have liked to post an idea, but I did not get to it, well you know time. It was not my highest priority. Project member #14

Creativity and empowerment

The visibility of the ideas in the Idea Exchange, the commenting and especially the ranking functionality provides for a democratic and transparent innovation process as it gives each employee a voice to bring up ideas, comment and ranking ideas thus influencing the process. It provides for open communication across the organization raising new values and ideas.

Concerns with the results of such a democratic ranking made the Innovation Team and Top Management to combine the online democratic ranking with a management based selection of another five ideas. Likewise management was given the final word when nominating the three finalist ideas. There is thus some opening up and letting go of some control by enhancing the transparency of the idea generation process and support a more open communication. However, management is still in control. Pure empowerment might have compromised the need of strategic anchoring of innovation with the business goal, as argued in the following quote:

> When resources are allocated then severity sets in. It would be crazy, well, it is not sure the democracy finds the best idea in relation to The Company business and strategy. It has to be the leaders who decides. Project leader #18

This is supported by the observation that some of the top ranking ideas in Idea Exchange were not really ideas, but more issues irrelevant for the company strategy. This points to a weakness of the online ranking functionality and how employees decide to buy shares into ideas. It turned out that employees buy shares to support a mix of good, funny and different ideas especially when they are related to their area of expertise as well as ideas from "friends" in the organization.

Innovation influence

The whole idea and outcome of the Idea Exchange event is to make the employees contribute with ideas that may help to improve the organizational processes based on their working experiences and knowledge Idea Exchange system is a way to disseminate ideas and knowledge about challenges and related solutions. Having the Idea Exchange event is a way to encourage employees to share their ideas about new ways to create value for the company and the customers. The Idea Exchange system seems to be strong in supporting communication about innovations as interesting or funny ideas are often discussed at lunch by employees

> Well regarding this one [a useful idea] a colleague told me about it. Try to look here, it is really good, just something for you. Project manager #18

Innovation implementation

The Idea Exchange concept ensures that at least the winning ideas are implemented. However, the lack of follow up on the majority of the ideas submitted has discouraged some participants (se earlier quote). To address this issue, the Innovation Team had considered of considering Idea Exchange platform as an incubator. An informal way of dissemination and possible implementation is when employees learn about others' ideas and experiences and get in contact with them to implement the ideas in their own project/department (see quote above).

5 Discussion and Conclusions

Our study reveals that idea competition tools may be used to rethink, encourage and eventually create a new/different innovation orientation in companies. As argued by Doherty and Doigh [20] the idea competition becomes a catalyst not only to implement espoused values but also to develop and rethink the approach to innovation and innovation practice in the organization. In addition it becomes a catalyst as it encourages and inspires innovative behaviors through the different design elements. Idea Exchange architecture and especially the three different roles made it potentially possible for all employees to participate whether or not they see themselves as innovation drivers. This creates a vehicle for exposing and changing the employees awareness of innovation. The idea competition event has created a new innovation orientation due both to the strategic approach behind the call for ideas as well as the allocation of resources for implementation.

Dobni [1] talks about a weaker or stronger innovation orientation as one common underlying approach within the company. Our study questions this understanding of one unified approach. We observe an innovation orientation with focus on collecting employees ideas for internal process innovations; an innovation orientation which is seen as complementary rather than in opposition to other innovation orientations in the company such as ad hoc innovation (e.g. [14]) through customer projects or innovation developed by top management. Also this type of innovation orientation is created occasionally as it is argued that it is difficult to create the needed critical mass and focus on an ongoing basis.

References

1. Dobni, C. B. (2010). The relationship between an innovation orientation and competitive strategy. *International Journal of Innovation Management, 14*(2), 331–357.
2. Brentani, U., & Kleinschmidt, E. J. (2004). Corporate culture and commitment: Impact on performance of international new product development programs. *Journal of Product Innovation Management, 21,* 309–333.
3. Chesbrough, H. W. (2003). *Open innovation: The new imperative for creating and profiting from technology.* Boston: Harvard Business School Press.
4. Andriole, S. J. (2010). Business impact of Web 2.0 technologies. *Communications of the ACM, 53*(12), 68–79.
5. McAfee, A. P. (2006). Enterprise 2.0: The dawn of emergent collaboration. *MIT Sloan management review, 47*(3), 20–28.
6. Alam, I., & Perry, C. (2002). A customer-oriented new service development process. *Journal of Services Marketing, 16*(6), 515–534.
7. Lakhani, K. R., & Kanji, Z. (2008). Threadless: The business of community. Harvard Business School Multimedia/Video Case, (pp. 608–707).
8. Nambisan, S., & Nambisan, P. (2008). How to profit from a better virtual customer environment. *MIT Sloan Management Review, 49*(3), 53–63.
9. Bjelland, O. M., & Wood, R. C. (2008). An inside view of IBM's innovation jam. *MIT Sloan Management Review, 50*(1), 32–40.

10. Standing, C., & Kiniti, S. (2011). How can organizations use wikis for innovation? *Technovation, 31*(7), 287–295.
11. Piller, F., Schubert, P., Koch, M., & Möslein, K. (2005). Overcoming mass confusion: Collaborative customer co-design in online communities. *Journal of Computer-Mediated Communication, 10*(4), article 8.
12. Piller, F. T., & Walcher, D. (2006). Toolkits for idea competitions: A novel method to integrate users in new product development. *R&D Management, 36*(3), 307–318.
13. Ibrahim, Y. (2010). The discourses of empowerment and Web 2.0: The dilemmas of user-generated content. In S. Murugesan (Ed.), *Handbook of research on Web 2.0, 3.0, and X.0: Technologies, business, and social applications* (pp. 828–845).
14. Gallouj, F., & Weinstein, O. (1997). Innovation in services. *Research Policy, 26,* 537–556.
15. Pliskin, N., Romm, T., Lee, A. S., & Weber, Y. (1993). Presumed versus actual organizational culture: Managerial implications for implementation of information systems. *The Computer Journal, 36*(2), 143–152.
16. Schein, E. H. (1985). *Organizational culture and leadership*. San Francisco: Jossey-Bass.
17. Hatch, M. J. (1993). The dynamics of organizational culture. *Academy of Management Review, 18*(4), 657–693.
18. Wenger, E. (1998). Communities of practice. Prentice Hall.
19. Doherty, N. F., & Doig, G. (2003). An analysis of the anticipated cultural impacts of the implementation of data warehouses. *IEEE Transactions on Engineering Management, 50*(1), 78–88.
20. Doherty, N. F., & Perry, I. (2001). The cultural impact of workflow management systems in the financial services sector. *The Services Industry Journal, 21*(4), 147–166.
21. Markus, M. L. (2004). Technochange management: Using IT to drive organizational change. *Journal of Information Technology, 19*(1), 4–20.
22. Ebner, W., Leimesister, J. M., & Kromar, H. (2009). Community engineering for innovations: The ideas competition as method to nurture a virtual community for innovations. *R&D Management, 39*(4), 342–356.
23. Bullinger, A. C., Neyer, A.-K., Rass, M., & Moeslein, K. (2010). Community-based innovation contests: Where competition meets cooperation. *Creativity and Innovation management, 19*(3), 290–303.
24. Hutter, K., Hautz, J., Füller, J., Mueller, J., & Matzler, K. (2011). Communitition: The tension between competition and collaboration in community-based design contests. *Creativity and Management, 20*(1), 3–21.
25. Yin, R. K. (1997). *Case study research design and methods*. Thousand Oaks: Sage Publications.
26. Goodman, L. A. (1961). Snowball sampling. *Annuals of Mathematical Statistics, 32*(1), 148–170.
27. Walsham, G. (1995). Interpretive case studies in IS research: Nature and method. *European journal of Information Systems, 4,* 74–81.
28. Miles, M. B., & Huberman, A. M. (1994). *Qualitative data analysis*. Thousand Oaks, California: Sage Publications. Second Edition.

Digitization, Accounting, Controlling, and Reporting

Accounting Information Systems: The Scope of Blockchain Accounting

Iacopo Ennio Inghirami ⓘ

Abstract Distributed Ledger Technology—of which Blockchain is an example—is revolutionizing different sectors, creating new challenges and new opportunities. In this paper, we will investigate the impact of this technology on Accounting and Accounting Information Systems (AIS). The adoption of a Distributed Ledger Accounting presents extremely interesting characteristics, eliminating or redefining the role of entities external to the company, such as Banks, Insurance Companies, Certified Public Accountants and Auditors. Furthermore, we will try to outline the impact of this technology on AIS by hypothesising possible paths of development.

Keywords Accounting information systems · Distributed ledger technology · Blockchain · Double entry accounting · Triple entry accounting

1 Introduction

Distributed Ledger Technology, the so-called Blockchain, is revolutionizing the Internet. On the other hand, the Internet itself is changing, following the requests of those who wish that it became not only a place of information exchange, but also a virtual place to exchange actual values.

In this paper, we will try to understand the Blockchain technology and its evolution. We will analyse in depth the Distributed Ledger Technology and its relationships with Accountability and Accounting. We will then analyse the impact of Blockchain on Accounting Systems and finally we will examine the changes to be made to Accounting Information Systems to exploit this technology.

Beyond the emphasis with which many researchers invite to welcome this new technology, we will try to understand if Distributed Ledger Technology really has the ability to revolutionize Accounting and Accounting Information Systems.

Some research questions emerge from this analysis:

I. E. Inghirami (✉)
University of Milano-Bicocca, Milan, Italy
e-mail: iacopo.inghirami@unimib.it

© The Editor(s) (if applicable) and The Author(s), under exclusive license to Springer Nature Switzerland AG 2020
R. Agrifoglio et al. (eds.), *Digital Business Transformation*, Lecture Notes in Information Systems and Organisation 38, https://doi.org/10.1007/978-3-030-47355-6_8

RQ1: What impact will the adoption of Blockchain technology have on business intermediaries?
RQ2: Will the Blockchain be universally adopted in the AIS of all companies?
RQ3: What could be the development paths of the AISs taking into account the Blockchain Technology?

2 Blockchain Definition

Distributed Ledger Technology (DLT) is a technological protocol that enables data to be exchanged directly between different contracting parties within a network without the need for intermediaries. The network participants interact with encrypted identities (anonymously). Each transaction is coded and added to an immutable transaction chain. This chain is distributed to all network nodes (ledgers), thus preventing the alteration of the chain itself [1]. Although the correct denomination of this technology is DLT, we will use the most appealing name of Blockchain in the rest of the paper.

2.1 Blockchain Technology in Details

The Blockchain can be seen as the distributed, decentralized, transparent and chronological database of transactions, sometimes also called the Ledger. The data in the blockchain (e.g. transactions) is divided into blocks. Each block is dependent on the previous one. The system in which a blockchain serves as the database comprises of nodes or "workers". These workers are responsible for appending new blocks to the blockchain.

A new block can only be appended after all nodes in the system reach a consensus, i.e. all agree that block is legitimate and contains only valid transactions. How the validity of transactions is determined and how the nodes compute new blocks, is regulated by the protocol. Blockchain is shared among all nodes in the system; it is monitored by every node and at the same time controlled by none. The protocol itself is responsible to keep the blockchain valid. According to the literature [2] there are three main categories of Blockchain applications:

Blockchain 1.0: Currency The currency and services associated with money transfers such as payment mechanisms and remittance services. Currently, there are hundreds of different types of cryptocurrencies with bitcoin remaining the biggest by market cup. The currencies may have different features such as being tied to a fiat currency or commodity, but their nature stays the same—they are used for payments and transfers of digital property.

Blockchain 2.0: Smart contracts It is a layer of smart-contracts, which are more sophisticated than just a currency. A 'smart contract' is a computer protocol intended to digitally facilitate, verify, or enforce the negotiation or performance of a contract. Smart contracts allow the performance of credible transactions without third parties. These transactions are trackable and irreversible. Nick Szabo, who coined the term in 1994, firstly proposed the adoption of smart contracts [3]. Smart contracts can represent shares of stocks, bonds, options, mortgages and smart property. While the 1.0 concept represents decentralization of money, the 2.0 concept is a decentralization of markets. All the technologies aiming at decentralization of relationships of different counterparties such clearing houses, banks, companies are covered by this concept. Some interesting examples are peer-to-peer lending services Btc-jam, Bitbond, Crowd-funding platform Koinify, bitcoin prediction markets Augur, Fairlay. A potential accounting system on Blockchain is, therefore, covered by the 2.0 concept as it is supposed to represent a smart-contract system where the transactions and automatically paid bills are executed and recorded. Almost since the introduction of Bitcoin and its underlying blockchain ledger, researchers began to explore other field where a blockchain technology might be of great use. With Blockchain 2.0 we introduce additional types of blockchains and reason about their potential in other fields beyond cryptocurrency.

Blockchain 3.0: Areas in government, health, science etc. It is a Blockchain applications system beyond financial markets and covers government, art, culture and science. Examples of 3.0 applications are Blockchain voting systems, Decentralized Domain Name system— Namecoin, anti-censorship applications like Alexandria and Ostel, and many other applications using immutability and transparency properties of blockchain to promote freedom, democracy and fair allocation of wealth.

2.2 Distributed Ledger Technology Features

An extensive literature illustrates in detail the technical characteristics of the Distributed Ledger Technology [2, 4]. DLT, of which Blockchain is an example, uses cryptographic tools and a distributed consensus process to create a significant innovation in traditional record keeping. It has three main features [1]:

- **Veracity**—multiple copies (as opposed to a single copy) of the complete historical record of ledger entries are each verified by consensus. Bogus entries are identified and eliminated by failure to reach consensus.
- **Transparency**—it is a public record of activity that can be seen by all market participants.
- **Disintermediation**—it operates using a peer-to-peer network, rather than requiring a specific central organization.

Disintermediation is the core feature that drives the benefits associated with distributed ledgers. Traditionally, systems that have centralized ledgers have required the participation of a trusted third party to maintain a record of transactions between organizations. A Distributed Ledger overcomes the need for a third party, which can be a significant benefit when there is no clear trusted central organization, or if the costs of intermediation are high [1].

Main applications of Distributed Ledger Technology so far have been in financial services, namely Bitcoin and all other cryptocurrencies. With Blockchain, we can imagine a world in which contracts are embedded in digital code and stored in transparent, shared databases, where they are protected from deletion, tampering and revision- In this world every agreement, every process, every task and every payment would have a digital record and signature that could be identified, validated, stored and shared. Intermediaries like lawyers, brokers and bankers might no longer be necessary [5].

To date, however, it has not made a significant impact on the core operations of the banking and payments systems, although many banks, including the Federal Reserve, the Bank of England and the Bank of Canada with its Jasper Project, are carefully assessing the possible implications of this technology [6, 7]. Moreover, many financial institutions are experimenting with broader uses like supply chain tracking and digital identity management [1].

2.3 Blockchain Applications

Although the Internet is a great tool to aid every sphere of the modern digital life, it is still highly flawed in terms of the lack of security and privacy, especially when it comes to FinTech and E-commerce [8]. Blockchain, the technology behind cryptocurrency, brought forth a new revolution by providing a mechanism for Peer-to-Peer transactions without the need for any intermediary body such as the existing commercial banks. Blockchain validates all the transactions and preserves a permanent record of them while making sure that any identification related information of the user is kept incognito. Thus, all the personal information of the users are sequestered while substantiating all the transactions. This is achieved by reconciling mass collaboration by cumulating all the transactions in a computer code based digital ledger. By applying Blockchain or similar cryptocurrency techniques, the users neither need to trust each other nor do they need an intermediator; rather the trust is manifested within the decentralized network system itself.

Bitcoin is just an exemplary use of the Blockchain. Blockchain is considered to be a novel revolution in the domain of computing enabling limitless applications such as storing and verifying legal documents including deeds and various certificates, healthcare data, IoT, Cloud and so forth. Tapscott indicated Blockchain to be the "World Wide Ledger", enabling many new applications beyond verifying transactions such as in: smart deeds, decentralized and/or autonomous organizations/government services etc [9].

Researchers propose these fields of application [10]:

- **Smart contracts.** As we have seen, a general definition of a smart contract would be a computer program that can automatically execute the terms of a contract. By being self-executing and having property ownership information embedded, they can solve the problems of counterparty trust. Smart contracts are trustless, autonomous, and self-sufficient. Instead of reinventing contractual relationships, smart contracts are making their formation and performance more efficient, cost-effective, and transparent [11]. Blockchain and Smart Contracts can work together to trigger payments when a pre-programmed condition of a contractual agreement is triggered. Smart Contracts are really the killer application of the cryptocurrency world. Using blockchain technology has made it much easier to register, verify and execute them. Moreover, open source companies like Ethereum and Codius are already enabling Smart Contracts using blockchain technology and many companies which operate on bitcoin and blockchain technologies are beginning to support Smart Contracts [12].
- **Domestic payments.** At a procedural level, the process of inter-bank clearing requires an intricate coordination of resource-intensive steps between banks, clearing houses, and the central bank. These steps are typically not executed at a constant basis, but rather as a processing cycle that happens several times a day. The outcome of it is that payment can often end up credited one or more days after their initiation, especially over weekends or holidays. The intricacy of the current system constitutes a procedural challenge for payment service providers, and highlights the need for a more efficient system for real-time payment, both domestically and internationally.
- **International payments.** To achieve real-time payments on an international scale, there will be a need to introduce foreign exchange (FX) market makers to the blockchain network. They will perform currency conversions on transactions between consumer bank accounts. Central bank participation on the network in a market maker capacity would also be needed between payment service providers in different currency jurisdictions. In this way, real-time payments could potentially be achieved on a cost-effective basis.
- **Trade finance.** Digitization and automation of trade processes has been ongoing for many years, but the banks' updated processes are still largely based around the logistics of handling physical documents. Many processes share similar character-istics but requires completely different IT systems and procedural steps to manage. An example here would be documentary collection, letter of credit and consign-ment. All of these processes follow roughly the same five steps: (1) Extension of credit to customer; (2) Informing the customer of credit status; (3) Banks open a communication channel regarding the customer; (4) Updating the status of goods from freight forwarder; (5) Execution of full or partial payment of funds based on certain criteria. Blockchain technology could bring the benefits of automation to these trades. Using cryptographic keys and multisignature wallets, one can create a replacement for traditional trade finance documents, which are stored on the blockchain as a Smart Contract. The document is updated by blockchain transactions as it moves through the steps of the trade process.

- **Capital markets.** When trading on the capital market, there exists a set of procedural steps that enable the trading of assets in a legally conforming fashion, as well as several custodian services revolving around facilitating the trade. A broad definition of these steps can be termed as such: (1) Create a representation of an asset, such as a currency, bonds, stocks, gold, etc.; (2) Enable a trade to take place between two or more stakeholders; (3) Balances must be recorded and kept; (4) The eventual liquidation of an investor's position.

3 Blockchain and Accounting: Literature Review

As we have seen, the applications of Blockchain have evolved since its first implementation in 2008. It is possible to find a vast literature on Blockchain, on its applications, on its strengths and weaknesses. In recent times some scholars have proposed the adoption of Blockchain in Accounting Systems.

3.1 Double and Triple Entry Bookkeeping

Modern Financial Accounting is based on a Double Entry system. Double Entry Bookkeeping (DEB) revolutionized the field of financial accounting during the Renaissance period [13, 14]. DEB solved the problem of managers knowing whether they could trust their own books. Double entry bookkeeping is a system of bookkeeping so named because every entry to an account requires a corresponding and opposite entry to a different account. The double entry has two equal and corresponding sides known as debit and credit. The left-hand side is debit and right-hand side is credit.

In the double-entry accounting system, at least two accounting entries are required to record each financial transaction. These entries may occur in asset, liability, equity, expense, or revenue accounts. Recording of a debit amount to one or more accounts and an equal credit amount to one or more accounts results in total debits being equal to total credits for all accounts in the general ledger. If the accounting entries are recorded without error, the aggregate balance of all accounts having Debit balances will be equal to the aggregate balance of all accounts having Credit balances.

Accounting entries that debit and credit related accounts typically include the same date and identifying code in both accounts, so that in case of error, each debit and credit can be traced back to a journal and transaction source document, thus preserving an audit trail. The accounting entries are recorded in the "Books of Accounts". Regardless of which accounts and how many are impacted by a given transaction, the fundamental accounting equation of Assets equal Liabilities plus Capital will hold.

However, to gain the trust of outsiders, independent public auditors also verify the company's financial information. Each audit is a costly exercise, binding the company's accountants for long times [15].

3.2 Triple Entry Bookkeeping

Blockchain technology may represent the next step for accounting: instead of keeping separate records based on transaction receipts, companies can write their transactions directly into a joint register, creating an interlocking system of enduring accounting records [16]. Since all entries are distributed and cryptographically sealed, falsifying or destroying them to conceal activity is practically impossible.

To explain the notion of Blockchain-based accounting some researchers use the term Triple-Entry Accounting which is described as an enhancement to conventional double entry accounting where the accounting entries of the involved parties are cryptographically sealed by a third entity (the Blockchain) [16–18].

Since the Blockchain is immutable to any data amendment it is impossible to falsify or delete the written accounting entries. Notably, the notion of triple-entry accounting was first time described in 2005 by Ian Grigg three years before Blockchain was invented [17]. Ian Grigg described the possibility of using crypto-graphically protected digital receipt to verify transactions occurred between different counterparts and stored by a third party and showing if any details in the records were changed or deleted. With the advent of Blockchain that processes can become auto-mated, cheap and even more reliable as the need for a third party holding the receipts in a centralized manner is superseded by a decentralized ledger.

Lazanis was first to coherently describe the possibility of Blockchain Accounting by conventional companies. He emphasizes that blockchain eliminates the need for trust in any intermediary such as bank or insurance company if a company voluntarily publishes its transactions on Blockchain [19].

The companies would benefit in many ways: standardization would allow auditors to verify a large portion of the most important data behind the financial statements automatically. The cost and time necessary to conduct an audit would decline consid-erably. Auditors could spend freed up time on areas they can add more value, e.g. on very complex transactions or on internal control mechanisms.

It is not necessary to start with a joint register for all accounting-entries. The Blockchain as a source of trust can also be extremely helpful in today's accounting structures. It can be gradually integrated with typical accounting procedures: starting from securing the integrity of records, to completely traceable audit trails. At the end of the road, fully automated audits may be reality [15]. Since companies are implementing Blockchain into their Enterprise Resource Planning (ERP) systems, particularly for tasks such as procurement and supplier management, the accountant's and the auditor's role has just evolved [4].

Blockchain's transparency gives visibility to all transactions for approved users, and this may decrease auditors' work with sampling and validating transactions.

However, this allows auditors more time to focus on controls and investigating anomalies. Meanwhile, opportunities are emerging for CPAs to use Blockchain technology as they expand their assurance services to areas such as cybersecurity and sustainability. Blockchain could enable a real-time, verifiable, and transparent accounting ecosystem. It has the potential to transform current auditing practices, resulting in a more precise and timely automatic assurance system [20, 21].

3.3   Real-Time Blockchain Accounting System

Another line of studies concerns Real-time Blockchain Accounting System (RBAS). RBAS is a software solution that enables transactions of currency, financial derivatives, and other digital documents between two or more counterparts, stores the transaction data in cryptographically protected blocks whose integrity is verified through the process of mining, and allows the composition of financial statements at any time [7].

For companies and their stakeholder to obtain all the benefits provided by the technology it is necessary that a RBAS possesses the following properties:

1. Transparency—the transactions must visible in real-time as it is the case with bitcoin.
2. Immutability—there must not be a programming possibility to change any data once they were entered, to ensure this, the company using the system must not control the mining power.
3. Accessibility—the data must be easily accessible to a broad range of stakeholders.

Financial statements are prepared at regular intervals and sum up what has happened in a firm's ledger throughout a certain period. An auditor then issues an opinion on the accuracy of the financial statements. Outsiders, such as investors and credit risk managers, have to trust both that the auditing is thorough and unbiased and that the firm has not given false information to the auditor. That is, the concept of trust is critical in both the preparation of the financial statement and in the auditing process.

This is where the Blockchain technology behind the bitcoin can play an integral role [22]. If a firm were to voluntarily post all of its business transactions on a blockchain, with a permanent time stamp on each transaction, the firm's entire ledger would be instantaneously visible and anyone could aggregate the firm's transactions into income statements and balance sheets in real-time.

That is, many of the things the auditor does in today's accounting world, the blockchain can possibly do much more efficiently and much timelier in tomorrows. By construction, if a firm kept all its transactions and balances on a blockchain, then the blockchain itself could, largely, replace the auditor in confirming the accuracy of the firm's accounting, thus avoiding potential moral hazard or agency problems [22]. In this sense, the only voice out of the chorus is Rückeshäuser. While agreeing with the adoption of a Blockchain Accounting, she believes that it alone is not enough to eliminate accounting fraud [23].

4 Blockchain and Accounting Information Systems

As mentioned above, companies are considering whether to integrate Blockchain-based procedures with their Enterprise Resource Planning (ERP) systems, particularly for tasks such as procurement and supplier management. Blockchain ledger-based technology can simplify the procurement process because it enables secure recording of transactions in a way that can lead to unprecedented transparency and increased operational efficiency [24].

However, with respect to Blockchain technology, it is necessary to understand: (1) what the application field really is; (2) how to implement it; (3) what the real advantages and disadvantages may be.

4.1 The Scope of Blockchain

Looking at the current literature regarding the Blockchain, we can observe that there is considerable confusion, at least from an accounting point of view. Our opinion is that the approach currently followed is strictly technical and does not take account of accounting rules.

An Accounting Information System (AIS) is a system that collects, stores and processes accounting data in order to manage a company. The core of an AIS is an Enterprise Resource Planning (ERP) system, that is the integrated management of main business processes, usually in real-time and mediated by software and technology.

ERPs implement Financial Accounting which is the field of accounting concerned with the summary, analysis and reporting of financial transactions related to a business. Financial Accounting strictly follows local and international rules, such as Generally Accepted Accounting Principles (GAAP) and International Financial Reporting Standards (IFRS) and uses the Double Entry paradigm. In other words, and as said before, Financial Accounting is based on a Double Entry system. We can therefore state that the transactions managed by ERP systems must implement the Double Entry rules. Furthermore, they must adhere to local and international standards that guarantee the correctness of data management.

We will call these transactions Internal Transactions, distinguishing them from other transactions that involve information exchanges between different companies, which we will call External Transactions.

Internal Transactions are stored in the Relational Databases of ERP systems following the logic of the Double Entry. Changing a transaction is impossible or extremely difficult. On the one hand, the internal consistency checks of the databases

Table 1 Scope of Blockchain

	Internal transactions	External transactions (actual–No BC)	External transactions (future–BC)
Physical layer	RDBs	Not formalized	DLT
Logical layer	Double entry self-balancing system	No checks	BC logic—smart Contracts
Control layer	External auditor	External auditor	DLT logic

exclude the possibility of removing and modifying a record, on the other it would be necessary to modify all the related entries of the Double Entry ledgers. The controls on Internal Transactions are carried out by external and independent Auditors. This not only guarantees the correctness of the information, but it is also required by current regulations. Automatic checks, even if they meet the needs, would not be enough from a legal point of view.

As regards External Transactions, we must distinguish between the current situation and a future situation in which DLT technologies are adopted. Currently, External Transactions are carried out using non-formalized channels, such as email messages, and there are no secure, shared and non-modifiable archives that contain the transactions themselves.

With the adoption of Blockchain these transactions could be included in a Distributed Ledger, thus achieving the security and sharing objectives we have seen. In addition to the physical storage in a formalized ledger, a logical control of the transactions would also be possible, for example by checking that they comply with the terms provided in a Smart Contract.

Finally, using Blockchain technology, it would be possible to obtain an automatic control of the transactions, which is currently not performed. Furthermore, the checks could not only be automatic, but also be carried out by interested parties that have access to the ledgers. We have summarized all these observations in Table 1.

4.2 How to Implement Blockchain: Blockchain as a Service (BaaS)

Claimed benefits of Blockchain include offering business value and efficiency gains by, for example, assisting compliance, asset tracking, supply chain management, and generally displacing intermediaries. The focus is particularly on multi-party scenarios (across organizations, departments, individuals, etc.), where the ledger provides a transparent and reliable source of facts across administrative domains [25].

As such, "Blockchain-as-a-Service" (BaaS) offerings are emerging to make Blockchain more accessible to businesses, by reducing the overheads of adoption. BaaS entails a service provider offering and managing various components of a

Table 2 Top 10 blockchain as a service providers [26]

Provider	Partners	Tool name	Cryptovalue
Microsoft	Microsoft, consensys, blockstack labs	Azure	Ethereum
R3	Barclays, Credit Suisse, Goldman Sachs, J. P. Morgan, and Royal Bank of Scotland, and more than 70 partners, including Bank of America and Wells Fargo	Corda	
HPE R3	HPE	Corda	
SAP cloud platform blockchain	SAP	Leonardo	
BitSE	BitSE, PricewaterhouseCoopers (PwC)	VeChain	
Blocko	Blocko, Samsung, LG CNS, Hyundai, other South Korean firms	Coinstack	Lotte card
Blockstream	Blockstream	Lightning charge, lightning network	Bitcoin
PayStand	PayStand		
Peer Ledger	Peer Ledger		
Deloitte	Deloitte	Rubix core	Ethereum

Blockchain infrastructure. The precise nature of a BaaS deployment depends on the service provider, application specifics, and the customer goals. Several IT solution companies provide BaaS solutions, see Table 2 [26].

Although there is a noteworthy academic literature about the Blockchain, its applications and the benefits that can be achieved with its adoption, there are no works related to real applications in Accounting Information Systems (AIS), as far as we know.

Many "big players" like Microsoft, SAP or Deloitte are starting to offer solutions that incorporate Blokchain-related technologies, typically based on a "Blockchain As A Service" approach as those that we have seen. However, these solutions are still at a prototype stage and the related documentation is halfway between a declaration of intent and a marketing proposal.

4.3   Final Considerations and Future Research Directions

The above-mentioned literature highlights characteristics, merits and advantages deriving from the adoption of DLT systems. However, no paper highlights the point of view of companies. As an example, what are the actual costs of implementing DLT systems? What are the real—not theoretical—advantages for the company deriving from the adoption of such systems?

As often happens in the field of IT, after an initial emphasis on the theoretical advantages of an innovation that feed great expectations, we are heading towards a phase of disappointment of these expectations [27].

In the current literature, some fundamental aspects are excluded or are not adequately investigated. As an example, we may argue that adoption of DLT-based systems only makes sense if:

(1) all or most of the members of the Value Chain adopt these systems;
(2) the costs of new disintermediation services are lower than the costs of current service providers;
(3) it is possible to adopt cryptocurrencies in order to take full advantage of the benefits offered by the Internet of Values.

Future research should investigate these aspects.

Point 1: it is very likely that to create an effective and efficient network it is necessary that most part of companies should be connected to a Blockchain. What happens if only some companies of a Value Chain adhere to a Blockchain? Point 2: Blockchain technology is convenient if the cost of intermediaries is high. However, some intermediaries may not be necessary: this is the case, as an example, of Small and Medium Enterprises (SME). SMEs are not obliged to have auditing procedures, so the benefits of such complex accounting are lost. Point 3: at present it is not clear if widespread use of cryptocurrencies is really possible, or if in the future it will be possible for everyone to use them. In response to this challenge, current financial systems could lower their costs, thus making the use of cryptocurrencies unattractive.

Finally, we would like to propose a crucial consideration: how will national and international legislation evolve? Most of the aspects exposed up to now have no specific reference legislation. Users of cryptocurrencies and smart contracts are absolutely not legally protected. This is currently the major obstacle to the spread of Blockchain technology.

5   Conclusions

Internet has changed: from the Internet of Information it has become Internet of Values. Blockchain is certainly one of the technologies that led to this transformation.

In conclusion, we can answer the Research Questions that we had placed in the introduction:

RQ1: What impact will the adoption of Blockchain technology have on business intermediaries?

Disintermediation is the core feature that drives the benefits associated with Distributed Ledgers. Traditionally, systems that have centralized ledgers have required the participation of a trusted third party to maintain a record of transactions between organizations. A Distributed Ledger overcomes the need for a third party, which can be a significant benefit when there is no clear trusted central organization, or if the costs of intermediation are high. Intermediaries such as banks, insurance companies and auditors will have to redefine their relationships with companies.

RQ2: Will the Blockchain be universally adopted in the AIS of all companies?

The adoption of DLT-based systems only makes sense if: (1) all or most of the members of the Value Chain adopt these systems; (2) the costs of new disintermediation services are lower than the costs of current service providers; (3) it is possible to adopt cryptocurrencies in order to take full advantage of the benefits offered by the Internet of Values. This is not the case, as an example, for Small and Medium Enterprises (SME).

RQ3: What could be the development paths of the AISs taking into account the Blockchain Technology?

Adopting DLT in an ERP system makes no sense because the current accounting logic is more reliable and efficient. For this reason, we consider it unlikely that new versions of ERP systems Blockchain-based will be created. Conversely, a company that wishes to implement truly effective and efficient intercompany solutions will use Blockchain technologies using "Blockchain as a System" (BaaS) platforms.

In conclusion, we can state that the Blockchain technology is extremely interesting and its adoption has great theoretical advantages. However, we will have to evaluate the implications and the costs of its use. Moreover, it remains to be seen what the steps will be for its introduction, especially considering that at present there are no studies that analyse these processes.

References

1. Chartered Accountants NZ (2017). *The future of Blockchain.* http://www.charteredaccountantsanz.com.
2. Swan, M. (2015). *Blockchain: Blueprint for a new economy*, 1st ed., O'Reilly.
3. Bartoletti, M. & Pompianu, L. (2017). *An empirical analysis of smart contracts: Platforms, applications, and design patterns.* arXiv preprint arXiv:1703.06322.
4. Pree, W. (2016). *Blockchain: Technology and applications.*
5. Benos, E., Garratt, R. & Gurrola-Perez, P. (2017). *The economics of distributed ledger technology for securities settlement.* https://doi.org/10.5195/ledger.2019.144.
6. Chapman, J., Garratt, R., Hendry, S., McCormack, A. & McMahon, W. (2017). Project Jasper: Are distributed wholesale payment systems feasible yet? *Financial System*, p. 59.
7. Potekhina, A. & Riumkin, I. (2017). *Blockchain–a new accounting paradigm: Implications for credit risk management.*
8. Miraz, M. H. & Ali, M. (2018). *Applications of blockchain technology beyond cryptocurrency.* arXiv preprint arXiv:1801.03528.

9. Tapscott, D., & Tapscott, A. (2016). *Blockchain revolution* (1st ed.). New York: Portfolio-Penguin.
10. Frøystad, P. & Holm, J. (2015). *Blockchain: Powering the internet of value*. http://www.evry.com.
11. Crosby, M., Pattanayak, P., Verma, S., & Kalyanaraman, V. (2016). Blockchain technology: Beyond bitcoin. *Applied Innovation Review, 2*, 6–10.
12. CoinMarketCap 07 (2017). *CryptoCurrency market capitalizations*. https://coinmarketcap.com/. Online Accessed June 17, 2018.
13. Pacioli, L. (1494). Particularis de Computis et Scripturis. In Summa de Arithmetica Geometria Proportioni et Proportionalita, Ff. 197v–210v. Venice, Italy: Paganino de Paganini.
14. Sangster A. (2016). The genesis of double entry bookkeeping. *The Accounting Review, 91*(1), 299–315.
15. Andersen, N. (2017). *Blockchain technology. A game-changer in accounting?* http://www.deloitte.com.
16. Coyne, J. G. & McMickle, P. L. (2017). Can blockchains serve an accounting purpose? *Journal of Emerging Technologies in Accounting, 14*(2), 101–111.
17. Grigg, I. (2005). *Triple entry accounting*. https://doi.org/10.13140/rg.2.2.12032.43524.
18. Mills, D. C., Wang, K., Malone, B., Ravi, A., Marquardt, J. C., Badev, A. I., Brezinski, T., Fahy, L., Liao, K., Kargenian, V. & Ellithorpe, M. (2016). *Distributed ledger technology in payments, clearing, and settlement*.
19. Lazanis, R. (2015). *How technology behind Bitcoin could transform accounting as we know it*. [online] Techvibes. Available at: https://techvibes.com/2015/01/22/how-technology-behind-bitcoin-could-transform-accounting-as-we-know-it-2015-01-22. Accessed 16 June, 2018.
20. Dai, J., & Vasarhelyi, M. A. (2017). Toward blockchain-based accounting and assurance. *Journal of Information Systems, 31*(3), 5–21.
21. Zhang, L., Pei, D. & Vasarhelyi, M. A. (2017) Toward a new business reporting model. *Journal of Emerging Technologies in Accounting September 2017, 14*(2), 1–15.
22. Byström, H. (2016). *Blockchains, real-time accounting and the future of credit risk modeling*. Department of Economics: Lund University.
23. Rückeshäuser, N. (2017). Do we really want blockchain-based accounting? Decentralized Consensus as enabler of management override of internal controls, in Leimeister, J. M.; Brenner, W. (Hrsg.): Proceedings der 13. Internationalen Tagung Wirtschaftsinformatik (WI 2017), St. Gallen, S. 16–30.
24. Tysiac, K. (2017). *Blockchain: An opportunity for accountants? Or a threat?*.
25. Singh, J. & Michels, J. D. (2017). *Blockchain as a service: Providers and trust*. Queen Mary School of Law Legal Studies Research Paper No. 269/2017.
26. Patrizio, A. (2018). *Top 10 blockchain as a service providers*. Datamation, March 27.
27. www.gartner.com/SmarterWithGartner.

Understanding Blockchain Adoption in Italian Firms

Adele Caldarelli, Luca Ferri, Gianluca Ginesti, and Rosanna Spanò

Abstract This study investigates individuals' blockchain adoption behavior focusing on the Italian setting, and gathering perceptions from information systems practitioners and entrepreneurs. The aim of the paper is to understand what are the factors that push organizational actors to use the blockchain. To this aim we embrace the second version of the unified theory of acceptance and use of technology (UTAUT). The model was estimated using the structural equation modeling with partial least square estimation (PLS-SEM). Our results show that performance expectancy and social influence are factors that have a strong positive effect on people intention to adopt blockchain. Surprisingly, the findings unveil that experience has a negative effect on blockchain use intention. This allows us to argue that the technology under scrutiny has such a disruptive nature that individuals with previous experience look at it with skepticisms as its implementation involves a full re-think of all routines and practices.

Keywords UTAUT · Blockchain · Italian firms

1 Introduction

The last years have been characterized by a raise in disruptive information and communication technologies (ICTs), that are challenging organizations to fully re-think their operational models [1]. Such emerging dynamics are putting on the table a number of questions, dealing with aspects of trust between the actors, accountability, transparency, collaboration, and knowledge sharing [2–5].

One particular technology, which is gaining momentum for its potential but at the same time poses extreme challenges is the blockchain [6–9]. Blockchain is already employed in a wide array of contexts [10–13], because virtually all transactions with blockchain are safer, more transparent, traceable and efficient [6, 7], with favorable impacts in terms of clients' trust [14]. The benefits ascribable to the blockchain,

A. Caldarelli · L. Ferri (✉) · G. Ginesti · R. Spanò
University of Naples Federico II, Naples 80126, Italy
e-mail: luca.ferri@unina.it

© The Editor(s) (if applicable) and The Author(s), under exclusive license to Springer Nature Switzerland AG 2020
R. Agrifoglio et al. (eds.), *Digital Business Transformation*, Lecture Notes in Information Systems and Organisation 38, https://doi.org/10.1007/978-3-030-47355-6_9

according to extant studies, are the amelioration of transparency and accountability [7, 15], the traceability of the operations and the fraud prevention [13, 14, 16], the cybersecurity and the data protection [7]. However, such benefits are achievable only if the technology is implemented in a manner acceptable to those involved. It is exactly to better tap into these issues that recent contributions are progressively exploring how individuals react when it comes to accepting to deploy this technology. Such studies fall into the domain of technology acceptance literature, which represents the main debate that this paper addresses [17–19]. Indeed, even if the studies on technology acceptance are steadily growing in number and scope [20–24], the blockchain seems still a quite unexplored area [20, 25], and open unanswered questions remain as for the drivers of the blockchain adoption.

Specifically focusing on accounting practices, the introduction of blockchain technology in firms could change the way in which records are created and stored triggering a deep revolution. Such a circumstance has been largely called upon, but is poorly deepened in literature. Thus, in the current study we rely upon the second version unified theory of acceptance and use of technology developed by Venkatesh et al. [18, 19] (namely UTAUT) to understand what are the factors that push organizational actors to adopt the blockchain.

To this aim, a Likert-based questionnaire was disseminated online between information systems practitioners and entrepreneurs. The questionnaire was divided into seven parts. The first part covered the respondents' personal information while the other six sections were about the different UTAUT theoretical constructs. Using the questionnaire results, a partial least square structural equation modeling (PLS-SEM) has been carried out in order to measure the effect of the theoretical constructs on people's intention to adopt the blockchain.

Our findings show that performance expectancy and social influence are factors that have a strong positive effect on people intention to adopt blockchain while experience has a negative effect on the use intention.

As for the remainder of this paper, Sect. 2 describes the features of the blockchain. Section 3, presents the theoretical framework and develops the hypotheses of the study. Section 4 describes the research design, Sect. 5 shows and discuss the results. Section 6 offers some concluding remarks.

2   The Features of Blockchain

Blockchain technology emerged in the crypto-currency market as a disruptive technology [26, 27] considered as a digital, distributed transaction ledger, that stores data creating identical copies, maintained on multiple computer systems, controlled by different entities [28, 29]. Although there is no an official definition of Blockchain, one of the commonly acknowledged formulations is the one proposed by Deloitte [29] according to whom *"anyone participating in a blockchain can review the entries in it; users can update the blockchain only by consensus of a majority of participants"*. In other words, Blockchain technology represents a distributed database (ledgers) that, performing in a synchronized environment (chain), validates information uploaded by users [6, 30–32]. This kind of technology implies the existence of a decentralized system where the validation activity (of transactions, contracts, etc.) cannot give rise to any kind of alteration [13]. Every data stored in a Blockchain represent information that can never be erased. From the business perspective, the Blockchain involves different entities as nodes in the transaction work and the process is being validated through cryptography [31]. Records of these transactions are stored as shared and decentralized ledger among all participating entities. Transactions are tamper-proof and are traceable thanks to the existence of a "genesis node". Indeed, data introduced in the chain are organized in blocks that shape a chain [10], and the current block is expected to store the information of the previous block. Blockchain transactions operate in a peer-to-peer network, in a decentralized way [13]. Thus, the transactions are validated and stored by a distributed consensus, and it is not necessary to have a central entity that validates the transactions. Consequently, o when someone store a set of transactions in the chain, information are recorded and validated by other computers of the same network.

Each block is unique, has its own identification code (hash) and it is connected with the preceding one making easier to have any kind of information history and to recover or verify previous transactions just exploring the previous blocks, generating more transaction security [32]. In this process, the transactions receive a unique sequence and time (timestamp) that cannot be changed: once a transaction is validated it cannot be modified [33, 34]. Furthermore, transparency of the operations is strengthened because the transactions are shared across the network, together with any useful information, thereby enabling all network actors to be timely informed.

Blockchain in itself can be termed as a meta-technology because it is the result of the integration of several other technologies such as software development, cryptographic technology, database technology, etc. [35]. Nowadays, firms that are looking at digital technologies, as enablers of competitive advantage or disruption innovation should consider the possibility to introduce blockchain technology in their activities.

While recent studies investigated the impact of Blockchain in supply chains, this technology could affect on several firm processes such as accounting practice, auditing activities (internal and external), information systems, quality activities, risk reduction, contract registrations.

Thanks to the benefits that Blockchain could provide to firms (i.e. cost reduction, efficiency improvement, quality improvement, risk reduction, flexibility) [8] almost all organizations want to take advantage of the great deal of improvements brought about by blockchain, which span enhanced process of adoption in Europe [29]. For example, authors examined how this technology has been an effective way to validate information about financial sector [36, 37], other authors showed how ticket events vendors are looking at using Blockchains to help prevent frauds [38]. Yet other authors focused on how this new technology could help in storing patient data securely and accurately in the health care sector [39]. Finally, some research focused on the possible use of blockchain in the public sector for recoding property transactions [40].

Table 1 Blockchain benefits for firms

Benefit	Explanation
Reliable and available	Because a wide circle of participants shares a blockchain, it has no single point of failure and is designed to be resilient in the face of outages or attacks. If any node in a network of participants fails, the others will continue to operate, maintaining the information's availability and reliability
Transparent	Transactions on the blockchain are visible to its participants, increasing auditability and trust
Immutable	It is nearly impossible to make changes to a blockchain without detection, increasing confidence in the information it carries and reducing the opportunities for fraud
Irrevocable	It is possible to make transactions irrevocable, which can increase the accuracy of records and simplify back-office processes
Digital	Almost any document or asset can be expressed in code and encapsulated or referenced by a ledger entry, meaning that blockchain technology has very broad applications, most as yet unimagined, much less implemented

Table 1, drawing from the above-cited contributions provides an overview of Blockchain benefits.

These key characteristics of blockchain technology open the door to disintermediating third parties from myriad transaction types, lowering transaction costs, and increasing the potential for innovation in every major industry. This technology can help to improve security and accountability of different firms' activities (i.e. financial transactions, micropayments, health records, corporate audits etc.).

Indeed, traditionally the double entry accounting system is in existence since the fifteen century. Blockchain removes the disadvantages of trust related issues associated with this system and thus reduces the friction in transaction process [41]. Blockchain will make transactions more instantaneous and cheaper [42]. For example, IBM has introduced a protocol for smart contracts that is based on the underlying blockchain technology.

3   Theoretical Framework and Hypotheses Development

Over the last years scholars have increasingly devoted attention to the development of models able to predict and understand information systems adoption behaviors [17–19, 43]. The majority of contributions revolves around individuals' attitudes, and attempted to adapt the theory of reasoned action (TRA) concepts [44] to this domain, by fostering the development of the TAM [17].

Before describing the adoption models' characteristics, it is important to remark that technology adoption represents the willingness within a group of users to employ technology for their benefit [45]. Adoption is not only related to the technology itself, but involves multiple levels and factors such as users' attitude and personality [18], social influence [46], trust [47] and enabling conditions [48].

From this perspective, the TAM proposed by Davis [17] examines the technology adoption devoting attention to the users' perception of its utility and ease of use. This model has been empirically verified and is largely accepted in literature [19, 49–52].

In addition to the TAM, the Theory of Planned Behavior (TPB) proposed by Ajzen [53, 54], which extends the TRA, is widely used to model the acceptance. The constructs included in TRA are behavioral attitudes, subjective norms, intention to use and actual use, as well as perceived behavioral control. TPB has been increasingly relied upon to comprehend the adoption dynamics of a variety of new information technology products and also to predict their levels of usage [55, 56].

However, some limitations of the above-cited models led to further explorations to encompass additional perspectives in the analysis. Further advancements have led to the unified theory of acceptance and use of technology (UTAUT) [18, 19], which ties together eight models from prior literature, that is TAM [17]; theory of reasoned action (TRA) [43]; motivational model (MM) [57]; theory of planned behavior (TPB) [54]; combined TAM and TPB (C-TAM-TPB) [58], model of PC utilization (MPCU) [48]; innovation diffusion theory (IDT) [59]; and social cognitive theory (SCT) [60].

The value of the UTAUT lies in the fact that it allows us to comprehend the role of performance expectancy, effort expectancy, social influence, and facilitating conditions as exogenous constructs for predicting the intention and use.

The fully encompassing approach of the UTAUT is particularly suitable to explore the issues forming the core of this paper on blockchain implementation. More specifically, for the purposes of the current study we refer to the UTAUT proposed by Venkatesh et al. [18], in order to include additional relevant dimensions such as the hedonic motivation, price value, and habit. This predictive model has proved its relevance in a number of contexts [61, 62] and is crucial in this paper to understand the main actors' motivations for blockchain adoption. In the UTAUT at the basis of the intention to use a technology there are four constructs: performance expectancy (expectation about performance or PE); effort expectancy (expectation on the effort to support or EE); social influence (social influence or SOI); facilitating conditions (conditions that make it possible to make the adoption of a technology less traumatic or FC).

Performance expectancy measures the level of expectation of IS actors with respect to improving the working condition due to the adoption of technology. The effect of performance expectancy on intention could be mitigated by personal factors such as age and gender. In our study performance expectancy refers to the degree to which an employee perceives that using the blockchain will improve their productivity and performance. On this regard it is worth noting that this new technology generates high expectations [8] and minimizes process complexity and uncertainty [63]. Previous contributions signal that the intention of individuals to adopt and to use a technology depends significantly on performance expectancy [18, 19, 64–66]. Therefore, we hypothesize that:

H1. Performance expectancy positively affects the intention to adopt blockchain.

Social influence stands for the level of influence that the opinion of the subjects of a user's social circle may have on a particular action. According to the authors, this construct is mitigated both by personal factors such as gender, age or experience, and by voluntariness in the use of technology. Social influence for the purposes of the current paper refers to the extent to which the employee comprehends the relevance of why others believe they should use the blockchain. The leading idea is that the opinions of colleagues, friends, family members impact one's choices [66, 67]. On this regard, literature has contended that social influence impacts the adoption of Internet-based banking [67, 68] and mobile government services [66, 69]. Several contributions have also emphasized that collaboration and the relational dimension are crucial and influence whether people are prone to adopt blockchain [66–69]. Therefore, we hypothesize that:

H2. Social influence positively affects the intention to adopt blockchain.

Facilitating conditions can be understood as the "*degree to which an individual believes that an organizational and technical infrastructure exists to support use of the system*" [19, p. 453]. In this paper, we consider employee's awareness of the resources available to sustain the blockchain implementation. Facilitating conditions influence both the adoption and use of a given technology [18, 19, 69–71]. Indeed, thanks to the existence of facilitating conditions users could be more incline to use the new technology and the degree of inefficiency related to technological change is significatively lower [71, 72]. Due to the importance of facilitating conditions and in light of previous literature we expect that the existence of conditions that could help people to use the new technology should have a positive effect on people intention to use blockchain. Therefore, we propose the following hypothesis:

H3. Facilitating conditions positively affect the intention to adopt blockchain.

Effort expectancy, represents the measure of the perception of simplicity expected in the use of the system. Literature posits that the relationship between effort expectancy and intention is likely to be moderated by gender, age, and above all experience. A common opinion is that the perceived ease of use positively influences the intention to adopt a certain technology, but that the lack of experience may play a limiting role [71, 72]. Therefore, we hypothesize that:

H4. Effort expectancy positively affects the intention to adopt blockchain
H5. Experience positively affects the intention to adopt blockchain.

4   Research Method

Questionnaire and reliability analysis

Table 2 Sample description

Measure	Item	n.	Percentage
Age	18–30	129	48.31
	30–40	81	30.34
	40–50	42	15.73
	50+	15	5.62
Gender	Male	139	52.06
	Female	128	47.94
Education	High school	22	8.24
	University degree	132	49.44
	Master	94	35.21
	Phd	19	7.12
Role	Accounting specialist	197	73.78
	Information system practitioner	66	24.72
	Other	4	1.50

For the purposes of our analysis, we disseminated a Likert based questionnaire among practitioners working in the information systems field during the period January-March 2018. In line with Venkatesh et al. [19] the questionnaire was divided into seven parts. The first part was about respondents' personal information (i.e., gender, age, experience and voluntariness to use). The other six sections were about the different UTAUT theoretical constructs. All constructs have been measured by employing a 6-point Likert scale ranging from (1) strongly disagrees to (6) strongly agree [73].

To ensure the reliability of the scale, a pretesting phase was carried out on sample of 72 scholars and professionals involved in blockchain initiatives [74]. The survey results of this sample were subjected to principal component analysis (PCA) in order to discern the correlation between the different components. No items were dropped after this analysis. Furthermore, we tested the same sample with Crombach's Alpha, which resulted in a satisfying score of 0.872.

Sample description

After the validation step, a survey was carried out between participants contacted by using blockchain thematic groups on social media (i.e. LinkedIn, Facebook). We considered as "thematic groups" all groups that have in the title the words "*Blockchain*" and "*Italy*". A total of 19 thematic group with more than 10 thousand people were found. For each group an invitation letter, explaining the aim of the study, has been sent. We collected a total of 322 observations. We excluded the responses of people with less than 3 years of experience in accounting or information systems fields and of those people that were not working for Italian firms. Our final sample consisted in 267 observations.

Table 2 provides few descriptive statistics of the sample. Table 2 provides the respondents' profile showing a similar distribution between male (52.06%) and female (47.94%) respondents. Also, in terms of age most respondents were between 18 and 30 years old (48.31%) and between 30 and 40 (30.34%) while just a little part of our sample has an age between 40 and 50 or 50+ (respectively 15.73% and 5.62%). With reference to the education level the 40.44% of respondents held a postgraduate degree or a master (35.21%), while just a little part of the sample has a Ph.D. (7.12%) or is not graduated (8.24%). Finally, with reference to the role in firms the great part of the sample work as accountant or accounting specialist (73.78%), the 24.72% is employed in information system field while a small part of the sample work in another field (1.5%).

5   Research Results and Discussion

The data gathered through the survey were analyzed using a Partial Least Square Structural Equation Modeling (PLS-SEM) approach in line with previous studies [75, 76]. This method is widely used in ICT literature and, more generally, in social sciences, because it is suitable for both large and small sample sizes, as well as for non-normal data.

We assessed the overall goodness-of-fit measure using the Chi-square test. This test is widely used to assesses the adequacy of a model in terms of its ability to reflect the variance and covariance of data [77]. Our test shows an overall Chi-square ratio of 661 with $p < 0.001$.

Because Chi-square is a test particularly sensitive to the size of the sample, we decided to test our model with other fit indices following the approach of other authors [76]. The results or our test are summarized in Table 3.

Table 3 Fit indexes

Index	Test results	Acceptable
Average path coefficient (APC)	APC = 0.118 $p < 0.001$	Yes
Average R-square (ARS)	ARS = 0.596 $p < 0.001$	Yes
Average adjusted R-square (AARS)	AARS = 0.582 $p < 0.001$	Yes
Average block VIF (AVIF)	AVIF = 3.355 (acceptable if <= 5, ideally <= 3.3)	Yes
Average full collinearity VIF (AFVIF)	AFVIF = 3.911, (acceptable if <= 5, ideally <= 3.3)	Yes
Simpson's paradox ratio (SPR)	SPR = 0.948, acceptable if >= 0.7, ideally = 1	Yes

Table 4 Research results

Hp n.	Relation	Path coefficient	Std. dev.	p-value
H1	PE.XP. -> BI	0.397	0.091	0.000
H2	SO.INF -> BI	0.401	0.067	0.000
H3	FA.CON. -> BI	0.256	0.082	0.000
H4	EFF.EXP -> BI	0.108	0.072	0.002
H5	EXP -> BI	−0.099	0.090	0.019
	Overall R-Square 0.596	Overall adjusted R-Square 0.582		

Finally, we carried out structural equation modeling in order to understand the effect of each theoretical construct on people intention to adopt blockchain technology. The following table (Table 4) presents the research results.

The explanatory power of the UTAUT was tested using the overall R-square. UATUT theoretical constructs explain the 59.6% of the total variance.

Performance expectation has a significant positive effect on people intention to adopt blockchain technology (coefficient 0.397 $p < 0.001$). This result suggests that every increase in the expectation about blockchain performance in firms could improve the people intention to abide by this technology. This result is compliant with the statement of several authors that discuss but not empirically demonstrate that there is a strong expectation about the performance of blockchain for practitioners that will push the use of this technology in firms [18, 19, 64–66]. Therefore, H1 is fully supported.

With reference to social influence, we found a strong positive effect on intention to adopt blockchain (coefficient 0.401 with $p < 0.001$). This results suggest that people will use this technology if there will be a high level of acceptance by social groups. These findings are compliant with those of other authors, which find that social influence impacts the adoption of new technologies [66–69]. On this regard, our results show that the relational dimension has a strong influence on people intention to adopt blockchain in compliance with the statement of other authors. Therefore, H2 is fully supported.

With reference to facilitating conditions, our results show the existence of a positive effect on the intention to adopt blockchain technology (coefficient 0.256 with $p < 0.001$). This result suggest that employee are disposed in adopt blockchain changing their working practices. This finding is compliant with the finding of Queiroz and Fosso-Wamba [20] that verified the positive effect of facilitating condition on blockchain use intention in different countries. Therefore, H3 is supported.

With reference to effort expectancy we found a positive and statistically significant effect on intention (coefficient 0.108 with $p < 0.01$) while experience has a negative effect on the intention to adopt blockchain technology (coefficient −0.099 with $p < 0.05$). These results suggest that of blockchain is perceived as a technology difficult to use. The negative effect of experience on the intention suggests that blockchain is perceived as something absolutely new so the past experience could represent a disadvantage because people should start over. More specifically, in this case the lack of experience plays a positive role in which people with higher experience have more difficulties in learning something completely new than less experienced people. Therefore, H4 and H5 are supported.

Finally, with reference to the personal variables, we found that gender and age do not have any statistically significant effect (both p- values are higher than 0.05) on the theoretical construct.

Our results show that social influence (H2) is the most important predictor in people intention to use blockchain technology. This is consistent with statement of other authors according whom the process of technology adoption depends strongly by social factors [67, 68]. Furthermore, consistent with prior literature, our results show that performance expectancy (H1) is another important predictor of intention to use [18, 19, 66]. Surprisingly, the experience of subject involved in the survey plays a negative role on the process of technology acceptance, a possible explanation of this phenomenon could be that blockchain technology is something completely new and different from other kind of technologies so people will need new skills in order to manage it.

6 Concluding Remarks

The current study is rooted in the increasing attention for the disruptive power of the most recent information and communication technologies (ICTs), that are completely changing the landscape of organizations and their daily routines, at both a strategic and an operational level, not to say from the perspective of internal and external relationships and dynamics of power [1].

Among others, the most prominent questions as to what concerns information systems implementation refer to the more nuanced face of concepts of trust, accountability, transparency, collaboration, and knowledge sharing within companies [3–5], that have nowadays a breadth and a content that has largely overcome their previously acknowledged semantic boundaries, and thus are changing in the perception of organizational actors as well influencing their propensity to change.

It is worth noting that the current paper addresses the on-going debate by devoting attention to the blockchain, considering its huge potential, its disruptive novelty, and the numerous interesting and risky challenges that it poses to organizations. We looked at the blockchain in the awareness that it is already in use in a number of contexts, due to its undeniable benefits [6, 8–13]. Likewise, in looking at the current dynamics the necessary premise is that any information systems need to be implemented in a manner acceptable to those involved to express in full its potential, otherwise it is played in parallel to the previous routines and represents only a waste of resources for the company.

An essential element is to understand how individuals behave when it comes to accepting to use this technology, which is the exact debate that we addressed in the paper [17–19] since there are still unanswered questions in this domain for the blockchain [20, 25].

Consequently, our aim was to understand what are the factors that push organizational actors to adopt the blockchain, by relying upon the second version unified theory of acceptance and use of technology developed by Venkatesh et al. (UTAUT) [18]. To this aim, thanks to a Likert-based questionnaire we gathered data among information systems practitioners and entrepreneurs on their personal information and on the UTAUT theoretical constructs. Then, a partial least square structural equation modeling (PLS-SEM) has been carried out in order to measure the effect of the theoretical construct on people intention to adopt the blockchain.

Our results show that performance expectancy and social influence are factors that have a strong positive effect on people intention to adopt blockchain. Surprisingly, experience has a negative effect on blockchain use intention, unfolding that the technology under scrutiny has such a disruptive nature that individuals with previous experience look at it with skepticisms as its use involves a full re-think of all routines and practices.

These results allow us to contribute to the literature in a twofold manner.

Firstly, they offer new bases for reflection given that on the one hand they confirm previously detected trends, while on the other they unveil new tendencies that help to gather a more complete picture of the phenomenon of the blockchain adoption and its multiple nuances and implications.

Secondly, they are the first empirical insights from Italy, a country with such strong cultural and contextual conditions influencing the change management dynamics, that they enlighten the need to tap even more closely into the role played by the surrounding environment in IS change choices.

Aside, it is also worth noting that trends as to what concerns experience and its negative impacts represent a very interesting issue that deserves far more attention. Indeed, they unveil fundamental areas of resistance that need to be seriously considered, as they need a rather different approach to the introduction of the tool in the company. Far more, it is important to notice that the real comprehension of such dynamics need to overcome the current quantitative approaches, towards the recourse to case studies and participant observation to better comprehend the whole processes.

Finally, before concluding, it is advisable to signal that these findings can be of some aid also to practitioners and policy makers, as they unveil areas that are fundamental to take care of over the changing phase, as well as possible triggers of conflict and rejection that need to be prevented. Not to say that the findings also allow us to start to reflect on possible institutional interventions and regulatory efforts by policy-makers to sustain and ease blockchain adoption phenomena.

References

1. Büyüközkan, G., & Göçer, F. (2018). Digital supply chain: literature review and a proposed framework for future research. *Computers in Industry, 97,* 157–177.

2. Morgan, T. R., Richey, R. G., Jr., & Ellinger, A. E. (2018). Supplier transparency: Scale development and validation. *The International Journal of Logistics Management, 29*(3), 959–984.
3. Tsanos, C. S., & Zografos, K. G. (2016). The effects of behavioural supply chain relationship antecedents on integration and performance. *Supply Chain Management: An International Journal, 21*(6), 678–693.
4. Wagner, S. M., & Buko, C. (2005). An empirical investigation of knowledge-sharing in networks. *Journal of Supply Chain Management, 41*(4), 17–31.
5. Stolze, H. J., Murfield, M. L., & Esper, T. L. (2015). The role of social mechanisms in demand and supply integration: An individual network perspective. *Journal of Business Logistics, 36*(1), 49–68.
6. Aste, T., Tasca, P., & Di Matteo, T. (2017). Blockchain technologies: The foreseeable impact on society and Industry. *Computer, 50*(9), 18–28.
7. Kshetri, N. (2017). Can blockchain strengthen the internet of things? *IT Professional, 19*(4), 68–72.
8. Kshetri, N. (2018). Blockchain's roles in meeting key supply chain management objectives. *International Journal of Information Management, 39,* 80–89.
9. Viriyasitavat, W., Da Xu, L., Bi, Z., & Sapsomboon, A. (2018). Blockchain-based business process management (BPM) framework for service composition in industry 4.0. *Journal of Intelligent Manufacturing,* 1–12.
10. Li, Z., Kang, J., Yu, R., Ye, D., Deng, Q., & Zhang, Y. (2018). Consortium blockchain for secure energy trading in industrial internet of things. *IEEE Transactions on Industrial Informatics, 14*(8), 3690–3700.
11. Veuger, J. (2018). Trust in a viable real estate economy with disruption and blockchain. *Facilities, 36*(1/2), 103–120.
12. Benchoufi, M., Porcher, R., & Ravaud, P. (2017). Blockchain protocols in clinical trials: Transparency and traceability of consent. *F1000Research, 6.*
13. Chen, Y. (2018). Blockchain tokens and the potential democratization of entrepreneurship and innovation. *Business Horizons, 61*(4), 567–575.
14. Biswas, K., Muthukkumarasamy, V., & Tan, W. L. (2017, December). Blockchain based wine supply chain traceability system. In *Future Technologies Conference.*
15. Zou, J., Ye, B., Qu, L., Wang, Y., Orgun, M. A., & Li, L. (2018). A proof-of-trust consensus protocol for enhancing accountability in crowdsourcing services. *IEEE Transactions on Services Computing.*
16. Lu, Q., & Xu, X. (2017). Adaptable blockchain-based systems: A case study for product traceability. *IEEE Software, 34*(6), 21–27.
17. Davis, F. D. (1989). Perceived usefulness, perceived ease of use, and user acceptance of information technology. *MIS Quarterly,* 319–340.
18. Venkatesh, V., Thong, J. Y., & Xu, X. (2012). Consumer acceptance and use of information technology: extending the unified theory of acceptance and use of technology. *MIS Quarterly, 36*(1), 157–178.
19. Venkatesh, V., Morris, M. G., Davis, G. B., & Davis, F. D. (2003). User acceptance of information technology: Toward a unified view. *MIS Quarterly,* 425–478.
20. Fosso Wamba, S., Kamdjoug, K., Robert, J., Bawack, R., & G Keogh, J. (2018). Bitcoin, Blockchain, and FinTech: A systematic review and case studies in the supply chain. *Production Planning and Control, Forthcoming.*
21. Liébana-Cabanillas, F., Marinković, V., & Kalinić, Z. (2017). A SEM-neural network approach for predicting antecedents of m-commerce acceptance. *International Journal of Information Management, 37*(2), 14–24.
22. Lin, F., Fofanah, S. S., & Liang, D. (2011). Assessing citizen adoption of e-Government initiatives in Gambia: A validation of the technology acceptance model in information systems success. *Government Information Quarterly, 28*(2), 271–279.
23. Mamonov, S., & Benbunan-Fich, R. (2017). Exploring factors affecting social e-commerce service adoption: The case of Facebook Gifts. *International Journal of Information Management, 37*(6), 590–600.

24. Wu, K., Zhao, Y., Zhu, Q., Tan, X., & Zheng, H. (2011). A meta-analysis of the impact of trust on technology acceptance model: Investigation of moderating influence of subject and context type. *International Journal of Information Management, 31*(6), 572–581.
25. Kamble, S., Gunasekaran, A., & Arha, H. (2019). Understanding the Blockchain technology adoption in supply chains-Indian context. *International Journal of Production Research, 57*(7), 2009–2033.
26. Nakamoto, S. (2008). Bitcoin: A peer-to-peer electronic cash system.
27. Mattila, J. (2016). *The blockchain phenomenon–the disruptive potential of distributed consensus architectures (No. 38).* The Research Institute of the Finnish Economy.
28. Pilkington, M. (2016). 11 Blockchain technology: Principles and applications. In *Research handbook on digital transformations* (p. 225).
29. Deloitte (2019), Deloitte's Global blockchain survey, available online at: https://www2.del oitte.com/content/dam/insights/us/articles/2019-global-blockchain-survey/DI_2019-global-blockchain-survey.pdf.
30. Swan, M. (2015). *Blockchain: Blueprint for a new economy.* O'Reilly Media, Inc.
31. Crosby, M., Pattanayak, P., Verma, S., & Kalyanaraman, V. (2016). Blockchain technology: Beyond bitcoin. *Applied Innovation, 2*(6–10), 71.
32. Khan, M. A., & Salah, K. (2018). IoT security: Review, blockchain solutions, and open challenges. *Future Generation Computer Systems, 82,* 395–411.
33. Herbert, J., & Litchfield, A. (2015, January). A novel method for decentralised peer-to-peer software license validation using cryptocurrency blockchain technology. In *Proceedings of the 38th Australasian Computer Science Conference (ACSC 2015)* (Vol. 27, p. 30).
34. Huckle, S., & White, M. (2016). Socialism and the Blockchain. *Future Internet, 8*(4), 49.
35. Mougayar, W. (2016). *The business blockchain: Promise, practice, and application of the next internet technology.* London: John Wiley & Sons.
36. Fanning, K., & Centers, D. P. (2016). Blockchain and its coming impact on financial services. *Journal of Corporate Accounting and Finance, 27*(5), 53–57.
37. Lamberti, F., Gatteschi, V., Demartini, C., Pranteda, C., & Santamaria, V. (2017). Blockchain or not blockchain, that is the question of the insurance and other sectors. *IT Professional.*
38. Cai, Y., & Zhu, D. (2016). Fraud detections for online businesses: A perspective from blockchain technology. *Financial Innovation, 2*(1), 20.
39. Clauson, K. A., Breeden, E. A., Davidson, C., & Mackey, T. K. (2018). Leveraging blockchain technology to enhance supply chain management in healthcare. *Blockchain in Healthcare Today.*
40. Catalini, C., & Gans, J. S. (2016). Some simple economics of the blockchain (No. w22952). National Bureau of Economic Research.
41. Davidson, S., De Filippi, P., & Potts, J. (2016). Economics of blockchain. Available at SSRN 2744751.
42. Peters, G. W., & Panayi, E. (2016). Understanding modern banking ledgers through blockchain technologies: Future of transaction processing and smart contracts on the internet of money. In *Banking beyond banks and money* (pp. 239–278). Cham: Springer.
43. Al-Sayyed, F., & Abdalhaq, B. (2016). Interventional factors affecting instructors adoption of E-learning system: A case study of palestine. *Journal of Theoretical and Applied Information Technology, 83*(1).
44. Ajzen, I., & Fishbein, M. (1980). Understanding attitudes and predicting social behaviour.
45. Samaradiwakara, G. D. M. N., & Gunawardena, C. G. (2014). Comparison of existing technology acceptance theories and models to suggest a well improved theory/model. *International technical sciences journal, 1*(1), 21–36.
46. Fishbein, M., & Ajzen, I. (1975). *Belief, attitude, and behavior: An introduction to theory and research.* Reading, Mass: Addison Wessley.
47. Gefen, D., Karahanna, E., & Straub, D. W. (2003). Trust and TAM in online shopping: an integrated model. *MIS Quarterly, 27*(1), 51–90.
48. Thompson, R. L., Higgins, C. A., & Howell, J. M. (1991). Personal computing: toward a conceptual model of utilization. *MIS Quarterly*, 125–143.

49. Szajna, B. (1996). Empirical evaluation of the revised technology acceptance model. *Management Science, 42*(1), 85–92.
50. Larasati, N., & Santosa, P. I. (2017). Technology readiness and technology acceptance model in new technology implementation process in low technology SMEs. *International journal of innovation, Management and Technology, 8*(2), 113.
51. Verma, P., & Sinha, N. (2018). Integrating perceived economic wellbeing to technology acceptance model: The case of mobile based agricultural extension service. *Technological Forecasting and Social Change, 126,* 207–216.
52. Davis, F. D. (1993). User acceptance of information technology: system characteristics, user perceptions and behavioral impacts. *International Journal of Man-Machine Studies, 38*(3), 475–487.
53. Ajzen, I. (1985). From intentions to actions: A theory of planned behavior. In *Action control* (pp. 11–39). Berlin, Heidelberg: Springer.
54. Ajzen, I. (1991). The theory of planned behavior. *Organizational Behavior and Human Decision Processes, 50*(2), 179–211.
55. Pattansheti, M., Kamble, S. S., Dhume, S. M., & Raut, R. D. (2016). Development, measurement and validation of an integrated technology readiness acceptance and planned behaviour model for Indian mobile banking industry. *International Journal of Business Information Systems, 22*(3), 316–342.
56. Issa, I., & Hamm, U. (2017). Adoption of organic farming as an opportunity for Syrian farmers of fresh fruit and vegetables: An application of the theory of planned behaviour and structural equation modelling. *Sustainability, 9*(11), 2024.
57. Bagozzi, R. P., Davis, F. D., & Warshaw, P. R. (1992). Development and test of a theory of technological learning and usage. *Human Relations, 45*(7), 659–686.
58. Taylor, S., & Todd, P. A. (1995). Understanding information technology usage: A test of competing models. *Information Systems Research, 6*(2), 144–176.
59. Moore, G. C., & Benbasat, I. (1991). Development of an instrument to measure the perceptions of adopting an information technology innovation. *Information Systems Research, 2*(3), 192–222.
60. Compeau, D. R., & Higgins, C. A. (1995). Computer self-efficacy: Development of a measure and initial test. *MIS Quarterly,* 189–211.
61. Hew, J. J., Lee, V. H., Ooi, K. B., & Wei, J. (2015). What catalyses mobile apps usage intention: an empirical analysis. *Industrial Management & Data Systems, 115*(7), 1269–1291.
62. Makanyeza, C., & Mutambayashata, S. (2018). Consumers' acceptance and use of plastic money in Harare, Zimbabwe: Application of the unified theory of acceptance and use of technology 2. *International Journal of Bank Marketing, 36*(2), 379–392.
63. Kim, H. M., & Laskowski, M. (2018). Toward an ontology-driven blockchain design for supply-chain provenance. *Intelligent Systems in Accounting, Finance and Management, 25*(1), 18–27.
64. Alalwan, A. A., Dwivedi, Y. K., & Rana, N. P. (2017). Factors influencing adoption of mobile banking by Jordanian bank customers: Extending UTAUT with trust. *International Journal of Information Management, 37*(3), 99–110.
65. Riffai, M. M. M. A., Grant, K., & Edgar, D. (2012). Big TAM in Oman: Exploring the promise of on-line banking, its adoption by customers and the challenges of banking in Oman. *International Journal of Information Management, 32*(3), 239–250.
66. Weerakkody, V., El-Haddadeh, R., Al-Sobhi, F., Shareef, M. A., & Dwivedi, Y. K. (2013). Examining the influence of intermediaries in facilitating e-government adoption: An empirical investigation. *International Journal of Information Management, 33*(5), 716–725.
67. Wang, X., White, L., Chen, X., Gao, Y., Li, H., & Luo, Y. (2015). An empirical study of wearable technology acceptance in healthcare. *Industrial Management and Data Systems.*
68. Zhang, Y., Deng, R. H., Liu, X., & Zheng, D. (2018). Blockchain based efficient and robust fair payment for outsourcing services in cloud computing. *Information Sciences, 462,* 262–277.
69. Ahmad, F., Ahmad, Z., Kerrache, C. A., Kurugollu, F., Adnane, A., & Barka, E. (2019). Blockchain in Internet-of-Things: Architecture, applications and research directions. In *2019 International Conference on Computer and Information Sciences (ICCIS)* (pp. 1–6). IEEE.

70. Huang, M., Wang, Q., Zhang, M., & Zhu, Q. (2014). Prediction of color and moisture content for vegetable soybean during drying using hyperspectral imaging technology. *Journal of Food Engineering, 128,* 24–30.

71. Oliveira, T., Thomas, M., Baptista, G., & Campos, F. (2016). Mobile payment: Understanding the determinants of customer adoption and intention to recommend the technology. *Computers in Human Behavior, 61,* 404–414.

72. Sabi, H. M., Uzoka, F. M. E., Langmia, K., & Njeh, F. N. (2016). Conceptualizing a model for adoption of cloud computing in education. *International Journal of Information Management, 36*(2), 183–191.

73. Lai, P. C. (2017). The literature review of technology adoption models and theories for the novelty technology. *JISTEM-Journal of Information Systems and Technology Management, 14*(1), 21–38.

74. Caldarelli, A., Ferri, L., Maffei, M., & Spanò, R. (2019). Accountants are from Mars, ICT practitioners are from venus. Predicting technology acceptance between two groups. In *Organizing for digital innovation* (pp. 27–38). Cham: Springer.

75. Caldarelli, A., Ferri, L., & Maffei, M. (2017). Expected benefits and perceived risks of cloud computing: an investigation within an Italian setting. *Technology Analysis and Strategic Management, 29*(2), 167–180.

76. Queiroz, M. M., & Wamba, S. F. (2019). Blockchain adoption challenges in supply chain: An empirical investigation of the main drivers in India and the USA. *International Journal of Information Management, 46,* 70–82.

77. Gangwar, H., Date, H., & Ramaswamy, R. (2015). Understanding determinants of cloud computing adoption using an integrated TAM-TOE model. *Journal of Enterprise Information Management, 28*(1), 107–130.

Improving Invoice Allocation in Accounting—An Account Recommender Case Study Applying Machine Learning

Markus Esswein, Joerg H. Mayer, Diana Sedneva, Daniel Pagels, and Jean-Paul Albers

Abstract Covering transactions between buyers and sellers, invoices are essential. However, not all invoices can be directly matched to a purchase order due to missing order numbers, differences in terms of the invoice amount, quantity and/or quality. Following design science research (DSR) in information systems (IS), the objective of this article is to propose a new kind of an account recommender by applying machine learning. We take a chemical company as our case study and build a prototype that today handles more than 500,000 invoices without purchase order per year more accurately and efficiently than manual work did before. Finally, we propose five design guidelines to drive future research as follows: (1) Truly understand the business need; (2) More data can only get you so far; (3) Give the machine a good starting position; (4) Computing power is crucial; (5) Do not burn your bridges yet (manual intervention).

Keywords Account recommender · Invoices without a purchase order ("SAP financials (FI) postings w/o a purchase order") · Cognitive-based automation · Machine learning (ML) · Nearest neighbor classification · Design science research (DSR) in information systems (IS).

1 Introduction

For business transactions between buyers and sellers (even for intercompany sales), *invoices* are essential [1]. Especially when companies are integrated in larger value chains, the yearly number of invoices reaches millions.

However, not all invoices can be directly matched to a purchase order due to missing order numbers or differences in terms of the invoice amount, quantity and/or quality. For *invoices without a purchase order*, finding the account in the enterprise

M. Esswein (✉) · D. Sedneva
University of Duisburg-Essen, 47057 Duisburg, Germany
e-mail: markus.esswein@uni-due.de

J. H. Mayer
Darmstadt University of Technology, 64283 Darmstadt, Germany

© The Editor(s) (if applicable) and The Author(s), under exclusive license to Springer Nature Switzerland AG 2020
R. Agrifoglio et al. (eds.), *Digital Business Transformation*, Lecture Notes in Information Systems and Organisation 38, https://doi.org/10.1007/978-3-030-47355-6_10

resource planning (ERP) system to be charged according to a predefined rule is a repetitive task. In other words: In terms of cost per booking, it is not efficient that qualified accountants perform such a kind of routine work.[1]

We propose that finding patterns in a big amount of (invoice) data and—more forward-looking—encapsulating the pattern in rules that can be used for predictions is a good use case for *automation* [2]. On the one hand, pattern matching is not new. Finding rules for information extraction and complementing predefined fields in a template was already addressed in the late 1990s [3]. On the other hand, automation recently gained new momentum by leveraging machine learning (ML) algorithms [4].

The term automation evolved from the Greek word "automatos," which means acting by its own will or by itself. With a focus on digitalization, it is defined as machines, tools, devices, installations, and information systems (IS) performing a set of activities without human intervention [5]. While Robotic Process Automation (RPA) targets rule-based activities such as routine tasks with structured data and deterministic outcomes [6], *cognitive-based automation* intends to perform activities which are typically performed by humans and, thus, require cognitive capabilities such as situational assessment, sensing, and monitoring [7]. *ML* enables cognitive-based automation to learn a task from a series of examples. Recognizing patterns and learning from them based on logical operations, ML seeks to perform a task more effectively the next time [8].

Over the last years, Finance departments prominently automated record-to-report (R2R) process activities, however, not yet addressing accounts payables (order to cash) and accounts receivables (purchase to pay) [9]. Focusing on invoice processing within the purchase-to-pay (P2P) process, the objective of this article is to propose *a new kind of an account recommender by applying ML*. We take a leading chemical company as our single case study and answer two research questions:

- Compared to manual work, what is the potential of ML to improve prediction accuracy and process efficiency when handling invoices without a purchase order?
- Which are first design guidelines[2] to implement ML in the accounting domain?

To create things that serve human purposes [13], finally, to create a better world [14], we follow Design Science Research (DSR) in IS [15]. The publication schema by Gregor and Hevner [16] gave us direction. We motivate an accounts recommender by applying ML (*introduction*). Based on the state-of-the-art, we identify several research gaps (*literature review*). To address these gaps, we adopt a single case study and build a prototype following the tenets of requirements engineering

---

[1]In terms of job enrichment, accountants may be thankful when they are relived from this task to gain more time for creative work such as commenting on the reasons for identified differences between purchase orders and corresponding invoices.

[2]In addition to the four types of DSR artifacts identified by March and Smith [10] and Hevner et al. [11]—constructs, models, methods, and instantiations—*design guidelines* are statements that prescribe what and how to build an artifact in order to achieve a predefined design goal. Thus, design guidelines contribute to theories that specify how IS artifacts should be designed based on kernel theories [12].

(*method*). We present functional requirements, the redesign of the P2P process, and the account recommender machine itself (*artefact description*). Emphasizing iterative "build" and "evaluate" activities [17], we then *evaluate* the prototype within our reference company and two other companies from different industries. Lessons learned are captured in design guidelines. Comparing these guidelines with prior work and examining how they relate back to this article's objective, we end with a summary, limitations of our work, and avenues for future research (*discussion and conclusion*).

2 Literature Review

2.1 Search Strategy

Following Webster and Watson [18], we started our four-step literature review with a (1) *journal search*. And, in doing so, we focused on leading IS[3] journals complemented by both proceedings from major IS conferences[4] and leading accounting journals.[5] For our (2) *database search* assessing the outlets we used ScienceDirect, EBSCOhost, JSTOR, and Google Scholar. Applying an iterative search process by updating our (3) *search string* whenever we identified new relevant[6] aspects in the reviewed outlets, we started with the keywords "finance" and "automation" (Fig. 1) and, in doing so, we focused on titles, abstracts, and keywords.

Due to the large number of hits in the thousands, we specified our search string with "financial accounting" and "finance transformation" as well "cognitive-based automation" and "recommender system." Furthermore, we included MIS Quarterly Executive, Harvard Business Review, and other "grey" literature to trace a first finding that the topic on hand is reflected in practitioners´ journals. We came up with 31 relevant hits.

Referring to more details such as different methods of ML, in a fourth and final step, we conducted a (4) backward and forward search [20]. In our *backward search* we reviewed (older) references cited in the articles we already identified, whereas

---

[3] Based on the senior scholars' basket of leading IS journals (2019): European Journal of Information Systems (EJIS); Information Systems Research (ISR); Information Systems Journal (ISJ); Journal of the Association for Information Systems (JAIS); Journal of Information Technology (JIT); Journal of Management Information Systems (JMIS); Journal of Strategic Information Systems (JSIS); MIS Quarterly.

[4] We followed the Association for Information Systems: Americas Conference on IS (AMCIS); European Conference on IS (ECIS); International Conference on IS (ICIS); Pacific and Asia Conference on IS (PACIS).

[5] Following Bandara et al. [19], we examined the best rated accounting journals of the German Association of Business Administration: Accounting Review; Journal of Accounting and Economics; Journal of Accounting Research.

[6] Classifying an article as relevant if its scope covered accounts payable activities more in detail or in a combination with ML.

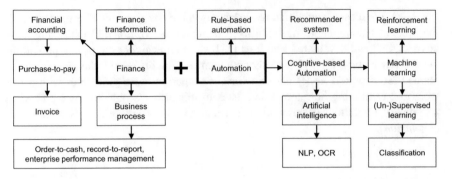

Fig. 1 Iteration of our initial search term "finance" and "automation" following the citation pearl growing approach [21]

our *forward search* covered additional sources citing the articles already identified to locate follow-up studies or newer developments on our topic of research. This led to another 17 hits. Hence, we ended up with a total of *48 relevant articles* (Fig. 2).

2.2 Gap Analysis

For our gap analysis, we structured these 43 outlets along four categories (Fig. 2): (1) Within the examined *business domains* we focused on financial accounting, information technology (IT), and complementing articles without a domain specification ("generic") [22]. (2) Regarding *automation*, we differentiate between rule-based and cognitive-based references. Within the latter, we focused on supervised, unsupervised, and reinforcement learning algorithms. (3) Focusing on the *research approach*, we distinguish empirical research, namely case studies, experiments, surveys, and interviews from conceptual research extending existing artifacts by logical reasoning. Regarding (4) the *type of contribution*, we differentiate constructs, models, methods, instantiations as well as design guidelines [10].

To analyze the number of co-occurrences of each pair, we computed *dyads between the components of our framework* [19]. For example, the number of articles covering financial accounting and cognitive-based automation is four (Fig. 2).

(1) **Business domain**: Our literature review shows a large number of 33 generic publications. However, some generic articles address problems related to financial and management accounting. For example, in their guide for ML applications, Witten et al. [2] present use cases like deciding whether to give a loan to a customer or not. Among the seven articles covering financial accounting, Wilson and Sangster [23] highlight the importance of rule-based automation for the finance function due their large volumes of numerical data to be processed. Van den Bogaerd and Aerts [24] look at the applicability of different computer-aided content analysis techniques. Codreanu et al. [25] provide a first

Financial accounting	Information technology	Generic and other	Rule-based	Cognitive-based	Other	Case study	Experiment	Survey	Interview	Conceptual	Sum	
Business domain			**Type of automation**			**Research aproach**						
						Empirical				Conceptual		
7	8	33	13	30	5	7	3	3	1	34	Sum	
2	5	6									13	Rule-based
4	2	24									30	Cognitive-based
1	1	3									5	Other
1	2	4	5	2	0						7	Case study
0	0	3	0	3	0						3	Experiment
1	1	1	3	0	0						3	Survey
0	0	1	0	1	0						1	Interview
5	5	24	5	24	5						34	Conceptual
4	1	11	4	10	2	1	0	1	1	13	16	Constructs
1	1	4	2	1	3	0	0	1	0	5	6	Model
1	2	11	3	11	0	3	1	0	0	10	14	Method
1	0	4	1	4	0	2	2	0	0	1	5	Instantiation
0	4	3	3	4	0	1	0	1	0	5	7	Guidelines

Darker values represent higher coverage

Right-side group labels: Type of automation (Rule-based, Cognitive-based, Other); Research approach — Empirical (Case study, Experiment, Survey, Interview), Conceptual; Type of contribution (Constructs, Model, Method, Instantiation, Guidelines).

Fig. 2 Literature systemization

overview of supervised and unsupervised ML techniques and their relation to online analytics processing (OLAP) in the accounting domain. Nolle et al. [26] test the accuracy of their deep learning auto-encoder on P2P data. However, their focus was on anomaly detection and they do not enhance their analysis with a case study.

(2) **Research approach**: None of the above-mentioned authors lay out concrete use cases. Only Bräuning et al. [27] introduce a learning algorithm and demonstrate relevance for a single use case recognizing actuarial gains and losses from occupational pension schemes. *ML* is applied in decision support of different

industries and application areas [28]. De Prado [29] covers ML for financial analysis, but only from an external perspective. There is only one case study for financial accounting. In line with our research objective, Veit et al. [30] demonstrate the application of ML to finance processes with their process mining tool. Overall, empirical research is clearly underrepresented in comparison to conceptual work (14 vs. 34).

Summarizing the findings from our first two clusters of research, we constitute a lack of research addressing concrete *ML use cases in the (financial) accounting domain*.

(3) **Type of automation**: There are a five rule-based automation case studies. For instance, Schmitz et al. [31] researched RPA at a large telecommunications operator, where more than a million transactions per month were automated in the course of one year. Aguirre and Rodriguez [32] cover RPA in the order-to-cash (O2C) process. With respect to *cognitive-based automation*, the foundations for ML and pattern recognition were laid out in Theodoridis and Koutroumbas [33] or Bishop [34]. In the late 1980s ML was established as an experimental science [35]. Caruana and Niculescu-Mizil [36] present a comparison of supervised learning algorithms like decision trees, support vector machines, neural nets, and k-nearest neighbors. They follow up their analysis with a comprehensive testing on different data sets, but none of them is accounting-related.

Among ML algorithms, *nearest neighbor classification* [37] is one of the most widely applied methods [38]. Knowledge discovery in databases was a well-regarded step ahead setting a framework for future work with the steps selection, preprocessing, transformation, data mining, and interpretation [39]. Efficiently splitting the available data into different sets for training algorithms and testing their performance against known data has also been subject to research in the 1980s [40]. In their study of ML in DSS, Merkert et al. [28] show that 30% use artificial neural networks while less than 5% use pattern recognition. More in line with our objective, Califf and Mooney [3] proposed a system for information extraction from documents to fill templates. However, their system was not integrated into a corporate environment and does not address information transformation, data mining, and interpretation.

(4) **Type of contribution**: Finally, we examined that constructs and methods exist for all types of automation. However, there is a lack of models, instantiations, and design guidelines. With respect to the latter, we did not find articles deriving design guidelines for financial accounting. Design guidelines for cognitive-based automation were given by five articles, among them Garcia et al. [38] with a taxonomy for nearest neighbor classification.

Summarizing our findings, we revealed a lack in addressing the potential of cognitive-based automation in (financial) accounting. To address this lack, we propose *a new kind of an account recommender by applying ML*. We take a leading chemical company as our case study and focus on two things: (1) examining prediction accuracy and process efficiency when handling invoices without a purchase order and (2) deriving first design guidelines to implement ML in the accounting domain.

3 Method

3.1 Case Study

Following Dul and Hak [41] *case studies* allow researchers to study artifacts in natural settings [42] and observe the situation in which activities take place. Case studies enable researchers to learn from practice (build on people's experiences and practices), understand the complexity of the process, and leverage the possibility of iteratively testing results in a *real world environment*. The results are analyzed in a qualitative manner [41]. In comparison to broader surveys, case studies provide in-depth information (esp., internal company data), and recognize the complexity and embeddedness of activities [43]. In the IS and accounting disciplines, case studies are a generally accepted research approach and have been employed for decades They are a proven way to research and contribute to theory building especially where only few studies exist [42].

We opted for a *single case study* and took a *leading chemical company* with revenues of more than 50bn USD and over 50,000 employees as our reference. Its financial processes are standardized worldwide and continuously optimized. Global Finance Transformation (GFT) has the central governance and harmonizes all financial processes running on a single SAP system. With the help of a network of process experts around the world, GFT is constantly seeking new (digital) technologies whilst promoting new solutions for process improvements. This way, we had the opportunity to assess multiple sources from different entities and experts. In doing so, the findings from the literature review gave us direction to ask the "right" question for both setting up a prototype and answering our research questions.

Following the tenets of *requirements engineering* [44], we differentiate between functional and non-functional requirements [45]. Focusing on the functional requirements, we examined internal documentations and archival records about invoice processing in the P2P process, conducted four semi-structured expert interviews[7] in the reference company, and analyzed key statements from these interviews along the guidelines of qualitative content analysis [46, 47]. Finally, we derived requirements for a prototype (Sect. 4) and set it up by applying an ML algorithm (Sect. 3.2).

The *P2P process* within our reference company starts with managing a requisition and comprises five steps from submitting a purchase order to invoice settling – predominantly administrative tasks as illustrated in Fig. 3 [48, 49]. While many rule-based tasks are already automated, the *invoice processing* still requires a lot of human input. The company receives around 4.8 million supplier invoices per year, out of which over 600,000 (13%) are related to a purchase order. This means a bundle of materials and services (even expense sheets from team lunches and client dinners) were requested without a purchase requisition and, thus, no purchase order is available ("FI postings w/o a purchase order"). After approving the order number,

---

[7]Interviewees were the head of the P2P process, a senior expert of R2R process, the head of the order-to-cash (O2C) process and a senior expert for accounts payable.

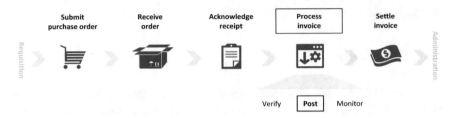

Fig. 3 P2P process of the reference company

invoice amount and/or quantity, finally, goods received, and the supplier of the invoice without purchase order, the invoice is posted to a manually determined general ledger (GL) account.

GFT set up a project team to develop a ML prototype that suggests *a general ledger-account within the SAP ERP* matching the content of the invoice (account recommender) according to a predefined rule. This should lead to both increasing prediction accuracy and a more efficient P2P process by reducing the manual workload.

3.2 Weighted K-Nearest-Neighbors

The k-Nearest-Neighbors (k-NN) algorithm is one of the *simpler classification algorithms*. It is a method, where a new object is assigned the class that occurs most frequently among the k observations in a given radius or neighborhood of the new observation [37]. As opposed to the simple k-NN algorithm, the distance-weighted k-nearest neighbor rule (dwk-NN) weighs the contribution of each of the k neighbors according to their distance to the new observation, giving greater weight to closer neighbors. The weights are taken from the interval [0–1]. The closest neighbor gets a weight of 1, the furthest of 0, and the others are scaled linearly on the interval in-between.

To determine the *optimal number of neighbors*, we computed the percentage of correct predictions at k from 1 to 20. Figure 4 shows the results. For example,

Fig. 4 K-NN algorithm: Accuracy against number of neighbors

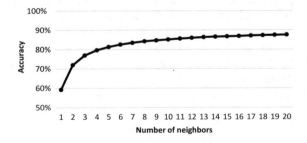

if $k = 1$ is chosen, the accuracy of the proposed forecast will be approximately 60%, whereas in the case of $k = 20$, the accuracy is 88%.

A decision for k should be a trade-off between the following two aspects: On the one hand, k should be large enough to avoid noisy decision boundaries that occur at very small k. On the other hand, it should be small enough so that only nearby samples are included. Choosing k too large will lead to over-smoothed boundaries and longer computation times without a proportional accuracy increase.

4 Artefact Description

4.1 Requirements Specification

Focusing on the functional requirements of an account recommender (Sect. 3), we derived the following six *functional requirements* (Fig. 3): (1) New invoices without a purchase order should be transmitted to the ML cloud right after arrival. Thus, they should be taken out of the standard workload basket and the usual rule-based automation process (incorporating Finance robots) should be stopped. (2) The account recommender should be able to handle all invoices, regardless of type and issuer. (3) The GL-account should be determined by comparing the billing attributes of the new invoice with historical data and their related postings to identify the best-fitting account. (4) If the estimate for the account has a likelihood of 80% or higher, the account should directly be written to the ERP system (without human interaction). If the likelihood is below 80%, the three best options should be returned as a choice. (5) The (human) approver should have the ability to override all propositions, even those above 80% likelihood. (6) The algorithm should remember account choices for retraining, which takes place every month.

4.2 Data Preparation and Feature Selection

Based on these requirements (Sect. 4.1), a data set was put together using historical invoice data of more than two million records in the period from 2010 to 2018. Each invoice includes over 200 fields. One of the most important steps in the preparation of data is the selection of *relevant features*. The reduction in the number of variables (the rejection of attributes that are weakly correlated with the target variable) not only increases the accuracy of the prediction, but also lowers the requirements for the computing resources. The most relevant variables for our use case were chosen after getting acquainted with the process of invoice processing. Criteria for selection included accounts payable employee experience, data availability in enough records, the information gain ranking for all attributes, and insights from the first iterations.

Table 1 Relevant invoice fields (independent variables)

Field name	Description	Examples
WC_USER	Invoice approver name	SMITHJ
VENDOR_NO	Account number of vendor or creditor	123456
REF_DOC_NO	Invoice number from vendor system	XX 12345
COMP_CODE	Company code	US01
CURRENCY	Currency key	USD
NET_AMOUNT	Net amount in document currency	500
GROSS_AMOUNT	Gross amount in document currency	600
INVOICE_IND	X if it is a normal invoice, blank if it is something else (e.g., a credit note)	X
CP_DOC_TYPE	Defines a kind of invoicing process	ID
SUPCOUNTRY_ISO	Country of the invoice (from vendor side)	US
DOC_DATE	Date of invoices	20180101

As a result, eleven fields were gathered, where "GL_ACCOUNT" is the dependent variable and the remaining features are independent variables (Table 1).

Based on these features, the supervised learning algorithm predicts a matching GL-account for a new invoice without a purchase order. Following the reasoning that some fields are more relevant for prediction than others, we iteratively assigned different weights to them. We then used *K-fold cross-validation* to randomly split the full dataset into K subsets of approximately equal size. $K - 1$ blocks were used to estimate the parameters of the model (train) and the one remaining block was used for testing the model's accuracy (test). The process was repeated K times, and each of the blocks was used once as a test set. Finally, the parameters of the resulting K models were averaged to get one estimate.

4.3 Results

The processing of invoices (step 4, Fig. 4) always starts with data extraction and validation (Fig. 5). If all data are available, the standard approval process is triggered. Otherwise, the type of data that is missing needs to be identified. In case of a missing GL account, the *account recommender* performs the necessary actions of (1) preparing the data, (2) computing a k-NN estimate, and (3) returning the GL account. Note that if the confidence level for a single GL account is too low, the account recommender returns three candidates from which the user has to select one account. For missing data other than the GL account, manual handling is still necessary. However, missing approvers have already been identified as an extension (Sect. 5).

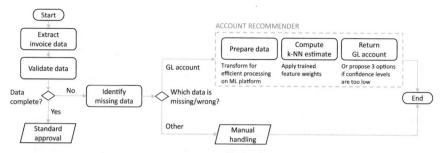

Fig. 5 Invoice processing for invoices with missing data

One key tuning parameter of our prototype is *coverage*, which means the ratio of invoices that are handled automatically by the prototype versus those for which three candidates are proposed. We tested the performance for three scenarios, 50, 75, and 100% coverage. Figure 6 clearly shows that it is impossible to have high prediction accuracy and high coverage at the same time. While the accuracy for 50% coverage is around 87%, it is only 59% for 100% coverage. In our trade-off scenario, the prediction accuracy is 72%.

Currently, the manual process requires at least five full time employees and can take up to one day of time. In contrast, for the three steps indicated in Fig. 6, the account recommender only needs a few seconds. However, *training* the model and retraining it with delta loads every week consumes more time than single predictions and is resource intensive. On a standard laptop, the process of initial model fitting and estimating the test set takes around 24 h, which is a strong argument for cloud computing.

Based on these results, we propose *five design guidelines* that sum up the lessons learned during the design and development of prototype as follows:

The first guideline addresses the fact that with a sensitive topic like thinking about *replacing human labor with machines*, the solution has to be all the better. More in detail, turning affected and most often reluctant accountants into engaged innovators

Fig. 6 Accuracy and coverage of three prediction models

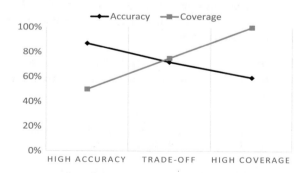

is a good facilitator for a successful digital transformation.[8] However, this can only be achieved if the prototype developer has a good business understanding and even a good relationship to the accountants and owners of the process to-be automated.

Design Guideline 1 *Truly understand the business need. Get yourself acquainted with the process and automate with the best possible user experience in mind.*

When training machines based on historical data, the *quality* of the training data is a crucial factor.[9] Although some algorithms are relatively robust against missing or erroneous data, the risk of replicating past mistakes hundreds of times exists. Hence, cleansing the initial training set from flawed data is an essential condition.

Design Guideline 2 *More data can only get you so far. While a broader training set generally leads to more accurate predictions, do not forget to provide good-quality data.*

Nowadays, most ML algorithms come paired with powerful feature selection and *iteratively adjust parameters* with methods like gradient descent. Still, most of the approaches to feature and weight selection are heuristics that start with a random or an all-equal-to-one initial configuration and often only reach a local optimum. In the presence of experts who have performed the task hundreds of times, initial configurations can be deduced that improve speed towards and accuracy of the final configuration.

Design Guideline 3 *Give the machine a good starting position. Using a combination of expert judgement and ML for feature selection and assigning weights speeds up the training process.*

Among the reasons why ML was not as prominently applied as it is today are the *hardware requirements* with increasing data volumes and complexity of tasks. Although business users were used to data loads over the night from traditional data warehouses, they are no longer as patient. While there has been significant progress in terms of single processing units, parallelization has had an even bigger impact on performance increases. Thus, distributing the workload of a ML use case over several machines is the most reasonable choice. A *cloud architecture* provides that, which is why the reference company chose to implement the prototype on one of the leading cloud platforms.

Design Guideline 4 *Computing power is crucial. Processing large amounts of data with ML requires resources that a cloud-based architecture is better suited for than local hardware.*

---

[8]The shared-service center employees of the reference company were the ones to identify use cases and develop an agenda for the broad introduction of rule-based and cognitive automation in their daily business.

[9]Training ML algorithms with biased and incomplete data has been subject to research for more than twenty years [50]. In the context of big data analytics, patching, and cleansing data in real time has become an important tool [51].

Despite the intelligence attributed to the machine and its far superior speed, there are always situations that require *human assessment, sensing, and monitoring* in a process as complex as invoice processing. As a result, in many cases the machine can only provide likely alternatives or make a choice based on probabilities of past data. Therefore, accountants should still have the option of overriding entries. Additionally, this may help build confidence since the accountant can experience first-hand what the machine does well and where it lacks behind. In turn, this knowledge can then be used to adjust parameters and improve the accuracy and coverage of the algorithm.

Design Guideline 5 *Do not burn your bridges yet. Keep a fallback solution for human workers to override entries and help the machine learn from experts' decisions.*

5 Evaluation

Evaluating the *relevance* of new artifacts is a major activity in DSR [52]. Gregor and Hevner [16] propose a number of dimensions such as validity, utility, quality, and efficacy.[10] Following our RQ 1, we evaluate our prototype focusing on prediction accuracy and process efficiency asking if the prototype outperforms the current standard of manual work in our reference company.

Following up on *prediction accuracy,* we had two unstructured interviews of roughly 30 min each. Evaluating different combinations of invoice fields as well as different levels of confidence and coverage, our first interviewee, the head of accounting of the reference company, told us that the automation should mitigate one of the bottlenecks in the finance back office. According to him, the process of determining approver and GL account (with cost center or project reference) sometimes take up to three weeks and it has not so good prediction accuracy rate than the prototype exposes (Sect. 4.3). The lead audit partner as our second interviewee pointed out that his company began to train a neural network that is fed all information on an invoice, including visuals, text positions, and the text information used in our prototype. He did not have comparable figures yet, however, acknowledged the eagerness of two of his clients to try it out.

In order to assess *process efficiency,* we conducted another four *interviews* during a workshop of a manager focus group, which is part of the Schmalenbach working group "Digital Finance"[11] and regularly meets to discuss trends in the digitalization of the Finance function. Interview partners were the head of GFT of our reference company, the head of accounting of a utility company, and a partner of an audit firm who has recently started implementing several ML prototypes for finance as well. The head of the GFT department laid out that the business case for the account

---

[10]Besides these goal- and activity-related dimensions, Prat et al. [53] add environment, structure, activity, and evolution as further evaluation criteria.

[11]Schmalenbach Gesellschaft für Betriebswirtschaftslehre e.V. https://www.schmalenbach.org/index.php.

recommender is very straight forward and amortization should be within a maximum of two years (Sect. 4.3). Today, our former prototype is being implemented to handle *more than 500,000 invoices per year* in the future more accurately and efficiently than manual work did before. Thus, our prototype results were very promising in its case environment.

Gaining further process efficiency, the working group discussed a feasible evolution of our prototype: An *approver recommender.* Based on a very similar model where only the "GL_ ACCOUNT" dependent variable is exchanged with "WC_USER" (the approver), this second use case is already on the list of future projects for GFT in 2020.

6 Discussion and Conclusion

Taking a single case study in a leading chemical company as our reference, the objective of this paper was firstly, to gauge the potential of ML in improving prediction accuracy and process efficiency compared to manual work and secondly, to lay out first design guidelines to successfully implement ML in the accounting domain. In doing so, we proposed a *new kind of an account recommender* which applies distance-weighted k-nearest neighbors to determine most probable general ledger accounts. We demonstrated three scenarios with different levels of coverage, prediction accuracy, and process efficiency. To drive future research, we proposed five design guidelines.

From 2020 on, our former prototype will be implemented to handle *more than 500,000 invoices without purchase order per year* more accurately and efficiently than manual work did before. *For practice*, our set of requirements and proposed areas of applying ML in the accounting domain should help companies to drive their implementation of cognitive-based automation whilst helping managers to improve the prediction accuracy and process efficiency of their finance back office. In addition, our design guidelines should help companies get started with ML for accounts payable. *For research* purposes, our approach is more comprehensive than mostly literature-based references like Fung [54]. As opposed to articles like Lacity and Willcocks [6], we followed DSR's iterative "build and evaluate" activities and deployed a prototype for more in-depth research. In comparison to Bräuning et al. [27] or Caruana and Niculescu-Mizil [36], we ensured the relevance of our design guidelines by evaluating them with experts from different companies.

However, our research reveals avenues for future research. Single case studies offer a broad range of advantages (Sect. 3), they have limitations in terms of validity and generalizability [55]. Thus, future research should approach the potential of ML in the accounting domain with the help of a quantitative approach or a *multiple case study*. Furthermore, we only presented our results using the k-nearest-neighbors algorithm. However, as Merkert et al. [28] pointed out, 30% of ML applications use *artificial neural networks*, which should be an interesting option for a future prototype.

Furthermore, the artifact itself faces limitations. Combining both findings from literature and expert interviews, we derived at six functional requirements. Despite our deep business understanding, further input factors could complement our findings. Thus, future research should extend our *set of input factors*. Overall, the research results should be interpreted carefully. *Generalizability* across companies is not possible due to differences companies may work – even in standardized domain such as accounting. Furthermore, *digitalization* and its transformational effects may lead to unforeseeable (technical) developments in the future. Nevertheless, ML is a rising topic and its application will become a game changer for the finance department and even beyond.

References

1. Taylor, G. J. (1985). *Accounting for business organisations: A practical approach*. London, UK: Palgrave.
2. Witten, I. H., Frank, E., Hall, M. A., & Pal, C. J. (2016). *Data mining: Practical machine learning tools and techniques*. Burlington, MA, USA: Morgan Kaufmann.
3. Califf, M. E., & Mooney, R. J. (1999). Relational learning of pattern-match rules for information extraction. In *National Conference on Artificial Intelligence*.
4. Onken, R., & Schulte, A. (2010). System-ergonomic design of cognitive automation: Dual-mode cognitive design of vehicle guidance and control work systems. In *Studies in computational intelligence* (Vol. 235). Berlin, Heidelberg: Springer.
5. Nof, S. Y. (2009). Automation: What it means to us around the world. In S. Y. Nof (Ed.), *Springer handbook of automation* (pp. 13–52). Berlin, Heidelberg, Germany: Springer.
6. Lacity, M. C., & Willcocks, L. P. (2017). A new approach to automating services. *MIT Sloan Management Review, 58*, 40–49.
7. Fast-Berglund, Å., Fässberg, T., Hellman, F., Davidsson, A., & Stahre, J. (2013). Relations between complexity, quality and cognitive automation in mixed-model assembly. *Journal of manufacturing systems, 32*, 449–455.
8. Simon, H. A. (1983). Why should machines learn? In R. S. Michalski, J. G. Carbonell, & T. M. Mitchell (Eds.), *Machine learning* (pp. 25–37). San Francisco, CA, USA: Morgan Kaufmann.
9. Plaschke, F., Seth, I., & Whiteman, R. (2019). *Bots, algorithms, and the future of the finance function*. Accessed February 12, 2019 from https://www.mckinsey.com/business-functions/strategy-and-corporate-finance/our-insights/bots-algorithms-and-the-future-of-the-finance-function.
10. March, S. T., & Smith, G. F. (1995). Design and natural science research on information technology. *Decision Support Systems, 15*, 251–266.
11. Hevner, A. R., March, S. T., Park, J., & Ram, S. (2004). Design science in information systems research. *Management Information Systems Quarterly, 28*, 75–105.
12. Chandra, L., Seidel, S., & Gregor, S. (2015). Prescriptive knowledge in IS research: Conceptualizing design principles in terms of materiality, action, and boundary conditions. In *48th Hawaii International Conference on System Sciences* (pp. 4039–4048). IEEE.
13. Simon, H. A. (1996). *The sciences of the artificial*. Boston, MA, USA: MIT Press.
14. Walls, J. G., Widmeyer, G. R., & El Sawy, O. A. (1992). Building an information system design theory for vigilant EIS. *Information Systems Research, 3*, 36–59.
15. vom Brocke, J., Winter, R., Hevner, A., & Maedche, A. (2020). Accumulation and evolution of design knowledge in design science research: A journey through time and space. *Journal of the Association for Information Systems*.

16. Gregor, S., & Hevner, A. R. (2013). Positioning and presenting design science research for maximum impact. *MIS Quarterly, 37,* 337–355.
17. Peffers, K., Tuunanen, T., Rothenberger, M. A., & Chatterjee, S. (2007). A design science research methodology for information systems research. *Journal of Management Information Systems, 24,* 45–77.
18. Webster, J., & Watson, R. T. (2002). Analyzing the past to prepare for the future: Writing a literature review. *MIS Quarterly, 26,* xiii–xxiii.
19. Bandara, W., Furtmueller, E., Gorbacheva, E., Miskon, S., & Beekhuyzen, J. (2015). Achieving rigor in literature reviews: Insights from qualitative data analysis and tool-support. *Communications of the Association for Information Systems, 37,* 154–204.
20. Vom Brocke, J., Simons, A., Niehaves, B., Riemer, K., Plattfaut, R., & Cleven, A. (2009). Reconstructing the giant: On the importance of rigour in documenting the literature search process. In S. Newell, E. A. Whitley, N. Pouloudi, J. Wareham, & L. Mathiassen (Eds.), *European conference on information systems* (Vol. 9, pp. 2206–2217). IT: Verona.
21. Rowley, J., & Slack, F. (2004). Conducting a literature review. *Management Research News, 27,* 31–39.
22. Stittle, J., & Wearing, R. (2008). *Financial accounting.* London, UK: Sage Publications.
23. Wilson, R., & Sangster, A. (1992). The automation of accounting practice. *Journal of Information Technology, 7,* 65–75.
24. Van den Bogaerd, M., & Aerts, W. (2011). Applying machine learning in accounting research. *Expert Systems with Applications, 38,* 13414–13424.
25. Codreanu, D. E., Popa, I., & Parpandel, D. (2011). *Accounting and financial data analysis data mining tools.* Galati, Romania: European Integration Realities and Perspectives.
26. Nolle, T., Seeliger, A., Mühlhäuser, M. (2016). Unsupervised anomaly detection in noisy business process event logs using denoising autoencoders (pp. 442–456). Springer.
27. Bräuning, M., Hüllermeier, E., Keller, T., & Glaum, M. (2017). Lexicographic preferences for predictive modeling of human decision making—A new machine learning method with an application in accounting. *European Journal of Operational Research, 258,* 295–306.
28. Merkert, J., Mueller, M., & Hubl, M. (2015). A survey of the application of machine learning in decision support systems. In *European Conference on Information Systems,* Münster, Germany.
29. De Prado, M. L. (2018). *Advances in financial machine learning.* Hoboken, NJ, USA: Wiley.
30. Veit, F., Geyer-Klingeberg, J., Madrzak, J., Haug, M., & Thomson, J. (2017). The proactive insights engine: Process mining meets machine learning and artificial intelligence. In *BPM (Demos).*
31. Schmitz, M., Dietze, C., & Czarnecki, C. (2019). Enabling Digital Transformation Through Robotic Process Automation at Deutsche Telekom. In N. Urbach & M. Röglinger (Eds.), *Digitalization cases: How organizations rethink their business for the digital age* (pp. 15–33). Cham: Springer.
32. Aguirre, S., & Rodriguez, A. (2017). Automation of a business process using robotic process automation (RPA): A case study. In *Applied computer sciences in engineering* (pp. 65–71). Springer.
33. Theodoridis, S., & Koutroumbas, K. (2009). *Pattern Recognition.* Burlington, MA, USA: Academic Press.
34. Bishop, C. M. (2006). *Pattern Recognition and Machine Learning.* New York, NY, USA: Springer.
35. Langley, P. (1988). Machine learning as an experimental science. *Machine Learning, 3,* 5–8.
36. Caruana, R., & Niculescu-Mizil, A. (2006). An empirical comparison of supervised learning algorithms. In *Proceedings of the 23rd international conference on machine learning* (pp. 161–168). ACM.
37. Cover, T. M., & Hart, P. E. (1967). Nearest neighbor pattern classification. *IEEE Transactions on Information Theory, 13,* 21–27.
38. Garcia, S., Derrac, J., Cano, J., & Herrera, F. (2012). Prototype selection for nearest neighbor classification: Taxonomy and empirical study. *IEEE Transactions on Pattern Analysis and Machine Intelligence, 34,* 417–435.

39. Fayyad, U., Piatetsky-Shapiro, G., & Smyth, P. (1996). From data mining to knowledge discovery in databases. *AI Magazine, 17,* 37–54.
40. Jain, A., & Chandrasekaran, B. (1982). Dimensionality and sample size considerations in pattern recognition practice. In P. R. Krishnaiah & L. N. Kanal (Eds.), *Handbook of statistics* (Vol. 2). Amsterdam: North-Holland.
41. Dul, J., & Hak, T. (2008). *Case study methodology in business research.* Oxford, UK: Butterworth-Heinemann.
42. Benbasat, I., Goldstein, D. K., & Mead, M. (1987). The case research strategy in studies of information systems. *MIS Quarterly, 11,* 369–386.
43. Yin, R. K. (2017). *Case study research and applications: Design and methods.* Thousand Oaks, CA, USA: Sage Publications.
44. Kotonya, G., & Sommerville, I. (1998). *Requirements engineering: processes and techniques.* Hoboken, NJ, USA: Wiley.
45. Sommerville, I. (2007). *Software engineering.* Boston, MA, USA: Addison-Wesley.
46. Kohlbacher, F. (2006). The use of qualitative content analysis in case study research. *Forum: Qualitative Social Research, 7,* 1–30.
47. Mayring, P. (2014). Qualitative content analysis: theoretical foundation, basic procedures and software solution. Klagenfurt.
48. Monczka, R. M., Handfield, R. B., Giunipero, L. C., & Patterson, J. L. (2015). *Purchasing and supply chain management.* Mason, OH, USA: Cengage Learning.
49. The Hackett Group. (2019). *Best practices and metrics for next-generation P2P.* The Hackett Group. Accessed March 08, 2019 from https://www.slideshare.net/carrfraser/hackett-trades hift-webinar-final.
50. Cortes, C., Jackel, L. D., & Chiang, W.-P. (1995). Limits on learning machine accuracy imposed by data quality. In U. Fayyad, R. Uthurusamy (Eds.), *International Conference on Knowledge Discovery and Data-Mining* (pp. 239-246), Montréal, Québec, Canada.
51. Saha, B., & Srivastava, D. (2014). Data quality: The other face of Big Data. In *IEEE International Conference on Data Engineering* (pp. 1294–1297). IEEE, Chicago, IL, USA.
52. Venable, J., Pries-Heje, J., & Baskerville, R. (2016). FEDS: A framework for evaluation in design science research. *European Journal of Information Systems, 25,* 77–89.
53. Prat, N., Comyn-Wattiau, I., & Akoka, J. (2014). Artifact evaluation in information systems design-science research—A holistic view. In *Pacific Asia Conference on Information Systems.*
54. Fung, H. P. (2014). Criteria, use cases and effects of information technology process automation (ITPA). *Advances in Robotics & Automation, 3,* 1–10.
55. Willis, B. (2019). *The advantages and limitations of single case study analysis.* E-International Relations Students. Accessed April 28, 2019 from https://www.e-ir.info/2014/07/05/the-adv antages-and-limitations-of-single-case-study-analysis/.

Performance-Based Funding in the Italian Higher Education: A Critical Analysis

Alberto Ezza, Nicoletta Fadda, Gianfranco Pischedda, and Ludovico Marinò

Abstract University performance is playing an increasingly important role in financing public institutions. This has resulted in higher competitiveness and stronger emphasis on efficiency and effectiveness and a propensity to hold universities directly accountable. However, assessment tools are not consistently able to measure the achievements of universities in a reliable way due to the lack of indicators that can assess performance objectively. Furthermore, the formulas that are frequently used to determine achievements are complex, and the raw data that feeds such formulas are not unfailingly reliable. The aim of this theoretical study is underlining the potential criticalities of the performance-based approach in the Italian higher education system by critically analysing three of the main mechanisms that are employed to determine resource allocation. The paper also highlights the derived effects that influence the strategic choices and consequent actions that are implemented by universities.

Keywords Performance-based funding · Higher education · Research · Performance management · Informative system · Italy

1 Introduction

Over the last few decades, the higher education (HE) system has significantly changed in line with New Public Management theories and marketization policies [2, 11]. In recent times, performance measurement and evaluation have become increasingly important with the aim of increasing competition within the system [29] as a means of enhancing efficiency [1]. Thus, governments have started to adopt different managerial tools, such as performance-based principles or reward-based resource allocation mechanisms, to achieve fairer and more efficient fund allocation practices. However, the attempt to measure all the activities carried out by public institutions can weigh down information systems due to the focus on complex indicators that cannot consistently measure results in an equitable manner.

A. Ezza (✉) · N. Fadda · G. Pischedda · L. Marinò
Department of Economics and Business, University of Sassari (Italy), Via Muroni, 25, 07100 Sassari, Italy
e-mail: alberto.ezza@uniss.it

R. Agrifoglio et al. (eds.), *Digital Business Transformation*, Lecture Notes in Information Systems and Organisation 38, https://doi.org/10.1007/978-3-030-47355-6_11

Despite the substantial empirical literature available on this topic, especially in relation to the impact of these reforms, there is still much research to be conducted in relation to the Italian higher education system (IHES) as a whole. To contribute to the debate on this topic, this work aims to point out the potential criticalities of performance-based logics in the IHES by theoretically examining three of the main mechanisms that are currently used to allocate resources to public universities within the IHES: the allocation of the state funding mechanism (FFO—Fondo di Finanziamento Ordinario), the budget for academic and administrative staff recruitment (Punti Organico-PO), and the extraordinary recruitment budget for fixed-term research fellows type B (Piano straordinario di reclutamento).

In particular, the study investigates, in depth, the characteristics of the performance-based principles that have been adopted in the last year by the Ministry with the underlying objective of identifying indicator peculiarities and criticalities. At the same time, it aims to ascertain what strategic responses universities can adopt to facilitate the achievement of a higher level of performance and, subsequently, secure more funds.

This paper is organized as follows. Section 2 will present a review of the existing literature on performance-based funding and the role performance information plays within the existing HE funding practices. Section 3 will outline the Italian situation with a specific focus on the reforms that have been implemented since 2010. Section 4 will describe three of the main mechanisms that are used to determine resource allocation across public universities in Italy and will include a thorough analysis of the indicators and performance measures that are in place. Finally, the conclusion will be presented in Sect. 5.

2 Performance-Based Funding in Higher Education

In recent decades, several reforms have promoted a managerial transformation of HE with the express intention of improving performance [7, 12] through the extensive use of performance measurement and assessment approaches. Performance information plays a fundamental role in budgeting decision [5]. Over the years, with the aim of substituting the traditional input-based approach with output/outcome-oriented models [28], different mechanisms of performance budgeting have been developed; however, the various approaches that are available can typically be categorised as one of two types [6, 30]: performance-based funding (PBF), which relies on the application of performance indicators directly, usually within a formula; and performance-based budgeting (PBB), which applies performance indicators in a more discretionary and indirect way.

PBF has been adopted to distribute funds more efficiently and facilitate the implementation of government policies. Indeed, by rewarding the highest-performing institutions, governments aim to increase the "value-for-money" of universities, and, eliminate or reduce the size of wasteful programmes [36]. It worth noting, as highlighted by the resource dependency theories [35], that organizations are more likely to adapt their strategy and managerial behaviour to meet the needs and target of funders. Consequently, public universities should be highly responsive to those targets defined by their main funders [19, 23, 32].

PBF logic strongly relies on the existence of a direct and deterministic relationship between policies (which result in goals and targets), incentives (higher shares of funds), the actions of universities (which change to achieve targets), and intended results [36]. Even if the rationale that underpin PBF is clear, there may be unintended consequences following its adoption. In fact, the implementation of PBF in HE can lead to some unpredictable impacts [34] and unintended results [14, 20].

The effectiveness of PBF programmes in HE (i.e., the capability of PBF to promote the achievement of the goals set at a governmental level) can be hampered by some factors. Regulators set indicators, which sit at the core of the PBF mechanism, to assess the performance of universities and drive the allocation of funds. However, as a PBF can only assess a limited extent of the activities in which universities engage [22, 40], the quality of the measures used and, concurrently, the reliability of the raw data collected and reported by the informative systems (both on an organisational and institutional level) have a direct impact on the effectiveness of a PBF [21]. In this sense, PBF has a limited ability to objectively identify the highest performing universities and, subsequently, allocate a higher share of funds to such institutions. As such, PBF can lead to inequitable funds distribution. Another potential weakness linked to this system lies in the inability of the indicators that are employed to comply with the institutional differences between the universities that result from diverse dimensions, be they size, institutional, vocational or due to localisation.

So, what are the potential unintended consequences of PBF adoption? First, implementing the PBF approach forces a government (and its agencies) and universities to bear high costs to meet information requirements. The cost of compliance is also high in terms of the higher workload that is created for university staff and the greater investments in informative systems and personnel. Furthermore, the cost of compliance can impact different universities in different ways due to heterogeneous institutional capacity [14]. Second, the higher competition for public subsidies can result in the adoption of policies that can reduce the diversity and specialisation of the institutional missions or programmes, since universities are incentivised to abandon those programmes that are not positively evaluated and, consequently, focus on specific activities [25]. Moreover, PBF can profoundly change student enrolment policies. Indeed, if indicators of students' success are included in the PBF formula, universities can refuse to enrol less-skilled students as a means of achieving higher performance [14]. If universities are publicly funded and education is considered a merit good [39, 41], these practices can seriously reduce the university's capability to achieve its institutional mission. Furthermore, PBF can reduce the overall quality of the education programmes that are available since the system motivates universities to remove the obstacles that can impede students' graduation. Even if, to some extent, this can be considered to represent a positive feature (universities are forced to increase their effectiveness), it can result in a reduction in the standard of education on offer.

Lastly, the adoption of PBF in a HE system that is characterised by a higher internal diversity can lead to an increase in inequalities. Indeed, the application of formulas can perpetuate and boost the existing inequalities [33] by over-favouring the best performing institutions and over-penalising the lower performing establishments [26]. This is particularly true if the diversity in performance can be explained by external factors [15] that are outside the control of public managers and are accountable for a high share of a university's results [42].

3   Performance-Based Funding in the Italian Higher Education System

IHES is the outcome of the season of reforms inspired by the New Public Management rhetoric and the European Union policies (Bologna process, Lisbon Strategy). The reforms aimed to increase the overall IHES performance in order to overcome the limited competitiveness, backwardness, and unfairness that characterised the IHES [10]. In particular, the funding system was remodelled in line with quasi-market [4, 31] and performance-based funding literature [24, 28].

Two main paths of reform should be considered: the global reform of 2010, and the reform of the funding mechanism in line with the PBF literature. IHES was profoundly changed with the introduction of L. 240/2010, which aimed to increase the autonomy, accountability and performance of universities [12, 13]. The so-called Gelmini Reform changed the overall landscape of the IHES by reorganising the governance mechanisms, strengthening the role and use of performance evaluation within the system, and promoting higher competition among universities.

The funding of IHES has also profoundly changed over the last few years. The latest evolution of allocative mechanisms was carried out during a phase in which the government significantly reduced the availability of resources [17]. The overall public funding dropped by 7.2% between 2006 and 2016 (−19.43% if the effect of inflation is eliminated), thereby increasing the degree of competitiveness among public universities.

The reform of IHES funding commenced in 1993 (L. 537/1993) and was amended in 1995 (L. 549/995) when the government created a unique source of public funding for universities (the so-called "Fondo di Finanziamento Ordinario") and promoted a shift to a lump-sum budget allocation process. After several trials of the PBF approach in IHES, the 2010 reform generated a strong impetus in the use of performance to determine public subsidy allocation.

In addition to the allocation of public subsidies, in 2012 (legislative decree 49/2012), a performance-based mechanism of allocating budgets for staff recruitment (both academic and administrative) was introduced. The allocation process is based on a metric named the Punto Organico (PO), which is the equivalent to the average cost of a full professor. This is used to measure and parametrize the costs of academic figures and the resources allocated to universities [16, 37]. In other words, using a set of weight defined ex ante (i.e., one associate professor equals 0.7 PO; one fixed-term research fellow varies from 0.4 to 0.5 PO; one executive equal 0.65 PO, etc.) this parameter expresses the resources that are available to universities. The budget that is allocated to universities on an annual basis (linked to the number and type of academics and administrative staff who left the universities the previous year) is shared among universities via a formula-based method that is based on two economic and financial parameters. Through the application of this formulaic approach, both the "best" and "worst" universities are identified, and the former are awarded a higher share of POs.

The underlying risk associated with the formula used to allocate funds to Italian universities is that is can serve to widen the gap between institutions by consistently rewarding performance that is only partially determined by universities' strategic and operative behaviours. In fact, the differences in socio-economic environments (e.g., regional wealth, occupational rates, etc.) could significantly impact performance and can explain perceptions that some areas of the country are more attractive than others (i.e., northern versus southern areas).

4 The Three Main Mechanisms for Resources Allocation in the IHES

The changes that have been introduced in terms of how resources are allocated in the IHES has created a landscape in which the primary use of performance can be found in the following three mechanisms: The state funding mechanism (FFO - Fondo di Finanziamento Ordinario), the budgets that are allocated for academic and administrative staff recruitment (PO), and the extraordinary recruitment budget that is apportioned for fixed-term research fellow type B[1] (Piano straordinario di reclutamento).

The critical analysis of these three funding mechanisms described along the lines of the latest regulation, determine which of the types of universities' activities are taken into consideration during the process of allocating resources as well as the performance areas of interest. Moreover, based on the classification of the funding mechanisms in higher education proposed by Jongbloed [27], each criterion of formula adopted to calculate the shares that are allocated have been categorized into input and output measurements. Input measurements are student enrolment figures and staff positions, while output measurements assess the results of the main activities conducted by the university in terms of education and research.

As Table 1 highlights, FFO is composed of a basic share (70%), a reward share (27%) and other specific interventions (3%).

---

[1] Type B research fellow (from now RTD-B), as regulated by the L. 240/2010 is a three-year contract that can lead to a tenure-track to became associate professor for those who achieved the national qualification.

Table 1 FFO Allocation criterion D.M. 587/2018

Shares	Basic (about 70%)		Reward (27%)
1	Student standard cost (22% FFO)	1	National research assessment—VQR 2011–2014 (16% FFO)
2	Historical funding (48% FFO)	2	Recruitment policies evaluation (5.5% FFO)
		3	Responsible autonomy (5.5% FFO)

The basic share is the sum of two elements: Historical funding and student standard cost share. Historical funding, which is not directly connected with current performance, is calculated as a percentage of the basic share of the previous year, while the standard cost share is determined through a demand-driven mechanism that weights the amount of resources allocated to each university against the number of regular students plus the number of students who are one year behind schedule (full-time equivalent—FTE). Within this model, students represent both the input and the users of educational services [3, 8, 38].

It is important to note that the demand-driven mechanism adopted in the IHES is mainly "virtual" since universities do not receive exactly the amount of funds defined by (standard cost of university * number of regular students). Indeed, "standard cost" is not a "fare" that is paid by the Ministry; rather, it is used as a parameter to allot the "basic share" to universities.

In terms of the second component of FFO, the reward share was introduced with the aim of allocating funds in association with teaching and research performance. However, the criteria adopted seems to steer competition more towards research quality than teaching quality. In fact, art. 3 of DM 587/2018 established that (approximately) 27% of the total amount of FFO will be based on:

- National research assessment–VQR (*Valutazione della Qualità della Ricerca*) 2011–14 (60% of the reward share, about 16% of the FFO). A periodic evaluation that aims to retrospectively assess the quality of research performed at a given institution.
- An evaluation of recruitment policies (20% of the reward share, about 5.5% of the FFO) that takes into account the effectiveness of research activity. However, it focuses purely on new recruits and also assesses the attractiveness of universities in terms of recruitment of fellow researcher or professor from other Italian universities, abroad or those awarded with a research project financed by the European Union.
- Responsible autonomy (20% of the reward share, about 5.5% of the FFO), aims to improve the autonomy of institutions. Universities can choose indicators from a list provided by the ministry that relate to three main dimensions: (1) Teaching, as assessed by students' performance; (2) Research, which is evaluated in terms of attractiveness in recruitment policies; and (3) Internationalization with regard to regular students, regular graduates and Ph.D. students from other countries.

Universities are required to choose between two of the three dimensions and select one indicator for each dimension.

The FFO is a mixture of historical, input and output-oriented allocation mechanisms. It should be noted that the basic share (see Table 2), which is still a significant amount (70%), is mainly linked to dimensional parameters (the input number of students) in both the cost standard allocation (with the number of FTE students) and historical funding. The latter is obviously related to the dimension of universities. The higher the number of students, the higher the basic share distributed to the providers. Looking at the reward share (see Table 3) an initial observation reveals that research activity is repeated in two of the three criteria adopted, which represents 80% of the reward share (about 21% of the FFO). Education assessment is relevant only with reference to the responsible autonomy, which accounts only for 5.5% of the FFO (20% of the reward share). Indeed, the focus of the results assessment, to which the resource allocation is related, is on the effectiveness of the research activities as evaluated through the quality of publications (output of research) produced by the academic staff and new recruits adopting the VQR. In this regard, it is noteworthy

Table 2 Elements of the basic share (about 70%)

	Student standard cost share (22% FFO)	Historical funding (48% FFO)
Simplified formula or criterion	No. of FTE students × unitary standard cost	Allocations of restricted funds
Focus on	Input (students)	Amount of resources allocated the previous year
Performance area	Economic efficiency	No direct connection with performance

Table 3 Reward share (27% FFO)

	VQR	Recruitment policy evaluation	Responsible autonomy
Activity area	Research	Research	(1) Education (2) Research (3) Internationalisation
Focus on	Output (academic staff)	Output (new recruits – academic staff)	(1) Regular student credits accumulated (output) (2) Attractiveness in recruitment policies (3) Regular students, regular graduate students, Ph.D. students from other countries
Performance area	Effectiveness	Effectiveness	Effectiveness

that the VQR results used to currently allocate funds spanned a previous temporal period, 2011–2014. This evaluation process is still disarrayed due to its not recurrent implementation. Indeed, the third-round exercise is going to start for the years 2015-2019, and further assessment criteria have yet to be published. The adoption of VQR results to distribute FFO over a period of several years led to the reiteration of resources allocated without differences from year to year. Doubtless, this is due to VQR mechanism assessment in relation to the period of the evaluation (research results achieved in four-five years).

PO is a metric that was first introduced in 2003 and later (2012) used in the PBF mechanism to allot annual recruitment budget. PO allocation is a complex mechanism that considers the number and type of employees (academic and administrative staff) who left each university in the previous year (turnover POs) and the financial efficiency of institutions, which is understood as the efficient use of resources with special reference to human resources expenses and indebtedness.

It is worth noting that there is no direct relationship between a university's turnover POs and the POs actually allocated since they are partially reallocated, and the following indicators are used to identify if a university is a good performer:

A.   Staff cost indicator, which is calculated as the ratio between personnel expenses and total revenues (i.e., the sum of public funds and tuition fees net of loan repayments);
B.   Economic and financial sustainability indicator, which is the result of the ratio between total revenues after reducing rents payable and personnel expenses plus amortization charges.

On the basis of the latest ministerial decree (DM n. 873/2018), a university is considered "virtuous" if indicator A <80% and indicator B >1. In this case, the best-performing universities are awarded with a higher share of POs than the worst-performing institutions. Following this classification, art. 2 of DM 873/2018 establishes three different groups:

1.   Worst-performing institutions (indicator A > 80% or indicator B < 1), which receive a maximum of 50% of their turnover POs;
2.   Virtuous institutions: (indicator A <80% or indicator B >1), which receive 50% of their turnover POs plus an additional budget that is identified through a complex formula that uses the 20% of the differences between two economic margins (20% of the difference between total revenues after reducing rents payable and personnel expenses plus amortization charges) to share the additional POs;
3.   Universities showing a severe financial crisis (see DM 353/2018) and indicator A >80% will not receive any funds for recruitment purposes (Table 4).

The PO allocation deals with the most arguable mechanism among the three analysed. First, the requirements that have to be respected to receive PO (see group 3) and the formula-based criteria adopted during the allocation process are purely financial indicators. Therefore, this mechanism rewards those universities that perform better in terms of financial efficiency; i.e., the weight of personnel expenses versus total revenues. This may not reflect dimensional variables and, as such, can prevent an

Table 4 PO allocation D. M. 873—2018

Indicators	Personnel expenses on the total revenues Economic and financial sustainability	
Performance area	Financial efficiency	
	Worst universities	Virtuous universities
Requirements	(Personnel expenses/total revenues (public funding plus students' fees) >80% or (Total revenues after reducing rents payable/personnel expenses plus amortization charges) <1	(Personnel expenses/total revenues (public funding plus students' fees) <80% or (total revenues after reducing rents payable/personnel expenses plus amortization charges) >1
PO allocated: basic share	50% turnover POs	50% turnover POs
PO allocated: additional share		20% margin (total revenues after reducing rents payable/personnel expenses plus amortization charges)

evaluation of the real personnel needs. However, although this criterion seems to encourage universities to reduce costs in proportion to total revenues, there is a need to clarify some underlying factors. In the total revenues an important role is played by the tuition level of students' fees whom total amount is proportional to the number of students and the unitary value of taxes. These factors are heavily influenced by contextual influences that are not completely within the universities' control. In fact, having the ability to attract students depends on the quality of the teaching offerings, the alignment between offerings and the labour market, a university's ability to facilitate an easy entry into the labour market due to the relationships between universities, and the economic and social fabric, etc. [8, 9]. These factors, in turn, depend on the socio-cultural and economic environment of the territory in which the university is located [16, 18]. Likewise, the tuition fees are correlated with the attraction and reputation of the university; that is, the higher the university's reputation, the higher the level of taxes the students pay. Finally, there is also a need to highlight that tuition fees can represent, at maximum, 20% of the total FFO (see Dpr. 306/1997) that is allocated to a university. However, the tuition fee-FFO ratio varies consistently throughout the country, and only northern universities can levy higher fees. In the period 2007–2016, for instance, the average fees paid by a student enrolled in a southern or insular university was about one half of that paid by a student who attended a northern university (from about 630 € to more than 1100 €).

With the objective of promoting new research recruitments, the Ministry periodically allocates specific resources for RTD-B as part of the recruitment budget. For the current year, the extraordinary budget—for a total of 1511 RTD-B—is allocated on the basis of the following indicators (DM 204/2019):

- 29% based on the mean number of academic staff in service in 2010 and 2018;

- 36% determined as follows: 90% according to the number of students, as set out in DM n. 587/2018 for FFO allocation, and 10% according to the number of financed grants for Ph.D. students;
- 18% according to VQR 11–14 assessment;
- 16% number of RTD-B in service in 2018 with national scientific qualification (abilitazione scientifica nazionale) multiplied by the ratio between the number of students, as set out in DM n. 587 for FFO allocation and number of academics in service in 2018.

The extraordinary recruitment budget for RTD-B is a combination of an input- and output-oriented allocation mechanism. However, looking at each of the criteria that is applied to assess the respective portion of the positions distributed, it is clear that input variables have a higher weight in the general formula. Input drivers represent about 65% divided by the mean of academics (29%) and number of students (36%). Therefore, as shown in Table 5, the output-based allocation pertains to the residual share that adopt the research results. Again, one criterion is the VQR (about 18%) while the latest part of position allotment is driven by another research output: the numbers of research fellows who obtained the national scientific qualification weighted on a structural parameter (n. students/n. academics). Also, this mechanism is mainly input oriented and, again, teaching results are not taken into consideration.

Table 5 Extraordinary recruitment budget for RTD-B-D. M. 204/2009 2019

N. (Total = 1511)	436	550	270	255
Approximate percentage	29	36	18	16
Simplified criterion	Mean value of academic position (years 2010-2018)	N. of FTE students (90%), N. of financed grant for PhD students (10%)	National research assessment—VQR 2011–2014	N. of research fellow with national scientific qualification * [n. of FTE students/n. academics]
Focus on	Input (academic staff)	Input (students)	Research output	Research output
Performance area	Dimensional parameter (no performance linked)	Dimensional parameter, students' attractiveness (no performance linked)	Effectiveness	Effectiveness, structural parameter

5 Conclusions

The purpose of this theoretical paper was to critically analyse the fundamental funding mechanisms of IHES with the aim of highlighting criticalities and the derived effects that influence the strategic choices and consequent actions taken by universities. Indeed, the motivation for introducing performance measurements within resource allocation practices was to substitute the traditional input-based approach with output/outcome-oriented models and to stimulate universities to increase performance through linking part of the funds that are distributed to reward shares or, rather, the output achieved. However, as a large amount of funding is input-oriented, it is anchored to dimensional parameters such as the number of students or academics. These are the basic share FFO (about the 70%), the 50% turnover PO and the two main portion of positions (about the 65%) in the recruitment budget for RTD-B. The predominance of input-driver related criterion in the IHES funding mechanisms triggers competition between universities in attracting students. In addition to the extensive use of input-based logic to allot funds, the choice of linking a relevant part of the FFO (about 48%) to previous allocation should be noted. The use of historical funding share serves to maintain the 'status quo' since it prevents extensive variation in the amount of funds allocated to universities. However, at the same time, using historical-based allocation can perpetuate gaps among universities and reduce the role of incentives linked to the PBF model.

The analysis highlights how the current system is extremely complex across all three of the mechanisms examined. Table 6 summarizes the targets that are encompassed in the three PBF mechanisms and shows the predominant outcomes of the actions that are motivated by the PBF mechanisms adopted in Italy.

It is worth noting that the repetition of some indicators/criterion, such as the dimensional indicator "number of students" and VQR results, which are used to determine the basic share of FFO and approximately 36% of the positions covered by the extraordinary recruitment budget for RTD-B, and the reward shares of the above mechanisms. In this regard, a questionable issue concerns the replication of the resource allocation due to the adoption of VQR results in the allotment of the reward shares over several years. The VQR exercise shows some issues in relation of evaluation process in relation to the disclosure of the assessment criteria provided at the end of the evaluation period. In terms of the reward shares, the deficiency of output related to the educational activity of universities stands out. These are only considered in the residual share "responsible autonomy" (20%) of FFO while they are not an allocation criterion in the distribution of PO, within which only financial indicators drive the PO assignment. The lack of adoption of educational outputs in the PBF mechanisms analysed emerges as one of the more questionable weakness considering the relevance of the education activity, which represents one of the key institutional missions of Italian universities.

Of the universities' behaviours that should be triggered by the resource allocation mechanisms, increasing student enrolment is the more relevant expected action as dimension indicators are the main resource allocation drivers. In fact, as previously

Table 6 Expected actions of PBF mechanisms

Target/focus	Used in	Expected outcomes (Rationale)
N. of FTE students	FFO basic share	Increase enrolment by improving quality and attractiveness
	Extraordinary recruitment budget for RTD-B	Promote higher efficiency of the formative path
Research productivity	FFO reward share—VQR	Increase in the quality of research
	FFO reward share—responsible autonomy	
	Extraordinary recruitment budget for RTD-B	Support a positive attitude toward external evaluation
Recruitment	FFO reward share	Increase universities' accountability of recruitment
		Increase the competition to attract "talent"
		Support the internationalisation of research
Education	FFO reward share—Responsible autonomy	Increase the overall students' productivity and the quality of the teaching path
Internationalisation	FFO reward share—responsible autonomy	Increase the internationalisation of education
Financial efficiency and cost control	PO (both indicators)	Reduce universities' expenditure with special focus on staff
		Increase the financial and economic sustainability of universities

argued, the number of students represents a key parameter in all three of the main funding mechanisms analysed, not only in terms of basic shares. This is reasonable in order to guarantee the financial sustainability of the overall system such that it is "giving more to the biggest". However, it is also a competitive incentive that should push universities to attract more students. Furthermore, the predominance of this dimension in funding allocation can limit the capability of PBF to promote higher performance in the IHES. Indeed, universities can be incentivized to mainly orient their strategies toward increasing the number of students enrolled, thereby limiting the effort that is invested in the dimension of performance, which is not adequately considered by the PBF. Is the number of students a factor that universities can manage? Can universities make decisions and take consequent actions that increase the number of students over the medium and long term? The attractiveness of a university is only partially conditioned by the quality and typology of the educational offerings. In this regard, universities should act to diversify or specialize their educational offerings [43, 44]. However, student choice is not necessarily the result of university quality and strategy. Indeed, the attractiveness of an institution is affected by context variables such as the socio-cultural and economic environment of the territory in which the university is located [8, 9, 17, 18]. As Table 6 shows, the other expected outcomes linked to the different targets that are included in PBF mechanisms are perhaps more within the control of universities; for example, they can modify their strategies and implement actions that aim to increase the internationalization or reduce staff expenditure. However, it is worth noting that these actions are linked to residual shares of resources.

Italian universities, as well as the ministry and the national agencies, are dealing with an overall increase in the cost of compliance. As highlighted by Dougherty and Reddy [14], the extensive use of PBF increases the costs of "producing" and managing the information and data required to comply with the informative needs that emerge from both outside and inside universities. Indeed, universities should produce and manage a large amount of micro and macro data to feed into the evaluation process and guarantee a management-by-objective approach.

Lastly, it is clear that the criterion adopted to allocate PO is questionable due to the absence of any effectiveness or output-related measures in the formula. This choice appears to be in contrast with of the main indication coming from the literature [27, 28] and the other mechanisms (FFO for instance) of PBF in Italy. In this sense, referring to the framework proposed by Jongbloed [28], IHES can be defined as a hybrid model since it clearly shares the assumption and objective of PBF while still strongly relying on input metrics instead of output/outcomes.

The analysis of the PBF systems adopted in the IHES highlights a further consideration. The use of layered and, sometimes overlapping, PBF mechanisms to allocate funds together with the high complexity of the system has increased the compliance costs that the universities and systems as a whole encounter. Universities have been forced to develop complex and costly informative systems to collect, report, and manage the information requested. This can have varying repercussions for universities according to their size; for example, bigger universities can benefit from economies of scale and, on the contrary, smaller universities that exhibit lower institutional capacity can potentially face an increase in the complexity and costs of their informative system [14]. In this sense, regulations should aim to achieve the right balance between the need to analytically assess the performance of universities and the requirement to manage information in a straightforward manner. It should also be noted that an increase in the complexity of the PBF can also reduce its readability and transparency, thereby limiting the role it plays in promoting higher accountability.

Examining these three models, there are issues that can lead to a reconsideration of some important peculiarities of PBF in IHES. First, despite the difficulty in finding accurate measures, it is necessary to properly consider educational indicators. Italian universities, in line with the traditional Humboldtian pattern, have to focus on both education and research. In this sense, the lack of proper performance indicators regarding education can push universities to focus only on research activities rather than education. Such a scheme can lead to the reduction of the quality of the educational programmes.

Secondly, the marketization policies imply that students and institutions can make their choices autonomously and on a rational basis. In reference to rationality, if universities do not know how their performance will be measured, are they able to rationally choose their strategy to improve performance? In this sense, the disclosure of the assessment criteria (e.g. VQR evaluation) must be provided at the beginning of the evaluation period. In this way, policymakers can properly link VQR (and, to a broader extent, PBF) to their political agenda and create incentives for institutions to adapt their strategy. At the same time, universities will have the correct information to plan accordingly.

Finally, using the number of students as one of the main funding allocation drivers can lead to an increase in the gaps between institutions. Indeed, the underlying assumption in using the number of students as a quasi-market metric is that students 'vote with their feet', implying that students are able to choose a university based on a rational evaluation of its quality and performance, yet they may also have insufficient information and be driven by external factors. In this sense, universities operating in a wealthier or more developed area of the country will appear more attractive than those located in other underprivileged areas, thus obtaining higher shares of funds. Considering the traditional shift that exists between the North and the South of Italy, policymakers should properly manage this potential shortcoming of PBF by introducing parameters into the formulas to address the differences between the areas of the country. Alternatively, the Italian government could modify the funding mechanism by juxtaposing PBF with some 'additional funds' to help those universities that underperform as a result of their location.

Acknowledgements This study contributes to the developmental project of the Department of Business and Economics of the University of Sassari ("Dipartimenti di Eccellenza 2018–2022") financed by the Italian Minister of Education.

References

1. Agasisti, T. (2009). Market forces and competition in university systems: Theoretical reflections and empirical evidence from Italy. *International Review of Applied Economics., 23*(4), 463–483. https://doi.org/10.1080/02692170902954783.
2. Agasisti, T., & Catalano, G. (2006). Governance models of university systems—towards quasi-markets? Tendencies and perspectives: A European comparison. *Journal of Higher Education Policy and Management., 28*(3), 245–262. https://doi.org/10.1080/13600800600980056.
3. Agasisti, T., & Pérez-Esparrells, C. (2010). Comparing efficiency in a cross-country perspective: The case of Italian and Spanish state universities. *Higher Education, 59*(1), 85–103. https://doi.org/10.1007/s10734-009-9235-8.
4. Bartlett, W., Le Grand, J.: The theory of quasi-markets. In *Quasi-markets and social policy* (pp. 13–34). Berlin: Springer.
5. Behn, R. D. (2003). Why measure performance? Different purposes require different measures. *Public Administration Review, 63*(5), 586–606. https://doi.org/10.1111/1540-6210.00322.

6. Burke, J. C., Minassians, H. P.: *Performance reporting: real. Accountability or accountability "lite": Seventh annual survey 2003.* Nelson A. Rockefeller Institute of Government, State University of New York.
7. Capano, G., et al. (2016). *Changing governance in universities.* London: Palgrave Macmillan UK. https://doi.org/10.1057/978-1-137-54817-7.
8. Cattaneo, M., et al. (2017). University spatial competition for students: the Italian case. *Regional Studies, 51*(5), 750–764. https://doi.org/10.1080/00343404.2015.1135240.
9. Chan, S.-J., & Lin, L.-W. (2015). Massification of higher education in taiwan: shifting pressure from admission to employment. *Higher Education Policy, 28*(1), 17–33. https://doi.org/10.1057/hep.2014.33.
10. Degli Esposti, M., & Geraci, M. (2010). Thirty years of higher-education policy in Italy: Vico's Ricorsi and beyond? *Bulletin of Italian Politics, 2*(2), 111–122.
11. Dill, D. (1997). Markets and higher education: an introduction. *Higher Education Policy, 10*(3–4), 163–166. https://doi.org/10.1016/S0952-8733(97)81764-3.
12. Donina, D., et al. (2015). Higher education reform in Italy: Tightening regulation instead of steering at a distance. *Higher Education Policy, 28*(2), 215–234.
13. Donina, D., & Paleari, S. (2018). New public management: global reform script or conceptual stretching? Analysis of university governance structures in the Napoleonic administrative tradition. *Higher Education.* https://doi.org/10.1007/s10734-018-0338-y.
14. Dougherty, K. J., et al. (2014). Performance Funding for Higher Education: Forms, Origins, Impacts, and Futures. *The ANNALS of the American Academy of Political and Social Science, 655*(1), 163–184. https://doi.org/10.1177/0002716214541042.
15. Estermann, T., et al. (2013). Designing strategies for efficient funding of higher education in Europe. DEFINE Interim Report, Brussels.
16. Ezza, A., et al. (2019). Il "grande gap": gli effetti del performance budgeting sulle politiche di reclutamento delle Università italiane. *Management Control, 2,* 99–121. https://doi.org/10.3280/MACO2019-002005.
17. Ezza, A., et al. (2017). Performance-based funding in public competition. lights and shadows in the Italian higher education system. *Journal of International Business and Economics, 17*(2), 5–22. https://doi.org/10.18374/JIBE-17-2.1.
18. Farhan, B. Y. (2016). Competitive behaviour in publicly funded academic institutions. *Interchange., 47*(4), 357–373. https://doi.org/10.1007/s10780-016-9283-9.
19. Fowles, J. (2014). Funding and focus: Resource dependence in public higher education. *Research in Higher Education, 55*(3), 272–287. https://doi.org/10.1007/s11162-013-9311-x.
20. Geuna, A. (2001). The changing rationale for european university research funding: Are there negative unintended consequences? *Journal of Economic Issues, 35*(3), 607–632. https://doi.org/10.1080/00213624.2001.11506393.
21. Geuna, A., & Martin, B. R. (2003). University research evaluation and funding: an international comparison. *Minerva, 41*(4), 277–304. https://doi.org/10.1023/B:MINE.0000005155.70870.bd.
22. Harnisch, T. L. (2011). *Performance-based funding: A re-emerging strategy in public higher education financing,* 12.
23. Herbst, M. (2007). Performance-based budgeting or funding. In *Financing public universities* (pp. 65–94). Dordrecht: Springer Netherlands. https://doi.org/10.1007/978-1-4020-9503-0_4.
24. Hicks, D. (2012). Performance-based university research funding systems. *Research Policy, 41*(2), 251–261. https://doi.org/10.1016/j.respol.2011.09.007.
25. Hillman, N. W., et al. (2014). Performance funding in higher education: Do financial incentives impact college completions? *The Journal of Higher Education, 85*(6), 826–857. https://doi.org/10.1080/00221546.2014.11777349.
26. Jeon, J., & Kim, S. Y. (2018). Is the gap widening among universities? On research output inequality and its measurement in the Korean higher education system. *Quality & Quantity, 52*(2), 589–606. https://doi.org/10.1007/s11135-017-0652-y.
27. Jongbloed, B.: Funding Higher Education: A Comparative Overview. (2008).
28. Jongbloed, B. (2004). *Funding higher education: options, trade-offs and dilemmas.*

29. Jongbloed, B. (2003). Marketisation in higher education, Clark's triangle and the essential ingredients of markets. *Higher Education Quarterly, 57*(2), 110–135. https://doi.org/10.1111/1468-2273.00238.
30. Jongbloed, B., & Vossensteyn, H. (2001). Keeping up performances: An international survey of performance-based funding in higher education. *Journal of Higher Education Policy and Management, 23*(2), 127–145.
31. Le Grand, J.: Quasi-Markets and Social Policy. The Economic Journal. 101, 408, 1256 (1991). https://doi.org/10.2307/2234441.
32. Liefner, I. (2003). Funding, resource allocation, and performance in higher education systems. *Higher Education, 46*(4), 469–489.
33. McKeown, M.P.: State Funding Formulas for Public Four-Year Institutions. (1996).
34. Nisar, M. A. (2015). Higher education governance and performance based funding as an ecology of games. *Higher Education, 69*(2), 289–302. https://doi.org/10.1007/s10734-014-9775-4.
35. Pfeffer, J., Salancik, G. R. (2003). The external control of organizations: a resource dependence perspective. Stanford University Press.
36. Rabovsky, T. M. (2012). Accountability in higher education: Exploring impacts on state budgets and institutional spending patterns. *Journal of Public Administration Research and Theory, 22*(4), 675–700.
37. Rossi, P. (2015). Il Punto Organico: una storia italiana. RT. *A Journal on Research Policy and Evaluation, 3*, 1.
38. Rothschild, M., & White, L. J. (1995). The analytics of the pricing of higher education and other services in which the customers are inputs. *Journal of Political Economy, 103*(3), 573–586.
39. Smethurst, R. (1995). Education: a public or private good? *RSA Journal, 143*(5465), 33–45.
40. Thornton, Z. M., & Friedel, J. N. (2016). Performance-based funding: State policy influences on small rural community colleges. *Community College Journal of Research and Practice, 40*(3), 188–203. https://doi.org/10.1080/10668926.2015.1112321.
41. Tilak, J. B. G. (2008). Higher education: a public good or a commodity for trade?: Commitment to higher education or commitment of higher education to trade. *Prospects, 38*(4), 449–466. https://doi.org/10.1007/s11125-009-9093-2.
42. Volkwein, J., & Tandberg, D. (2008). Measuring up: Examining the connections among state structural characteristics, regulatory practices, and performance. *Research in Higher Education, 49*, 180–197. https://doi.org/10.1007/s11162-007-9066-3.
43. van Vught, F. (2007). *Diversity and differentiation in higher education systems*, 22.
44. Widiputera, F., et al. (2017). Measuring diversity in higher education institutions: A review of literature and empirical approaches. *IAFOR Journal of Education, 5*(1), 47–63.

People, Organizations, and New Ways
of Working in the Information Age

Organizational Impacts on Sustainability of Industry 4.0: A Systematic Literature Review from Empirical Case Studies

Emanuele Gabriel Margherita⬤ and Alessio Maria Braccini⬤

Abstract There is an increasing interest in Industry 4.0 (I40) applications for organizations to act sustainable. Indeed literature agrees the adoption of I40 technologies promises various organizational benefits which lead to the achievement of an enduring sustainability and competitive advantage for organizations. However, there is a lack of a study which provides transparency confirming and summarizing those spawned organizational benefits. This paper aims at addressing this gap performing a systematic literature review analyzing I40 empirical case studies for detecting the spawned I40 organizational impacts on sustainability. We employed the triple bottom line (TBL) concept as sensitive device to confront different studies distinguishing among the sustainability dimensions, namely the economic, social and environmental dimensions. We then categorize and group I40 organizational impacts according to TBL dimensions. The review portrays an initial empirical knowledge regarding the I40 organizational impacts on sustainability since 18 I40 empirical case study have found. Furthermore, the literature review reveals that I40 applications mainly impact the economic dimension whereas few applications generated benefits for the remaining dimensions.

Keywords Industry 4.0 · Organizational impacts · Organizational benefits · Sustainability · Internet of things · Literature review · Cyber physical system

1 Introduction

Nowadays due to the climate change and a constant increasing of pollution, acting sustainable has become the requirement and priority for organizations [22].

Within this landscape, Industry 4.0 (henceforth I40) is a trendy industrial initiative which aims at innovating production processes towards sustainable practices through the use of advanced digital technologies into the assembly line [13, 19]. However, even though there is a consensus in literature that I40 leads to positive organizational

E. G. Margherita (✉) · A. M. Braccini
Department of Economics Engineering Society and Organization—DEIM, University of Tuscia, Via Del Paradiso, 47, 01100 Viterbo, Italy
e-mail: emargherita@unitus.it

© The Editor(s) (if applicable) and The Author(s), under exclusive license to Springer Nature Switzerland AG 2020
R. Agrifoglio et al. (eds.), *Digital Business Transformation*, Lecture Notes in Information Systems and Organisation 38, https://doi.org/10.1007/978-3-030-47355-6_12

impacts on sustainability [13, 19], there is a lack of studies that provide transparency summarizing and confirming these premises [28]. To address this gap, we perform a systematic literature review of I40 empirical case study detecting the I40 organizational impacts on sustainability. We use the Triple Bottom Line (henceforth TBL) concept as sensitive device since it allows to study the sustainability in a holistic way embracing the economic, environmental and social dimensions [12]. Therefore, we detected I40 organizational impacts which affected positively the three dimensions. Our investigation answers the following questions: "*What are the organizational impacts on sustainability of Industry 4.0?*"

The reminder of this article is organized as follows. Section 2 describes the foundational concepts of I40 and TBL. Section 3 illustrates the research method. Section 4 is devoted to the results of the literature review. Section 5 discusses the findings proposing future directions for the research. The paper concludes in Sect. 6 proposing implications for researchers and practitioners.

2   Related Literature

In this section, we portray the Triple Bottom Line, Industry 4.0 initiative, the related technologies and their organizational impacts on sustainability.

2.1   The Triple Bottom Line

Developed by Elkington, the TBL describes sustainability in a holistic way. The TBL encompasses three dimensions: environmental, social, and economic [12, 14]. TBL supports organizations to address sustainability issues providing accounting measures for all the dimensions.

Indeed, the environmental dimension refers to organizational practices which account the currently environmental issues like ozone depletion and climate change. More specific, this dimension embraces practices which avoid consuming natural resources as well as practices for alleviating CO_2 and polluted gas emissions. Moreover, this dimension encourages practices dedicated to the recycling of resources, the regeneration and purification of resources, as well as redesigning of processes and products to minimize resource usage, in terms of raw materials, water, and energy that even alleviate the pollution issue [14, 17].

The social dimension refers to organizational attitude to treat and develop people as a capital within the organization for creating value. As such, this dimension considers as main driver the enrichment of work tasks and a more suitable and safer workplace which also are the means to improve the quality of life and society [14, 29].

The economic dimension refers to organizational attitude to make profit as well as protecting the other two dimensions. More specific, the economic dimension of

Fig. 1 The TBL
organizational impacts [14]

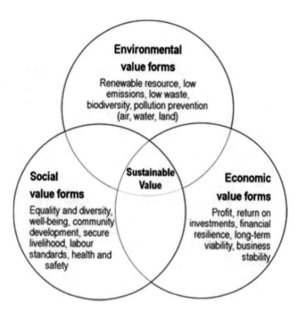

the TBL is related to with economic and financial performance dimensions of the organization. In addition, organization supports both long-term economic growth and the community growth encouraging the increasing of the personal income, paying taxes and promoting actions in order to support the other two dimensions [14, 34].

Finally, Fig. 1 punctuated the organizational impacts that TBL embraces for each dimension which we employed as a sensitive device for detecting organizational impacts on sustainability.

2.2 Industry 4.0

I40 is an industrial initiative launched by German government in 2011. I40 aims at innovating production processes in industries which promises several organizational impacts for organizations. The initiative goal is the development of cyber-physical systems (henceforth CPS) which allow the interconnection between machines and human resources as well as the machine self-decision making [19]. In fact, this latter feature allows to predict and address malfunctions in assembly line by machineries without human interactions [25].

The realization of these organizational impacts goes through an effective implementation of a mix of advanced technologies which enables CPS. These technologies have presented as follows:

- Internet of things (henceforth IoT) describes the operation, in which physical products and machinery are equipped with sensors like Radio-Frequency Identification (RFID henceforth) in order to capture, process, and communicate in real-time data to humans as well as other machineries. These technology requires sensors and actuators to acquire and communicate through a WIFI network [44].
- Big Data refers to technologies allowing to analyze a massive set of unstructured or semi-structured data, which is not possible to analyze by traditional data process methods owing to their complexity in order to reveal patterns, trends, and associations, especially relating to human behavior and interactions [19].
- Additive manufacturing is an "umbrella term" which employs different technologies, such as 3D printing, to produce a high quality real objects by adding material rather than by mechanically removing or milling material from a solid block [2].
- Virtual Reality, Augmented Reality and Hologram are advanced technologies which aim at designing products, operation planning, factory layout planning, system maintenance through specific hardware and software without using real materials [20, 33].
- Cloud manufacturing is the cloud computing technology that is applied to the manufacturing area. Indeed, Cloud manufacturing is mainly employed for its ability to make the entire manufacturing plant integrated and capable of distributing machines as a service [4, 30, 47].

Regarding the I40 organizational impacts, there is a consensus in literature which connects the interoperability of I40 technologies to positive organizational impacts on sustainability [13, 19]. Indeed, I40 seminal paper explained the full potential and the promising organizational impacts of I40. With regards to the economic dimension, I40 leads to a higher process flexibility, higher decision making, chance to create new services and products [15]. Whereas in terms of the environmental and social dimension, I40 leads to energy savings and a better work life balance for employees [19]. In line with this, a similar industrial initiative to I40 called Industrial Internet undertaken in U.S., which employed the same technologies, have agreed on these benefits [13].

As a result, because of a plethora of technologies deployed in I40 and industrial initiatives with different names around the world, the knowledge of I40 organizational impacts and I40 empirical studies resulted fragmented. To address this gap, Kang et al. [20] performed a non-systematic literature reviewed both initiatives portraying core technologies, benefits and empirical case studies, respectively. On the other hand, Piccarozzi et al. [37] performed a rigorous and systematic literature review of I40 in management literature focusing only on I40 without considering Industrial Internet and individual technologies. Therefore, a systematic literature regarding I40 organizational impacts on sustainability which includes keywords from both initiatives and technologies is still lacking.

3 Research Method

Our investigation aims at detecting I40 organizational impacts on sustainability from I40 empirical case studies. First of all, we conducted a rigorous [6] and systematic literature review applying the protocol by Webster et al. [46]. Table 1 shows the details of literature search we performed over the SCOPUS database of indexed scientific publications in February 2019.

Because of various and similar initiatives, the query contains "Industry 4.0" and keywords which researchers frequently employed as a synonym of I40 applications like internet of things, smart factory, cyber physical systems [37] as well as Industrial Internet which is an equivalent initiative developed in U.S. [13]. In addition, we used a set of secondary keywords, namely implementation, application and adoption since they point to empirical adoption of the I40.

We encompassed in the database only papers containing industrial empirical case studies which adopted I40 technologies. Since I40 is also used as a buzz word which refers to the interconnection of technologies, the initial hits of our research included several papers from different sectors as smart building, agriculture and e-health. Accordingly, we excluded those papers as well as theoretical survey papers which is also the cause of the cause of the large drop between the initial hits (386) to the first exclusion step (25). Still, an author and reference forward and backward search was conducted to ensure exhaustiveness [35, 46].

The final query produced 18 entries which have employed as database to identify the I40 organizational impacts. Figure 2 shows the publication trend. Hence, afterwards we accomplished the literature review research, we conducted qualitative coding techniques to explore and elucidate the various organizational impacts on sustainability. We maintain a qualitative rigor following the canons by [8]. We employed as a sensitive device all the organizational impacts of the TBL in Fig. 1. More specific, we considered all the benefits which I40 technologies led to the

Table 1 Literature search for empirical I40 case studies

Item	Description
Source	Scopus
Query	TOPIC: "industry 4.0" OR "industrial internet" OR "internet of thin*" OR "smart factor*" OR "cyber physical system*" AND "implementation*" OR "application*" OR "adoption*" Refined by: LANGUAGES: (ENGLISH), Subject Area: Business, Management and Accounting, Source Type: Journals
Hits	386
Papers retained after • Title and abstract selection • Full-text selection • Backward and forward search	25 10 18

Fig. 2 Publication trend of
the empirical I40 case study

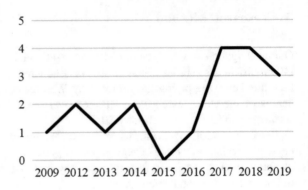

organization for each paper. We then distinguished those benefits according to
the three sustainability dimensions of the TBL, namely the economic, social and
environmental dimension.

4   Results

The literature review search revealed 18 I40 empirical case studies in which the
I40 applications led to organizational impacts on sustainability. We summarized
organizational impacts in Table 2.

With regards to the organization impacts on economic dimension, all the I40
applications fully supported this dimension. Indeed, the literature review showed
I40 application which improved various back-end processes realizing cost reduction
and higher efficiency. As a matter of fact, there is a general consensus stating that IoT
applications into inventory management and warehouse management improved the
efficiency and effectiveness of the supply chain management reducing the inventory
inaccuracy and the time of receiving the goods by consumers [9, 18, 36]. Still, Reif
et al. [38] added that providing workers decision support via head-mounted displays
significantly reduces the required time for the picking process.

Moreover, according to Mourtzis et al. [31] and Sayar et al. [40] I40 applications, particularly IoT, provided new avenues to deliver enhanced services. While
3D printing applications affected positively small medium production of products allowing organization to produce different goods [1]. Likewise, I40 affords
an improved managerial decision-making capability in organizations, thanks to the
improved analytics capabilities of the data produced by the digital infrastructures.
Indeed, Shahbaz et al. [42] proposed a data mining techniques in manufacturing
industry in order to deliver information to improve the product manufacturing life
cycles and eventually the economic performance of the industry. Furthermore, Lee
et al. [26] argued that I40 allows predictive analysis on the organizational processes
and providing a promptly maintenance on production mistakes.

Table 2 Industry 4.0 Organizational Impacts on Sustainability by authors

Authors	I40 organizational impacts		
	Economic dimension	Social dimension	Environmental dimension
Goyal et al. [18]	RFID embedded in inventory management reduced inventory inaccuracy		
Cui et al. [9]	RFID implemented within supply chain management improved the efficiency and effectiveness		
Lee et al. [24]	Warehouse management with RFID system improved productivity	Improved employee morale	
Reif et al. [38]	Virtual reality improved picking system efficiency		
Zhang et al. [50]	IoT Real time scheduling systems		Reuse of the materials
Shahbaz et al. [42]	Big data and data mining to improve the product manufacturing life cycles		
Shin et al. [43]	Big data and analytics model maintained technical efficiency		Analytics model predicted energy consumption
Thiede et al. [45]	Continuous energy monitoring reduces energy costs		CO_2 reductions
Lee et al. [26]	Big Data and predictive analysis reduced production mistakes		
Yuan et al. [48]	CPS enhanced operational agility and improvement of competitiveness	Reduction of safety incident	
Liang et al. [27]	CPS and Big data generated Productivity improvement.		CPS and big data generated energy saving
Sayar et al. [40]	IoT generated new valuable services		
Schulze et al. [41]	Production processes resulted more efficient thanks to CPS		CPS reduced water usage

(continued)

Table 2 (continued)

Authors	I40 organizational impacts		
	Economic dimension	Social dimension	Environmental dimension
Kembro et al. [21]	IoT and sensors technology improved warehouse management	Safer workplace	
Braccini et al. [5]	Robotics improved productivity and product quality	Safer work environment, less intense work-load and job enrichment	Reduction of CO2 emission and natural resources
Mourtiz et al. [31]	Robotics generated new and advanced services		
Pero et al. [36]	RFID improved the efficiency of the supply chain		
Ardanza et al. [1]	3D printing improved the efficiency of small and medium production		

Whit regards to I40 organizational impact on environmental dimension, the literature revealed that those impacts are generally connected to the former dimension since the improvement of production processes led to a reduction of energy consumption and natural resources. Indeed, according to Liang et al. and Shahbaz et al. [27, 43] the analysis of the big data through an analytic and predictive model allows to predict and reduce the energy consumption with the maintenance of technical efficiency within organization. Analogously, Strange et al. [45] presented a CPS study where the application led to productivity improvement energy saving and with a resulting reduction of CO_2 reduction.

Finally, a more articulated research proposed by Zhang et al.[50] showed how the IoT can reinvigorate the remanufacturing processes allowing a real-time production scheduling method which combined with a mathematical model achieve cost reduction, dynamic management of re-manufacturable resources, and energy consumption decrease.

With regards to I40 organizational impacts on social dimension, the literature review found that researchers have paid little attention on it revealing only 3 case studies with stressed on this dimension. As a matter of fact, Lee et al. [24] explained as warehouse management systems improved the productivity increasing the employee morale. Whereas Yuan et al. [48] considered in toto the Smart Factory adoption for oil refinery demonstrating its operational agility, the improvement of economic competitiveness, but also on the reduction of safety incident.

Finally, Braccini et al. discussed I40 application of robotics and big data where workforce participated in the system design [5]. This user centric approach [11] led to the various organizational impacts with affect positively all the three sustainability dimensions of TBL. Indeed, the production quality increased together with productivity. The continuous energy consumption monitoring reduced CO_2 emission and usage of natural resources. Beyond that, organization obtained a safer work environment characterized by a less intense workload and job enrichment of tasks.

5 Discussion and Future Directions

Table 2 allows us to answer our research question summarizing the results of our systematic literature review of I40 organizational impacts on sustainability. Table 2 depicts an initial stage of the I40 initiative. Indeed, most of the I40 applications concerns individual technologies (e.g. 3d printings, big data or IoT) rather than a mix of technologies which enable the full potential of I40. Figure 3 shows the technologies adopted in the empirical I40 case studies. Within the case studies, the most studied technology is the IoT in the warehouse and inventory management leading to several benefits along the supply chain which impacted mainly the economic dimension. Conversely, 3d printing and virtual reality appeared only in one case study respectively. Therefore, we argue that there is a need for further studies in order to understand the advantages of these technologies. Researchers should focus on 3d printings when they are in a key role within the organizational strategy producing a small amount of high customized goods for fulfilling individual customer [49].

The systematic literature review also revealed that several I40 applications did not reach both the two features of I40 initiative since the CPS has not implemented in all empirical case studies. Further research should focus on this issue investigating the adoption barriers which impede the CPS implementation as well as how to address them. As a matter of fact, the cybersecurity will become increasingly important in a I40 context requiring more studies for addressing this issue.

Furthermore, we noticed that most of the studies underpinned a deterministic technological approach. Indeed, I40 organizational benefits have connected to the delivery of the technical systems without considering the social systems and the

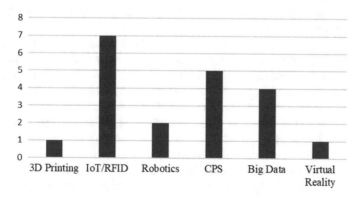

Fig. 3 Industry 4.0 technologies adopted into empirical I40 case studies

complex interaction between humans, machines, and the environmental aspects of the organizations. These studies employed a perspective at organizational level presenting organizational needs in terms of poor productivity and weak coordination among units which are then addressed by I40 technologies. The social systems, composed by workers and their values, are not mentioned during the adoption process. The I40 technologies themselves lead to benefits which rely on their predetermined functionalities. However, these I40 technologies, following this perspective, improved only the economic dimension of sustainability without considering the remaining two dimensions. Accordingly, we suggest encompassing the social system and environmental issues during the I40 adoption to fully exploits its benefits employing a socio-technical perspective [19]. Indeed, the socio-technical perspective stated that in order to enhance the organization's efficiency, manager should optimize the technological and social systems conjointly, otherwise the optimization of only system leads to inefficiency. Therefore, we argue that researchers should apply a socio-technical perspective during I40 adoption to deliver positive organizational impacts over all TBL dimensions. Thus, we encourage management to encompass the worker participation in the design and implementation of the new I40 systems in order to accomplish I40 organizational impacts on the social dimension [32]. Whereas, in order to generate positive organizational impacts on the environmental dimension, I40 technologies should be shaped following a green orientation rather than the currently orientation. That considers as main purpose the cost reduction without considering the reuse of resources as well as the stemming of the pollution [19]. As a matter of fact, Braccini et al. showed how a I40 application led to positive organizational impacts over the three dimensions through a green mind-set of management and a worker participation in the I40 adoption [5].

To conclude proposing a novel research avenue, we noticed that studies from the database adopted the lean production within I40 context. Indeed, lean production played a vital role in the mass production systems which is devoted to improved product quality with the aim of satisfying customers [23]. Thus, recent studies claimed that I40 and lean production can support each other [7, 39]. Accordingly, to advance our research regarding I40 organizational impacts, researchers should also consider lean production as a driver for those impacts studying also the interplay with I40 and sustainability.

To sum up, Table 3 photographed the state of the arts regarding the I40 organizational impacts on sustainability. The economic dimension is well accomplished since I40 technology functionalities mainly impact this dimension through cost reduction and a higher process efficiency. Still, those studies employed a perspective at the organizational level. Whereas, there is a lack of studies which employed a group and individual perspective. Further studies should focus on addressing this gap showing in which way the interrelation between individual worker or worker groups and I40 technologies support the economic dimension.

On the other hand, little attention has been paid on organizational impacts on the environmental dimension. Due to the environmental issues which dominated our world, this dimension is increasingly become more important. To support this dimension, I40 technology vendor and researchers should embrace purposes of the Green

Table 3 Organizational Impacts of Industry 4.0 on Sustainability by TBL

I40 Organizational Impacts by TBL		
Environmental dimension	Economic dimension	Social dimension
• Reduced natural resources • Reduced CO_2 emissions • Energy Saving	• New valuable services • Improved production efficiency and quality • Improved supply chain management • Reduced inventory inaccuracy • Improved productivity	• Improved employee morale • Safer work environment • Less intense work load • Job enrichment

Manufacturing combining with I40 initiative [16]. Indeed, Green Manufacturing aims at developing green innovation and new green products. Green Innovation refers to innovation which is characterized by energy conservation, pollution prevention and environmental management as well as produce products easy to recycle and less polluting.

Finally, the social dimension is not prominent in the literature. Few studies covered this dimension where organizational benefits often are generated by a positive externality. Information systems (IS) researchers should concentrate on this dimension as implications of I40 technologies on social systems have not investigated yet. IS researchers, employing an individual and group perspective, should pay attention on how I40 technologies should change the way of working and how these I40 technologies improved work conditions answering questions regarding new competences needed to handle these technologies and how I40 improve the quality of working life.

6 Conclusions, Implications and Limitations

Our investigation is motivated by the identification of I40 organizational impacts on sustainability dimensions which have detected from a systematic literature review of I40 empirical case studies. The literature review portrayed an initial empirical knowledge regarding the I40 organizational impacts on sustainability as 18 I40 empirical case studies have been found. Even though, I40 leads to the several organizational impacts on the economic dimensions, further studies and I40 applications are required to fully exploits the two remaining researches. This lack is due to the technologic determinism perspective which surrounded the selected studies. We argue for a socio-technical perspective to address this gap. Beyond, we also argue for further investigations at individual and group level to advance the knowledge regarding the I40 benefits.

The investigation proposed presents both implication for practitioners and researchers. Regarding the implication for practitioners, Table 2 can be seen as a repository of existing effective I40 implementations. It is useful for practitioners since it highlights the spawned organizational impacts acknowledging the role of the modern technologies such as internet of things, cloud, big data, robotic systems, 3D printing.

Regarding the implication for researchers, the literature review summarized our knowledge regarding I40 initiatives, these advanced technologies and their positive organizational impacts on sustainability proposing new avenues. Still, the investigation also opens for socio-technical approach in order to maximize organizational impacts for I40. This triggers further consideration regarding the "fit" between the two systems in terms of job satisfaction, knowledge, task structure and social value [32].

Furthermore, Table 2 can be used to improve IS theories like the adaptive structuration theory which is a meta-theory for accounting the change by a technology within the sociotechnical systems [3]. Indeed, from these I40 case studies we can detect and extend the construct of technology dimensions for I40 [10]. Indeed, Bostrom et al. 2009 claimed for "further research exploring and identifying a complete set of features and dimensions [of technologies] would be useful" (pg. 27) [3]. Finally, the study limitation is that we employed SCOPUS database. This does not cover all the accessible sources of I40 and similar initiatives. Accordingly, an interesting avenue to extend our literature review, is to embrace further database such as Web of Science (WOS), EBESCO and JSTOR.

References

1. Ardanza, A., et al. (2019). Sustainable and flexible industrial human machine interfaces to support adaptable applications in the Industry 4.0 paradigm. *International Journal of Production Research.*
2. Bassi, L. ()2017. Industry 4.0: Hope, hype or revolution? In *RTSI 2017—IEEE 3rd International Forum Research and Technologies for Society and Industry. Conference Proceedings* (2017).
3. Bostrom, R. P., et al. (2009). A meta-theory for understanding information systems within sociotechnical systems. *Journal of Management Information System, 26*(1), 17–48.
4. Braccini, A. M. (2011). *Value generation in organisations.*
5. Braccini, A. M., Margherita, E. G. (2019). Exploring organizational sustainability of Industry 4.0 under the triple bottom line: the case of a manufacturing company. *Sustainability, 11*(1), 36.
6. Vom Brocke, J., et al. (2009). *Reconstructing the giant: On the importance of rigour in documenting the literature search process.* Syst: European Conference on Information.
7. Chen, D. Q., et al. (2010). Information systems strategy: Reconceptualization, measurement and implications. *MIS Quarterly, 34*(2), 233–259.
8. Corbin, J. M., & Strauss, A. L. (1990). Grounded theory research: Procedures, canons, and evaluative criteria. *Qualitative Sociology, 13*(1), 3–21.
9. Cui, L., et al. (2017). Investigation of RFID investment in a single retailer two-supplier supply chain with random demand to decrease inventory inaccuracy. *Journal of Cleaner Production, 142,* 2028–2044.
10. DeSanctis, G., & Poole, M. S. (1994). Capturing the complexity in advanced technology use: Adaptive structuration theory. *Organization Science, 5*(2), 121–147.
11. Eason, K. (2014). Afterword: The past, present and future of sociotechnical systems theory. *Applied Ergonomics, 45*(2), 213–220.
12. Elkington, J. (1997). *Cannibals with forks—Triple bottom line of 21st century business.* Stoney Creek, CT: New Society Publishers.

13. Evans, P. C., Annunziata, M. 2012(). *Industrial Internet: pushing the boundaries of minds and machines.*
14. Evans, S., et al. (2017). Business model innovation for sustainability: towards a unified perspective for creation of sustainable business models. *Business Strategy and the Environment.*
15. Fatorachian, H., Kazemi, H.: A critical investigation of Industry 4.0 in manufacturing: theoretical operationalisation framework. *Production Planning and Control, 7287*, 1–12.
16. Feng, Z., & Chen, W. (2018). Environmental regulation, green innovation, and industrial green development: An empirical analysis based on the spatial Durbin model. *Sustainability, 10*, 1.
17. Glavič, P., & Lukman, R. (2007). Review of sustainability terms and their definitions. *Journal of Cleaner Production, 15*(18), 1875–1885.
18. Goyal, S., et al. (2016). The effectiveness of RFID in backroom and sales floor inventory management. *International Journal of Logistics Management, 27*(3), 795–815.
19. Kagermann, H., et al. (2013). *Recommendations for implementing the strategic initiative INDUSTRIE 4.0.* Working Group. Acatech, Frankfurt am Main, Ger.
20. Kang, H. S. et al. (2016). Smart manufacturing: Past research, present findings, and future directions. *International Journal* of Precision *Engineering* and *Manufacturing-Green Technology, 3*(1), 111–128.
21. Kembro, J. H., et al. (2017). Network video technology: Exploring an innovative approach to improving warehouse operations. *International Journal of Physical Distribution & Logistics Management, 47*(7), 623–645.
22. Kiel, D., et al.: *Sustainable industrial value creation: Benefits and Challenges of Industry 4.0.*
23. Koukoulaki, T. (2014). The impact of lean production on musculoskeletal and psychosocial risks: An examination of sociotechnical trends over 20 years. *Applied Ergonomics, 45*(2), 198–212.
24. Lee, C. K. M., et al. (2017). Design and application of Internet of things-based warehouse management system for smart logistics. *International Journal of Production Research, 7543*(October), 1–16.
25. Lee, C. K. M., et al. (2015). Research on IoT based cyber physical system for industrial big data analytics. *IEEE International Conference* on *Industrial Engineering* and *Engineering Management* (IEEM) (pp. 1855–1859).
26. Lee, J., et al. (2013). Recent advances and trend in predictive manufacturing systems in big data environment. *Manufacturing Letters, 1*, 1.
27. Liang, Y. C., et al. (2018). Cyber physical system and Big Data enabled energy efficient machining optimisation. *Journal of Cleaner Production, 187*, 46–62.
28. Liao, Y., et al.: Past, present and future of Industry 4.0 - a systematic literature review and research agenda proposal. *International Journal of Production Research, 55*(12), 3609–3629.
29. Littig, B., Griessler, E. (2005). Social sustainability: A catchword between political pragmatism and social theory. *International Journal of Sustainable Development, 8*(1/2), 65.
30. Margherita, E. G., Braccini, A. M. (2020). IS in the cloud and organizational benefits: An exploratory study. In: Lazazzara, A., Ricciardi, F., Za, S. (Eds.) *Exploring digital ecosystems. Lecture notes in information systems and organisation*, vol. 33. Cham: Springer.
31. Mourtzis, D., et al.: Modelling and quantification of industry 4.0 manufacturing complexity based on information theory: A robotics case study. *International Journal of Production Research.*
32. Mumford, E. (2003). *Redesigning human systems.* Idea Publishing.
33. Nee, A. Y. C., et al. (2012). Augmented reality applications in design and manufacturing. *CIRP Annual Manufaturing Technology, 61*(2), 657–679.
34. Norman, W., & Macdonald, C. (2004). Getting to the bottom of the triple bottom line. *Business Ethics Quarterly, 14*(2), 243–262.
35. Okoli, C., & Schabram, K. (2010). A Guide to conducting a systematic literature review of information systems research. *Sprouts Working Paper on Information Systems, 10*(26), 1–50.
36. Pero, M., & Rossi, T. (2014). RFID technology for increasing visibility in ETO supply chains: A case study. *Production Planning and Control, 25*(11), 892–901.

37. Piccarozzi, M., et al. (2018). Industry 4.0 in management studies: a systematic literature review. *Sustainability, 10*(10), 3821.
38. Reif, R. Günthner, W.A. (2009). An augmented reality supported picking system. In: *WSCG 2009 Full Paper Proceedings*, Plzen, Czech Republic, February 2–5, 2009.
39. Sanders, A., et al.: Industry 4.0 implies lean manufacturing: Research activities in Industry 4.0 function as enablers for lean manufacturing. *Journal of Industrial Engineering Management, 9*(3), 811–833.
40. Sayar, D., & Er, Ö. (2018). The Antecedents of successful IoT service and system design: Cases from the manufacturing industry. *International Journal of Design, 12*(1), 67–78.
41. Schulze, C., et al. (2018). Cooling tower management in manufacturing companies: A cyber-physical system approach. Journal of Cleaner Production.
42. Shahbaz, M., et al. (2012). Data mining methodology in perspective of manufacturing databases. *Life Science Journal, 9,* 3.
43. Shin, S., et al. (2014). Predictive analytics model for power consumption in manufacturing predictive analytics model for power consumption in manufacturing. *Procedia CIRP, 15*, 153–158.
44. Strange, R., Zucchella, A.: Industry 4.0, global value chains and international business. *Multinational Business Review, 25*(3), 174–184.
45. Thiede, S. (2018). Environmental sustainability of cyber physical production systems. *Procedia CIRP, 69*(May), 644–649.
46. Webster, J., & Watson, R. T. (2002). Analyzing the past to prepare for the future: Writing a literature review. *MIS Quarterly, 26,* 2.
47. Xu, X. (2012). From cloud computing to cloud manufacturing. *Robotics and Computer-Integrated Manufacturing, 28*(1), 75–86.
48. Yuan, Z., et al. (2017). Smart manufacturing for the oil refining and petrochemical industry. *Engineering, 3,* 1–4.
49. Zawadzki, P., Zywicki, K. (2016). Smart product design and production control for effective mass customization in the industry 4.0 concept. *Management and Production Engineering Review, 7*(3), 105–112.
50. Zhang, Y., et al. (2018). The 'Internet of Things' enabled real-time scheduling for remanufacturing of automobile engines. *Journal of Cleaner Production, 185,* 562–575.

Industry 4.0 and the Global Digitalised Production. Structural Changes in Manufacturing

Giovanna Morelli, Cesare Pozzi, and Antonia R. Gurrieri

Abstract The globalization process and the new digitalized production have rapidly changed the structural organizational models of major economies. To avoid the commoditization trap, globalization and price-advantage erosion, manufacturing industries are moving fast from mass to customized productions. They have servitized business operations, taking advantages of the new emerging and digitized technologies within the scenario of Industry 4.0 (I4.0). This paper recalls the most significant debate on the new industrial paradigm, and investigates its impact on the manufacturing sector, focusing on Italian SMEs. It evaluates the effects on labour division, organizational models of production (agents-machines-organization), the "new" power structure, and the economy as a whole. It investigates the effects of technology on the labour market and organizational models with respect to SMEs and networks, concluding that I4.0 could be an effective driving force for networking SMEs, despite the reduction of employees in manufacturing is likely to continue.

Keywords Industry 4.0 · Servitization · Globalization · Labour division

1 Introduction

In the last decades, the process of globalization and the digital transformation of the industrial production have changed economic systems all over the world, leading to a significant impact on life, the way people work and the functioning of markets. The socio-political context has deeply changed. The large increase on the extent of the market followed the pervasive process of globalization, the new technological

G. Morelli (✉)
University of Teramo, via R. Balzarini 1, 64100 Teramo, Italy
e-mail: gmorelli@unite.it

C. Pozzi · A. R. Gurrieri
University of Foggia, Largo Papa Giovanni Paolo II, 71100 Foggia, Italy
e-mail: cesare.pozzi@unifg.it

A. R. Gurrieri
e-mail: antoniarosa.gurrieri@unifg.it

© The Editor(s) (if applicable) and The Author(s), under exclusive license to Springer
Nature Switzerland AG 2020
R. Agrifoglio et al. (eds.), *Digital Business Transformation*, Lecture Notes in Information
Systems and Organisation 38, https://doi.org/10.1007/978-3-030-47355-6_13

opportunities offered by technical progress, and a more genuine attention to the environmental problems identified a new way of producing in the changing world. Time after time, industries have experienced deep structural changes in the production organization; services have been more incorporated into final outputs, and the most significant driver of change—across all industries—is the changing nature of work itself. The manufacturing industries are currently moving from mass production to customized one, acknowledging a strategic competitive advantage to the talent of providing individually designed products and services to every customer through high process flexibility and integration. We are facing a new "industrial revolution", the Fourth Revolution (FIR), with a simultaneous radical change in the economic strategies and in the social roots of the society.

The "smart" factory, on which it is based the new paradigm, opens outward implementing new production models and exploiting sizes far superior to those known so far. The creation of a global supply chain allows sharing data, information and production systems not only within the single system, but networking several organizations in real time, reducing operational costs and increasing productivity. In this scenario, Industry 4.0 (I4.0) radically reshapes production and market models so far adopted, thanks to its flexibility in connecting worldwide via web not only machinery and plants but also products, workers and consumers.

Over the past two decades, the structural and technological change associated with the rapid progress in Information and Communication Technology (ICT) imposed a deep reconsideration of the theoretical foundations of production and exchange of the entire economic system. The increase in digitalization, the process of progressive globalization of value chains, and the arising interconnection of people and systems through the exchange of information in real time make the difference. It enforces to better define and evaluate the final effects on products, machines and procedures, and their capabilities to adapt them quickly to the new environment. Innovation, as the result of the integration of science and technology, is always more cross-sectoral, and has a simultaneous widespread effect on products, processes and methods to be used. It becomes to be much more invasive for economic operators, deeply changing the traditional relationship between producers and consumers.

Two features of the FIR are still remarkable: the rapid technological change, and the growth of inequalities. The final effects on the division of labour, in terms of employment and wages caused by the rapid advances and the raised reliance on technology, the expected productivity increases, and cost reductions are still uncertain [1, 2]. In the near future, if industrial policies will not be supported by ad hoc actions on the supply side of the economy (labour market), the gap between employment and productivity will increase, magnifying, but not recomposing, social inequalities [3].

I4.0 identifies the FIR, namely the automation of manufacturing production and the change in the labour market based on the digitization of robotics and automation, using ICT and intelligent production processes. Recently, the «Centre facilitant la recherche et l'innovation dans les organisations» (CEFRIO) suggested a more comprehensive definition, including a series of initiatives to improve processes, products and services that allow decentralized decisions based on real-time data acquisition [4]. Internet of Things (IoT), Industrial Internet, Smart Manufacturing and Cloud based Manufacturing are the key concepts of this construction. The machine-to-machine interaction associated to Internet opens the way for join-interfirm production systems that allow the design and control of the production chain all over the entire process.

The FIR involves a complex interconnection of the latter, starting from development and ending with distribution to after-sales services. Automation uses robots and smart technologies that move and develop through networking. However, the shift from a mechanical production to an "intelligent" one entails a potential loss of manual labour. Robots replace man, causing difficulties in skill-labour upgrading. It usually takes a long time and, potentially, drives to technological unemployment. The devices, and even the products themselves, have chips enclosing information on where/how/when they should be processed. As a result, archiving systems also send the order by themselves. The fast reorganization of cheaper and smaller production runs is a plus. Smart and customized products include a deep knowledge of the entire production process and of consumer applications, and independently lead their way through the supply chain. The purpose of the automation pyramid towards the controlling auto-systems manages to a great amount of extracted, visualized and used data.

The aim of this work is to investigate the impact of I4.0 on the manufacturing sector, focusing on Italian SMEs, and the effects of technology on work and organizations. Our research hypothesis is to investigate the relationship between production organization and the "new" power structure determined by I4.0, and its effectiveness on the economy. In a word, the «political economy of industry». What are the changes in the organization of production (agents-machines-organization)? What is the final effect on the social division of labour after the introduction of the FRI? Does it hurt the development of capitalism, as we know it today? Does it create a larger disparity between worker classes?

The paper is structured as follows. Section 2 gives an overview of the relevant literature on I4.0 paradigm. Section 3 offers some descriptive evidence on the effects of technology on work and organizational models with respect to SMEs. Section 4 presents the strategic benefits in terms of value creation associated to networking. Section 5 discusses the economic insights related to the transformation of organizational models in the labour market, while Sect. 6 concludes.

2   The Industry 4.0 Paradigm

The term I4.0 was introduced at the 2011 Hannover Messe, in Germany [5], and denotes the transformation of "traditional" industries by the IoT, data and services.[1] It relates to the FIR, which offers, in terms of industrial policy, very different characteristics related to the three previous revolutions. It is based on the production of cybernetic systems using heterogeneous data and knowledge integration, where its core is the ever-closer integration of digital technologies in manufacturing processes [6].

On the other hand, also the three industrial revolutions of the past were all triggered by fundamental technical changes: the introduction of water- and steam-powered mechanical manufacturing at the end of the eighteenth century, the division of labour at the beginning of the twentieth century, and the introduction of programmable logic controllers for automation purposes in manufacturing in the 1970s. They revealed to be a sequence between different forms of manufacturing "regimes" in the production organization they followed. The forth revolution is encouraged by the Internet, which allows communication between humans, as well as machines, controlled or monitored by computer-based algorithms throughout large networks.

The definition of I4.0 proposed by Kagermann et al. [7] is very promising: "a new level of value chain organization and management across the lifecycle of products". Applying the new paradigm, firms are willing to achieve a higher level of operational efficiency and productivity, as well as of automation, not only using Internet technologies and advanced algorithms, but also adding value and managing knowledge inside the production process. A major objective of this industrial strategy is the simultaneous integration, within a single network, of large and small firms, helping the latter to overcome the traditional lock-in access to new technologies.

Among the main pillars of I4.0 are digitization, optimization and customization of production, automation and adaptation, human-machine interaction (HMI), added value services and activities, automatic data exchange and communication. The theoretical foundations of I4.0 have the great advantage of scalability (Cloud Computing), which it makes possible to increase or decrease the use of resources, according to the production schemes. Other added value are interoperability, i.e. the ability of two systems to understand each other to use functionality of one another, virtualization, decentralization, real-time capacity, service orientation and modularity [8].

Although I4.0 produces value creation results, by gains in productivity and efficiency, developing "new" business models, it could have both, positive and negative effects, on employment and wages due to the disruptive outcome of the technological change on the labour market. Technological progress biased toward hi-specialization (or skill biased) can lead, at the same time, to a higher wealth effect on behalf of a low number of people, where substantially reducing the employment opportunities of others. Today, automation systems can easily replace repetitive jobs at a much lower cost per hour than a worker salary.

---

[1] The form of numbering (4.0) it uses, the same as for software release, emphasizes more both the high computer content, and the digital character of this revolution.

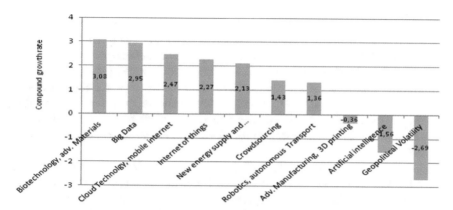

Fig. 1 Drivers of change-effect on employment. Compound growth rate (2015–2020), in %
Source Elaboration on World Economic Forum (2016)
Note The compound growth rate, real and estimated, shown on Y axis, shows the effects of the drivers of change on employment. Estimated employment effects have been converted into a compound growth rate, i.e. the mean growth rate over the specified period of time if employment had grown or declined at a steady rate, which is unlikely to be the pattern observed in reality. It can be thought of as a useful measure of growth over multiple time periods

Figure 1 shows active workers in the most innovative technological sectors.

At a first glance, it would seem that Big Data, mobile Internet, IoT and robotics have the potential to create "new" jobs. On the contrary, the negative value of geopolitical volatility risks being the greatest threat to job creation and employment itself. The negative values of artificial intelligence and 3D printing would be explained as the typical results of highly technological and competitive sectors, which, as such, require specific skills. The changes imposed by I4.0 could bring new employment opportunities and/or they result in a shift of retrained workers. Nowadays, the main challenge is "job restructuring", since some of the less skilled jobs will quickly disappear in the near future.

On the one hand, productivity gains achieved through the use of "smart" technologies can help to increase employment and the demand for consumers with additional income (compensation effect), whereas on the other hand the use of new technologies and production processes can also destroy jobs (redundancy effects). No systematic evidence exists whether the latter applied on I4.0 will prevail in the long term, leading to technological unemployment [5]. Moreover, even the digitalisation of business processes entails the automaticity of workers, whose added value will "create" new output and solutions. The digitalization also helps to determine changes in "traditional" business models, and introduces the "smart" economy as a way of generating value.

The I4.0 paradigm deals with:

1. *Supply chain and logistics*: technology and IoT, in particular, improve supply chain efficiency by providing more detailed and up-to-date information, mitigating the "bullwhip effect", reducing supply chain inefficiencies with adequate forecasts, and lessening copying due to product traceability [9];
2. *Security and privacy*: since all devices are wireless, they are highly exposed to information intrusion. The growing global networking increases the need to protect industrial systems, production lines, and plants from cyber-attacks. The data transfer and their storage in the cloud must not be subject to unauthorized access;
3. *Intelligent infrastructure*: "smart" devices improve flexibility, reliability and efficiency in infrastructure operations. Here, the added value is in terms of reduced operating costs and improved safety, and refers mainly to smart, cost-efficient, high capacity, user-friendly transportation infrastructures, smart cities, and intelligent mobility management;
4. *Healthcare*: sensors, integrated in domotics environment or smartphone applications, screen patients and send information to specialists. They are integrated in many different "things", and are able to generate and transmit "granular" information in real time through software and hardware technologies using Big Data and automatic systems, thus improving the quality and variety of the offer. The result is a positive network effects with increasing returns from data production, as in all markets where knowledge comes from them [10]. Big Data Analytics, for example, transform data into soft information in real time, which, applying automation and artificial intelligence techniques, favours decision-making [11].

The integration and real-time analysis of a huge amount of data will optimize resources in the production process, and enable better performances. The development of algorithms to manage data is one of the main challenges of I4.0, as the pervasive integration of ICT into production components always generates also larger, different data sets. By facilitating information and knowledge, the IoT improves the efficiency and effectiveness of knowledge development and management in I4.0. Therefore, manufacturers and retailers will not dominate production decisions. Instead, customers will be more involved in quality decisions and product customization. The disadvantages of heterogeneous data will compromise industrial development, but Big Data management (data mining, data classification and data storage) can help to mitigate the problem [12]. The use of artificial intelligence in production processes involves an innovation in terms of organizational culture. It increases creativity and result orientation. Moreover, Háša and Brunet-Thornton [13] argue that managerial innovation involves fast time-to-market approaches through the creation of intelligent, flexible and qualified production structures, suitable for overcoming risky and heterogeneous step-by-step markets. It is therefore essential to implement qualified strategies for human capital formation, so that not only the manager, but also the entire workforce will be competitive.[2]

---

[2]Schneider and Spieth [14] sustain that the innovation of business models is a relevant source of unique sales proposals and strategic differentiation in highly competitive market contexts.

3 The Industry 4.0 Action and the Small-Medium Enterprises

According to the traditional paradigm of the value creation process based on a strict good-dominant logic, large firms are more competitive in R&D capabilities and complementarities, therefore are able to outperform small firms. The in-house activities are the most important source of innovation that validates the existence of a lock in closed innovation model. The consumer-agent remains outside the enterprise and does not contribute to co-create new value for the manufactured output, tangible or intangible. However, over the past several decades, new perspectives have emerged that have a revised logic focused on intangible resources, the co-creation of value, and relationships. The globalization process with the opening to the outside world has its advantages. In a global market with a rapid circulation of knowledge flows, rich in venture capital and in massive labour mobility, firms could not indeed afford to innovate themselves. The service-dominant (S-D) logic becomes prominent due to the increasingly use of data-intensive technologies. As a result, open innovation systems arise [15].

A closed innovation model is based on innovations developed exclusively by firms themselves; it is costly and requires control. The innovation process is only settled within clearly defined company boundaries, as it is (and remains) an internal action where R&D investments are a strong entry barrier to outsider competition. When the innovation process opens up beyond company boundaries, from the generation of ideas to development and marketing, innovation arises through the interaction of internal and external ideas, taking advantages of the potential strategic use of the environment, technologies, processes and sales channels [16]. In both cases, the aim of the firm is the same: to develop promising innovative products, services or business models, in order to increase one's own innovation. It is an example of nice collaborative networking made by the integration of science and technology.[3]

In a global market with a rapid circulation of knowledge flows, abundant presence of venture capital and labour mobility, firms could not afford to innovate themselves. Gassmann [17], and subsequent theoretical papers, considers open innovations as fundamental, especially for management innovation; Lichtenthaler [18] recalls that the existence of a new paradigm for open innovation implies either technology exploitation, or technology acquisition. This is true for small firms too [19]. Networks are able to use outside knowledge for a specific need of internal network enterprises, without passing for the internal vertical integration. In this context, I4.0 could be crucial in SMEs development. I4.0 could be of help by improving the flow of information across the entire system, allowing better control and real time adaptability to the demand. However, despite the tools of I4.0 requiring large investments and a high level of competence [20], the decentralization of information and decision-making

---

[3] Among the determinants that leads to the open innovation logic, Chesbrough [16] clearly specifies the increasing mobility of workers and the division of labour. In the last decades, the technological success of several open source software, such as web applications and operating systems apps (Android and iOS), has played an important role in spreading open innovation culture.

would allow SMEs with a greater flexibility and competitive capacity, and a better managerial capabilities.

Finally, the conceptual paradigm of I4.0 can also be used to transform the nature of products and services provided by organizations. Porter and Heppelmann [21] explain how artificial intelligence change the current process control system, overcoming the traditional approach to production planning and control, and reaching different levels of performance. Setting simple monitoring tools help to reach the most complex goals. Since each level requires investments and specific skills, it is essential to classify I4.0 initiatives in terms of the desired goal to which a given management capacity corresponds. To this end, I4.0 initiatives for SMEs can be implemented through technological groups (Internet of objects, Big Data or Cloud Computing (CC)), in which each of them represents different means to implement the desired capacity [4].

In order to improve the instrumental skills of SMEs, a three-step process could be undertaken: monitoring (analysis of the decision-making process); control (use of algorithms for historical data analysis); optimization and autonomy (analysis of monitoring data and consequent autonomy of behaviour). Furthermore, since performance indicators are expression of corporate strategies, SMEs could improve their indicators (lower costs, better quality, greater flexibility and productivity, reduction in delivery times) resorting to technological investments [22].

One of the main goals of I4.0 is the synchronization of flows along the entire supply chain (flexibility). CC platforms should be used as collaboration structures between firms [23]. Bonfanti et al. [24] show that Italian artisan enterprises and small businesses who introduced and implemented new digital tools (e.g. 3D digital model) recorded a reduction in operational costs, and an increase in production demand. On the one hand, CC is widely used between SMEs (e.g. document sharing, servicing, collaboration, distributed production, and resource optimization). In practice, CC platforms introduce a new business culture, from corporate individuality to network sharing between partners, moving first from partner search, to risk sharing, to the CC platform at the end. There is evidence that Italian artisan firms use CC to offer products and services online, thus strengthening customer loyalty and providing access to new markets.

With respect to productivity, an increase could take place at the plant level, or at the level of calculation (algorithms) of the production plans forecasting internal flow disturbances and changes in customer requests, or calculating algorithms based on IoT data on a CC platform. Its use shortens design time, promotes collaboration between all network partners, and facilitates the synchronization of the entire production processes. Concerning the use of Big Data in I4.0, Ren et al. [23] suggest a CC platform dedicated to SMEs that exploits IoT data using MapReduce algorithms. However, due to the their traditional low investment in R&D, there are no successful cases for the planning or control of production processes through the use of these technologies which help to organize data. Simulation models for SMEs have also been proposed. Barenji et al. [25] present a method (Prometheus) to develop a software application for planning simulation, based on both dynamic demand, and production variations. Denkena et al. [26], on the contrary, start from the idea that most SMEs do not have reliable data to introduce the IoT and RFID technology to manage the flows and facilitate the implementation of Lean Manufacturing. Constantinescu et al. [27] develop the Just In Time Information Retrieval (JITIR) to eliminate the problem of excess data that flow into the IoT. In relation to CPS (Cyber physical systems), or complex systems that incorporate processing algorithms, the cases of applicability to SMEs are known. Givehchi et al. [28] refer that SMEs apply CPS for production planning and control, although the low level of their internal skills, and consequently the lack of ability to process complex algorithms, remains a constraint.

4 Network of SMEs in Industry 4.0

The network of legally independent organizations that share common skills in order to exploit a business opportunity are identified as virtual companies. Collaborative Manufacturing [29] and Collaborative Development Environments [30] are important for SMEs strategies since they increase flexibility. In a collaborative network, risks can be balanced and combined resources expand the range of perceivable market opportunities. The organization in networks amplifies the available capacities without the need for further investments. Therefore, firms in collaborative networks can adapt to volatile markets and reduce product life cycles with ease.

A strong coordination capacity is needed to aggregate spatially separate production processes and to integrate information (data) that comes from the different production sites. Clusters of SMEs, and networks in particular, manage to implement product and process innovation, resulting in "open winners", as the case of the industrial districts. The availability of product data throughout the network is essential for the global optimization of the production processes. The maintenance of the global competitive advantage occurs for the enterprises in collaborative networks, for the single unit through the maintenance of the basic competences, for the group through the externalization of other activities.

The key features of networks are generative knowledge and cognitive clusters (accessible from anywhere). However, in the era of I4.0, the operating chains that manage the multilocalized and interconnected transformation of intangible products and services could represent the key feature. If the more technological sectors seem to be able to cope well with the FRI, also the Italian manufacturing industry seems to organise itself to the transformation and innovations imposed by the markets. The creativity and flexibility of man will be an added value: therefore the study and analysis of systems for the valorisation of people in factories remains of great relevance. The new evolution will not only touch all industrial sectors, as it embraces transversal technologies, but it will have a strong impact on processes and products.

The main problem related to virtual networks is information sharing, as leaders/owners of SMEs do not share information they preserve [31]. Therefore, while, on one hand, information sharing can lead to innovation, on the other it could generate asymmetric action due to opportunistic behaviour (learning tenders), and higher coordination costs resulting from antagonisms and competition between firms.

Advanced visualization techniques of context-sensitive data via virtual reality can be used to illustrate information for effective collaboration. Local availability and understanding of global production data is essential for real-time intervention in a changing environment.

The idea of I4.0 is based on the concept of a modular enterprise that combines new business models for "smart" supply chain management. Thus, the importance of a flexible network of relationships consisting of autonomous, but interdependent, fragments of production within the organizational structure usually connected through ICT systems. For this reason, I4.0 seems to be a valid tool to activate processes of reindustrialisation and industrial competitiveness all around the world. It uses cyber-physical systems and dynamic production networks to create flexible and open value chains, as well as 3D printing, Big Data, IoT and the Internet of Services, which are all facilitators of intelligent production and logistics processes [7].

However, despite I4.0 points towards horizontal integration, value chains could develop complex and intertwined manufacturing networks, where supply chains could be fragmented [32]. Division would reduce barriers to entry for SMEs, and could lead to the creation of new business models. It calls for the Italian economy to recover from the slowdown and speed up. The production development cycle will lower its costs, reduce delivery times, the potential of 3D printer and manufacturing will increase; the spread of robots proceed at very high rates. From the growing diffusion of digital technologies, it is reasonable to expect significant network effects: companies will have to adapt their business models, above all, to manage the Big Data available.

The new I4.0 paradigm is a positive opportunity to globalization because it amplifies positive trends, making it possible to resort to suppliers (source of localization) and to share knowledge in manufacturing activities. Thus, it is the necessary link between man and machine, and the training and requalification of digital workers are the required step to compete. In addition, digital platforms are a strong means of cooperation among firms, which co-located SMEs can exploit to compete at a broader level. In this process, the role of policy makers and institutions is fundamental, since it should support the migration from a traditional way to do business to a "new" technological one.

5 The Industry 4.0 and the Labour Market

Along with FIR characteristics, one of great relevance is the convergence between industrial production technology and science, which allows entrepreneurs the opportunity to choose tools that are more suitable, i.e. those offered by their integration, to gain a better competitive position in the "new" value chains. Innovation, as the result of science and technology integration, is a crucial element for the development of the global industry.

Recently, the Italian Ministry of Economic Development, in order to spread I4.0 culture, identifies three different areas for policy actions. These are the scientific and technological strategy of culture innovation, promoting measures for supporting investments in human capital digitalization and in firms' innovation; the political perspective towards innovation, encouraging public incentives for supporting "I4.0 firms"; the perspective of business management towards digitalization, favouring innovation hubs, and high competence centres for the local dissemination of basic knowledge on I4.0 technologies. However, the applicability of I4.0 policies has many limits, such as the digital organizational form (agents-internal-work organization), the implementation of ad hoc policies, and the interaction between them.

The transformation of organizational models follows the growing fragmentation of production in several global value chains, where the single production process is the result of the convergence between the "real" world of manufacturing plants and the "virtual" world of IoT. Consequently, a system of goods and services suitable for I4.0 challenges should be flexible and adaptable to both, the external and internal environment. Inside the "black box", in a cyber-physical atmosphere, economic operators interact together and with a complex network of machines, physical goods, and digitalized devices. Entrepreneurs must manage the pre-existing organization and digitalization of markets in real time, and I4.0 tools embody the opportunity to adapt the firm's organizational system. A new (advanced) business model should reconsider both, the role of the individual agent in the digitalization, and the entire organizational structure. Products are not only gradually assembled along the production chain, like before, but using digital devices all means of production (workers, machines, network) can intercommunicate and specify detailed further steps of activities. "Technical" division of labour goes under stress.

Frey and Osborne [33] highlight some criteria to identify which jobs are exposed more than others to the risk of automation. These are routine (manual and cognitive tasks involving explicit rule-based activities) and non-routine (digital intensive) jobs and, following recent technological advances, digitalization is now spreading to non-routine extents. In this respect, because of the technological evolution, the effects on I4.0 labour division is very significant, and it is in large part related to the process of deskilling, especially if we consider the technologies adopted by Big Data and IoT.

Thanks to them, a wide range of non-routine cognitive tasks could be digitalized with a scalability of human labour. The continuous identification and resolution of digital problems, due to a fast technological progression, will lead to a growing specialization of digital work. The man-machine replacement can be limited by identifying elements that only the worker-man possesses, such as the ability to manipulate or assemble objects in a singular and non-automatic way (finger and manual dexterity), creative (ability to present clever ideas) and social intelligence (persuasion, assistance). In advanced manufacturing, machines can easily replace jobs that require routine and standardized tasks. Jobs losses are mainly due to inadequate skills of the workers, who are unable to keep up with the innovation rate of growth. In fact, on the one hand investments in education-digitalization are low but, on the other hand, the speed at which technical progress moves does not allow the demand for skill-labour to be able to adapt quickly.

In Italy, several reforms have been introduced in recent years (e.g., Jobs Act, 2014 for the labour market, La Buona Scuola, 2015 for education; school-work transition

Table 1 Italy. Firms' actions for facing the lack of I4.0 skills, 2017 (in %)

	Size classes in number of persons employed (%)				
	1–9	10–49	50–249	+250	Total[a]
New employees	11.1	33.7	50.7	55.7	17.7
Qualification of workers	37.2	60.1	69.0	78.8	43.6
External collaborations	35.9	42.1	47.7	43.3	37.7
No actions	32.0	10.8	5.7	3.2	26.2

Source Elaboration on Italian Ministry of Economic Development (2018, Table 4.10)
[a]In Table 1, the total exceeds 100% because the interviewed firms involved in the survey had the option of choosing more than one answer

projects, at regional level). In the period 2017–2020, thanks to I4.0, incentives for 13 billion Euros have been allocated to firms to be invested in technologies in order to qualify them with the high skills required. According to a survey of the Italian Ministry of Economic Development (IMED), a large number of firms used human capital training (43.6% of the answers), and preferred outsourcing solutions (37.7%) to overcome the obstacles in the application of I4.0 (Table 1).

Only less than one third of all responses (26.2%) provided by the firms confirmed that they have not yet implemented any corrective action, while a 17.7% of the respondent decided to hire new employees. Indeed, from a dimensional point of view, some substantial differences emerge. Larger firms are more reactive; they rely mainly on staff training and new employees, while micro and small ones, in addition to training, use relatively more services and external collaborations. The smaller firms (10–49 employees), accounting for less than 11% of the total, fail to take actions to solve positively the "digitalization problems"; instead, only 11.1% of the micros (1–9 employees) make new hires, while 32% choose not to take action.

Following the IMED survey, in 2017, the so-called "I4.0 firms", because of the adoption at least of one of the new technologies considered in FIR, cover only 8.4% of the entire population of active enterprises in industry, excluding construction, substantially differing from 86.9% representing the traditional firms that do not use new technologies and confirmed not to be intended to use it in the next three years. Data concern a well-structured, small but representative sample of 23,700 industry and service firms of different sizes distributed throughout the country. At regional level, I4.0 technology is more widespread in the Northern and Central Italy (in italics related data for these macroareas); Piedmont (11.8%), Veneto (11.7%), Trentino (10.9%) and Emilia Romagna (10.6%) stand out, both in 4.0 "smart manufacturing", and in firms that have planned to introduce 4.0 technological actions (Table 2).

On the other hand, the innovation of intelligent production systems faces limits due to the rapid migration of data, the integration of new systems in existing production facilities and databases (which already have very high entry costs). Concerning organization, the main problem is that intelligent systems based on decentralized and automated self-organization collide with the traditional organizational scheme of production, causing paradox of (organizational) inertia. SMEs with limited resources

Table 2 Italy. I4.0 technology disseminations by selected regions and macroareas (in italics) (%), 2017

Regions	Traditional firms	Traditional firms with planned I4.0 measures	I4.0 firms
Piedmont	81.8	6.4	11.8
Lombardy	86.1	4.2	9.7
Trentino A.A.	83.9	5.2	10.9
Veneto	80.5	7.8	11.7
Friuli V.G.	86.4	4.1	9.5
Northern Italy	*85.8*	*4.7*	*9.5*
Tuscany	92.1	3.3	4.3
Marche	89.5	3.5	7.0
Lazio	86.7	5.3	8.0
Central Italy	*89.5*	*3.8*	*6.5*
Abruzzi	89.4	3.7	6.9
Molise	88.3	3.0	8.7
Apulia	90.2	5.1	4.6
Calabria	88.3	4.8	6.8
Sicily	91.0	2.0	7.0
Southern Italy	*89.8*	*3.7*	*6.3*
Italy	*86.9*	*4.7*	*8.4*

Source Elaboration on Italian Ministry of Economic Development (2018, Table 4.2)

could fail in a "smart" factory perspective, but networking would allow sharing and/or training of the necessary skills. With respect to the geographical macro-areas, the South shows a higher proportion (89.8%) of traditional firms compared to a below country average of 85.8% in the North, with more than three points higher percentage (9.4%) due to the presence of I4.0 firms than in the South. Southern and Central Italy differ slightly from the North due to firms that have introduced I4.0 measures.

Technology, machines and algorithms complete human work in data and information processing, technically supporting humans for some complex assignments integrating numerous physical and manual tasks. Nowadays, the limit of machines and algorithms concerns some work activities with high communication and interaction. Therefore, where for some fields it is possible (Fig. 2: Information and data mining, job related information, technical activities performing, and so on) to foresee that in the near future machines and algorithms can increasingly replace human work, for others (Fig. 2: Administering, Managing and Advising), this substitution is not so easy. Some work tasks have thus far remained overwhelmingly human.

According to the World Economic Forum (WEF 2018) estimates, the information, processing and transmission of an organization's data and research activities will be performed by automation technology with a potential average increase (30%) of labour productivity in all sectors.

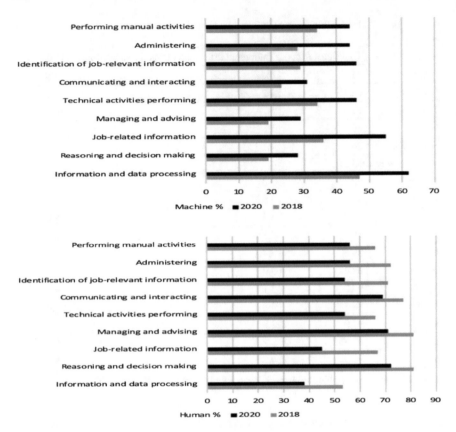

Fig. 2 Human/machine (hours worked)—projections %
Source Elaboration on World Economic Forum (2018)

Since I4.0 represents an opportunity for firms to compete at increasing speed, the challenge will consist in the ability to apply the 4.0 paradigm also to the intentional and decision-making processes of men. Although I4.0 may lead to a decrease in the employment levels of less qualified workers, higher skills can stimulate competition.

Big Data and algorithms could allow testing new products and services on customers anywhere in the world, customizing the company offer, reducing development costs, product launch and adaptation. The growth of digital platforms for product distribution (e.g., Amazon) can facilitate the entry of small businesses into global markets. On an institutional level, new internal and external structures must emerge that are suitable for the regulation of a more complex reality where, within the smart manufacturing, products, people and machines can be related via internet and interact simultaneously. The result, at the industrial policy level, is a reduction in organizational costs as integrated firms, since hierarchies are able to better control the production process at all levels thanks to the increasingly complete integration between science and technology.

Some interesting features arise from the analysis of WEF 2018 survey data. I4.0 disrupts as well as creates jobs for improving both, productivity and quality, of existing work of human employees. Figure 2 shows the projections of hours worked by man and machine in the period 2018–2020 explaining the potential of new technologies towards jobs innovation. At a first reading, data on human labour indicate a decrease in almost all the economic sectors. The most involved are Information and data processing, Job related information, Identification of job relevant information and Technical activities performing, and in general those which require a highly automation processes, where the presence of man can be easily partially replaced by the machine. On the contrary, the predominance of man over the machine would persist in the planning and strategic sectors (e.g. managing and advising; reasoning and decision making) where, despite an expected absolute decrease in human presence over the period, it is possible to believe that the complete machine-man substitution cannot take place as they are areas in which human abilities still act as a fly-wheel.

6 Conclusions

In the new competitive environment, I4.0 has been changed competition scheme, as the competitive phenomenon also extends to supply chains. Innovation and time, i.e. the frequency by which new or significantly updated product versions are introduced, denote the real competitive advantage, as they have an insightful effect on the life cycle of outputs, changing the firm production and organizational structure.

What are the major changes? When a firm uses I4.0 tools, it assumes that it is open to cultural changes, to operate new management strategies. Men and machines have an essential role in doing this. The acquired knowledge that represents the "social capital" of the firm, using Big Data and the IoT, is able to compete in a global perspective, in which the value chain of production changes radically. Consequently, smart firms will face a persistent increase in the knowledge content of outputs, strengthening the prominence of intangible assets in production. The main reasons lay in the increase in the extent of the market induced by globalization that pushes firms to boost the knowledge content of products, including more innovation, so to remodel them frequently and exploit new competitive advantages [34]. A consequence is the changes in the international economic scenario, which have gradually shifted the foundations of industrial competitiveness from a static to a dynamic cost competition that companies attempt to implement, improving their learning skills and creating knowledge faster than the competitors do.

Such an increasingly complex competitive setting has its origins in different phenomena such as market globalization, continuous socio-cultural changes, political-financial instability and the increasingly abrupt development of new technologies. These events are inevitably leading to a significant improvement in the ability of firms to innovate their production processes, goods and services, and to approach new markets in a new and unconventional way.

The division of labour will be still affected: the decrease of employees in manufacturing is likely to continue as machines will replace workers, and the remaining ones must be qualified to a higher level of education and capabilities in order to handle the new technologies. Unfortunately, many Italian firms, especially of medium-small size, are still vulnerable to face the new challenge and show a severe handicap compared to their foreign competitors. It seems they are far from understanding the ongoing culture according to which "smart" factory opens outward using new model and dimensions, superior to those previously known. The firm becomes an "open place" that looks to the future, closely connected to the territory, the research system, the entire community.

Skills gaps in human capital formation remain one of main problem of Italy, both with respect to workers and managers. This lack would accelerate in some cases the trends towards automation, but it also block the adoption of new technologies and, therefore, hinder business growth. A solution might be both investments in the formation of specific skills, suitable for worker recycling, and in favouring collaborative practices between small firms. The changes due to the introduction of new technologies aim to increase labour productivity in all sectors, in order to move competition among firms from the reduction of the labour cost to the ability of exploiting new technologies to integrate and improve human work. The traditional business models are under stress, and the technological progress open the opportunity for the firms to reduce working time and to grow and expand rapidly.

In order to spur innovation within emerging sectors fostering development, new industrial policies are needed: they will involve activities where knowledge networks are still weak and concern to the open question that technological and digital diffusion entails. Moreover, the FIR has bounded new paths in the mobility of workers and in the international division of labour. A further research direction that has not yet fully tested and explained might be the total effect on the labour market, since it is still persistent a deep heterogeneity and asymmetry in human capital formation among countries. The introduction of suitable strategies to favour new relationships between manufacturing and services following the theoretical scheme of S-D logic will play an important role, as well as strategies for a more complete international opening.

References

1. Arntz, M., Gregory, T., & Zierahn, U. (2016). *The risk of automation for jobs in OECD countries: A comparative analysis* (OECD Social, Employment and Migration Working Papers No 189). Paris: OECD Publishing.
2. Baldwin, R. (2016). *The great convergence: Information technology and the new globalization.* Cambridge: Harvard University Press.
3. Acemoglu, D., & Restrepo, P. (2018). The race between machine and man: Implications of technology for growth, factor shares, and employment. *American Economic Review, 108*(6), 1488–1542.
4. Danjou, C., Rivest, L., & Pellerin, R. (2016). *Industrie 4.0: des pistes pour aborder l'ère du numérique et de la connectivité [Industry 4.0: Paths to the Era of Digital and Connectivity].* CEFRIO.

5. Roblek, V., Mesko, M., & Krapez, A. (2016). A complex view of industry 4.0. *SAGE Open, 6*(2), 1–11.
6. Bianchi, P., & Labory, S. (2018). The political economy of industry. In I. Cardinale & R. Scazzieri (Eds.), *The Palgrave handbook of political economy* (pp. 1–36). London: Palgrave Macmillan.
7. Kagermann, H., Helbig, J., Hellinger, A., & Wahlster, W. (2013). *Recommendations for implementing the strategic initiative INDUSTRIE 4.0: Securing the future of german manufacturing industry* (Final Report of the Industrie 4.0 Working Group). Frankfurt: National Academy of Science and Engineering, Federal Ministry of Education and Research.
8. Schumacher, A., Erol, S., & Sihn, W. (2016). A maturity model for assessing industry 4.0 readiness and maturity of manufacturing enterprises. *Procedia CIRP, 52*, 161–166.
9. Flügel, C., & Gehrmann, V. (2009). Intelligent objects for the internet of things: Internet of things—Application of sensor networking logistic. In H. Gerhäuser, J. Hupp, C. Efstratiou, & J. Heppner (Eds.), *Constructing ambient intelligence, communications in computer and information science.* Berlin: Springer.
10. Pang, Z., Zhengb, L., Tianb, J., Walterc-Kao, S., Dubrovab, E., & Chen, Q. (2015). Design of a terminal solution for integration of in home health care devices and services towards the internet-of-things. *Enterprise Information Systems, 9*, 86–116.
11. Quaglione, D., & Pozzi, C. (2018). Big data economics: The features of the ongoing debate and some policy remarks. *L'industria, Rivista di Economia e Politica Industriale, 34*(1), 3–16.
12. Morelli, G., & Spagnoli, F. (2017). Creative industries and big data: A business model for service innovation. In S. Za, M. Dragoicea, & M. Cavallari (Eds.), *Exploring services science.* Berlin: Springer.
13. Háša, S., & Brunet-Thornton, R. (Eds.). (2017). *Impact of organizational trauma on workplace behaviour and performance.* Hershey: IGI Global.
14. Schneider, S., & Spieth, P. (2013). Business model innovation: Towards an integrated future research agenda. *International Journal of Innovation Management, 17*(01), 15–27.
15. Bellini, F., & D'Ascenzo, F. (2018). L'evoluzione dei modelli di produzione nella logica della co-creazione di valore. In F. D'Ascenzo & F. Bellini (Eds.), *Produzione, Logistica e Trasformazione Digitale.* Padova: CEDAM.
16. Chesbrough, H. (2003). The era of open innovation. *MIT Sloan Management Review, 4*(33), 35–41.
17. Gassmann, O. (2006). Opening up the innovation process: Towards an agenda. *R&D Management, 36*(3), 223–228.
18. Lichtenthaler, U. (2008). Open innovation in practice: An analysis of strategic approaches to technology transactions. *IEEE Transactions on Engineering Management, 55*(1), 148–157.
19. Lecocq, X., & Demil, B. (2006). Strategizing industry structure: The case of open systems in low-tech industry. *Strategic Management Journal, 27*, 891–898.
20. Ruessmann, M., Lorenz, M., Gerbert, P., Waldner, M., Justus, J., Engel, P., & Harnisch, M. (2015). *Industry 4.0: The future of productivity and growth in manufacturing industries* (Vol. 9). Boston: Boston Consulting Group.
21. Porter, M., & Heppelmann, J. E. (2014). How smart, connected products are transforming competition. *Harvard Business Review, 92*, 64–88.
22. Raymond, L. (2005). Operations management and advanced manufacturing technologies in SMEs. *Journal of Manufacturing Technology Management, 16*, 936–955.
23. Ren, L., Zhang, L., Tao, F., Zhao, C., Chai, X., & Zhao, X. (2015). Cloud manufacturing: From concept to practice. *Enterprise Information Systems, 9*, 186–209.
24. Bonfanti, A., Del Giudice, M., & Papa, A. (2018). Italian craft firms between digital manufacturing, open innovation, and servitization. *Journal of the Knowledge Economy, 9*(1), 136–149.
25. Barenji, A. V., Barenji, R. V., Roudi, D., & Hashemipour, M. (2017). A dynamic multi-agent-based scheduling approach for SMEs. *The International Journal of Advanced Manufacturing Technology, 89*(9–12), 3123–3137.

26. Denkena, B., Schmidt, J., & Krüger, M. (2014). Data mining approach for knowledge-based process planning. *Procedia Technology, 15,* 406–415.
27. Constantinescu, C., Mattoo, A., & Ruta, M. (2015). *The global trade slowdown. Critical or structural?* (Policy Research Working Paper 7158). World Bank Group.
28. Givehchi, M., Haghighi, A., & Wang, L. (2015). Generic machining process sequencing through a revised enriched machining feature concept. *Journal of Manufacturing Systems, 37,* 564–575.
29. Lin, H. W., Nagalingam, S. V., Kuik, S. S., & Murata, T. (2012). Design of a global decision support system for a manufacturing SME: Towards participating in collaborative manufacturing. *International Journal of Production Economics, 136*(1), 1–12.
30. Mendikoa, I., Sorli, M., Barbero, J. I., Carrillo, A., & Gorostiza, A. (2008). Collaborative product design and manufacturing with inventive approaches. *International Journal of Production Research, 46*(9), 2333–2344.
31. Msanjila, S. S., & Afsarmanesh, H. (2008). Trust analysis and assessment in virtual organization breeding environments. *International Journal Production Research, 46*(5), 1253–1295.
32. Dujin, A., Geissler, C., & Horstkötter, D. (2014). *INDUSTRY 4.0: The new industrial revolution.* Munich: Roland Berger Strategy Consultants.
33. Frey, C. B., & Osborne, M. (2017). The future of employment: How susceptible are jobs to computerisation? *Technological Forecasting and Social Change, 114,* 254–280.
34. Bianchi, P., & Labory, S. (2018). *Industrial policy for the manufacturing revolution.* Cheltenham: Edward Elgar Publishers.

Managing Online Communities and E-WOM: Prosumers' Characteristics and Behaviors in the Food Service Sector

Claudia Dossena and Francesca Mochi

Abstract Nowadays having a good online corporate reputation is a valuable resource for organizations, especially in the food and beverage service sector. Potential diners frequently rely on people's opinions shared online in choosing a new restaurant. In so doing, online communities are gaining increasing importance in influencing the customer journey. This research aims to better understand the prosumers' use of social media (i.e. people that are both consumers and social media users and that contribute to create digital contents) in choosing a restaurant and reviewing it online. In particular, we want to investigate if prosumers' characteristics or habits, can influence their use and perception of social media, such as looking for information, writing feedbacks, and trust online reviews. In this paper we will focus on two main prosumers' characteristics or habits: the frequency of going to a restaurant and the willingness to try new restaurants. Our main findings suggest that prosumers that frequently go to a restaurant have a different approach to social media being more inclined to used them both for gathering information and for reviewing their experience. Similarly, we find that prosumers that have an "explorative" behavior (i.e. enjoy to frequently try new restaurants), use social media differently from prosumers that have a "loyal" behavior, i.e. that choose the same and familiar restaurant. In this explorative study we adopted a quantitative methodology by using a survey on 315 Millennials prosumers. Theoretical and managerial implications are also developed.

Keywords Prosumers · Social media platforms · Food service sector · Online reputation · Online attractiveness

C. Dossena (✉) · F. Mochi
Università Cattolica del Sacro Cuore, Milan 20123, Italy
e-mail: claudia.dossena@unicatt.it

F. Mochi
e-mail: francesca.mochi@unicatt.it

R. Agrifoglio et al. (eds.), *Digital Business Transformation*, Lecture Notes in Information Systems and Organisation 38, https://doi.org/10.1007/978-3-030-47355-6_14

205

1   Introduction

Social media platforms provide extensive opportunities for consumers to share online their evaluations about organizations, their products and/or services. In recent years, an increasing number of opinion platforms, that offer consumers' online reviews and ratings, have been introduced. Opinion websites and social media platforms allowed the arise of online communities in which users can spread their opinions and have access to other people reviews (e.g. [1]), thus having a profound effect on consumers' purchase decisions and behaviors.

Social media's bi-directional communication characteristic develops large-scale word-of-mouth (WOM) networks in online environments (e-WOM). Online reputation mechanisms allow the members of a community to submit their opinions, thus influencing online corporate reputation. Online communities related to social media are now available for many categories of products, including hotels, restaurants, books, electronic goods, and games. In particular, for restaurants online communities are channels that connect potential diners with many other diners. Numerous web sources enable users to easily spread their reviews and share their experiences online, such as opinion platforms (e.g. TripAdvisor), social networks (e.g. Facebook) and Google Reviews. In this way, everybody can access user-generated reviews even more easily than in the past.

Online communities evolve during time and co-evolve with the daily contributions of users, thus constantly changing. In this sense consumers are now defined as prosumers (i.e. people that are both consumers and users and that are co-creator of contents [2]). This aspect and the widespread of e-WOM, highlight the relevance of an effective online community management and the awareness that social media are now essentials tools for business [3, 4].

Currently, some authors have investigated the e-WOM phenomenon, the content of reviews, their credibility and trustworthiness in the hospitality industry (e.g. [2, 5]). However, to our knowledge only few works focused on the food service sector (e.g. [3]). Moreover, in literature there is a lack of studies that focus on users' profiles, their characteristics and online behaviors.

This research aims to better understand the prosumers' use of social media such as choosing a restaurant and/or reviewing it online. In particular, we want to investigate if prosumers' features or habits, such as frequency of going to a restaurant, or willingness to try new restaurants can influence their use and perception of social media, such as looking for information, writing feedbacks, and trust online reviews.

The study is explorative, thus the methodology that we used is an explorative survey to assess the main topics of interest concerning prosumers' behaviors in searching for restaurants and rating their experience, especially considering the use of social media and digital devices.

2   Theoretical Framework

Researchers noted that consumers are becoming "hyper-digital", using connected devices every day or multiple times a day. As a consequence of the massive use of mobile devices for gaining information and giving feedbacks, the literature shows that digital tools replace human contacts with technological interactions, from the information research stage through booking a place at a restaurant to give a feedback about the experience [6].

Before the advent of social media, word of mouth (WOM) was the most useful tool for marketing research and the most influential source for information exchange [4]. Furthermore, previous researchers noted that in the hospitality sector and especially in the food service one, consumers mainly trust the WOM [3]. WOM is the transfer of information from one customer to another in a way that has the potential to change their preferences, purchase behavior, and interaction with each other [3, 7]. However, nowadays the e-WOM is even more used as a method to reach information.

e-WOM is defined as "any positive or negative statement made by potential, actual, or former customers about a product or company, which is made available to a multitude of people and institutions via the Internet" [8, p. 39]. e-WOM takes place in a more complex technologically mediated context whereas traditional WOM occurs normally in a face-to-face fashion, with participants in close proximity [9]. Unlike traditional WOM, e-WOM spreads more widely and rapidly due to e-WOM's unique characteristics. In particular, e-WOM is directed at multiple individuals, is anonymous and is available at any time [6]. Consequently, the potential impact of e-WOM on customers' decision-making processes can be more powerful than the impact of traditional WOM [10].

Although there is still a lack in literature in investigating e-WOM concerning restaurants, there is an increasing consumer reliance on e-WOM when choosing a restaurant [3, 11].

Websites and social media allow users to be influenced by the e-WOM about the restaurant choice [12, 13]. Those tools have completely reshaped the hospitality industry scenario and changed the sources customers use/trust to search for hotels, locate restaurants, place orders, make reservations, plan trips and share experiences [14].

Unlike traditional forms of communication (i.e. TV, newspaper, advertisement on street) communication through social media is bi-directional: consumers are not only receivers of information, but they are active participants in content and information creation, opinion sharing, e-WOM creation and co-creator of value for the restaurant [12]. In effect, previous research considers them as "prosumers" (combining the words "producer" and "consumers") thus describing the consumers' ability to openly share their product/service experiences [2]. The prosumers' co-creation of content and sharing of experiences affect the brand-image of the restaurants [15] and influence other prosumers' behaviors.

Previous research considers the use of different social media platforms such as Facebook, TripAdvisor, Yelp, etc. In particular, Facebook and TripAdvisor are the social media that seemed more used by customers when choosing the hotel [16, 17], however we still do not know the prosumers' preferences concerning the food service sector. In the food service literature there are some studies that investigate how different social media are able to make big data analytics useful both for the customers and the restaurant managers [18], however only few contributions investigate which are the main social media platforms used by prosumers and how they impact their consumption behaviors.

Researchers also start to investigate the content of reviews, their credibility and trustworthiness. To quantify the credibility of reviewers, [19] we consider two key dimensions: expertise and trustworthiness of the reviewers, which can be extracted from reviewers' contribution histories and number of helpful votes [20]. Previous research shows that positive and negative reviews are perceived differently in the level of trustworthiness: negative reviews are usually perceived as more reliable than positive ones [21]. However, at the stage of evaluating the gathered information, people perceive as more important the negative information they have gained about the products and services and consider them more meticulously than positive information [22, 23]. Customers may attach more importance to negative information in order to be prepared in advance for certain negative characteristics of the purchased products and services.

Previous managerial literature informed us about certain prosumers' behaviors such as searching information on particular social media platforms (e.g. Facebook and TripAdvisor) [18] or rely more on negative comments and reviews than on positive ones [21, 23]. However, at the best of our knowledge, literature does not consider the influence of prosumers' characteristics and the impact on their choices and behaviors. In particular, we are interested in exploring if people that frequently goes to the restaurant have a different approach to social media being more inclined to use them both for gathering information and for reviewing their experience. Similarly, we want to analyze if prosumers that have an "explorative" behavior (i.e. enjoy to frequently try new restaurants), use social media differently from prosumers that have a "loyal" behavior, i.e. that choose the same and familiar restaurants. Indeed, previous research shows that restaurants can strategically engage "loyal users" and convert them to advocates and serve as "hubs" for users who trust friends' recommendations [12].

Our paper is thus exploratory and aims at understanding if there are some characteristics or habits that can influence prosumers' behavior and choices and how this can impact the restaurants owners and other prosumers.

3 Methodology

The aim of the study is explorative, thus the methodology that we used is an explorative survey to assess the main topics of interest concerning prosumers' characteristics and behaviors in searching information about new restaurants and rating their experiences.

The overall sample was composed by Millennials (minimum 18 years old, maximum 20 years old, mean age 19 years old). The millennial generation is generally defined as those born between 1981 and 2000 [24] and is reported to be more technologically advanced than the previous generations [25]. Millennials have always known and been immersed in technology [26] and within the generally accepted millennial age cohort has now emerged the 'Generation C', formed by those born after 1990. These Generation C consumers were born into a digital world and, as such, are frequently referred to as digital natives [27] and they love content creation, form active communities rather than remain passive, and they gravitate toward social media sites where they can participate in discussions about different ideas and products

Bowen and McCain [28] reported that Millennials share their personal experiences with products and learned from others' reviews through social media. For Millennials, social media are a mean to connect to each other, as they crave social interaction and want to share everything [29]. Furthermore, Millennials are replacing baby boomers as the major travel and food consumers segment [30]. At least in the US, a large portion of Millennials' expenditure is primarily spent in the restaurant industry, they eat out an average of 3.39 times per week, and the frequency is almost twice that of the rest of the population [31]. Moreover, Millennials treat dining out as a social event, and meeting for food and beverage is one of the most common ways to spend time with friends and relatives [32]. For all those reasons, they seem to represent the adequate sample for exploring the use of social media in the food service industry.

The questionnaire was spread among 380 Millennials that were homogeneous in age and background. In effect they all are studying at the same Italian University and at the same bachelor course (economics), furthermore they were homogeneous in wealth, habits and they live in the same area (Milan). Among those 380, the respondents were 315 students. 55% of them were female.

In the first analysis, in order to reveal Millennials' behaviors and preferences, we divided the sample into groups to reveal if there are some prosumers' characteristics or habits that can influence their use and perception of social media platforms in the food service sector. At first, we consider the Millennials' tendency to go to a restaurant as a multi-categorical independent variable that split our sample in 4 groups thus allowing us to run ANOVAs. The first group (participants never go to a restaurant) is actually not present in the results as no one has declared that. We thus remain with only 3 groups: the second group (participants rarely go to a restaurant), the third (participants often go to a restaurant) and last one (participants always/every day go to a restaurant) (Fig. 1).

Our dependent variables concern the mean of research of information about a restaurant, the check for the reliability of online reviews, the online comparison of their restaurant experience with those made by other prosumers, the willingness to write a review after being at the restaurant and the use of smartphones and app to make a reservation or to order with a delivery service. All those variables are single item variables and we used a 4-point Likert scale in order to avoid the mid-point category thus forcing the indifferent respondents to make a choice and, as the sample is made by students, to avoid their desire to please the interviewers or appear helpful

Fig. 1 Groups according to the frequency of going to a restaurant

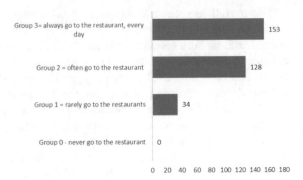

or not be seen to give what they perceive to be a socially unacceptable answer (for discussion about the Likert scale points see [33, 34]).

In the second analysis, we divided the sample in 4 groups depending on their willingness to try new restaurants, the first group is composed by Millennials that do not want to try new restaurants, but trust the few that they already know (we will call them the "loyal" prosumers), while the fourth group is composed by Millennials that always want to change the restaurant and try new ones (we will call them the "explorer" prosumers) (Fig. 2).

The single items dependent variables used a 4-points Likert scale and concern the mean of research of information about restaurants, the willingness to read positive and negative comments to understand the restaurant strength and weaknesses, the willingness to move with cars (30 km) to try a restaurant with good online reviews, the tendency to compare the experience with those made by others, the willingness to write a review and to use social media for making a reservation and ordering food delivery.

Fig. 2 Groups according to the tendency to try new restaurants

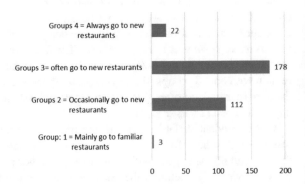

4 Results and Discussion

First of all, from our descriptive statistics, we found that 92.4% of our sample use Internet to search information at least once a day, so they are all proficient in using the web. Furthermore, 96.2% of our sample use the mobile device to search information about restaurants, thus confirming the literature about the relentlessly trend of use mobile devices for searching information that overcome the use of laptop and PC [6].

In the first analysis the sample was divided in 4 groups depending on the frequency of going to the restaurant (form never to always/every day), however, as stated before, no one responded "never", thus the results that we present show only 3 groups.

We ran multiple one-ways ANOVAs in order to explore our data (Table 1).

Table 1 Prosumers' behavior comparison depending on their frequency of going to a restaurant

Dependent variables	Groups	Mean	Standard deviation	Significance
Search for information on FB	1	1.41	0.701	0.021
	2	1.84	0.818	
	3	1.80	0.830	
Search for information on specialistic blogs	1	1.53	0.788	0.009
	2	1.64	0.791	
	3	1.91	0.920	
Search for information on restaurant website	1	2.56	0.824	0.170
	2	2.83	0.814	
	3	2.87	0.923	
Search for information on comparison platforms (e.g. TripAdvisor, the Fork)	1	2.91	1.083	0.218
	2	3.16	0.811	
	3	3.19	0.817	
Check for the reliability of online reviews	1	1.91	1.311	0.05
	2	2.50	1.363	
	3	2.50	1.328	
Comparing experience online after being in a restaurant	1	1.29	0.462	0.042
	2	1.54	0.698	
	3	1.63	0.825	
Write a review after being in a restaurant	1	1.29	0.579	0.026
	2	1.66	0.724	
	3	1.63	0.742	
Use social media to make a reservation	1	1.91	0.866	0.042
	2	2.10	0.877	
	3	2.29	0.886	
Use social media for food delivery	1	1.82	0.834	0.000
	2	2.07	0.871	
	3	2.44	0.924	

$N = 315$; Groups: 1 = rarely go to the restaurant ($n = 34$), 2 = often go to the restaurant ($n = 128$) 3 = always go to the restaurant, every day ($n = 153$)

ANOVAs results show us that prosumers in our sample mainly use Facebook (p-value $= 0.021$) and specialistic blogs (p-value $= 0.009$) to search for information about a restaurant, however we have found non-significant the use of restaurant website and comparison platforms such as TripAdvisor and the Fork. Probably for those social media platforms the differences in mean among the groups are non-significant, i.e. they all use those social in a similar way and frequency. Those results partially contrasted with the literature that assessed that both Facebook and TripAdvisor were the most used platforms in the hospitality industry [16, 17, 35]. Results also show that the more you are inclined to go to the restaurant the more you rely on social media as information tool as the significant means differences among groups can show. Results on Table 1 show that people that have a higher score in going to restaurants for lunch or dinner (group 2 and 3), have a higher mean score in checking the reliability of online reviews (p-value $= 0.05$). Therefore, prosumers that frequently go to a restaurant significantly exploit online opinions but also have a more careful approach in trusting online reviews. Furthermore they are more willing to compare their experience with the reviews of others after having lunch or dinner (p-value $= 0.042$), i.e. their 'online experience' is not limited to the phase before the dinner (to search information) but it keeps on also after having dinner, in order to confirm their opinions. Similarly, those people are also the ones that more frequently write a review after their experience at the restaurant (p-value $= 0.026$). Lastly, the results show that the more the prosumers go to restaurants the more they use social media not only for acquiring information and write reviews, but also to make reservation (p-value $= 0042$) and to exploit the food delivery options (p-value $= 0.000$).

From these results we can infer that prosumers that frequently go to the restaurant, strongly rely on information found on social media platforms and e-WOM as their decision will influence not only an occasional night, but probably every day since they often or always go to restaurant. They are also prone to exploit social media in an active way for various purposes such as sharing their experience or use them to reserve a table.

Starting from these results, we deepened our investigation by dividing the sample in a different way. As the previous results show us that the people who frequently go at restaurants are also those that are more proactive on social media, we decided to compare the behaviors of people that frequently change restaurant (the explorer ones) with people that are not so willing to change (the loyal ones). We run a series of one-way ANOVAs where the independent variable is multi-categorical and composed by 4 groups depending on the participants' frequency of trying new restaurants (Table 2). Therefore, the sample were divided in 4 groups, from $1 =$ almost never change the restaurant, to $4 =$ almost always change the restaurant. This distribution of the sample allows us to understand and compare the behaviors of the people that are very loyal to a single or few restaurants with those that always want to change the choice of the restaurant and are prone to try new ones.

First of all, as shown in Table 2, we again found the significance of searching information about a restaurant on specialistic blogs (p-value $= 0.043$) as well as on general blogs (p-value $= 0.033$), the search on other social media was found

Table 2 Prosumers' behavior comparison depending on their frequency of trying new restaurants

Dependent variables	Groups	Mean	Standard deviation	Significance
Search for information on specialistic blogs	1	2.00	1.732	0.043
	2	1.68	0.830	
	3	1.75	0.856	
	4	2.23	0.922	
Search for information on non-specialistic blogs	1	2.33	1.528	0.033
	2	1.44	0.695	
	3	1.52	0.730	
	4	2.27	1.120	
Search for information on comparison platforms (e.g. TripAdvisor, the Fork)	1	2.33	1.528	0.204
	2	3.07	0.856	
	3	3.21	0.828	
	4	3.18	0.853	
Search for information on social media (e.g. Facebook)	1	2.00	1.732	0.108
	2	1.64	0.781	
	3	1.82	0.789	
	4	2.05	1.046	
Read positive comments to understand the restaurant strengths	1	2.00	1.00	0.045
	2	3.31	1.014	
	3	3.32	1.065	
	4	3.73	1.985	
Read negative comments to understand the restaurant weaknesses	1	2.00	1.00	0.043
	2	3.50	1.930	
	3	3.60	1.117	
	4	3.86	1.082	
Willing to move 30 km to eat in a restaurant with good reviews	1	1.67	1.155	0.013
	2	2.39	1.211	
	3	2.58	1.305	
	4	3.52	1.555	
Comparing experience online after being in a restaurant	1	2.00	1.732	0.000
	2	1.33	0.566	
	3	1.65	0.784	
	4	1.95	0.844	
Write a review after being in a restaurant	1	2.00	1.732	0.000
	2	1.38	0.587	
	3	1.70	0.719	
	4	2.00	0.926	
Use social media to make a reservation	1	1.33	0.577	0.000
	2	1.90	0.859	
	3	2.28	0.857	
	4	2.77	0.813	

(continued)

Table 2 (continued)

Dependent variables	Groups	Mean	Standard deviation	Significance
Use social media for food delivery	1	1.67	0.577	0.009
	2	2.01	0.865	
	3	2.34	0.920	
	4	2.45	1.011	

$N = 315$; Groups: 1 = Mainly go to familiar restaurants ($n = 3$), 2 = Occasionally go to new restaurants ($n = 112$), 3 = often go to new restaurants ($n = 178$), 4 = Always go to new restaurants ($n = 22$)

not significant probably because every group use other social media (Facebook, TripAdvisor, Google Review) at a similar intensity.

However, we found significant differences in means among groups concerning the attention to positive and negative comments and reviews. It seems that the more you are willing to change restaurants and try new ones, the more is the attention towards both positive comments (p-value = 0.045) and negative ones (p-value = 0.043). Positive comments are read in order to understand the strengths of a restaurant, while negative ones are taken into count in order to understand the weaknesses of the restaurant. This is partially in contradiction with previous literature that stated that negative reviews are the most taken into count and perceived as reliable [21].

Furthermore, the more the people assume an "explorative" behavior, always trying new restaurants, the more they are prone to go far away (at least 30 km) in order to reach restaurants that have very good reviews (p-value = 0.013). In this case the differences in means among groups are very strong showing an exponential increasing of the willingness to go far for those that always want to try new restaurants (mean = 3.52) particularly if compared with those that prefer the familiar ones (mean = 1.67).

Results show that participants that love to change restaurants and those that trust only few well known one share a similar behavior as they both compare, post consumption, their experience with those shared online by other users by looking at reviews or comments (p-value = 0.000, mean group 1 = 2.00; mean group 4 = 1.95) even more than the groups with preferences in between (mean group 2 = 1.33; mean group 3 = 1.65).

The results show similar conclusions about writing online reviews. The ones that write the most are those that are loyal to few restaurants (mean group 1 = 2.00), probably they post positive reviews to promote the restaurant they love, and those that always change their restaurant choice (mean group 4 = 2.00; p-value = 0.000).

Lastly, again, it seems that the more you are an "explorer" of restaurants the more you use social media to make a reservation (p-value = 0.000) or to use the food delivery option (p-value = 0.009).

5 Conclusions

5.1 Theoretical and Managerial Implications

Our research tries to develop two different literature, the social media literature by considering social media platforms and online communities, and hospitality industry literature, especially the food and beverage service sector, by considering the prosumers' behavior in choosing a restaurant and reviewing it. Furthermore, the paper aims at investigating how prosumers' characteristics or habits, i.e. the frequency of going to a restaurant and of being prone to change restaurants, can impact the use of social media platforms. Thus, also e-marketing literature can benefit from our explorative study since it opens up a new debate on the prosumers' profile.

The study, even if exploratory, can give some interesting suggestions also to practitioners. Firstly, restaurant managers have to be aware that there are some prosumers' characteristics or habits that influence their use of social media. For instance, restaurant managers should be aware that Facebook and specialistic blogs are social media mainly used by prosumers that frequently go to the restaurant. Moreover, those people that frequently go to the restaurant are prone to check the reliability of reviews and also after the experience at the restaurant they tend to compare their experience with those of the others by re-screening the reviews. This means that people that frequently go to the restaurants, and that probably are those more valuable for restaurant managers, are also those that are more careful in checking comments and reviews and that re-think and re-evaluate the restaurant experience even after the lunch or dinner is over. Similarly, those people are the ones that actively use social media platforms and also use them as a tool for simplifying their lives by using online reservation apps or food delivery options thus evaluating those services tools and expecting them from a restaurant. Lastly, restaurant managers should consider that loyal customers and the "explorer" ones can perceive and use social media in different ways. The explorer ones are more prone to consider both positive and negative comments and are willing to choose a restaurant that is far away if it has very good online reviews. They are also those that are more active in using online reservation tools and food delivery. However, the two groups (loyal and explorer) can also show behaviors similarities, as they both are really inclined to write reviews and to re-examine online comments after being at the restaurants. Restaurants can strategically engage "loyal users" and convert them to advocates and serve them as "hubs" for users who trust friends' recommendations [12].

5.2 Limitations and Future Research

Our study presents some limitations, first of all the sample is composed only by students, it could be interesting to develop the same study but with a less homogeneous sample in order to understand if differences in age, digital literacy, past experience can influence the use of social media in terms of information research, trust in reviews, writing of comments.

Furthermore, our research only considers few prosumers' habits or characteristics (i.e. frequency of going to a restaurant and willingness to change the restaurant), but future research can consider other prosumers' characteristics, also by involving personal traits (e.g. openness to experience, extraversion) or competencies (e.g. digital skills, communication skills).

Lastly, future research can also investigate not only the prosumers' perspective but also the influence of prosumers' behaviors on restaurant managers.

References

1. Breazeale, M. (2009). Word of mouse: An assessment of electronic word-of-mouth research. *International Journal of Market Research, 51*(3), 297–318.
2. Fine, M. B., Gironda, J., & Petrescu, M. (2017). Prosumer motivations for electronic word-of mouth communication behaviors. *Journal of Hospitality and Tourism Technology, 8*(2), 280–295.
3. Fox, G., & Longart, P. (2016). Electronic word-of-mouth: Successful communication strategies for restaurants. *Tourism and Hospitality Management, 22*(2), 211–223.
4. Hussain, S., Guangju, W., Jafar, R. M. S., Ilyas, Z., Mustafa, G., & Jianzhou, Y. (2018). Consumers' online information adoption behavior: Motives and antecedents of electronic word of mouth communications. *Computers in Human Behavior, 80,* 22–32.
5. Cheung, C. M., & Lee, M. K. (2012). What drives consumers to spread electronic word of mouth in online consumer-opinion platforms. *Decision Support Systems, 53*(1), 218–225.
6. Litvin, S. W., Goldsmith, R. E., & Pan, B. (2018). A retrospective view of electronic word-of-mouth in hospitality and tourism management. *International Journal of Contemporary Hospitality Management, 30*(1), 313–325.
7. Libai, B., Bolton, R., Bugel, M., Ruyter, K., Gotz, O., Risselada, H., et al. (2010). Customer-to-customer interactions: Broadening the scope of word of mouth research. *Journal of Service Research, 13*(3), 267–281.
8. Hennig-Thurau, T., Gwinner, K. P., Walsh, G., & Gremler, D. D. (2004). Electronic word-of-mouth via consumer-opinion platforms: What motivates consumers to articulate themselves on the internet? *Journal of Interactive Marketing, 18*(1), 38–52.
9. King, R. A., Racherla, P., & Bush, V. D. (2014). What we know and don't know about online word-of-mouth: A review and synthesis of the literature. *Journal of Interactive Marketing, 28*(3), 167–183.
10. Jeong, E., & Jang, S. S. (2011). Restaurant experiences triggering positive electronic word-of-mouth (eWOM) motivations. *International Journal of Hospitality Management, 30*(2), 356–366.
11. Obal, M., Burtch, G., & Kunz, W. (2011). How can social networking sites help us? The role of online weak ties in the IMC mix. *International Journal of Integrated Marketing Communications, 3*(2), 33–47.
12. Ghiselli, R., & Ma, J. (2015). Restaurant social media usage in China: A study of industry practices and consumer preferences. *Worldwide Hospitality and Tourism Themes, 7*(3), 251–265.
13. Gregory, S., & Kim, J. (2004). Restaurant choice. *Journal of Foodservice Business Research, 7*(1), 81–95.
14. Sigala, M., Christou, E., & Gretzel, U. (Eds.). (2012). *Social media in travel, tourism and hospitality: Theory, practice and cases.* Ltd: Ashgate Publishing.

15. Siuda, P., & Troszynski, M. (2017). Natives and tourists of prosumer capitalism: On the varied pro-prosumer activities of producers exemplified in the Polish pop culture industry. *International Journal of Cultural Studies, 20*(5), 545–563.
16. Jeacle, I., & Carter, C. (2011). In TripAdvisor we trust: Rankings, calculative regimes and abstract systems. *Accounting, Organizations and Society, 36*(4), 293–309.
17. Scott, S. V., & Orlikowski, W. J. (2012). Reconfiguring relations of accountability: Materialization of social media in the travel sector. *Accounting, Organizations and Society, 37*(1), 26–40.
18. Li, J., Xu, L., Tang, L., Wang, S., & Li, L. (2018). Big data in tourism research: A literature review. *Tourism Management, 68,* 301–323.
19. Wang, Y., Chan, S. C. F., Leong, H. V., Ngai, G., & Au, N. (2016). Multi-dimension reviewer credibility quantification across diverse travel communities. *Knowledge and Information Systems, 49*(3), 1071–1096.
20. Lee, H. A., Law, R., & Murphy, J. (2011). Helpful reviewers in TripAdvisor, an online travel community. *Journal of Travel and Tourism Marketing, 28*(7), 675–688.
21. Kusumasondjaja, S., Shanka, T., & Marchegiani, C. (2012). Credibility of online reviews and initial trust: The roles of reviewer's identity and review valence. *Journal of Vacation Marketing, 18*(3), 185–195.
22. Ahluwalia, R. (2002). How prevalent is the negativity effect in customer environments? *Journal of Consumer Research, 29,* 270–279.
23. Sahin, I., Gulmez, M., & Kitapci, O. (2017). E-complaint tracking and online problem-solving strategies in hospitality management: Plumbing the depths of reviews and responses on TripAdvisor. *Journal of Hospitality and Tourism Technology, 8*(3), 372–394.
24. Steadman, M. (2008). What small CPA firms are doing to recruit and retain staff. *CPA Journal, 78*(7), 61–63.
25. Blain, A. (2008). The millennial tidal wave: Five elements that will change the workplace of tomorrow. *Journal of the Quality Assurance Institute, 22*(2), 11–13.
26. Wesner, M. S., & Miller, T. (2008). Boomers and millennials have much in common. *Organization Development Journal, 26*(3), 89–96.
27. Williams, D. L., Crittenden, V. L., Keo, T., & McCarty, P. (2012). The use of social media: An exploratory study of usage among digital natives. *Journal of Public Affairs, 12*(2), 127–136.
28. Bowen, J. T., & Chen McCain, S. L. (2015). Transitioning loyalty programs: A commentary on the relationship between customer loyalty and customer satisfaction. *International Journal of Contemporary Hospitality Managemen, 27*(3), 415–430.
29. Bleedorn, G. (2013). Say hello to the millennial generation. *ABA Bank Marketing, 45*(1), 24–28.
30. Bowen, J. (2015). Trends affecting social media: Implications for practitioners and researchers. *Worldwide Hospitality and Tourism Themes, 7*(3), 221–228.
31. Jang, Y. J., Kim, W. G., & Bonn, M. A. (2011). Generation Y consumers' selection attributes and behavioral intentions concerning green restaurants. *International Journal of Hospitality Management, 30*(4), 803–811.
32. Nyheim, P., Xu, S., Zhang, L., & Mattila, A. S. (2015). Predictors of avoidance towards personalization of restaurant smartphone advertising: A study from the Millennials' perspective. *Journal of Hospitality and Tourism Technology, 6*(2), 145–159.
33. Chang, L. (1994). A psychometric evaluation of 4-point and 6-point Likert-type scales in relation to reliability and validity. *Applied Psychological Measurement, 18*(3), 205–215.
34. Garland, R. (1991). The mid-point on a rating scale: Is it desirable. *Marketing Bulletin, 2*(1), 66–70.
35. Pantano, E., & Di Pietro, L. (2013). From e-tourism to f-tourism: Emerging issues from negative tourists' online reviews. *Journal of Hospitality and Tourism Technology, 4*(3), 211–227.

Identification of IT-Needs to Cope with Dynamism in Collaborative Networked Organizations—A Case Study

Ronald van den Heuvel, Rogier van de Wetering, Rik Bos, and Jos Trienekens

Abstract Collaborative Networked Organizations (CNOs) are increasingly common in current dynamic markets. The participants in a CNO try to achieve a common goal while acting on market opportunities. Information technology (IT) facilitates collaboration between participants within a CNO. In this paper, we show how CNOs cope with network-dynamics related to their IT-needs. Two sub-characteristics of network dynamics, respectively many-to-many relations and inter-action patterns, will be investigated. In the end, we are trying to answer the question regarding what IT-needs CNOs have, to cope with CNO-dynamism. Based on a literature review we developed a framework on CNO-dynamism and executed a multi-case study within four CNOs. We conclude that all framework components are recognized within the CNOs. CNOs appeared to mainly cope with dynamics by using collaborative platforms, task management systems, and conference facilities.

Keywords Collaborative networked organizations (CNOs) · CNO-dynamism · IT-needs · IT-alignment · Multiple case study

1 Introduction

Organizations that operate in highly turbulent markets demand more agility from their strategic partners and suppliers. In response to rapidly changing customer demands and wishes, organizations are forced to collaborate and jointly create products and

R. van den Heuvel (✉) · R. van de Wetering · R. Bos · J. Trienekens
Faculty of Management, Science and Technology, Open University of the Netherlands, Heerlen, The Netherlands
e-mail: ronald.vandenheuvel@ou.nl

R. van de Wetering
e-mail: rogier.vandewetering@ou.nl

R. Bos
e-mail: rik.bos@ou.nl

J. Trienekens
e-mail: jos.trienekens@ou.nl

© The Editor(s) (if applicable) and The Author(s), under exclusive license to Springer Nature Switzerland AG 2020
R. Agrifoglio et al. (eds.), *Digital Business Transformation*, Lecture Notes in Information Systems and Organisation 38, https://doi.org/10.1007/978-3-030-47355-6_15

219

services [1]. Collaborative networks (CN) have become a common organizational form in these dynamic markets to innovate and collaborate, allowing these organizations to cope with the dynamics at hand. A collaborative networked organization (CNO) is comprised of multiple participants whose aim is to achieve common goals [1–3]. Achieving a state of Business/IT-Alignment (BITA) between the participants in the CNO appears to be a valuable endeavor that could provide benefits on agility and performance [4].

Extant literature on BITA predominantly focuses on uni-minded organizations (as opposed to networked organizations); it does not consider the networked dynamics "lens" [4–7]. The alignment frameworks dedicated to uni-minded organizations are based on hierarchical structures and governed within one organization. Within a CNO, multiple, participating organizations have their own governance structures. BITA could provide organizational benefits to these CNOs. It is this networked perspective on alignment within CNOs that is unique to the current dynamic times; this perspective is not yet part of the current body-of-knowledge.

The goal of this paper is to provide insight into the need for IT systems (described as IT-needs) to overcome or react to (described as coping with) the network-dynamics that a CNO encounters. This CNO-dynamism influences the CNO via market dynamics, network dynamics between partners and dynamics related to reconfigurations of the CNO itself. This results in our research question:

RQ: *What IT-needs do CNOs have to cope with CNO-dynamism?*

To answer this research question, we use the "Dynamic and self-regulating networks" characteristic presented by Van den Heuvel et al. [8] and focus, as part of this characteristic, on the interrelations and interactions between participants within the CNO. We focus on two operational (system/process) characteristics: "many-to-many relations" and "interaction patterns." Many-to-many relations and interaction patterns are typical for collaborative environments, where multiple organizations work together.

Via a systematic literature review (SLR) we created a framework to structurally gather results in the case study. The case study consists of 15 interviews over 12 organizations that participate in the CNOs. Semi-structured interviews were used to gather insight into IT-needs, and the results were transcribed and coded to answer the research question.

Our results can help practitioners to determine the needed IT when creating a CNO to can cope with dynamism. Researchers can use our results to get a better insight into these IT-needs to extent BITA models that fit CNOs and their dynamics.

Section 2 describes the theoretical background. Section 3 describes the methodology of the SLR, framework development, the case study, and coding. Section 4 describes the framework that is used within the case study. Section 5 outlines the results. We finalize this paper with a discussion (Sect. 6) and a conclusion (Sect. 7).

2 Theoretical Background

2.1 Networked Organizational Context

CNs are complex networks of organizations that cannot achieve their goals by themselves. These CNs are not hierarchically structured, are evolutionary, and are continuously interacting with the environment [9]. When we talk about organized collaboration, the term Collaborative Networked Organization (CNO) is used [10].

Walters and Buchanan [9] describe that these organizations have benefits compared to hierarchical networks. A few of the benefits are: leverage via best capabilities, higher speed due to reduced management and increased IT usage, agility, independence, and interdependence [9]. The rationale behind "increased IT usage" within a CNO is that CNOs need to communicate and IT is needed to facilitate this communication [10, 11].

2.2 Business/IT-Alignment (BITA)

BITA has been popularized by Henderson and Venkatraman [12] in the Strategic Alignment Model (SAM). Henderson and Venkatraman [12] state that "the inability to realize value from IT investments is, in part, due to the lack of alignment between the business and I/T strategies of organizations." Organizations should embrace a process of continuous adaptation and change in order to achieve alignment. BITA "refers to applying Information Technology (IT) in an appropriate and timely way, in harmony with business strategies, goals and needs" [13] and leads to an increase in agility and performance [4]. Within this paper, we define alignment as strategic and operational alignment as described by Bagheri et al. [14], where strategic alignment is the fit between business strategy and IT strategy and operational alignment is the alignment between business processes and supportive information systems.

The extant literature shows that a higher degree of alignment within an organization provides benefits to the firm [4]. Current models for BITA do not address the 'networked lens' that we see within a collaborative environment [8].

2.3 Many-to-Many Relations

CNOs are networks of participating entities, where entities can be a variety of types like organizations, humans, or systems. An important aspect is the bi-directional, reciprocal way of exchanging resources [15] which show bi-directional interaction existing between participants in a CNO. If we consider the dynamics of a CNO and the vast number of participants collaborating within the CNO, many relations can exist. Each participant and organization can take part in multiple other organizations, resulting in many-to-many relations which could have an epistatic nature.

Ahuja [16] argues that the number of relations, specifically direct ones, can positively affect the innovative output of the organization. The relationships influence the output via knowledge sharing, complementarity, and scale. The power of relations and their impact on the innovative output is essential for the dynamism that CNOs experience. While the benefits of indirect relations are low compared to direct relations, they still contribute to innovative power.

2.4   Interaction Patterns

The created interaction patterns are the connections between the entities during collaboration. Jaakkola et al. [17] describe collaboration in Information Systems (IS) research as information processing by humans and computers, the information transfer between them and the transformations needed in the transfer itself. Camarinha-Matos [18] describes collaboration as "a more demanding process in which entities share information, resources, and responsibilities to jointly plan, implement, and evaluate a program of activities to achieve a common goal and therefore jointly generating value." Entities can manifest in various forms, such as organizations, humans, and systems.

Dynamism in CNOs, whether it is facilitated by internal or external change, forces collaboration to evolve and thus results in ever-changing interaction patterns. These internal or external interaction patterns need to be taken into account when looking at CNO-dynamism as a whole [19].

3   Research Methodology

Our research comprises a literature review (3.1) that forms the basis for our framework (3.2) used in the case study (3.3), which is executed via interviews. The interviews were transcribed and coded (3.4) to gather insights into IT-needs (see Fig. 1).

3.1   Literature Review

Two SLRs were conducted for each of the sub-characteristics. The execution was based on Saunders et al. [20]. We selected articles based on the following characteristics: peer-reviewed, age (10 years, or seminal paper), language (English). The search query was based on the components CNO, BITA, dynamic and self-regulating network (DSN) extended with the sub-characteristic interaction patterns (IP) or

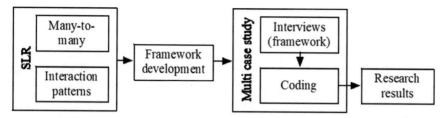

Fig. 1 Research model

Table 1 Results SLR on many-to-many sub-characteristic

Building blocks	Results
CNO + BITA + MM	73
CNO + BITA + Dynamics + MM	28
CNO + BITA + Self-regulating + MM	1
CNO + BITA + Dynamics + Self-regulating + MM	0

Table 2 Results SLR on interaction patterns sub-characteristic

Building blocks	Results
CNO + IP	4
BITA + IP	1
DSN + IP	19
CNO + DSN + IP	0

many-to-many (MM) relations. We executed the search by combining the mentioned components to create search queries executed on EBSCO host (Academic Search Elite, Business Source Premier and E-journals). Additional literature was gathered by using backward searching. The literature found during the review was analyzed and used to create the framework (see Tables 1 and 2).

3.2 Framework Development

The material from the SLRs was reviewed and analyzed to create the framework that was used during the case study interviews. The framework components were grouped into themes. Section 4 contains the framework, based on the theme CNO, relation (many-to-many relations), and interaction (interaction patterns).

3.3 Case Study Approach

The selection of organizations is based on heterogenous non-probability sampling advised by Saunders et al. [20]. Organizations needed to meet the following qualifications: The CNO is operational or has been in the last six months; A clear goal for the collaboration is available; At least one IT specialist and one business specialist are available for the semi-structured interviews within the CNO; Collaboration exists between three or more partners (to account for many-to-many relations); Within the case study, a minimum of three interviews are executed within a CNO. If the requirements could not be met, the case would be discarded. We aimed at four organizations within the same sector with goals related to IT service management (ITSM).

The interviews were held in a semi-structured manner based on the framework and an interview guide. The semi-structured interview provided us with the flexibility to discuss specific topics within the interview guide. Specifically, experiences were asked within the interview to focus on real effects instead of expected outcomes. A trial interview was held to test the interview guide. The participant received an introduction letter to increase the understanding of the research topic and to level the knowledge between the participants within the study. Interviews were conducted face-to-face, recorded, and transcribed. The transcriptions were provided to the participant for validation [20]. All transcripts are anonymized to provide confidentiality and anonymity.

3.4 Coding Procedure

Quantitative coding was used to analyze the transcripts of the interviews inspired by the methods of Muhr [21]. Closed-coding was used to set a base codebook, based on the interview guide, that was used by all three researchers. Each researcher independently coded and used open-coding to extend the codebook. Codes that were created during the coding process were shared within the research team to align coded phenomena. After closed and open-coding we used axial coding to find relations between the codes.

The first author reevaluated the codes in the transcripts. An independent researcher evaluated the process and, via selective bi-directional inter-coding, validated the coded interviews based on the transcribed text and codes. We retrieved an inter-coder agreement beyond 90% of these transcripts, providing us with sufficient confidence in our analysis [22].

4 Network Dynamics Framework

The framework created from the literature review contains three main themes. The first theme is CNO, which provides insight into CNO-related characteristics to classify the CNOs and topology. The second theme is the relation, which provides insight into the connection between participants within the network. The third theme is interaction, which provides insight into the relation itself. The first theme is descriptive for the CNO the second and third are possible influencers of CNO-dynamism.

4.1 Theme CNO

There are multiple forms of CNOs structured in the taxonomy provided by Camarinha-Matos and Afsarmanesh [23], and this taxonomy is still evolving.

Based on the SLR, we found the following components related to the theme "CNO": CNO goal, CNO type, and CNO life cycle. Cheikhrouhou et al. [24] describe two topologies of networks—vertical and horizontal. We called this CNO Type, where vertical CNOs try to extend their capabilities and horizontal CNOs try to extend their capacity to fulfill a business goal. Camarinha-Matos and Afsarmanesh [25] describe five stages of the life cycle of the CNO: L1 Creation: In this phase, the CNO and its components are created or acquired, and the legal structure is formed; L2 Operation: CNO is operational and moving towards its intended goal; L3 Evolution: In this phase, the CNO is changed in daily operation. L4 Dissolution: In this phase, the CNO is ended, commonly when they achieve their goal. This phase is common for short-term CNOs; L5 Metamorphosis: The CNO fundamentally changes its goal or structure. This stage is common for long-term partnerships where the L4 is too destructive for the assets that are available within the CNO.

These CNO-related components provide insight into the CNO and could potentially identify relations between CNO-components, and the dynamics related components many-to-many and interaction patterns.

4.2 Theme Relation (Many-to-Many Relations)

Based on the SLR, we found the following components related to the theme "relation": trust, entity role, relation type, tie form, tie strength, and embeddedness.

Cheikhrouhou et al. [24] mention five types of trust in their paper: competence, contractual, relational, indirect, and negative trust. Cheikhrouhou et al. [24] define these types of trust as: Competence trust is founded by the belief a partner has the competence to achieve the goals. Contractual trust is based on economic or "formal" aspects of a relationship. Relational trust includes human aspects of the economic relations that could allow developing or improving relations while indirect trust focuses on the external factors and components that can indirectly influence trust between partners in a CNO. Last, we have negative trust, defined as the difference of power between two partners in a considered relation. "If the relation is not on the same level from the point of view of both companies, this can lead to a source of conflict between the partners" [24].

Grefen et al. [1] describe two non-hierarchical types of entity roles within a network: hub, a focal firm distributing communications through the network, and contact point, a focal firm acting as a contact point to a client party for accepting orders and distributing them through the network [1].

A connection between two or more actors in the network results in interdependency [16, 26]. Ahuja [16] describes three relation types: direct ties—the arrangement of direct inter-firm linkages between a firm and its network partners, which primarily serves as sources for resources, and information. Indirect ties—inter-firm linkages between a firm and its indirect partners, via partners of its partners, which primarily serves as a source for information. Structural holes—a structural hole is a gap between parties that have a relationship with a central organization but not with each other, resulting in the possibility of receiving different information within the network [16].

Wulf and Butel [27] found that the position of a participant in the network influences their ability to achieve sustainable competitive advantage (tie form). They describe a difference between business eco-systems and business networks. In these two constellations, the structure is viewed from a governance and a relationship point of view. The governance point of view relates to the CNO. The structural part describes the difference between formal and informal ties. Formal ties are related to hierarchical structures governed by contracts (prescribed) or ownership, whereas informal ties are related to social organizational structures where there are informal relationships between individuals and are the basis for collaboration and knowledge transfer (emergent) [28].

When communication takes place mutually and frequently, strong ties exist [27]. They can reduce cost, reduce monitoring and integration costs, and improve information flow. Thus strong cohesion can be instigated [29]. "Weak ties provide access to non-redundant information" [30]. Strong ties and weak ties are part of the framework where the "strongness" relates to frequent mutual interaction and infrequent distant interaction (tie strength).

Osman [26] studied the influence of formal versus informal ties to the embeddedness of the participant within the CNO. Embeddedness is the degree of centrality of any company within the social network. Strong embeddedness refers to an organization which has many close ties with which it is in frequent contact, it may be the hub with many spokes; weak embeddedness is where the organization does not actively take part in ties within the (social) network.

These components provide the ability to gather data about the relations within the CNO, related to dynamics and how IT-needs change based on these relations.

4.3 Theme Interaction (Interaction Patterns)

In the theme "interaction" we identified interaction mode, locale, time, the goal of the interaction, structures, and level of formality as relevant components. These components describe how a relation is used. We will describe the components in the following text.

The modes as described by Oukes and von Raesfeld [31] are as follows: Interaction create mode: "The creation of innovative solutions by an organization and its counterpart beyond the scope of their initial agreement to align their interests and preserve the relationship"; Interaction acquiesce mode: "The compliance of an organization to the action of its counterpart or situation even at the expense of its own short-term interests"; Interaction compromise mode: "The partial compliance of an organization to the action of its counterpart or situation. They renegotiate the relationship's agreements in a relationship preserving manner"; Interaction manipulate mode: "The persistent efforts of an organization to act regardless of the ideas and preferences of its counterpart. It tries to shape, change or redefine the counterpart's actions or the situation by overpowering its counterpart"; Interaction avoid mode: "An organization's lack of intention to react to the action of a counterpart or situation"; Interaction defy mode: "An organization's dismissal of a counterpart's action or situation. It may either try to benefit from the relationship at the expense of its counterpart's interests, or it ends the relationship".

Another aspect is the locale the interaction takes place in. We identified two dimensions relevant for our research based on Camarinha-Matos and Afsarmanesh [19], namely Endogenous—Interactions that lie within the CNO-network, and Exogenous—Interactions between actors outside the CNO-network. Additionally, we see a difference between synchronous and asynchronous communication [32], classified in our study as "time."

Clark et al. [32] indicate that there are three types of goals an actor tries to accomplish with an interaction. These are Consensual: Both Actors are in agreement; Responsive: An actor expects an answer from another actor; Elaborative: Interaction between two actors until the goal is reached. While the study focuses on student interaction, we think these types of goals can help understand the dynamics within CNOs and their interaction patterns.

Wagner et al. [33] describe the common human (H)/computer (C) communication model. This model describes the transfer of knowledge between two parties where the combination can be H-H, H-C/C-H, and C-C. These combinations need to be facilitated in knowledge transfer. We define H-H interaction as a biological interaction, H-C/C-H as a formal interaction, and C-C as a technical interaction. Within our study, this component is called "Structures."

The level of formality is also a component we see that influences the interaction pattern. We combined these communication models with formal and informal levels where formal communication follows specific guidelines and has lower sequential variety, and informal communication is more ad hoc and has a higher sequential variety [34].

These components provide the ability to the framework to gather data about the way a relation is used, how they react to dynamism, and how this influences IT-needs.

4.4 Framework

The described themes provided a framework to structure and analyze the cases for our study. The framework is meant to provide a basis to discuss IT-needs in relation to dynamism in CNOs. The framework components can be viewed in Table 3.

Table 3 Network dynamics framework

Theme CNO	
CNO goal	[35]
CNO type (horizontal, vertical)	[24]
CNO life cycle (initiation, foundation, operation, evolution, metamorphosis, dissolution phase)	[35]
Theme relation	
Trust (competence, relational, contractual trust)	[24]
Entity role (hub, contact point)	[1]
Relation type (direct tie, indirect tie, structural gap, tie value)	[16, 26, 31]
Tie form (formal, informal tie)	[27, 36]
Tie strength (strong, weak tie)	[27, 30]
Embeddedness (strong, weak embeddedness)	[27]
Theme interaction	
Interaction mode (interaction create, interaction acquiesce, interaction compromise, interaction manipulate, interaction avoid, interaction defy mode)	[31]
Locale (endogenous, exogenous)	[19]
Time (synchronous, asynchronous)	[32]
Goal of interaction (consensual, responsive, elaborative)	[32]
Structures (biological, formal, technical)	[17, 33]
Levels of formality (formal, informal)	[34]

Table 4 Identified IT-needs

T1	Collaboration tooling	T5	Process support tooling
T2	Document templates	T6	Knowledge sharing
T3	Task management tooling	T7	Documentation tooling
T4	Conference facilities	T8	Forum

5 Case Study Results

5.1 Organizations

This case study comprises four CNOs with a network size ranging from 4 to 50+ participants. The CNOs have an ITSM focus and, at a minimum, one party has extensive IT knowledge in the ITSM project space.

CNO 1 and 2 show a vertical topology; CNO 4 shows a horizontal topology. CNO 3 shows both types. CNO goals were related to providing a service, ranging from IT consolidation to project management. In total, 12 organizations participating in one of the four CNOs took part, resulting in 15 interviews spread over the organizations.

5.2 Case Study Results

During the analyses, the components most related to IT-needs and dynamics were CNO life cycle, interaction mode, and interaction structure, followed by trust, relation type, time, and level of formality. The least found components were entity role, CNO goal, CNO type, and locale. We did not see any influence by CNO goal and CNO type and therefore these components are omitted from the results. Only CNO life cycle was used for theme CNO. The identified IT-needs are listed in Table 4.

The IT-needs are mapped to the components of the framework (vertical axis) and the CNOs (horizontal axis) (Table 5). Each component describes the high-level findings.

From the case study, we confirmed that IT is crucial to facilitate collaboration for a CNO. Collaboration tooling (T1) and conference facilities (T4) are mentioned frequently as an IT-need related to the majority of the framework components. The components trust, relation type, embeddedness, and time were also discussed frequently. IT-needs T1 and T4 were mentioned to increase trust, facilitate direct relations, strong embeddedness, and (a)synchronous communication. T1 is not only focused on office tooling but also a shared environment for specific tools used within the CNO. An example is 3D drawing tools. The intensity for the IT-need T4 increases when there are direct and strong ties as opposed to only providing and using T1 as a shared environment (relation type and tie strength). When participants in the network

Table 5 High-level results per CNO

	CNO 1	CNO 2	CNO 3	CNO 4	Needs
Theme CNO					
CNO life cycle	Evolution decreased dynamics	Evolution increased dynamics	All phases were recognized	All phases except dissolution	T1, T3, T4, T5
Theme relation					
Trust	Competence and relational. Informal communication increased trust	Contractual and after evolution competence and relational	Relational. Minimalistic agreements, high amount of trust	Competence, contractual	T1, T3, T4
Entity role	Hub, contact point	Hub	Hub, contact point	Hub	T1, T4, T6
Relation type	Direct	Indirect, after evolution direct	Direct	Direct	T1, T3, T4, T5
Tie form	Formal and when dynamics increased, informal	Formal and after evolution informal	Informal	Formal	T1, T4
Tie strength	Strong	Weak and after evolution strong	Strong	Strong	T1, T4, T6
Embeddedness	Strong	Weak, decreased dynamics, created misalignment, lowered trust	Strong	Weak	T1, T4
Theme interaction					
Interaction mode	Acquiesce, create	Avoid and manipulate to gain a dominant role and increase trust	Compromise, acquiesce and create	Acquiesce, create	T1, T2, T3, T4
Locale	Exogenous	Exogenous	Endogenous	Endogenous and exogenous	T1, T4, T8
Time	Synchronous	Asynchronous and moved to synchronous	Asynchronous at initiation. Moved to synchronous	Endogenous: synchronous. Exogenous: asynchronous	T1, T3, T4, T5
Goal of interaction	Consensual, responsive, elaborative	Consensual, responsive, elaborative	Consensual, responsive	Elaborative	T1, T2, T4, T5

(continued)

Table 5 (continued)

	CNO 1	CNO 2	CNO 3	CNO 4	Needs
Structures	Biological and later formal and technical	Technical at the beginning and then biological	Biological and formal	Biological and formal	T1, T3, T4, T5
Levels of formality	Informal. Later formality increased due to tooling	Formal with goal to increase trust. After increase, informal to increase dynamics	Informal, which provided a basis to cope with dynamics	Formal and informal	T1, T2, T3, T4, T8
IT-needs	T1, T2, T3, T4	T1, T3, T5	T1, T3, T5, T6	T1, T3, T7, T8	

work on different components of an assignment, defining used tooling and collaborating via T1 is extended by integrating the work to a combined result during the creation of a product.

When discussing trust, interviewees mentioned that when competence and relational trust increases, informal ties, strong embeddedness, and synchronous interaction in a biological structure is preferred. T1, T3, T4, and T5 were mentioned as IT-needs related to these components. Contractual trust (mainly in the initial life cycle phase) did also trigger the IT-need for T1 and T4 to facilitate collaboration.

When discussing how CNOs cope with dynamics, informal ties and an informal level of formality were mentioned. The related IT-needs were T1, T3 and T4.

Interviewees did not mention technical communication structure to cope with dynamics. Within the cases, tooling was used to optimize processes between participants (T5), and in the evolvement of the CNO more tooling was introduced to optimize biological, formal, and technical communication.

Indirect relations were also recognized and it was mentioned that the collaboration relied on email and in some cases T3 and T5.

Exogenous relations were mentioned to be supported by asynchronous communication and facilitated by T5 and T8. When the interaction in exogenous relations increases, T1 and T4 were mentioned as an IT-need to cope with dynamics.

Overall, we can see that when interaction increases (which in the cases is related to increased dynamics) the move to more "active" relations and interaction patterns are visible. These increased communication paths are then supported mostly by T1 and T4, sometimes by T2, T3 and T5 and in some cases T6 and T7. T8 (Forum) is often seen as a method to cope with asynchronous, indirect communication, and exogenous relations.

6 Discussion, Limitations, and Future Research

In this section, we will discuss IT-needs within CNOs to cope with CNO-dynamism.

The interviewees recognized all components in the model, which validates the model we created. The framework was not extended based on the result. We got valuable information about IT-needs of CNOs and the IT-needs to cope with dynamics.

When the relationship and interaction were exogenous and formal, and the tie strength was weak, the communication regularly was asynchronous via email or a forum (T8). In some cases, supported via supportive systems (T5). When the relationship and interaction moved to tie strength strong, tie form informal and embeddedness was high. Moreover, T1 and T4 were mentioned as an IT-need. When dynamics are introduced in a CNO, the interviewees indicated a preference for synchronous, informal communication in a biological and formal structure, resulting in the need for T1 and T4. We cannot state that dynamism forces T1 and T4 or if dynamism forces active interaction and therefore the need for T1 and T4. Still, the need to cope with dynamism triggers the IT-need for the collaborative environment (T1) and conference facilities (T4).

The IT-need for task management tooling (T3) was mentioned in relation to dynamics related to trust, relation type, interaction mode, time, and structure within all CNOs. When dynamics occur, the number of tasks to execute increased and tooling that supports that was needed. The IT-needs document templates (T2), knowledge sharing (T6), and documentation tooling (T7) were not mentioned related to dynamics, and thus we think that these are not used to cope with dynamics within the CNO.

IT-needs did not drastically change related to the CNO life cycle. Dynamics cannot be planned and therefore facilitating a collaborative environment (T1), task management tooling (T3), and conference facilities (T4) from the beginning of the CNO could be part of general requirements.

The topic of technical structures was not frequently addressed and did not result in an IT-need. We expected this to be a more prominent topic especially with the ITSM focus within the CNOs. Technical structures were mentioned as a possible improvement for the CNO. The lack of technical structures could be related to the goal-oriented focus of the CNOs within our study.

Our model could be extended by different research fields. For instance, media synchronicity [37] could provide more insight into biologic communication from a process perspective differentiated in a conveyance and convergence stage, to in the end, tailor it to the CNOs specific need. Also, electronic negotiation [38] could be used to facilitate technical communication, still this was not specifically mentioned as a method to cope with dynamism within our study.

Overall, we noticed that trust was a central and important topic within our interviews. Trust (specifically competence and relational) was mentioned combined with other characteristics like a direct relation type, strong ties, and a high amount of communication (biological). Leading to strong relations. The component-time and locale were often mentioned together. Mainly in the combination of asynchronous/exogenous and synchronous/endogenous. All IT-needs are, as expected, related to collaboration and interaction. When discussing dynamics mainly IT-needs T1, T3, and T4 were mentioned. Mostly in the context of increased informal and synchronous communication.

In this study, we focused on the relationship between participants and not all "dynamic and self-regulating" characteristics. Our characteristics are on an operational level, where others are related to strategy (landscape of organizations) or governance topic (dynamic partnering, maturity). We expect that analyzing the other characteristics will be useful. Also, the lack of technical structures was not expected. We do not know why these technical structures were not present, but we would have expected that these structures would be an IT-need to cope with dynamism in a prosperous CNO. These points show room for future research.

These results can help practitioners in determining the needed IT systems when participating in a collaborative organization so that they are prepared to cope with the dynamism they could encounter as a CNO. From a research perspective, these results provide more insight into IT-needs that help cope with the dynamism CNOs can encounter. Within our broader research program, we will try to create guidelines and hopefully a new BITA model that could facilitate CNOs and specifically their operational BITA between the participants that take part in the CNO. To in the end provide a model that is more suitable for these networked organizations with their vast number of configurations, and fill a gap within the body-of-knowledge on this topic.

Our study does have some limitations that future research should seek to address. First, our SLR and thus our framework finds it basis in the paper of Camarinha-Matos and Afsarmanesh [2] where they introduce the scientific discipline around CNOs. We tried to keep our search queries as broad as we can, but the concept of CNO is part of our search queries. By using backward searching we broadened our scope, still could have limited our SLR, our framework, and thus our results. Second, dynamism is a phenomenon that changes over time. Our research was cross-sectional and thus replicating the study over time could gather more valuable insights. Third, CNOs consist of and are formed by multiple participants. The vast number of configurations a CNO can have based on capabilities, the configuration of the participant, and other characteristics create complex objects to analyze [39]. We gather results within our study and agree that generalization based on these configurations is hard. By using common aspects of the CNOs, like goals and type of participants within a CNO, we tried to limit this effect. Still, we think that multiple studies will result in valuable additional data to research this topic. Last, by using transcribed interviews, intensive coding frameworks, and cross-referencing the codes between the interviewers, we tried to limit observer bias; however, we cannot guarantee that no bias entered the research. We do think we mitigated this risk adequately by applying a rigorous method of coding and analyses based on theory from Yin [40] and adding validation from external researchers.

7 Conclusion

By following an explicit research methodology we derived results regarding IT-needs in CNOs having to cope with dynamism.

First, collaboration tooling (T1), document templates (T2), task management tooling (T3), conference facilities (T4), process support tooling (T5), knowledge sharing (T6), documentation tooling (T7) and a forum (T8) are IT-needs within a CNO.

Second, collaboration tooling (T1), task management tooling (T3), and conference facilities (T4) are IT-needs to cope with CNO-dynamism. T1, T3, and T4 facilitate informal, synchronous, biologic communication that is mentioned as a preferred method of interaction to cope with dynamism. Third, when trust is lacking, informal and face-to-face communication is mentioned as a method to increase trust, which can be facilitated via the IT-need T1, T3, and T4. Last, we notice that technical structures were not mentioned as an IT-needs.

Via a rigorous research process; creating a framework via systematic literature reviews and using this framework in our multi case study in four CNOs (15 interviews over 12 organizations), coding the results and validating these codes, we succeeded in identifying IT-needs that are used to cope with the dynamics a CNO encounters. Our results can help CNOs determine their IT-needs upfront and the framework could help CNOs to identify their IT-needs. Scientifically we extended the body-of-knowledge with more insights in IT-needs to cope with CNO-dynamism.

Acknowledgements This paper was created with the help of Manon van Rooijen—van der Bas, Merel Visser, and Danny van Maanen.

References

1. Grefen, P., Mehandjiev, N., Kouvas, G., Weichhart, G., & Eshuis, R. (2009). Dynamic business network process management in instant virtual enterprises. *Computers in Industry, 60*(2), 86–103.
2. Camarinha-Matos, L. M., & Afsarmanesh, H. (2005). Collaborative networks: A new scientific discipline. *Journal of Intelligent Manufacturing, 16*(4–5), 439–452.
3. Grefen, P. (2013). Networked business process management. *International Journal of IT/Business Alignment and Governance (IJITBAG), 4*(2), 54–82.
4. Coltman, T., Tallon, P., Sharma, R., & Queiroz, M. (2015). Strategic IT alignment: Twenty-five years on. *Journal of Information Technology, 30*(2), 91–100.
5. Bernus, P., Noran, O., & Molina, A. (2015). Enterprise architecture: Twenty years of the GERAM framework. *Annual Reviews in Control, 39,* 83–93.
6. Van den Heuvel, R., Trienekens, J., Van de Wetering, R., & Bos, R. (2016). Business/IT-alignment adaptation in dynamic networked environments. In *PRO-VE2016*, Porto, Portugal.
7. Cuenca, L., Boza, A., Ortiz, A., & Trienekens, J. J. M. (2014). Business-IT alignment and service oriented architecture—A proposal of a service-oriented strategic alignment model. In S. Hammoudi, J. Cordeiro, & L. Maciaszek (Eds.), *Proceedings of the 16th International Conference on Enterprise Information Systems (ICEIS 2014)* (Vol. 3, pp. 490–496). SCITEPRESS-Science and Technology Publications, Lda.

8. Van den Heuvel, R., Trienekens, J., Van de Wetering, R., & Bos, R. (2017). Toward CNO characteristics to support business/IT-alignment. In L. M. Camarinha-Matos, H. Afsarmanesh, & R. Fornasiero (Eds.), *Collaboration in a data-rich world. PRO-VE 2017. IFIP Advances in Information and Communication Technology* (Vol. 506, pp. 455–465). Cham: Springer.
9. Walters, D., & Buchanan, J. (2001). The new economy, new opportunities and new structures. *Management Decision, 39*(10), 818–834.
10. Camarinha-Matos, L. M., Afsarmanesh, H., Galeano, N., & Molina, A. (2009). Collaborative networked organizations—Concepts and practice in manufacturing enterprises. *Computers & Industrial Engineering, 57*(1), 46–60.
11. Concha, D., Espadas, J., Romero, D., & Molina, A. (2010). The e-HUB evolution: From a custom software architecture to a software-as-a-service implementation. *Computers in Industry, 61*(2), 145–151.
12. Henderson, J. C., & Venkatraman, N. (1993). Strategic alignment: Leveraging information technology for transforming organizations. *IBM Systems Journal, 32*(1), 472–484.
13. Luftman, J. (2004). Assessing business-IT alignment maturity. In *Strategies for information technology governance*. Hershey, PA: IGI Global.
14. Bagheri, S., Kusters, R. J., & Trienekens, J. J. M. (2015). Business-IT alignment in PSS value networks-linking customer knowledge management to social customer relationship management. In S. Hammoudi, J. Cordeiro, & L. Maciaszek (Eds.), *Proceedings of the 17th International Conference on Enterprise Information Systems (ICEIS 2015)* (Vol. 3, pp. 249–257). SCITEPRESS-Science and Technology Publications, Lda.
15. Parmigiani, A., & Rivera-Santos, M. (2011). Clearing a path through the forest: A meta-review of interorganizational relationships. *Journal of Management, 37*(4), 1108–1136.
16. Ahuja, G. (2000). Collaboration networks, structural holes, and innovation: A longitudinal study. *Administrative Science Quarterly, 45*(3), 425–455.
17. Jaakkola, H., Henno, J., Thalheim, B., & Mäkelä, J. (2015). Collaboration, distribution and culture-challenges for communication. In *38th International Convention on Information and Communication Technology, Electronics and Microelectronics (MIPRO)* (pp. 657–664). Opatija, Croatia: IEEE.
18. Camarinha-Matos, L. M. (2009). Collaborative networked organizations: Status and trends in manufacturing. *Annual Reviews in Control, 33*(2), 199–208.
19. Camarinha-Matos, L. M., & Afsarmanesh, H. (2007). A comprehensive modeling framework for collaborative networked organizations. *Journal of Intelligent Manufacturing, 18*(5), 529–542.
20. Saunders, M., Lewis, P., & Thornhill, A. (2016). *Research methods for business students* (7th ed.). Harlow: Pearson Education Limited.
21. Muhr, T. (2018). *Scientific Software Development GmbH*. Berlin, Germany: ATLAS.ti (8.2). http://www.atlasti.com/.
22. Boudreau, M.-C., Gefen, D., & Straub, D. W. (2001). Validation in information systems research: A state-of-the-art assessment. *MIS Quarterly*, 1–16.
23. Camarinha-Matos, L. M., & Afsarmanesh, H. (2012). Taxonomy of collaborative networks forms: FInES task force on collaborative networks and SOCOLNET—Society of collaborative networks. In *Roots and wings*. European Commission.
24. Cheikhrouhou, N., Pouly, M., & Madinabeitia, G. (2013). Trust categories and their impacts on information exchange processes in vertical collaborative networked organisations. *International Journal of Computer Integrated Manufacturing, 26*(1–2), 87–100.
25. Camarinha-Matos, L. M., & Afsarmanesh, H. (2008). *Collaborative networks: Reference modeling*. New York: Springer Science + Business Media, LLC.
26. Osman, L. H. (2017). The pattern of inter-organizational level of connectivity, formal versus informal ties. *Jurnal Komunikasi, Malaysian Journal of Communication, 33*(1), 59–79.
27. Wulf, A., & Butel, L. (2017). Knowledge sharing and collaborative relationships in business ecosystems and networks. *Industrial Management & Data Systems, 117*(7), 1407–1425.
28. Caimo, A., & Lomi, A. (2015). Knowledge sharing in organizations: A Bayesian analysis of the role of reciprocity and formal structure. *Journal of Management, 41*(2), 665–691.

29. Franco, M., & Haase, H. (2015). Inter-organizational cooperation in community health organizations: A competence-based perspective. *International Journal of Health Care Quality Assurance, 28*(2), 193–210.
30. Levin, D. Z., & Cross, R. (2004). The strength of weak ties you can trust: The mediating role of trust in effective knowledge transfer. *Management Science, 50*(11), 1477–1490.
31. Oukes, T., & von Raesfeld, A. (2016). A start-up in interaction with its partners. *IMP Journal, 10*(1), 50–80.
32. Clark, D. B., Sampson, V., Weinberger, A., & Erkens, G. (2007). Analytic frameworks for assessing dialogic argumentation in online learning environments. *Educational Psychology Review, 19*(3), 343–374.
33. Wagner, H.-T., Beimborn, D., & Weitzel, T. (2014). How social capital among information technology and business units drives operational alignment and IT business value. *Journal of Management Information Systems, 31*(1), 241–272.
34. Becker, M. C. (2005). A framework for applying organizational routines in empirical research: Linking antecedents, characteristics and performance outcomes of recurrent interaction patterns. *Industrial and Corporate Change, 14*(5), 817–846.
35. Camarinha-Matos, L. M., & Afsarmanesh, H. (2008). On reference models for collaborative networked organizations. *International Journal of Production Research, 46*(9), 2453–2469.
36. Grant, R. M., & Baden-Fuller, C. (2004). A knowledge accessing theory of strategic alliances. *Journal of Management Studies, 41*(1), 61–84.
37. Dennis, A. R., & Valacich, J. S. (1999). Rethinking media richness: Towards a theory of media synchronicity. In *Proceedings of the 32nd Annual Hawaii International Conference on Systems Sciences* (pp. 1–10). Maui, HI: IEEE.
38. Bichler, M., Kersten, G., & Strecker, S. (2003). Towards a structured design of electronic negotiations. *Group Decision and Negotiation, 12*(4), 311–335.
39. Van de Wetering, R., Mikalef, P., & Helms, R. (2017). Driving organizational sustainability-oriented innovation capabilities: A complex adaptive systems perspective. *Current Opinion in Environmental Sustainability, 28*, 71–79.
40. Yin, R. K. (2014). *Case study research: Design and methods* (5th ed.). Los Angeles: Sage.

Unwrapping Efforts and Difficulties of Enterprises for Digital Transformation

Haruka Ikegami and Junichi Iijima

Abstract Since the late twentieth century, Information Technology (IT) has made a fundamental transformation in our society through automation, a process known as the third Industrial Revolution. More recently, in the twenty-first century, there has been a farther stage of transformation through IT called "Digital Transformation." However, enterprises are struggling with aligning suitable digital strategies and actions for Digital Transformation, since there is a fundamental complexity in IT management, and a scarcity of research relating to how enterprises could systematically approach Digital Transformation. Therefore, we conducted eight interviews as a case study to explore key strategic themes for those enterprises regarding Digital Transformation. We applied directed content analysis for the interviews and obtained detailed descriptions that fully explain Digital Transformation in Japanese enterprises. From our results, three key topics have been discovered for the enterprises to consider for Digital Transformation: (1) Customer Experience, (2) Strategic Intent, and (3) Ecosystem. The results of our research contribute to a better understanding of what struggle enterprises have experienced with Digital Transformation by showing a practical approach for real businesses, as well as by demonstrating the possibilities for future research.

Keywords Digital transformation · IT-capability maturity framework · Directed content analysis · Customer experience · Strategic intent · Ecosystem

1 Introduction

The tech wave has been building for a long time but it has accelerated in recent years [34]. Since the third Industrial Revolution in the late twentieth, we have benefited from increased automation by electronics and information technology. In the

H. Ikegami (✉) · J. Iijima
Tokyo Institute of Technology, Meguro, Tokyo 152-8550, Japan
e-mail: ikegami.h.ac@m.titech.ac.jp

J. Iijima
e-mail: iijima.j.aa@m.titech.ac.jp

R. Agrifoglio et al. (eds.), *Digital Business Transformation*, Lecture Notes in Information Systems and Organisation 38, https://doi.org/10.1007/978-3-030-47355-6_16

twenty-first century, we stand on the brink of a technological revolution that will fundamentally alter the way we live, work, and relate to one another [28]. The latest digital technologies such as SMACIT (Social, Mobile, Analytics, Cloud, and Internet of Things) will enable us to achieve things that were impossible a decade ago, and many occupations, institutions and industries that are established today will not survive this transition intact [20]. This transition is referred to as Digital Transformation. Digital Transformation can be understood as the changes that have been caused by the digital technology in all aspects of human life [31].

For instance, Burberry Group PLC, a London-based apparel company, committed to a digital future by offering the comfort of cross channels and the expansion of its presence in mono-brand websites for operations based on the shop-in-shop concession with T-Mall and Amazon [13]. The company engages its customers and showcases its brand seamlessly across its physical and digital channels by revamping its online assets and building a strong, engaging experience on social media [33]. The new offerings to consumers include such as fitting products in their 500 stores spread across 50 countries with RFID tags that give manufacturing information or dressing recommendations to the shoppers' mobiles in addition to providing product information and digital contents through Snapchat's Snapcode, Facebook's chatbots and its own channel on Apple Music [21]. As this example shows, the use of different digital tools has facilitated the process of communication between company and the consumer [13].

Prior research on Digital Transformation has been carried out in various industries such as automotive [15, 24, 27], media [32], healthcare [1] and music industry [4]. Based on these, we have learned that the impact of Digital Transformation can be a radical and disruptive change. Since Digital Transformation strategies cut across various other strategies at the same time, as shown in prior studies, complex coordination efforts might be needed [22]. While many decision makers sense technological changes and the resulting competitive context shifts, which can potentially have a profound impact on their organizations, it is not yet clear, how the organizations should prepare and what steps are needed in order to respond appropriately to these threats arising from Digital Transformation [2]. Overall, decision makers need to think more about the role of digital technologies in influencing not only the business strategies of individual firms but also the nature of the industry, the sources of value creation, and location of value capture [3].

Our research complements prior research from the perspective of enterprises that stumble on Digital Transformation in the initial phase by comprehensively analyzing enterprises across industries. This paper explores their current efforts and difficulties regarding Digital Transformation, and it aims to identify difficulties that the enterprises have. Additionally, this paper will suggest a practical way for enterprises to approach digital transformation in their business. Our research questions in this paper are as follows:

RQ 1: Where do enterprises stumble on Digital Transformation?
RQ 2: How can those enterprises approach Digital Transformation?

To answer the research questions above, we conducted a case study with eight enterprises. For the study of the case, we introduced a directed content analysis [16] as analysis method and a capability maturity framework, IT-Capability Maturity Framework [18] as conceptual background, particularly its part that is specialized in managing organizations' IT function [11].

This paper is organized as follows: following introduction, the next section describes the conceptual background of this study, a maturity framework used to measure and grasp the maturity of Digital Transformation in enterprises. Next, we describe our research methodology and results in the third section, and insights based on the analysis result in the fourth section. Finally, the paper concludes by addressing our theoretical contributions and avenues for future research.

2 Conceptual Background: IT-Capability Maturity Framework

Our study is based on cross-industry case studies in their initial phase of transformation, which is often perceived as ill-defined, random and mysterious [26]. The IT-Capability Maturity Framework (IT-CMF) allows us to study such situation more comprehensively due to its focus on IT management capabilities [17].

There are three reasons why we chose to apply the IT-CMF in this study. First, the framework is an innovative and systematic framework, representing an emerging blueprint of key IT capability processes, and acting as an assessment tool [6]. Second, over 150 assessments have been performed across 80 leading Fortune 500 firms [7], which enables the survey result to be compared with their benchmark data. Third, the framework is easy for practitioners to understand and leverage [9]. While other IT management frameworks such as CoBIT and ITIL have contributed to describing a set of good practices in IT-related processes [14], IT-CMF has competitiveness in its practice-oriented structure and it can be used to avoid spending too much time on complicated process diagrams [30].

IT-CMF is a high-level process capability maturity framework for managing the IT function within an organization [11]. It was created by Innovation Value Institute (IVI), co-founded in 2006 by Maynooth University in Ireland and Intel. From the point of a maturity model, the created analysis technique has been proved to be valuable in measuring the different aspects of a process or an organization, and it has been well-established academically for its model structure, assessment method and support availability [25]. This result indicates that IT-CMF is one of the state of the art maturity models.

IT-CMF consists of 37 management disciplines which are defined as Critical Capabilities (CCs) [18]. For each capability, IT-CMF incorporates a comprehensive suite of maturity profiles, assessment methods, and improvement roadmaps, expressed in such a way that businesses can use them to guide discussions on setting goals and evaluating performance [18]. Based on the framework and its defined capabilities,

Table 1 Seven digital business behaviour themes [18]

Digital business behaviour theme	Definition
DBB_01 Planning and Execution Management	Establishing a coherent direction and actions regarding how digital can assist the organization to compete and thrive
DBB_02 Ecosystem Management	Leveraging the capabilities of, and creating synergies amongst, participants involved in the value chain supporting digital business objectives
DBB_03 Delivery and Operations Management	Providing the digital enablement across the organization
DBB_04 Talent Development and Organizational Design	Aligning leadership, skills and management structures in support of the organization's digital business objectives
DBB_05 Investment and Financial Management	Improving the return on investment from IT-related resources
DBB_06 Information Exploitation Management	Leveraging data to improve decision-making and business outcomes
DBB_07 Risk, Control, and Cyber Security Management	Mitigating threats to digital business objectives, and enforcing regulatory obligations, standards, policies and guidelines

IVI offers seven processes for Digital Transformation from the management point of view. These are called the "Seven Digital Business Behaviour Themes" (Table 1), which serve as guidelines for our analysis.

3 Research Methodology and Findings

In this research, we followed a directed content analysis approach [16] for our case studies. This approach is defined as a research method for the subjective interpretation of the content of text data through the systematic classification process through the coding and identifying themes or patterns [16]. The reason why we selected to utilize this methodology is that it can provide knowledge and understanding of the phenomenon under study [12].

3.1 Case Selection

Selection of the cases began with a broader survey to understand the overall state of digital transformation in enterprises. This was then followed up with more detailed qualitative, open-ended interviews to collect detailed views from participants [8]. With this goal in mind, we conducted an online survey ahead of the case studies. The survey was conducted on 45 people from 45 different Japanese enterprises via Google Forms during October and November 2018. The reason why we chose to target Japanese enterprises for this research is based on the fact that academic research on enterprises' Digital Transformation in the Japanese context is still lacking in comparison to studies carried out in European countries [29], the United States [10], and even other Asian countries such as China [35], India [23], South Korea [19] and ASEAN countries [5]. If the environments or conditions where enterprises are undergoing changes differ, then the enterprises themselves would be different. Therefore, further research regarding Digital Transformation in Japanese enterprises is needed.

Among the 45 enterprises, 73.3% are IT User enterprises in Finance (8.9%), Manufacturing (20.0%) and other industries (44.4%), with 66.7% of respondents being large enterprises with over 1000 employees. In addition, the survey consists of four sections, A through D. Section A is for profile information followed by Sections B to D that focus on the digital readiness assessment based on IT-CMF. Section B consists of five questions on the intensity of digitization (e.g. "Is central to the organization's success leveraging a diversified portfolio of digital technologies?"). Section C consists of five questions on breadth or reach of digitization (e.g. "Are business processes digitally transformed across the organization?"). Section D consists of seven sub-sections based on Seven Digital Business Behaviour Themes (e.g. "Does the organization have an agreed upon and shared a business-aligned digital strategy that can rapidly adapt to turbulent business conditions?"). Interviewees answered each question on a scale of 1–4.

We analyzed the answered results, and the result of how interviewee companies are ready for Digital Transformation are shown in Fig. 1. Figure 1 indicates the attainment level of digital readiness, which is calculated by the percentage of the sum in Sections B, C and D. According to the total percentage, we categorize the

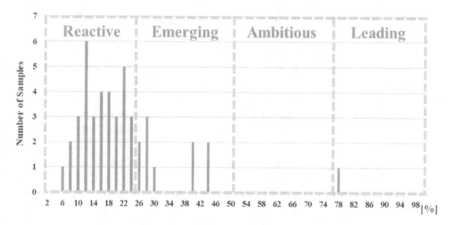

Fig. 1 Attainment level of digital readiness in Japanese enterprises

result into four stages of digital readiness: reactive (0–25%), emerging (25–50%), ambitious (50–75%) and leading (75–100%).

From this result, it can be seen that 77.8% of the enterprises belong to the reactive stage and 20.0% belongs to the emerging stage. This result shows that Japanese enterprises have just started taking actions for Digital Transformation. In the following section, we focus on Section D, which refers to Seven Digital Business Behavior Themes as the first step for our research.

3.2 Case Studies

For the first research question, "Where do enterprises stumble on Digital Transformation?", we conducted follow-up interviews on eight Japanese enterprises (Table 2). As theoretical sampling, we selected one enterprise for an interview to avoid bias in the attainment level of digital readiness, industries and company size, every time we finished analysing one enterprise. We finished selecting with eighth enterprise, reaching data saturation. Titles of the interviewees included Manager and Head of Digital Transformation.

3.3 Interviews and Analysis Method

Each interview was conducted in a semi-structured manner based on open-ended questions [16] for approximately 60 min. The analysis was carried out by two authors as follows:

- We asked each interviewee questions which were prepared in advance to correspond to their measurements and mindset for Digital Transformation along the Seven Digital Business Behaviour Themes, and if necessary, asking additional questions. In addition to the interview, we used complementary documents such as Integrated Reports and strategy papers (available for five out of the eight enterprises) for additional sources of data for the analysis.
- For each company, we transcribed all the recordings of the interviews and the complementary documents, identified the key descriptions related to Digital Transformation through open coding. Each description was labelled with descriptive titles.
- While paying attention to prevent the result from having an arbitrary bias, we extracted the labelled descriptions according to the Seven Digital Business Behaviour Themes in order to gain a complete and systematic picture of the enterprise's Digital Transformation activities. We lastly looked over the data of each company and coding result to ensure the validity of coding.

Table 2 Overview of eight interviewee enterprises

Company	Digital readiness (%)	Industry	Number of employees	Key objectives of digital transformation
Alpha	77.4	IT service	1100	To provide digitalized products/services and optimize the back-office operation
Beta	43.7	Consulting	10	To provide digitalized products/services for better customer engagement
Gamma	38.8	Electric	100,000+	To provide digitalized products/services
Delta	26.2	Manufacturing	100,000+	To provide digitalized products and optimize the back-office operation
Epsilon	24.7	Manufacturing	250	To optimize the back-office operation
Zeta	17.7	Social infrastructure	700	To provide digitalized products and optimize the back-office operation
Eta	13.1	Manufacturing	950	To provide digitalized products and optimize the back-office operation
Theta	11.3	Finance	7500	To provide digitalized services

3.4 Result of Directed Content Analysis

From the total analysis across all the 8 companies, we acquired 19 descriptions (between 2 and 3 descriptions for each theme) as shown in Table 3.

The detailed results of the directed content analysis are described according to the seven themes in this section. We would like to note that the following describes the summary of the aggregated empirical findings from all the companies, and as such, not all of the descriptions apply to each company.

Table 3 Coding result in directed content analysis	DBB_01	Lack of leaders to draw fundamental designs
		Middle-down management siloed by department
		Low information mobility due to complex organization structure
	DBB_02	Closed ecosystem
		Strengthening recruitment and education system internally
		Fixed relationship by traditional business practice
	DBB_03	Undeveloped integration of old and new systems
		Traditional vertical organization structure
	DBB_04	Lack of leaders with sufficient knowledge to realize DX
		Suboptimal utilization of human resources due to localized focus
		Pushed assignment
	DBB_05	Low investment budget for digital activities
		Execution within the previously approved budget
		Difficulty of evaluating by indicators such as ROI
	DBB_06	Undeveloped of data collection process
		Lack of quantitative and qualitative data collection
		Under developed data sharing systems and digital marketing
	DBB_07	Building an internal risk management policy only
		Enhancing operation management in internal security

3.4.1 Planning and Execution Management (DBB_01)

The enterprises, especially large ones, have often middle-down management within each department, and there is no common agreement in the enterprise regarding Digital Transformation. They also have worked on digitalization by for example creating a special department for Digital Transformation. However, due to a lack of the leaders' skills, which can draw the fundamental strategy design, the degree of influence on digitization remains at an improvement level instead of at a transformation level. Such vertical and siloed organizational structures lead to the low mobility of information.

3.4.2 Ecosystem Management (DBB_02)

In the enterprises, there is little incentive to create a joint platform due to a want to maintain the current balance between each other's competitive advantage within the industry. The enterprises try making up for resources that are necessary for Digital Transformation through in-house recruitment or by strengthening the education system. Moreover, they often have an account with specific fixed third parties owing to traditional business practice in Japan, and subcontracting enterprises tend to be treated with scepticism.

3.4.3 Delivery and Operations Management (DBB_03)

Many large enterprises have a complicated organizational structure, which slows down information transmission speed leading to a lethargic and inflexible operations styles. Most decision makers are veterans who have low motivation to change, and can even have a negative influence on their department due to vertical structure. Therefore, these enterprises are struggling with integrating old and new systems on a department level. Additionally, collected data is not in a form that can be used to optimize products and services through the use of analytics.

3.4.4 Talent Development and Organizational Design (DBB_04)

While the top management in the enterprises are engaged in activities to improve the organization's digital capabilities, they lack the latest knowledge related to IT and digital. However, since the pace of Digital Transformation is rapidly accelerating, the top managers are not able to catch up even if educated from this current situation. In addition, the overall structure of the organization has not been visualized due to its complicated organization structure, which leads to a suboptimal allocation of human resources due to a focus on the local optimum. Employees use digital technologies without understanding the underlying mechanisms used by the process. Instead they just carry out the work given to them by their bosses, which can be considered as a push assignment that ignores individual skills.

3.4.5 Investment and Financial Management (DBB_05)

Among these enterprises, the proportion of the new digital budget is low due to existing IT investment and overestimated risk. They promote Digital Transformation through activities such as setting up a fixed budget amount, but at such a low budget ratio that it is not always tied to the business results. They evaluate the cost-effectiveness of digital investment based on performance indicators such as Return On Investment (ROI). However, using such indicators can have a bad influence on a digital investment since it does not immediately lead to an immediate improvement in performance but instead should be continued over a longer time period.

3.4.6 Information Exploitation Management (DBB_06)

These enterprises require an enormous time and resources to collect data since the data collection process is not well established due to a huge number of legacy systems and manual processes. Data integration has not progressed and does not meet the criteria required for analytics from both points of quantity and quality. Regarding information sharing, information on the site is not shared real-time to the top management, hence they invest a significant amount of money in traditional activities such as TV commercials and leaflets particularly in marketing.

3.4.7 Risk, Control, and Cyber Security Management (DBB_07)

The enterprises recognize that dealing with cyber security matters is indispensable, and establish and maintain risk management policies within the enterprises even when external cloud services are used. However, as the range of digital services used widens, there can be concerns on the security risk of business partners' part which cannot be fully grasped by the enterprise. Moreover, the enterprises sometimes have not considered the security risks concerning employees' use of personal data.

4 Insights on Digital Transformation of Enterprises

Based on the presented case studies, which showed what enterprises struggle with and lack for their Digital Transformation, we would like to identify what the enterprises must do and seek in order to answer the second research question, "How can those enterprises approach Digital Transformation?". We reorganized the seven themes by considering how the themes are related to each other based on our recursive discussion (Fig. 2).

In an ambitious digitally transformed world, an enterprise firstly considers customers since all the business activities start with its customers (DBB_01). In order to offer a better customer experience, the enterprise seeks to utilize digital technologies (DBB_06) and build an investment portfolio flexibly (DBB_05). To realize the portfolio, the decision makers design the whole organization and tries optimize the assignment of human resources (DBB_04). Furthermore, for the designed ambitious organization and digital technology utilization, the enterprise reforms its IT infrastructure (DBB_03), and finally, utilizes external resources effectively to realize all of the activities mentioned before (DBB_02). In addition, it handles its risk management policy of the whole ecosystem (DBB_07).

As shown in Fig. 2, the seven themes can be captured from three points of view, customers, enterprises and suppliers. For each point of view, we offer three key topics, Customer Experience, Strategic Intent and Ecosystem, which showed a lack in the interviewee companies but are indispensable for them to achieve Digital Transformation.

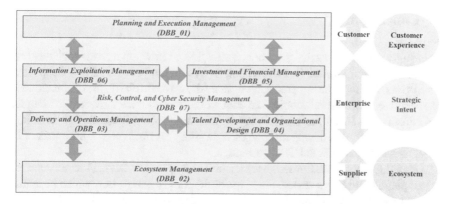

Fig. 2 Restructured seven digital business behaviour themes and three keywords

First, Customer Experience. All business activities begin with customers. Digital transformation makes it possible to realize customer experience that is close to the needs of each customer. In order to respond to the diverse customer needs, it is necessary for the enterprises to adapt flexibly and agile through Digital Transformation. While top management must not only decide the direction of the whole enterprise but also have its own vision of business with digital technologies. The enterprise must also be able to break down the vision into concrete action plans. Additionally, the employees, as well as the top management, must engage in designing customer experience increasingly from customer points of view.

Second, Strategic Intent. Since enterprises that are lagging behind in Digital Transformation have too many things to deal with. As a result, trying in a blank way would not be effective. From the point of Information Exploitation Management, for instance, it is important to tackle the development of the data collection process as the first action since it can be valuable in terms of both quality and quantity. However, due to the wide range of data collection, priority must be given on the basis of strategic initiatives in activities such as the development of data collection. For anything other than that, the top management needs to have strategic intent to realize their vision.

Third, Ecosystem. What Japanese enterprises currently have worked on is optimization of digitalization at a department level which is not as transformation but on an improvement scale. In addition, in order to further increase in the impact of Digital Transformation, it is indispensable to cooperate with other enterprises both in the same and different industries. In order to achieve Digital Transformation, it is necessary to involve stakeholders, inside and outside of the enterprise, and aim towards the optimization of the entire ecosystem, which would increase the impact of Digital Transformation on not only their own enterprise but also on the suppliers and the whole ecosystem.

5 Conclusion

This study aimed to clarify the current situation of how enterprises make efforts and struggle with Digital Transformation by researching case studies on Japanese enterprises. Through the directed content analysis, we could clarify the characteristics of specific efforts and difficulties the studied companies have in regards to Digital Transformation. From the analysis result, this study could illustrate the three key topics that enterprises having difficulties in Digital Transformation must consider in order to accomplish Digital Transformation.

This study has several limitations as it is still an in-progress work. First, the number of samples should be increased. Since the difficulties of enterprises, which have just started tackling Digital Transformation, are changeable and difficult to summarize, we need to collect a large sample of enterprises with different backgrounds. Second, the scope of this study could be limited. We only focused on Japanese enterprises and it would be difficult to apply the results for enterprises in other countries. In order to have a more comprehensive grasp of the situations in enterprises' Digital Transformation, we plan to further analyse enterprises in other countries as well.

References

1. Agarwal, R., Gao, G., DesRoches, C., & Jha, A. K. (2010). Research commentary—The digital transformation of healthcare: Current status and the road ahead. *Information Systems Research.*
2. Berghaus, S. (2016). The fuzzy front-end of digital transformation: Three perspectives on the formulation of organizational change strategies. In *BLED 2016 Proceedings.*
3. Bharadwaj, A., EI Sawy, O. A., Pavlou, P. A., & Venkatraman, N. (2013). Digital business strategy: Toward a next generation of insights. *MIS Quarterly, 37*(2), 471–482.
4. Bourreau, M., Gensollen, M., & Moreau, F. (2012). The impact of a radical innovation on business models: Incremental adjustments or big bang? *Industry and Innovation, 19*(5), 415–435.
5. Box, S., & Lopez-Gonzalez, J. (2017). The future of technology: Opportunities for ASEAN in the digital economy. In The ASEAN Secretariat, S. S. C. Tay, & J. P. Tijaja (Eds.), *Global megatrends: Implications for ASEAN economic community* (pp. 37–60).
6. Carcary, M. (2011). Design science research: The case of the IT capability maturity framework (IT CMF). *The Electronic Journal of Business Research Methods, 9*(2), 109–118.
7. Costello, T. (2010). A new management framework for IT. *IT Professional, 12*(6), 61–64.
8. Creswell, J. W. (2002). *Research design: Qualitative, quantitative, and mixed methods approaches* (p. 21). Sage.
9. Curley, M. (2008). Introducing an IT capability maturity framework. In J. Filipe, J. Cordeiro, & J. Cardoso (Eds.), *Enterprise information systems. ICEIS 2007. Lecture Notes in Business Information Processing* (Vol. 12). Berlin, Heidelberg: Springer.
10. Cziesla, T. (2014). A literature review on digital transformation in the financial service industry. In *BLED 2014 Proceedings.*
11. Donnellan, B., & Helfert, M. (2010). The IT-CMF: A practical application of design science. In R. Winter, J. L. Zhao, & S. Aier (Eds.), *Global perspectives on design science research. DESRIST 2010. Lecture Notes in Computer Science* (Vol. 6105). Berlin, Heidelberg: Springer.
12. Downe-Wamboldt, B. (1992). Content analysis: Method, applications, and issues. *Health Care for Women International, 13*(3), 313–321.

13. Escobar, A. (2016). The impact of the digital revolution in the development of market and communication strategies for the luxury sector (fashion luxury). *Central European Business Review, 5*(2), 17–36.
14. Haes, D. S., & Grembergen, V. W. (2015). Chapter 5: COBIT as a framework for enterprise governance of IT. In *Enterprise governance of information technology: Achieving alignment and value, featuring COBIT 5* (Vol. 2, pp. 103–128). Springer.
15. Hanelt, A., Piccinini, E., Gregory, R. W., Hildebrandt, B., & Kolbe, L. M. (2015). Digital transformation of primarily physical industries—Exploring the impact of digital trends on business models of automobile manufacturers. *Wirtschaftsinformatik Proceedings*.
16. Hsieh, H., & Shannon, S. (2005). Three approaches to qualitative content analysis. *Qualitative Health Research, 15*(9), 1277–1288.
17. Innovation Value Institute. (2019). *How to approach digital transformation in your organization.* Accessed February 14, 2019. https://ivi.ie/enabling-your-business-for-digital-transform ation/.
18. Innovation Value Institute. (2019). Accessed February 14, 2019. https://ivi.ie/about/.
19. Lee, J. (2009). Contesting the digital economy and culture: Digital technologies and the transformation of popular music in Korea. *Inter-Asia Cultural Studies, 10*(4), 489–506.
20. Loebbecke, C., & Picot, A. (2015). Reflections on societal and business model transformation arising from digitization and big data analytics: A research agenda. *Journal of Strategic Information Systems, 24*(3), 149–157.
21. Marr, B. (2019). *The amazing ways Burberry is using artificial intelligence and big data to drive success.* https://www.forbes.com/sites/bernardmarr/2017/09/25/the-amazing-ways-bur berry-is-using-artificial-intelligence-and-big-data-to-drive-success/#7b382d7f4f63. Accessed May 19, 2019.
22. Matt, C., Hess, T., & Benlian, A. (2015). Digital transformation strategies. *Business & Information Systems Engineering, 57*(5), 339–343.
23. Pasti, S., & Ramaprasad, J. (2015). The BRICS journalist within the changing dynamics of the early 21st century. *African Journalism Studies, 36*(3), 1–7.
24. Piccinini, E., Hanelt, A., Gregory, R. W., & Kolbe, L. M. (2015). Transforming industrial business: The impact of digital transformation on automotive organizations. In *International Conference on Information Systems*.
25. Proença, D., & Borbinha, J. (2016). Maturity models for information systems—A state of the art. *Procedia Computer Science, 100,* 1042–1049.
26. Rhea, D. (2003). Bringing clarity to the "fuzzy front end". In B. Laurel (Ed.), *Design research: Methods and perspectives* (pp. 145–154). MIT Press.
27. Riasanow, T., Galic, G., & Böhm, M. (2017). Digital transformation in the automotive industry: Towards a generic value network. In *European Conference on Information Systems*.
28. Schwab, K. (2016). *The fourth industrial revolution: What it means, how to respond.* World Economic Forum. https://www.weforum.org/agenda/2016/01/the-fourth-industrial-rev olution-what-it-means-and-how-to-respond/. Accessed May 17, 2019.
29. Schweer, D., & Sahl, J. C. (2017). The digital transformation of industry—The benefit for Germany. In F. Abolhassan (Ed.), *The drivers of digital transformation.* Management for Professionals. Cham: Springer.
30. Sharifi, M., Ayat, M., Rahman, A. A., & Sahibudin, S. (2008). Lessons learned in ITIL implementation failure. In *Information Technology 2008. ITSim 2008* (pp. 1–4).
31. Stolterman, E., & Fors, A. C. (2004). Information technology and the good life. In B. Kaplan, D. P. Truex, D. Wastell, A. T. Wood-Harper, & J. I. DeGross (Eds.), *Information systems research. IFIP International Federation for Information Processing* (Vol. 143). Boston, MA: Springer.
32. Utesheva, A., Cecez-Kecmanovic, D., & Schlagwein, D. (2012). Understanding the digital newspaper genre: Medium vs. message. In *European Conference on Information Systems*.
33. Westerman, G., & Bonnet, D. (2015). Revamping your business through digital transformation. *MIT Sloan Management Review*.

34. Westerman, G., Bonnet, D., & McAfee, A. (2014). *Leading digital*. Harvard Business Review Press.
35. Yu, H. (2017). *Networking China: The digital transformation of the chinese economy.* Champaign: University of Illinois Press.

Coordinating Innovation in Digital Infrastructure: The Case of Transforming Offshore Project Delivery

Mina Haghshenas and Thomas Østerlie

Abstract The relationship between digitalization, digital innovation, and digital transformation is an emerging topic in information systems (IS) research. Whereas IS researchers widely acknowledge that digitalization underpins both digital innovation and digital transformation, just how and by what mechanisms link digital innovation with digital transformation remains underexplored. Differentiating between 'digital infrastructure innovation' and 'innovation in digital infrastructure', this paper contributes towards current discussions by empirically elaborating how the open-ended and generative potential of digital innovation in practice has to be negotiated against the installed base of technical and organizational arrangements in digital transformation. We pursue this argument through a case study of digital innovation coordination in an inter-organizational digital innovation project with the goal of instigating digital transformation within the offshore construction industry.

Keywords Digital innovation · Digital infrastructure · Digital transformation · Digital delivery

1 Introduction

Digitalization[1] impacts on central aspects of industrialized society, ranging from the reshaping of individual organizations to the transformation of entire societal sectors and industries. At the same time, digitalization transform the very character of innovation as the open-ended and generative capacity of digital technologies challenge fundamental assumptions about innovation boundaries, agency, and the process-product relationship [2]. While Information Systems (IS) researchers

---

[1] Drawing upon Tilson et al. [1] we understand digitalization as the socio-technical processes through which digital technologies become infrastructural to work and organizing.

M. Haghshenas (✉) · T. Østerlie
Norwegian University of Science and Technology, Høgskoleringen 1, 7491 Trondheim, Norway
e-mail: mina.haghshenas@ntnu.no

T. Østerlie
e-mail: thomas.osterlie@ntnu.no

© The Editor(s) (if applicable) and The Author(s), under exclusive license to Springer Nature Switzerland AG 2020
R. Agrifoglio et al. (eds.), *Digital Business Transformation*, Lecture Notes in Information Systems and Organisation 38, https://doi.org/10.1007/978-3-030-47355-6_17

251

widely acknowledge the relationship between digital innovation and the transformative impacts of digitalization, just how and by what mechanisms the two are linked remains an issue of much debate among IS researchers [3–7].

In this paper, we contribute towards these discussions through a case study of digital innovation for transforming project delivery in the offshore construction industry. Through this case study, we empirically elaborate how the open-ended and generative potential of digital innovation in practice has to be negotiated against the installed base of technical and organizational arrangements in digital industrial transformation. This argument supplements ongoing discussions about the open-ended possibilities of digital technologies in IS research [e.g. 3] by emphasizing how digital innovation unfolds within the confines of existing industrial, organizational, and technological structures. To this end, we empirically demonstrate that digital innovation network dynamics emerge through the interplay between generativity and installed base.

We pursue our argument through an analysis of digital innovation in the Open Industry Platform (OIP, pseudonym for maintaining anonymity), an industry-level collaboration project in the offshore construction industry. Specifically, we follow the challenges OIP faces in transitioning from a stage of mobilizing industry support for the project towards a full-scale digital innovation project. Emphasizing how digital innovation is negotiated towards an installed base of existing socio-technical arrangements, this paper can be regarded as a response to Nambisan [6] call for more research on institutionalized aspects (i.e. installed base) of digital innovation. More specifically, this paper contributes to theory on digital innovation networks in three ways. First, we empirically demonstrate and draw implications of a temporal, evolutionary dimension to digital innovation networks. Second, we elaborate upon and substantiate the need for coordinating mechanisms to evolve as digital innovation networks change. Third, by arguing for the embeddedness of digital innovation networks in other network structures and its implications for digital innovation. We also draw practical implications for coordinating large-scale and complex digital innovation projects.

2 Digital Innovation Coordination and Digital Infrastructure

While digital innovation is by now a well-established topic in IS research [2, 8], IS researchers approach it somewhat differently. On the one hand, there are those who emphasize digital innovation as processes, products, or business models that are new and enabled by IT [e.g. 8]. This paper, however, draws upon a recombination approach to digital innovation [9]. Emphasizing digital innovation as producing novel products through new combinations of digital and physical components, this approach emphasizes digital technologies' generative and open-ended potential enabled through the key characteristics of being editable, re-programmable, and with functionality that can be procrastinated until the point of use [3]. This differentiates digital innovation from earlier forms of IS innovation [10] by two distinguishing features: the changing role of digital technology in innovation from operand to operant resources, and a shift in innovation locus from firm-centric to innovation networks.

Pervasive digitization changes the role of digital technologies from an enabler for innovation (operand resource) to a trigger for innovation and medium through which innovation unfolds (operant resource) [11]. Digital technologies as operant resource conflates innovation product with process [11], with attention shifting towards reconfiguration [9] of innovation processes and the generativity unleashed by digital resources. Pervasive digitalization also shifts innovation locus from firm-centric to innovation networks. Innovation no longer unfolds within a single company, but through a network of actors [1].

Digital innovation affords, as such, new modes of coordination. Based on the two distinguishing characteristics of digital innovation, Lyytinen, et al. [4] forward a framework for innovation network coordination that characterizes innovation networks along the two axes of (1) heterogeneity of operant resources, and (2) distribution of coordination and control within the innovation network structure. Through this framework, they forward that there is limited need for social and cognitive translation when innovation networks consist of "a homogenous pool of actors and related tools that are readily identified" (ibid., p. 58). Lyytinen et al. define cognitive translate as "a generative process whey innovation knowledge is identified, produced, refined, integrated and evaluated partially through digital means in its movement towards (…) being stabilized in a new product" (p. 55), and social translation as the processes through which "an innovation process, by necessity transforms the social space of the actors in the innovation network" (p. 56). As such, in networks of actors consists of heterogenous operant resources, coordination mechanisms' need to support social and cognitive translation. Specifically relevant to this paper is what Lyytinen et al. [4] characterizes as 'anarchic' digital innovation networks; i.e. networks with operant resource heterogeneity and distributed control and coordination as 'anarchic'. These networks are characterized by collaboration of self-adjusting actor-to-actor networks driven by opportunistic behavior with "actors spontaneously sensing and responding to their continued market relevance and viability/sustainability" [12].

Digital infrastructures offer a pertinent example of anarchic innovation networks. Digital infrastructures underlie pervasive digitalization of organizational life [1]. Drawing upon a network perspective on infrastructure [cf. 13], Tilson et al. [1] characterized digital infrastructure as "shared, unbounded, heterogeneous, open, and evolving socio-technical systems comprising an installed base of infrastructure capabilities and their user, operations, and design communities". Digital infrastructure innovation is, as such, subjected to heterogeneous and distributed actors' independent choices beyond the control of any central actor [14]. A key challenge is, as such, handling the different interests. However, as Sørensen [14] notes, specific control mechanisms are needed to coordinate and balance distributed action for digital infrastructure innovation to be successful.

While there is some research on coordination in networks of heterogeneous operant resources and distributed control and coordination, Lyytinen et al. [4] argued that the main challenge in digital infrastructure innovation is to actualize digital innovation in such networks. The degree of alignment between network actors is a particular challenge pertinent to this paper. Swanson and Ramiller [15] forwards the notion of 'organizing vision' to explain the productive capacity industry buzzwords have in mobilizing and shaping actors' expectations and opportunities in innovative application of digital technologies. Similarly, Pollock and Williams [16] shows how industry analysts' classifications of different digital technologies influence the trajectories of emerging classes of digital technologies. While both studies show coordination across heterogeneous networks, they do so among loosely aligned actors. While some mechanisms function in loosely aligned networks (such as organizing visions), other mechanisms are needed as networks become more closely integrated and aligned; as in digital infrastructure innovation. Furthermore, while IS scholars acknowledge the importance of digital innovation coordination, Nambisan [6] argues there is still lack of knowledge about institutionalized aspects of innovation. In the case of digital infrastructure innovation, such institutional aspects include the installed base of organizational, technical, and financial investments [17]. As such, digital innovation coordination needs to encompass the tension between the generativity and open-ended potential of digital innovation [3] with the digital infrastructure's installed base.

3 Methods and Materials

This paper draws upon the authors' engagement with digitalization of offshore construction projects over the past three years. The empirical data are mainly from the first author's embedded case study [18] of OIP (project title along with company names have been anonymized). OIP is a collaborative project among companies throughout the offshore infrastructure industry. The project aims at developing an industry-wide system for digital exchange of technical information in offshore construction projects.

Participant observation [19] has been the first author's main data collection method for the case study. The author has been embedded with an OIP project team located at HostCo, the company responsible for project management of the joint project, from November 2018 through April 2019. During this period, the author spent 3–4 full days a week at HostCo, for a total of 54 days of participant observation. The author was provided with office space together with the project team and OIP management, with full access to observing meetings, spending time talking with the project team and management, as well as contributing by maintaining the project's document repository. Data from observations have been written in a field notes journal [20].

The first authors' participant observation has been supplemented with both authors' interviews and analysis of documents related to the project and the overall transition towards digital delivery of offshore construction projects. We have individually and together done 24 semi-structured interviews [21] with OIP's project participants including software engineers, domain experts, management-level participants and the project initiators.

We have conducted data analysis and collection in parallel. Initial data analysis was informal, aimed at narratively analyzing observations and interviews to form an overall understanding of the project. Over time, data analysis turned more systematic through coding of interview transcripts and fieldnotes for concepts and topics. During this process, we supplement the emerging analysis by sampling from the second authors' fieldnotes from participating in meetings and workshops related to digitalization of offshore construction projects at the industry level. Throughout this process, we sought to relate aspects of the emerging analysis back to different potential theoretical venues. In this paper, we draw upon literature on digital innovation networks and mechanisms for coordinating these.

4 Case Setting: Digital Offshore Project Delivery

The Open Industry Platform project sought to establish a system for digital exchange of technical information shared by all companies throughout the Engineering, Procurement, and Construction (EPC) industry. The EPC industry delivers offshore infrastructures such as pipelines, new production facilities, and more recently offshore windmill parks through large and complex infrastructure projects. The main contractor (usually referred to as 'the EPC company') subcontracts and outsources much of the project activities through a heterogeneous ecology of subcontractors, vendors, and service companies with different specialties. OIP was, to this end, organized as a collaborative project between key companies representing different stakeholders in this ecology.

Digital delivery is considered the next step of digitalization in the EPC industry. While practically every individual company have digitalized their activities, digital delivery is "the use of integrated software and processes across the project ecology" [22]. Technical information is the basis towards which companies in EPC projects verifies that individual pieces of equipment fulfil technical and regulatory requirements. Furthermore, forwarding the project as the transition 'from document-centric to data-centric' exchange of technical information, the initiators projected how OIP would not merely replace existing work processes. Seeking to mobilize industry support for the project during the first six months of 2018, OIP's initiators forwarded the project as the missing piece in transitioning towards digital delivery of EPC projects:

> What we are doing is a game changer, and can make tremendous changes to how we are working in large [offshore] construction projects (…) (OIP project participant, fieldnote excerpt)

However, upon project initiation in mid-2018, HostCo—the service company given responsibility for hosting and managing OIP—quickly faced problems. Reflecting upon this a few months into the project, a key project participant observed:

"So, I now see that the project has been somewhat oversold in that the foundations of the project is more based on, let's say, hopes and aspirations rather than being expressions of a clear plan [of project goals and how to achieve them]." (Interview excerpt)

Labelling the initial months of the project a 'preparatory phase' prior to commencing the project proper in early 2019, HostCo worked to operationalize 'hopes and aspiration' through which the project initiators had sought to mobilize support for the project.

To facilitate a transition to digital exchange of technical information, OIP was to consolidate, update, and digitize existing standards that specify the informational elements required for different classes of equipment used on offshore installations. There is currently no single standard that completely specifies what information should be supplied for different equipment classes. Rather, they are distributed across over 50 different national and international standards (as well as company-specific documents). With little or no coordination among different standardization bodies, the standards are often overlapping and sometimes even downright contradictory. To this end, OIP was organized around two related activities at project initiation:

One activity was to update existing national guidelines by consolidating existing standards on technical information required of different classes of equipment

The other activity was to develop a core technology (OIP Core) for digitally expressing the requirements laid down in the updated national guidelines

The content of these activities, however, remained underspecified. As such, moving from 'hopes and aspirations' towards concrete project outcomes and activities turned problematic. OIP's participants spent most of 2018 seeking to operationalize the project vision into concrete technical features, and a plan laying out what activities are to be done by whom, when, and how. With this came a shift in focus for the activity to develop OIP Core. More than developing technology in support of digitizing the updated national standards, they came to focus on methods for expressing and processing digital requirements in general. Throughout this period, participants involved in updating the national standard repeatedly raised questions about OIP's functional focus, and the appropriateness of OIP Core's general requirements handling features for their activities on updating national guidelines for technical information and what they perceived as a lack of progress in this activity.

As such, how OIP's vision was to be operationalized into activities and materialized into concrete outcomes (plans, reports, revised standard, designs, executing software) remained contested as HostCo prepared to scale up the project for the second phase; the project proper. Consequently, when it came to mobilizing funding for the project proper in early 2019, most of the participating companies were hesitant. Several expressed the view that OIP was lacking a clear direction to meet the needs of the industry. As a key stakeholder put it:

Isn't it discouraging that we have conducted a first [preparatory] phase of the project and no-one really knows what the outcome of this has been or how to progress from here? (Fieldnote excerpt)

As the preparatory phase came to a conclusion, several of the key companies involved in the project openly considered pulling out OIP, possibly even terminating the project entirely.

5 Analysis: Digital Infrastructure Innovation Versus Innovation in Digital Infrastructure

Conflicting views on the nature of digital innovation in OIP lie at the core of the controversy threatening OIP's continuation after the preparatory phase. Echoing Schumpeter, Henfridsson et al. [3] forward that "[r]ecombination is at the heart of innovation" (p.89). Rather than conceiving of digital technologies as pre-packaged applications or services, Henfridsson et al. (ibid., p.90) forward the notion of digital resources, "entities that serve as building blocks in the creation and capture of value from information". The technical approach chosen for OIP, which all participants agreed upon, followed a similar logic. Rather than developing a self-contained application, OIP was to provide a digital resource—the OIP Core—that its participants could freely integrate with their own technical and organizational arrangements. While agreeing on this, whether OIP Core would form the basis of a new infrastructure for digital EPC project delivery or simply provide functionality to be inserted in existing technical and organizational arrangements remained contested throughout the project period.

We conceptualize this as an unresolved tension between divergent views on the nature of digital innovation in OIP; between an emphasis on digital infrastructure innovation versus an emphasis on innovation in digital infrastructure. We draw the line of demarcation between the software engineers developing OIP Core, on the one hand, and the domain experts tasked with updating national guidelines on informational requirements for different classes of equipment on the other. Emphasizing the open-ended, transformative, and generative potential for a large-scale transition from document-based to data-oriented requirements handling, the software engineers regarded OIP as digital infrastructure innovation. The domain experts emphasized the need for OIP Core to take into account operators' and EPC companies' installed base of financial, technical, and organizational investments in digital EPC project delivery in general, and digital exchange of technical information in particular. As such, they viewed OIP as a form of innovation in digital infrastructure (Table 1).

5.1 Innovation Focus

Organized around two related activities, OIP faced two possible points of departure at project initiation: (1) focus on updating national guidelines for technical information, or (2) focus developing a technology for expressing the requirements laid down in the

Table 1 Digital infrastructure innovation versus innovation in digital infrastructure

	Digital infrastructure innovation	Innovation in digital infrastructure
Description	Innovation of the infrastructure for digital EPC project delivery through OIP	OIP as an innovative part of existing technical and organizational arrangements for digital EPC project delivery
Innovation dimension		
Focus	Technology-driven	Use-oriented
Trajectory	Start afresh with new technology	Build on existing activities
Outcome	OIP as digital platform outside of installed base	OIP integrated as system for digital exchange of technical information within installed base

updated national guidelines. There were discussions from onset of the project about which of these two activities to consider as driver of project activities. The software engineers working on OIP Core advocated that developing the technological basis of the project should be central to proceeding with updating the national guidelines. Although the domain experts agreed that the updated national guidelines should be digitized from the onset, their view on OIP Core's role in the project diverged from that of the software engineers:

> The goal is to update the standards [national guidelines for technical information]. The technology [OIP Core] is to support this process, rather than setting the premises for the standardization. (Fieldnote excerpt, OIP initiator)

At the onset of the preparatory phase, HostCo donated the results from a company-internal project for digitally expressing requirements on a machine-readable form. Their argument was that building on this as the technological basis for OIP would give the project a 'flying start'. The donated technology, which became OIP Core, was a technology for digital requirements handling in general. This aligned well with HostCo's other business areas in requirements validation and verification:

> "We [HostCo] are working with requirement in very broad scale and large volume. Much of what we are doing is about creating rules and publishing guidelines where most of them are based on industry standards. The complexity in understanding set of rules is work intensive. (….) It [OIP Core] will provide computer assistant requirement management by which we can move the burden of knowing and applying complex rules to the computer and then improve quality." (Interview excerpt, software engineer)

Deciding to use HostCo's general digital requirement technology for OIP Core emphasized requirements handling and its transformative potential on digital EPC project delivery. While the technology provided the domain experts with a format for unambiguously expressing requirements, they remained uninterested as their focus was on how digital technologies could simplify time-consuming and error-prone aspects of their work. As such, within the first months of OIP, the disagreement on project driver came to be drawn between the software engineers seeking to establish development of OIP Core, on the one hand, and the domain experts wanting technological development to be driven by the user needs for updating the national standards, on the other hand.

The software engineers attributed the domain experts' skepticism of digital requirements handling in general as a failure to grasp OIP Core's generative potential. As such, they translated the domain experts' objections to OIP Core's emphasis on digital requirements handling as a form of user resistance. As a software engineer noted:

> I have been in the oil and gas industry for many years myself, and I know that this is an extraordinary conservative business. Engineering and engineers by themselves are particularly conservative and procedurally oriented, right? And used to doing things the way they have always done. (Interview excerpt)

From the domain experts' point of view, however, software engineers failed to grasp OIP's role in the wider context of transitioning towards digital EPC project delivery:

> We were introduced to an application which [the software engineers] believe is the best solution. But as we moved on, we understood this was only a small piece of the bigger picture. This is the drawback of [HostCo] having the potential solution in-house. (Interview excerpt, domain expert)

The domain experts attributed the focus on digital requirements handling to a lack of domain knowledge among the software engineers. The operators' domain experts argued the software engineer's insistence on digital requirements handling's generative potential failed to appreciate that the recipient and end-user for the technical information generated during an EPC project are the operators' life-cycle information departments.[2]

> The emphasis kind of changed towards the HostCo technology rather than focusing on the technical [information] requirements. I think they gave too much focus on that (…). In a way the work was done on the technology [OIP Core], it is kind of difficult to understand how that would work before agreeing upon what we want to digitalize and used that engine for. (Interview excerpt, management-level stakeholder operator)

Similarly, the EPC companies' domain experts argued that focusing on digital requirements handling failed to acknowledge key competitive dynamics in EPC projects. While technical information is the basis for validating that delivered equipment fulfils technical requirements, requirements validation efficiency is a key competitive factor among companies in the EPC ecosystem. All companies therefore have internal systems for requirements validation already. Moving such functionality to the digital infrastructure would undermine these companies' organizational and technological investments in requirements validation efficiency. As such, the disagreement over OIP Core's functional scope was not solely about functionality per se, but also on whether OIP's focus should be on digital infrastructure innovation or innovation in digital infrastructure.

---

[2]Life-cycle information departments are responsible for providing technical information to internal departments as well as subcontractors in relation to operations and maintenance activities.

5.2   Innovation Trajectory

OIP is infrastructural in ambition and scope. The offshore industry's interest organization clearly signals OIP's infrastructural ambitions by concluding their report on future competitiveness with

Digitalization: collaboration, sharing, openness, standardization. OIP is the foundation.

This statement reflects what Star and Ruhleder [23] refers to as the 'common-sense view' of infrastructure as "substrate (...) something upon which something else 'runs' or 'operates'". The conclusion forwards the ambition of OIP as the substrate for "collaboration, sharing" to underpin digital EPC project delivery. OIP is infrastructural in scope in its focus on cross-domain standardization. Henfridsson and Bygstad [13] describes a relational perspective on infrastructures. This perspective emphasizes infrastructures as socially embedded and coordinated across social worlds and standards. Companies throughout the EPC industry tend to spend an inordinate amount of time sifting through technical equipment information. Different suppliers provide the information on differing formats and with differing information depending upon the customer. In worst case, the same supplier can provide the same customer with differing information for the same piece of equipment as operators have limited standardization of technical information across their development projects. OIP is, as such, infrastructural in scope as standardizing the information elements to be provided for specific classes of equipment is key to coordinating across the different social worlds involved in EPC projects.

Both of these perspectives of OIP's infrastructural aspects are well acknowledged among the participating companies, and link closely with the view of OIP as digital infrastructure innovation; the innovation of the infrastructure for digital EPC project delivery. Less acknowledged, however, is how OIP is also innovation in digital infrastructure.

OIP had been preceded by a series of smaller, independent, yet related collaborative projects focusing on different aspects of digital exchange of technical information. Companies have, in the past, pursued digital EPC project delivery internally. The effect has been that vendors, subcontractors, and EPC companies spend much effort on transferring data and information to and from different companies' digital delivery systems. Key stakeholders throughout the EPC industry (including OIP's initiators) have therefore sought to consolidate and move internal systems onto what they referred to as 'the common arena' over the past years. All participating companies, apart from HostCo, have previous investments in at least some of these projects. In mobilizing participants for OIP, the project initiators therefore highlighted the importance of OIP as a continuation and consolidation of these past projects. The domain experts' objections to OIP Core's emphasis on digital requirements handling, can be understood as a failure by the software engineers to acknowledge that OIP is not developed in isolation, but within an installed base of financial, technological, and organizational investments [17] made by companies throughout the EPC ecosystem.

The domain experts' objections to OIP Core's emphasis on digital requirements handling was, as such, not solely a critique of the software engineers' lack of domain knowledge. They also found the focus on digital requirements handling to lack an appreciation of the need for continuity with previous industry efforts towards establishing an infrastructure for digital exchange of technical information in EPC projects:

> I have participated in [a previous project on identifying informational element requirements for technical information] from 2015 to 2018 on behalf of my company. (...) From our side, (...) the OIP project is to use the results from previous initiatives. How can we say that the [previous] project is OIP's background without continuing it? (Interview excerpt, domain expert)

Having attributed the domain experts' objections to a lack of understanding of digital requirements handling's transformative potential, the software engineers responded to the critique by organizing a workshop. The goal of this workshop was to instill an understanding of digital requirements handling's transformative potential among the domain experts by explaining the technical basis of OIP Core. Yet, as a management-level participant noted in the aftermath of the workshop:

> It isn't that the domain experts don't understand OIP Core. It's that they fail to see how it builds on and extends their existing work on identifying and standardizing the information elements' requirements for [different classes of] equipment. (Fieldnote excerpt)

Emphasizing the generative potential of digital requirements handling, the software engineers failed to acknowledge the other participants' previous investments in digital exchange of technical requirements. Indeed, by translating the other participants' objections to OIP Core's focus on digital requirements handling as a form of user resistance (as elaborated in 5.1 above), the software engineers failed to acknowledge that the other companies have previous financial, technological, and organizational investments in the digital exchange of technical information that they seek to further through OIP. Unresolved, the conflicting views of digital innovation escalated into suspicions over HostCo's ulterior motives to use OIP Core to re-configure the digital EPC ecosystem around their product offerings.

5.3 Innovation Outcome

The EPC industry draws upon a wide array disparate, frequently overlapping, and to a certain degree even redundant digital systems for creating, exchanging, and storing information in a single infrastructure project or for an installation. The degree to which companies in the EPC industry implement digital delivery varies greatly. Most energy companies have their own internal systems for digital project delivery that all subcontracted companies are required to use. Similarly, all EPC companies have their own systems for digital delivery that their subcontractors and vendors are required to use. Even the large equipment vendors have their own internal systems for digital delivery. Some of the systems used are commercial software offering with a higher or lesser degree of tailoring to fit individual companies' organizational practices. Others are custom-built for individual companies. The situation is made further complex as the same company may assume different roles across different EPC projects (such as having the role of EPC company in one project, while functioning as vendor of a particular piece of equipment in another EPC project).

How OIP fit into this picture remained challenging for everyone involved. Deciding upon developing a digital resource that the participants could integrate with existing technical and organizational arrangements made it possible to progress without deciding upon the issue. However, as focus for OIP Core shifted towards digital requirements handling, the operators and EPC companies raised questions over the overall architecture OIP was working towards. The underlying concern was about the implications such architectural decisions would have for the (re-)configuration of the digital EPC ecosystem. OIP's participants envisioned two scenarios. One, that OIP would be "an open industry platform that translate different companies' practices into shared technical requirements which helps the industry to improve efficiency and cut cost" (HostCo presentation). Such a digital platform would obviate and replace functionality in the companies' existing systems (such as requirements management), moving it into the platform and the 'common arena'. The other scenario was for a bare minimum but fully standardized system providing a lingua franca for the digital exchange of technical information between companies' existing systems.

HostCo and the software engineers working on OIP Core were the main proponents OIP aiming towards becoming a digital platform. Domain experts on the other hand advocated for the second scenario; to have a shared standardized system that can fit to their existing technical arrangements.

> In our company, we are using a tool for our requirement management in which we can create specification to have the traceability of the requirements. (...) The tool that is developing in OIP project would then communicate with the system we are using now (Interview excerpt, domain expert)

> The tool we are using is not a competitor to the OIP product, but it is a facilitator providing dynamic information administration. We would use the engine [OIP Core] that comes out of the OIP project to build on our system (Interview excerpt, domain expert)

Focusing on developing the OIP Core based on the first scenario, failed to encompass the existing systems' functionality. While, domain experts translated HosCo's tendency for development of open platform as their effort for gaining generative potential over OIP's outcome, software engineers referred to their lack of acknowledgment of the existing system' functionality in order to dispense with the overlapping and redundant systems. Indeed, divergent focus on the digital infrastructure innovation and innovation in digital infrastructure lead to the conflicting views over architectural aspects of OIP's outcome.

6 Discussion and Conclusion

The above analysis contributes to theory on digital innovation networks in three ways. First, by introducing the temporal dimension in our analysis, we demonstrated digital innovation networks as dynamic and evolving over time. Lyytinen, et al. [4] argue that "the speed and scope of pervasive digitization have created an increasingly dynamic and complex set of social processes in digital product innovation" (p. 52), affording new modes of coordination. How and by what mechanisms to coordinate is contingent upon the taxonomy's two axes of digitizing as operand and operant resource. Including the temporal dimension emphasizes digital innovation networks as ongoing and dynamic, not merely fixed or static entities. As such, not only are the social processes of digital innovation dynamic and complex. They also evolve over time as the configuration of the digital innovation network shifts and evolves. The above analysis traces this as the configuration of companies involved with OIP moved from the pre-project phase of distribution with no centralized control (i.e. anarchic network) towards a more federated innovation network with HostCo as its focal form. Introducing a temporal dimension to digital innovation networks also brings out the tensions that can arise out of such changes. We showed this with regards to modes of coordination. 'From document-centric to data-centric' was an effective organizing vision [15] in mobilizing and coordinating companies' efforts in the loosely coupled, anarchic EPC network. Yet, as the participating companies became more integrated and aligned as a federated network in OIP, this abstract slogan became an ongoing source of confusion as well as contention among project participants seeking to enroll it in favor of their interpretation of project scope and focus.

This argument is similar to Gardet and Mothe [24] observation that different coordination mechanisms are needed as innovation networks evolve. Their observation is grounded in studies of innovation networks in general. Our second contribution is therefore to elaborate upon and substantiate this observation in the context of digital innovation network theory. OIP drew a subset of EPC sector companies closer together in a federated innovation network with HostCo as focal firm. This network came to be coordinated through a centralized project structure with hierarchies and division of labor distributed among sub-projects, along with a work plan with milestones and deliverables. While these mechanisms are well suited to distributing and coordinating more or less clearly defined tasks or activities and for tracking progress through deliverables with deadlines, they do not address what Lyytinen et al. [4] refers to as knowledge and resource heterogeneity resulting from network participants coming from different organizations as well as professional and disciplinary knowledge domains. As Carlile [25, p. 556] notes in the context of new product design "[a]s difference in the amount and/or type of domain-specific knowledge increases between actors, the amount of effort required to adequately share and assess each other's knowledge also increases." Framed in the Lyytinen et al. [4] terminology, with increasing knowledge heterogeneity comes the need for modes of coordinating between professional and knowledge domains.

While HostCo recognized that the organizing vision 'from document-centric to data-centric' was inadequate as coordinating mechanism for OIP phase 1, they did not fully acknowledge its function as translator between heterogeneous knowledge domains. Carlile [25, p. 556] traces the complexity of collaborating across disciplinary and professional knowledge domains increases with (a) knowledge heterogeneity, (b) dependence between different knowledge domains, and (c) the novelty of the project. While knowledge heterogeneity did not change from pre-project to phase 1, the big difference was that the dependencies across knowledge domains increased, actualizing differences in type and amount of domain knowledge. Drawing upon Carlisle's notion of 'knowledge translation' as a mode of coordinating across heterogeneous knowledge domain, Lyytinen et al. [4] observe that coordination across knowledge domains requires both cognitive and social translation. The unresolved tension between the divergent views on the nature of digital innovation in OIP (i.e. 'digital infrastructure innovation' vs. 'innovation in digital infrastructure') can as such be interpreted as a failure by OIP management to acknowledge the need for coordinating mechanisms in support of cognitive translations across heterogeneous knowledge domains.

OIP management sought to address this issue by giving the workshop on OIP Core. This workshop constituted a form of knowledge transfer from software engineers to domain experts, whereas—thinking in terms of Carlile [25] notion of collaborating across disciplinary knowledge domains—what was needed was a translation between the differing knowledge domains to develop an understanding of OIP goals, processes, and outcome. As such, the workshop solidified the tensions between software engineers and domain experts. Furthermore, digital requirements handling challenges existing industry and professional structures. Such questions are resolved through social translations, that "involve constant interaction and political positioning among innovation network participants [whose] perspective are often in conflict, but they still need to find a way to modify and align their interests into temporary dialectic synthesis" [4, p. 56]. Therefore, the ending of OIP phase one can be understood as a failure to negotiate the open-ended and generative potential of OIP Core as envisioned by HostCo's software engineers, against the installed base of previous investments among the EPC sector companies' knowledge base, technical know-how, standards, and existing tools. This leads us to the third and final theoretical contribution, the embeddedness of digital innovation networks.

OIP shares a similar structure to Boland et al. [26] digital innovation network centered on a key firm. Boland et al.'s study shows that the focal firm enforces a transformation throughout the network of subcontractors and vendors delivering goods and services. While HostCo assumed a similar position in the innovation network, its ability to enforce an agenda did not match that of Boland et al.'s focal firm. A key difference between the two cases is the broader network of companies the two digital innovation networks are embedded in. While Boland et al. offers a case study of designing and constructing a novel building, the 3D construction drawing tools enabling such novel design are in more or less widespread use throughout the construction industry. As such, the installed base of technological know-how, disciplinary knowledge was to a large degree already oriented around 3D drawings. In the case of OIP, however, there was no such alignment of the installed base. Rather, OIP's outcome needed to fit with the participating companies previous technological and organizational investments in different approaches to digital delivery. While it is not correct to say that OIP management did not acknowledge this, our analysis illustrates how digital innovation coordination needs to encompass the tension between generativity and open-ended potential of digital innovation [3] with the digital infrastructure's installed base.

The practical implication of our study relates to networks of projects' participants. Due to the fact that digitalization changes the way innovation unfolds, from a single firm to the networks of actors, considering the heterogeneity and distributed features of innovation networks are at the core. Based on the networks' configuration (whether it is heterogenous or homogenous, centralized or decentralized), coordination needs to be considered as an evolving and achieved accomplishment. Respectively, the first feature characterizes that although networks of actors may not be changed through the project, new modes of coordination are required as projects progress to the next stage. In our case, the reason why challenges arise was lack of proper coordination and ability to align the coordination mechanisms to the changes when projects progress to the next phase (i.e. from preparatory phase to the project proper).

More importantly, the embeddedness of innovation networks may exist in large-scale projects. For instance, as we showed in our case, the project network was embedded in an industry network which made some challenges in coordination mechanisms. Therefore, differentiating the industry level and organizational level strategies is vital in coordinating such complex and large-scale projects.

In concluding, by focusing on the innovation networks we have provided insights about how and why challenges arise during large-scale and complex projects, yet future researches are needed to discuss the possible solutions in coping with such challenges. For instance, future studies can investigate different coordination mechanisms (especially the ones used in more heterogeneous and distributed networks of actors) and how they affect the project progress.

References

1. Tilson, D., Lyytinen, K., & Sørensen, C. (2010). Research commentary—Digital infrastructures: The missing IS research agenda. *Information Systems Research, 21*(4), 748–759.
2. Nambisan, S., Lyytinen, K., Majchrzak, A., & Song, M. (2017). Digital innovation management: Reinventing innovation management research in a digital world. *Mis Quarterly, 41*(1).
3. Henfridsson, O., Nandhakumar, J., Scarbrough, H., & Panourgias, N. (2018). Recombination in the open-ended value landscape of digital innovation. *Information and Organization, 28*(2), 89–100.
4. Lyytinen, K., Yoo, Y., & Boland, R. J. (2016). Digital product innovation within four classes of innovation networks. *Information Systems Journal, 26*(1), 47–75.
5. Monteiro, E. (2018). Reflections on digital innovation. *Information and Organization, 28*(2), 101–103.

6. Nambisan, S. (2018). Architecture vs. ecosystem perspectives: Reflections on digital innovation. *Information and Organization, 28*(2), 104–106.
7. Osmundsen, K., Iden, J., and Bygstad, B. (2018). Digital transformation: drivers, success factors, and implications. In Editor (Ed.)^(Eds.), Book digital transformation: Drivers, success factors, and implications' (2018, edn.), pp.
8. Fichman, R. G., Dos Santos, B. L., & Zheng, Z. E. (2014). Digital innovation as a fundamental and powerful concept in the information systems curriculum. *MIS Quarterly, 38*(2).
9. Yoo, Y., Henfridsson, O., & Lyytinen, K. (2010). Research commentary—The new organizing logic of digital innovation: an agenda for information systems research. *Information Systems Research, 21*(4), 724–735.
10. Swanson, E. B. (1994). Information systems innovation among organizations. *Management Science, 40*(9), 1069–1092.
11. Nambisan, S. (2013). Information technology and product/service innovation: A brief assessment and some suggestions for future research. *Journal of the Association for Information Systems, 14*(4), 1.
12. Lusch, R. F., & Nambisan, S. (2015). Service innovation: A service-dominant logic perspective. *MIS Quarterly, 39*(1).
13. Henfridsson, O., & Bygstad, B. (2013). The generative mechanisms of digital infrastructure evolution. *MIS Quarterly*, 907–931.
14. Sørensen, C. (2013). Digital platform and-infrastructure innovation. In H. Higashikuni (Ed), Mobile strategy challenges (In Japanese). Tokyo: Nikkan Kogyo Shimbun Ltd.
15. Swanson, E. B., & Ramiller, N. C. (1997). The organizing vision in information systems innovation. *Organization Science, 8*(5), 458–474.
16. Pollock, N., & Williams, R. (2010). The business of expectations: How promissory organizations shape technology and innovation. *Social Studies of Science, 40*(4), 525–548.
17. Monteiro, E. (1998). Scaling information infrastructure: The case of next-generation IP in the Internet. *The information Society, 14*(3), 229–245.
18. Yin, R. K. (2017). Case study research and applications: Design and methods. Thousand Oaks: SAGE.
19. Jorgensen, D. L. (1989). *The methodology of participant observation* (pp. 12–26). Thousand Oaks: SAGE.
20. Fetterman, D. M. (2009). Ethnography: Step-by-step. Thousand Oaks: SAGE.
21. Kvale, S., & Brinkmann, S. (2009). Interviews: Learning the craft of qualitative research interviewing. Thousand Oaks: SAGE.
22. Lobo, S., & Whyte, J. (2017). Aligning and reconciling: Building project capabilities for digital delivery. *Research Policy, 46*(1), 93–107.
23. Star, S. L., & Ruhleder, K. (1996). Steps toward an ecology of infrastructure: Design and access for large information spaces. *Information Systems Research, 7*(1), 111–134.
24. Gardet, E., & Mothe, C. (2011). The dynamics of coordination in innovation networks. *European Management Review, 8*(4), 213–229.
25. Carlile, P. R. (2004). Transferring, translating, and transforming: An integrative framework for managing knowledge across boundaries. *Organization Science, 15*(5), 555–568.
26. Boland, R. J., Lyytinen, K., & Yoo, Y. (2007). Wakes of innovation in project networks: The case of digital 3-D representations in architecture, engineering, and construction. *Organization Science, 18*(4), 631–647.

Digital Ecosystems for Business
Innovation and Digital Transformation

Organizational Capabilities for Social Media Management: How Restaurant Managers Approach to the Digital Ecosystem

Claudia Dossena and Francesca Mochi

Abstract Digital platforms and social media are now widespread and their diffusion enables the development of digital ecosystems where organizations, users and firms' stakeholders virtually meet, share knowledge, influence each other and co-evolve. In order to effectively manage and exploit digital ecosystems, organizations require to evolve their processes and capabilities. The paper aims are threefold: (1) understanding how restaurant managers perceive and approach the digital ecosystem, (2) investigate how they concretely manage the digital ecosystem, and (3) comprehend what organizational competences are perceived as useful to effectively manage the digital ecosystem. We adopt an explorative approach through a qualitative analysis of 54 companies in the food and beverage service sectors.

Keywords Digital ecosystem · Social media · Organizational competences

1 Introduction

The Web and, in particular, social media have radically changed the business landscape, with relevant consequences on organizations' knowledge management activities. Basically, social media stand for open participation and user-interaction, e.g. through user groups and online communities, forums, blogs, wikis and social network sites [1]. Through social media, stakeholders have a powerful medium to share knowledge and information. From this perspective, the Web is a fundamental information source for organizations, especially for what concerns stakeholders' opinions. Due to the increasing easiness and user-friendliness of online publishing processes, especially if compared to traditional media, every Web user is now able to communicate unmediated and unchecked contents via simple and widely used publishing tools,

C. Dossena (✉) · F. Mochi
Università Cattolica del Sacro Cuore, 20123 Milan, Italy
e-mail: claudia.dossena@unicatt.it

F. Mochi
e-mail: francesca.mochi@unicatt.it

R. Agrifoglio et al. (eds.), *Digital Business Transformation*, Lecture Notes in Information Systems and Organisation 38, https://doi.org/10.1007/978-3-030-47355-6_18

269

thus affecting firm's legitimation and reputation [2]. E-word of mouth communication (e-WOM) is a major part of online consumer interactions, particularly within the environment of online communities [3]. Modern social media make easier and virulent the diffusion of comments, anecdotes, opinions, and this can be both profitable and problematic for online reputation. Park and Lee [4] demonstrate that just one negative comment can contribute to worsen the reputation within an online forum, while the perception of a positive reputation is merely proportional to the number of positive comments. Therefore, online reputation is a resource cumulated in time, it is also quite 'fragile' and quickly damageable [5–7]. This makes more important the proactive interventions in managing the environment of online communities. In academic world many authors have studied online reputation both at an individual and a firm level, focusing mainly on the opportunities and threats of e-WOM [8, 9]. From an empirical point of view, a growing number of organizations are developing a digital strategy [10, 11] or are developing processes of digital transformation [12, 13]. However, despite the increasing attention paid from both academics and practitioners on how to approach to the digital world, there isn't a dominant reference model or best practices yet [14]. In particular, there is a need for a deeper understanding of the digital competences required to effectively explore and exploit the opportunities coming from the digital platforms. The diffusion of digital platforms enables the development of digital ecosystems where organizations, users and firms' stakeholders virtually meet, influence each other and co-evolve. Consequently, organizations require to evolve their processes and capabilities in order to manage this digital ecosystem.

Drawing on from those premises our research questions are the following:

- how restaurant managers perceive and approach to the digital ecosystem,
- how they concretely manage the digital ecosystem
- what organizational competences are useful to effectively manage the digital ecosystem.

In order to answer our research questions, we follow an explorative approach through a qualitative analysis of 54 businesses in the food and beverage service sectors. With this research we thus expect to find some answers about how restaurant managers approach and manage the digital ecosystem and the competences and behaviors that managers may adopt.

The research aims at contributing to the digital ecosystems' literature, the e-HRM literature and the IS literature. Furthermore, it will offer managerial implications of digital ecosystems' effectiveness and on the behaviors and capabilities that the HR, managers and firms owners have to monitor, search and promote among employees and themselves. Lastly, it will give managerial suggestions on how to deal with e-WOM and reputation issues.

2 Theoretical Framework

2.1 e-WOM and Social Media Management in the Food and Beverage Service Sector

Previous literature in hospitality and tourism management noted that consumers are becoming "hyper-digital", an "always-on consumer, using connected devices every day or multiple times a day" [15]. Before the advent of the Internet, word of mouth (WOM) was the most useful tool for marketing research and the most influential source for information exchange [9]. e-WOM is defined as "any positive or negative statement made by potential, actual, or former customers about a product or company, which is made available to a multitude of people and institutions via the Internet" [16: p. 39]. Fox and Longart [8] investigated restaurant marketers' use of social media as part of an integrated marketing communication strategy. They highlighted some relevant recommendation to restaurant marketers in order to create a positive e-WOM for the restaurant (e.g. maintain fluid and flexible communication, adapt tactics by the channel, i.e. by the social media platform used, give stickiness to the content in order to avoid boredom and predictability, adapt the social media strategy to include mobile devices in order to follow the increasing trends towards mobile consumption of social media). Similarly, Ghiselli and Ma [17] examine the use of social media by restaurants in China. Their results suggest that even if restaurants are not very active on the four main Chinese platforms (WeChat, Dianping, Baidu and Meituan), actually they are making efforts to improve their social media presence, especially upscale restaurants. Surprisingly, international chains are doing worse than domestic restaurants, but the authors stated that this probably is due to the fact that social media landscape in China is drastically different from that in the West. Although consumers seem to appreciate online ordering and online payment, they are not provided widely. Ghiselli and Ma [17] also adopt the consumers' perspective and investigate the extent to which consumers are using social media to obtain information about dining options. They found that 85% of participants (a total of 254 responses were considered) use social media to search for restaurants; 15% of participants indicated they use social media to search for restaurants almost every time. Older participants were less likely to use social media to search for restaurants, as they trust friends' recommendations more. The authors also investigated the usage of different social media for the restaurant selection (e.g. Dianping, WeChat, Baidu, Meituan, Tripdvisor), they found that those social media were almost equally used when looking for restaurants. Moreover, they investigated the willingness to receive update information from the social media pages of the restaurants (69% of the participants were willing to receive social media updates at least once a week). Lastly, they investigate some consumers preferences and highlight that consumers "prefer (in order): real-time updates (e.g. special offers), GPS/location and direction services, online menu information, online ordering (for delivery and carryout), average spending/expectation, a social function (likes, share with friends, check in where you have been, rating, etc.), online payment, new menu items, reservation/waiting time and an interaction function (leave message, provide feedback)" [17: p. 257]. Similarly to Ghiselli and Ma [17], in 2011 Jeon and Jang [18] investigate which restaurant experiences trigger customers to engage in positive e-WOM. The results show that restaurants' food quality positively influences customers to spread positive e-WOM, because diners want to help the restaurant; also satisfactory service and a superior atmosphere triggered positive e-WOM. On the contrary, price fairness did not drive diners toward e-WOM. As previous research shows us, web sites and social media allow users to be influenced in the restaurant choice by the e-WOM [17, 19]. Those tools have completely reshaped the hospitality industry scenario and changed the sources customers use/trust to search for hotels, locate restaurants, place orders, make reservations, plan trips and share experiences [20].

2.2   Digital Competences in the Hospitality Industry

Social media have significantly impacted the tourism system [21] since they are widely adopted by travelers to search, organize, share, and annotate their travel stories and experiences through blogs and microblogs (e.g., Blogger and Twitter), online communities (e.g., Facebook, Qzone RenRen, TripAdvisor and TheFork), media sharing sites (e.g., Instagram, Flickr, Pinterest, and YouTube), social bookmarking sites (e.g., Digg), social knowledge sharing sites (e.g., Wikitravel), and other tools in a collaborative way. Social media are useful for managing customer relationships with their unique ability of attracting customers through in-depth, focused, and user-generated content, engaging customers through social interactions, and retaining customers through relation building with other members [22]. Dellarocas [23] also suggested that social media provide tourism companies with unprecedented opportunities to understand and respond to consumer preferences. Analyzing the comments on online communities such as TripAdvisor, organizations are able to better understand what their guests like and dislike about them and their competitors. Consequently, tourism businesses have been integrating social media platforms into their websites to enhance customers' travel information searching experience [24, 25]. Leung et al. [26] reviewed and analyzed social media-related research articles in tourism and hospitality sectors. Adopting both the consumers' and the suppliers' perspectives, the authors found that consumer-centric studies generally focus on the use and impact of social media in the research phase of the travel planning process. Supplier-related studies in tourism and hospitality sectors [27] have concentrated closely on the role of social media in supporting marketing activities—especially on promotion [26, 28]—communication mechanisms, both internal and external to the organizational boundaries, [27, 29], management function [30], and research area, training and learning processes [31]. However, what are the main organizational competences required for effectively managing social media remains still unclear both for academic scholars and practitioners. Roy e Dionne [32] investigated how 4 SME (inns and restaurants) perceive social media and how they use it to sustain their day-to-day work. In their multiple case study they found that all the businesses developed the social media platform internally even though some organizations had difficulties in doing so. The choice of content to publish on social media platforms is usually not related to a formal and specific marketing strategy, but it is mostly based on the personal choices of the person in charge of the platforms monitoring. The 4 SMEs are aware that they are not exploiting social media to the extent they could or should. Lack of time, lack of technological knowledge and lack of knowledge on how to evaluate their performance on social media are only some of the reasons that explain the underuse of social media platforms. In tourism literature, Schmallegger and Carson [27] used case studies to discuss the challenges tourism organizations face when using blogs to five key functions—promotion, product distribution, communication, management and research. Ayeh et al.[33] explored Hong Kong practitioners' perceptions of social media and concludes that organizations apply a variety of strategies in day-to-day management: organizations employ a variety of social media platforms in order to maintain high exposure to potential and existing customers, they continuously update the company's account in order to ideally raise the users interest, they assign a staff member to be responsible for answering enquiries and comments through social media platforms, and they post positive reviews on the social media to maintain a positive image and online reputation. However, the capabilities, competences and personal attributes needed to apply a strategy in managing social media remain still unclear. Munar [30], focusing on social media strategies for destination management organizations, argued that social media require a new communication culture and training, but this is not enough to succeed.

3 Methodology

We adopted two different methodologies, firstly, we used structured interviews in order to assess the familiarity and use of digital platforms and to assess the restaurant managers perceptions on the use of digital platforms. Our sample of the structured interviews is based on 54 restaurants. To deepen our understanding regarding the organizational competencies needed to efficiently manage digital ecosystem, we have also developed in-depth semi-structured interviews with 19 restaurant managers that have also participated to the structured interview. Thus, among the 54 restaurants of our sample, 19 agreed to be further interviewed. By analyzing the social media pages of those restaurants (i.e. TripAdvisor, Google rating, Facebook, JustEat and Deliveroo) we found that all the 19 were active online—with an institutional account on at least three different digital platforms—and with a good online reputation [with feedback ratings higher than 4 (out of 5) in Google, Facebook, Tripadvisor, JustEat and Deliveroo and higher than 8 (out of 10) in TheFork]. This seems to highlight an auto selection bias of our sample, only those restaurants that are interested in the use of social media for their business activity actually agreed to be further interviewed with the semi structured interview.

To analyze the semi-structured interviews, we adopted the Gioia's methodology to assess qualitative rigor [34]. Our analysis consisted of multiple, iterative readings of the interview transcripts, and the identification of dimensions of first-order concepts uttered by respondents regarding the use and management of social media. We concentrate our study on the restaurants of Milan, one of the most well known northern Italian cities in the key tourism generating markets [35]. The majority of respondents is male (74%) and with an age between 21 and 68 years old. All respondents are restaurant managers and/or owners. Our sample is heterogenous in terms of dimensions, typology and average cost for a dinner. We have considered both very small restaurants and medium restaurant chains (with more than a restaurant in Milan). We excluded from our analyses the big food service chains, since we decided to focus on SMEs because they are the majority of businesses in the food service sector in Italy. We included in our sample different typologies of restaurants: Italian restaurant, ethnic cuisine, pizzeria, vegan cuisine, regional cuisine, gourmet cuisine. The sample is mixed also in terms of average cost for a dinner: less than 10 euros a person (9% of the sample), between 10 and 25 euros (35%), between 25 and 50 euros (44%), more than 50 euros a person (11%).

4   Results and Discussion

4.1   How Restaurant Managers Perceive the Digital Ecosystem

In our sample there are two polarized positions regarding the evolution of the ecosystem in the food and beverage service sector. Some interviewees seem enthusiastic about how their ecosystems are changed, especially thanks to the diffusion of social media. Those people see digital ecosystem as a new world, a harbinger of opportunities for the development of their business. Other interviewees have a more circumspect attitude to social media, since they recognize in this new ecosystem also potential threats for their business. In Table 1 we compared different positions of restaurant managers and owners as emerged by in-depth interviews. The semi-structured interview data were grouped and coded into four first-order themes [34].

Competitiveness and market shares

The majority of the interviewees perceive digital ecosystem as fundamental for the success of their business (66.7% of respondents) and the remaining one third of the sample declares that even if digital world is important, there are also other important things for their business. Social media can be an effective means to reach more users (through a greater visibility) and to increase customers if this visibility is combined to a positive online reputation. According to 50 (out to 54) respondents, the Web

Table 1 How restaurant managers and owners perceive digital ecosystems

Theme	Pros	Cons

Competitiveness and market shares	• Increase visibility
	• Increase attractiveness
	• Offer improvement:
	  – Listening customers through reviews and feedback
	  – Copying competitors' best practices
	  – Offering digital experiences
		• Increase market competition

Communication	• Increase communication between the restaurant and customers • More direct communication • Voice of the cunstomers	• Possible conflicts and misunderstandings • High costs (in terms of time and competences required)
Transparency	• High transparency • Democratization of the web	• Low transparency • Fake reviews
Customer education	• More informed customers	• "know-all" customers

is an effective channel to have visibility. Digital platforms are perceived differently according to their ability to give a greater visibility to a restaurant: Google (53 out of 54), TripAdvisor (46 out of 54), Instagram (45 out of 54), restaurant website (43 out of 54), Facebook (43 out of 54), thematic blogs and forums (28 out of 29), food delivery websites (28 out of 54), YouTube (18 out of 54), generalist blogs and forums (16 out of 54), LinkedIn (8 out of 54). To efficiently managing digital ecosystem, restaurants can also use social media for increasing their attractiveness. About two thirds of respondents believe the majority of their customers searches for online information about a restaurant, independently by the customer age (i.e. everybody, and not only younger customers, use online platforms as information source) (43% of respondents) or if customers are under 30 (26%). Moreover, thanks to the digital ecosystem, restaurants can improve their offer through at least three different ways:

• Exploiting customers' feedbacks and reviews online: according to 45 (out of 54) restaurant managers, social media are effective channels to listen customers' opinions and, consequently, improve their offer. About 82% of the sample perceives customers' feedbacks and reviews useful for improving their services. According to respondents, constructive feedbacks are given by young and extrovert customers, with great familiarity with social media tools and high instruction levels. The remaining one third perceives customers' feedbacks as means for venting frustration. In an in-depth interview, a restaurant owner declares: "*online reviews and comments are driven by emotions and not by the desire to give a constructive opinion*";

• Copying competitors' best practices: 43% of respondents declare to frequently search for information about competitors' activities; 39% of restaurant managers

monitor competitors' online activity at least occasionally. Only 18% of respondents don't search for information about competitors;
- Offering digital experiences: according to in-depth interviews, managing in a synergetic way the real and in the digital world, restaurants can offer an extra service to their customers, i.e. a digital experience.

Even if digital ecosystem is generally perceived positively by respondents, some restaurant managers complain about a generalized increase of market competition, also because of the diffusion of social media. In particular, through food delivery platforms a lot of new cooking businesses have arisen.

Communication

Restaurant managers speculate that their customers are very active online. In restaurant managers opinion, often (28% of respondents) their customers leave online reviews, or at least occasionally (72%).

Social media can increase communication between restaurants and their stakeholder, enabling a more direct communication. Of course, social media, enhance a better listening of customers opinions, expectations and desires. As argued in managerial literature, thanks to their interactivity, social media significantly empower users, increasing the voice of the customers. However, social media are also a useful tool for giving voice to restaurant managers. 81% of respondents declare that the direct communication with the customer enables restaurant managers to transform a negative comment in a business opportunity. However, there are also restaurant managers in an opposite position, that perceive social media as something that mediates relationships and hinders communication. The written form and the asynchronous communication can lead to conflicts and misunderstandings. Moreover, surprisingly some restaurant managers highlight high communication costs. Indeed, even if social media have apparently very low costs, somebody argue that the management of the digital ecosystems has high costs, especially in terms of time and competences required.

Transparency

Some restaurant managers and owners believe in the democratization of the Web, especially for the high transparency, the lack of filters and control in sharing user-generated contents within social media. However, most of them adopt a skeptical position about transparency in the digital ecosystem, especially in negative reviews. 83% of respondent declares to have read at least an online comment and thought that it was a fake review. About two third of the sample believes that highly negative comments may be fake reviews left by competitors in order to intentionally damage their online reputation. In general, e-WOM is perceived as less truthful and corresponding with reality than traditional WOM. Moreover, some respondents with technological competences are aware that for having a good online reputation you can "simply" pay social media agencies and develop Search Engine Optimization (SEO) and Search Engine Marketing (SEM) activities. One interviewee implicitly cites Asch conformity effect, i.e. the influence of the group majority on an individual's judgment. A restaurant owner declares *"if users read very positive comments about a restaurant, when they have to judge (or rank) their personal experience they tend to conform with the group majority"*. However, some digital platforms (e.g. Google) are recognized as more credible than others (e.g. Tripadvisor).

Customer education

In in-depth interviews, some interviewees recognize in the social media also an educational role for customers. This cookery education is also reinforced by the spreading of cooking TV shows. Moreover, thanks to social media, customers are now more informed and more aware than in the past. They pay more attention to the quality of raw material, to original or traditional recipes, and also to plating. For the majority of restaurant managers, this is an important advantage for their businesses. However, some interviewee also argue that now almost everybody considers his(her) self an expert and a great culinary critic, even if he(she) has not adequate competences. And even worse, he(she) expresses and shares his(her) opinions through social media.

4.2 How Restaurant Managers Approach to the Digital Ecosystem and How They Manage It

Restaurant managers and owners approach to digital ecosystems in a variety of ways. As expected, all the interviewees use the Web, and in particular social media and the restaurant website, for marketing purposes. However, as argued in the previous paragraph web platforms are used also for other purposes, i.e. for improving the restaurant offer, for benchmarking activities, for efficiently managing relationships with partners and suppliers, for engaging customers, for increasing brand awareness, for internal and external communication, for educating customers and spreading cookery culture, for CRM activities, for getting sponsorships, improving booking (online booking), and e-recruitment.

In Fig. 1 we reported the digital platform used by respondents.

Many restaurant managers highlight the appropriateness in using different digital platforms depending on the content of the message and its aim. These digital platforms are managed both internally and in outsourcing. 49 restaurants managers (out of 54) internally manage the digital ecosystem, personally or through internal collaborators, after an adequate training. 5 interviewees give in outsourcing the management of the digital channels to communication agencies, web agencies or social media managers. Notably, even if some restaurant owners have technological and digital competences, they choose to externalize the digital platforms management to more specialized people. Restaurant managers feel to have adequate technological skills to manage social media, these latter perceived as intuitive and user-friendly tools. The choice to give in outsourcing social media management relies in perceived difficulties to correctly communicate within online communities. Many restaurant managers

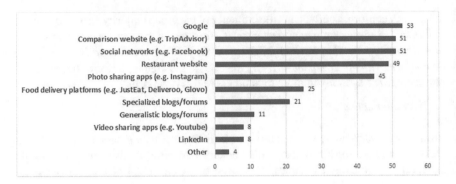

Fig. 1 Presence in the digital platforms

declare to have inadequate communication skills for the digital ecosystem, this latter perceived with high degrees of complexity, dynamism and heterogeneity. Moreover, 8 restaurant owners (out of 54) declare to use ad hoc web tools for monitoring the web.

Regarding Web monitoring activities, 63% of respondents declare that they don't perceive difficulties or critical issues in monitoring social media. However, web monitoring is described as an activity particularly time-consuming. Nevertheless, the majority of respondents continuously (daily or at least one time a week) monitors online activities only on selected digital platforms: Google, TripAdvisor, Facebook and Instagram. Another issue related to social media monitoring relies in understanding the truthfulness of online reviews. Interviewees identify fake reviews by looking at some review or reviewer characteristics such as very generic review and with a lack of details, reviews that are too similar to other reviews, that describe situations that don't confirm to reality and that are left by users with ambiguous profiles. In order to improve online reputation, restaurant managers pay great attention in writing and in replying to online reviews. From this perspective, restaurants in our sample adopt very different strategies. About a quarter of respondents reply to all comments, both positive and negative ones. 31% of respondents reply only to comments in specific digital platforms, perceived as strategic ones. 20% of restaurant managers choose to reply only to negative reviews (a respondent says *"reply is extremely important and, in case, also apologize"*). The remaining respondents (14 out of 54) reply only occasionally (a respondent argues *"the better strategy is never reply, either to positive or negative reviews, since 'the customer is always right"*).

For writing on digital platforms, communication capabilities are essential for message efficacy. Interviewees declare that communication has to be clear, brief and linear and different communication style is needed accordingly to the social media used.

Table 2 Relevant competences for restaurants managers

Aggregate dimension	Macro themes
Communication	• Language coherency • Message efficacy
Customer management	• Negotiation and conflict management • Customers understanding • Customers management processes
People's engagement	• Brand identity • Storytelling
Restaurant management	• Organizational change • Food and service quality and creativity
Social media management	• Awareness about the characteristics and differences of social media
Imitation	• Recognition of best practices • Implementation of best practices

4.3 What Organizational Competences Are Useful to Effectively Manage the Digital Ecosystem

Table 2 reports the systematization of the interviews by showing the competences that the interviewees explicitly or implicitly reveal as fundamental to effectively exploit digital ecosystems for their business. We adopted the Gioia's methodology [34] to aggregate the competences in macro themes and aggregate dimensions. We unified those competencies in 6 aggregate dimensions: communication, customers management, people engagement, restaurants management, social media management and imitation. Those dimensions allow us to understand which competencies are relevant for the interviewees. Notably, digital and technological competences are not perceived as relevant. Technological capabilities are left to more IT-specialist people, since managers do not need to know how to use the technology, but they would benefit from greater understanding of how it can be used and what can be achieved.

Communication

Respondents consider communication as a core competence to effectively communicate with users in a digital ecosystem. Restaurants owners and managers mainly focus their attention on language coherency and message efficacy. Language coherency refers to the attention that the interviewees pay to the use of different communication style accordingly to the social media used, the content of the message and the customers that have to receive the message. For example, the use of LinkedIn is related to a formal communication, it mainly reaches professionals and could be used for posting CSR initiatives or to promote the brand identity of the restaurant. Facebook, on the other hand, is used for a more informal communication, to promote new menus or promotional deals. Moreover, different social media and different language styles allow a different use of jokes, slogans and photos. The language style depends also on the type of restaurant, an elegant restaurant usually adopts a more formal communication, while a fast food relies on informal one. Respondents also highlight the importance of effective message by giving examples of the qualities that a message must have such as clarity, linearity, sincerity and transparency as well as charisma and surprise. Moreover, the message must contain valuable information for the customers.

> The message posted on social media has to be simple and clear, brief and strict to the point in order to be easily comprehensible from everyone

> It is better to write sincere messages, to show transparency and thus avoid possible critics

Customers management

The second set of competencies that the interviewees identified are related to customers management. They highlight the relevance to have negotiation competencies in order to resolve conflicts smoothly, to understand the customers' needs and preferences and to engage in customers management processes also using CRM software. In particular, in negotiation and conflict management interviewees mainly focus on the ability to detect fake comments and reviews posted on their social media pages and the ability to answer in a polite way but at the same time discrediting the fake reviews, thus sometimes obtaining visibility and competitive advantage.

People's engagement

Some respondents have focused on the competence of being able to engage people. In order to engage potential customers, it is essential to know the restaurant strengths and promote them. Managers need to build a strong brand identity to be recognizable and different from others. Furthermore, building a strong identity helps to engage and retain employees and promote a strong organizational culture. Lastly, there is nothing such as a good story to engage people and to obtain their attention, and our results show that promoting a good story about the restaurant and practicing storytelling is a competence that is valued by some of the respondents.

Restaurant management

Managing a restaurant comprises a lot of competencies and the overcome of frequent problems or unexpected events. However, social media could help to manage restaurants and to promote internal change too. The interviewees, although only few of them, show that social media could be a useful tool to promote organizational change and improve food and service quality and creativity. Customers' comments and reviews work as a check of the customers' evaluation of quality and can thus reveal if something went wrong during a specific day, thus promoting a constructive change in the work processes or in the plates offered. Furthermore, the wide competition that restaurants are facing due to the spread of social media reviews, are an incentive to improve not only the quality of food and service but also the aesthetic presentation of the plates and the creativity and innovation of the product.

Social media management

As previously argued, some restaurants managers declare to rely on external social media managers or social media agency, while others internalize the management of digital ecosystems. However, when social media are used to improve competencies such as negotiation management, organizational change management, creativity and innovation, they are mainly managed internally in the organizational boundaries. The majority of restaurant managers is aware of the necessity to use digital platforms in different ways depending on the platform itself, and on the purpose and content to share. Some of them are also aware that there are tricks that can be used in order to increase the visibility of posts, such as posting on certain day hours or carefully plan the frequency of a new post. Lastly, they are aware about the need to have coherency of information among every social media page they owned and the website as well, however due to time restriction this is not easily implemented.

Imitation

Lastly, there is one interviewee that declares to not be obsessed with digital and social media competencies, because the relevant and first competence to own is to understand who are the best players on the market and their social media strategies in order to imitate them.

> I only need to recognize which are the best practices in dealing with social media platforms from other restaurants that seem effective in using them. Once I have understood those best practices I simply try to replicate them on my social media

5   Conclusions

Theoretical and managerial implications

Our study leads to some relevant theoretical and managerial implications. Firstly, our study gives an original interpretation of the web, recognized as a digital ecosystem where organizations, users and firms' stakeholders virtually meet, influence each other and co-evolve. Secondly, the present work focuses on the food and beverage service sector, that is still insufficiently investigated [8, 17]. In particular, we investigate how restaurant managers perceive and approach to the digital ecosystem, how they manage social media, and what organizational competences are useful to effectively manage the digital ecosystem. It is an attempt to investigate the competencies that seem more relevant for effectively dealing with social media in the food and beverage sector thus enriching both social media literature and hospitality one. Moreover, the research aims at contributing to the digital ecosystems' literature, the e-HRM literature and the IS literature. The study also offers some relevant managerial implications for practitioners regarding how restaurant managers concretely manage digital ecosystem in day-by-day activities and what organizational competences a restaurant manager should have according to how social media can be used and what organizational purposes can be achieved. An interesting result is that some restaurant managers use social media as a knowledge source for improving their offer and their processes. From this perspective, restaurants could reinterpret digital capabilities as a tool for continuously explore and exploit external knowledge shared within online community. The social media are thus a tool that allow knowledge sharing and that promote the transformation of organizational processes. Lastly, in this contribution we try to give some managerial suggestions on how to deal with e-WOM and reputation issues, e.g. how to write an effective message and how to manage and reply to negative reviews. Social media can show competitors best practices in dealing with negative reviews that can be imitated by other restaurants thus sharing knowledge about problem solving competencies and negotiation abilities.

Limitations and future research

The research has some limitations, first of all the sample is still small, and a future research can continue the data gathering for enriching the explorative study. The sample is also composed by restaurant in the same Italian city. This criterium was chosen in order to be able to compare the restaurants, however, future research can replicate the study in other cities or Countries. Furthermore, there is the chance of auto-selection bias of the sample of the second semi structured interviews. The sample is indeed composed by a subgroup of the first sample that agree to further investigate the use and perceptions of social media in the food and service sector. Furthermore, the comparison with other Countries could reveal different approaches in managing the digital ecosystems.

Lastly, a longitudinal investigation could be useful in order to understand if with time and practices the restaurant managers and owners acquire new competences and change their perception about the use of social media for their businesses.

References

1. Gorry, G. A., & Westbrook, R. A. (2009). Winning the internet confidence game. *Corporate Reputation Review, 12*(3), 195–203.
2. Francesconi, A., Dossena, C., & Francesconi, A. (2015) A strategic and organizational perspective for understanding the evolution of online reputation management systems. In: L. Mola, F. Pennarola & Za, S. (Eds.), From information to smart society—Environment, politics and economics (pp. 49–61). New York: Springer.
3. Brown, J., Broderick, A. J., & Lee, N. (2007). Word of mouth communication within online communities: Conceptualizing the online social network. *Journal of Interactive Marketing, 21*(3), 2–20.
4. Park, N., & Lee, K. M. (2007). Effects of online news forum on corporate reputation. *Public Relations Review, 33*(3), 346–348.
5. Alsop, R. J. (2004). Corporate reputation—Anything but superficial: The deep but fragile nature of corporate reputation. *Journal of Business Strategy, 25*(6), 21–29.
6. Grant, M. (2005). *Contemporary strategic analysis* (5th ed.). Oxford, UK: Blackwell.

7. Hall, R. (1993). A framework linking intangible resources and capabilities to sustainable competitive advantage. *Strategic Management Journal, 14,* 607–618.
8. Fox, G., & Longart, P. (2016). Electronic word-of-mouth: Successful communication strategies for restaurants. *Tourism and Hospitality Management, 22*(2), 211–223.
9. Hussain, S., Guangju, W., Jafar, R. M. S., Ilyas, Z., Mustafa, G., & Jianzhou, Y. (2018). Consumers' online information adoption behavior: Motives and antecedents of electronic word of mouth communications. *Computers in Human Behavior, 80,* 22–32.
10. Porter, M. E., & Heppelmann, J. E. (2015). How smart, connected products are transforming companies. *Harvard Business Review, 93*(10), 96–114.
11. Bughin, J., & Van Zeebroeck, N. (2017). The best response to digital disruption the best response to digital disruption. *MIT Sloan Management Review, 58*(4), 80–86.
12. Zhu, K., Dong, S., Xu, S. X., & Kraemer, K. L. (2006). Innovation diffusion in global contexts: determinants of post-adoption digital transformation of European companies. *European Journal of Information Systems, 15*(6), 601–616.
13. Kane, G. C., Palmer, D., Phillips, A. N., Kiron, D., & Buckley, N. (2015). Strategy, not technology, drives digital transformation. *MIT Sloan Management Review and Deloitte University Press, 14,* 1–25.
14. Pucihar, A., Kljajić Borštnar, M., Ravesteijn P., Seitz, J., Bons, R. (2018). Digital transformation: meeting the challenges. In A. Pucihar, et al. (Eds.), *31st BLED eConference: Digital Transformation: Meeting the Challenges,* Slovenia: Conference Proceedings.
15. Litvin, S. W., Goldsmith, R. E., & Pan, B. (2018). A retrospective view of electronic word-of-mouth in hospitality and tourism management. *International Journal of Contemporary Hospitality Management, 30*(1), 313–325.
16. Hennig-Thurau, T., Gwinner, K. P., Walsh, G., & Gremler, D. D. (2004). Electronic word-of-mouth via consumer-opinion platforms: what motivates consumers to articulate themselves on the internet? *Journal of Interactive Marketing, 18*(1), 38–52.
17. Ghiselli, R., & Ma, J. (2015). Restaurant social media usage in China: A study of industry practices and consumer preferences. *Worldwide Hospitality and Tourism Themes, 7*(3), 251–265.
18. Jeong, E., & Jang, S. S. (2011). Restaurant experiences triggering positive electronic word-of-mouth (eWOM) motivations. *International Journal of Hospitality Management, 30*(2), 356–366.
19. Gregory, S., & Kim, J. (2004). Restaurant choice. *Journal of Foodservice Business Research, 7*(1), 81–95.
20. Sigala, M., Christou, E., & Gretzel, U. (2012). *Social media in travel, tourism and hospitality theory, practice and cases.* CA: Ebrary.
21. Xiang, Z., Du, Q., Ma, Y., & Fan, W. (2017). A comparative analysis of major online review platforms: Implications for social media analytics in hospitality and tourism. *Tourism Management, 58,* 51–65.
22. Wang, Y., & Fesenmaier, D. R. (2007). Collaborative destination marketing: A case study of Elkhart county, Indiana. *Tourism Management, 28,* 863–875.
23. Dellarocas, C. (2003). The digitization of word of mouth: Promise and challenges of online feedback mechanisms. *Management Science, 49*(10), 1407–1424.
24. Fuchs, M., Scholochov, C., & Höpken, W. (2009). E-Business adoption, use, and value creation: An Austrian hotel study. *Information Technology and Tourism, 11*(4), 267–284.
25. Sanchez-Franco, M. J., & Rondan-Cataluña, F. J. (2010). Virtual travel communities and customer loyalty: Customer purchase involvement and web site design. *Electronic Commerce Research and Applications, 9*(2), 171–182.
26. Leung, D., Law, R., & Lee, H. A. (2011). The perceived destination image of Hong Kong on Ctrip. com. *International Journal of Tourism Research, 13*(2), 124–140.
27. Schmallegger, D., & Carson, D. (2008). Blogs in tourism: Changing approaches to information exchange. *Journal of Vacation Marketing, 14*(2), 99–110.
28. Akehurst, G. (2009). User generated content: the use of blogs for tourism organizations and tourism consumers. *Service Business, 3*(1), 51–61.

29. Pantelidis, I. S. (2010). Electronic meal experience: A content analysis of online restaurant comments. *Cornell Hospitality Quarterly, 51*(4), 483–491.
30. MunarMunar, A. M. (2010). Digital exhibitionism: The age of exposure. Culture Unbound. *Journal of Current Cultural Research, 2*(3), 401–422.
31. Isacsson, A., & Gretzel, U. (2011). Facebook as an edutainment medium to engage students in sustainability and tourism. *Journal of Hospitality and Tourism Technology, 2*(1), 81–90.
32. Roy, A. & Dionne, C. (2015) How SMEs evaluate their performance in reaching and attracting customers with social media? In P. Peres & A. Mesquita (Eds.), *ECSM2015*-Proceedings of the 2nd European Conference on Social Media (pp. 390–397), Portugal: Porto.
33. Ayeh, J. K., Leung, D., Au, N., & Law, R. (2012). Perceptions and strategies of hospitality and tourism practitioners on social media: An exploratory study. In M. Fuchs, F. Ricci & L. Cantoni (Eds.), *Information and communication technologies in tourism 2012* (pp. 1–12), Wien: Springer.
34. Gioia, D. A., Corley, K. G., & Hamilton, A. L. (2013). Seeking qualitative rigor in inductive research: Notes on the Gioia methodology. *Organizational Research Methods, 16*(1), 15–31.
35. De Carlo, M., Canali, S., Pritchard, A., & Morgan, N. (2009). Moving Milan towards Expo 2015: designing culture into a city brand. *Journal of Place Management and Development, 2*(1), 8–22.

Achieving Trust, Relational Governance and Innovation in Information Technology Outsourcing Through Digital Collaboration

Giovanni Vaia, William DeLone, Daria Arkhipova, and Anna Moretti

Abstract Through an explorative case study, this paper provides insights on how the adoption of a digital collaboration tool (i) can create a more trust-based relationship between ITO client and suppliers, and (ii) can foster collaborative relationships that result in both operational and strategic innovation outcomes. Our case study is based on an ITO project developed by Infocert, the first Certification Authority in Italy, having issued and managed more than 4,500,000 qualified certificates of digital signature. Our findings show how digital collaboration can affect trust before and during the engagement phase of the IT outsourcing process. The digital media tool increased communication flexibility and supported temporary relationships based on explicit rather than implicit agreements. This case, therefore, highlights how the use of a digital collaboration tool can change relational governance in a short time frame as trust among client and suppliers switched swiftly from affective attitudes to a more objective relations based on competencies.

Keywords IT outsourcing · Outsourcing governance · Trust · Digital collaboration · Operational innovation · Business process innovation · Strategic innovation

G. Vaia (✉) · D. Arkhipova · A. Moretti
Ca' Foscari University of Venice, San Giobbe 873, Cannaregio, 30121 Venice, Italy
e-mail: g.vaia@unive.it; giovanni.vaia@gmail.com

D. Arkhipova
e-mail: daria.arkhipova@unive.it

A. Moretti
e-mail: anna.moretti@unive.it

W. DeLone
American University, 4400 Massachusetts Ave NW, Washington, DC, USA
e-mail: wdelone@american.edu

R. Agrifoglio et al. (eds.), *Digital Business Transformation*, Lecture Notes in Information Systems and Organisation 38, https://doi.org/10.1007/978-3-030-47355-6_19

1 Introduction

In an economy increasingly characterized by dispersed production networks and disintegrated supply chains, firms are gradually turning to outsourcing relationships for an increasing number of steps in their value creation processes. How to manage and govern the resulting thick network of outsourced relations is now a key factor for achieving competitive advantage. This phenomenon, from the beginning of the century, has had a great boost from Internet that offered an immense opportunity for selecting and interacting with suppliers. In recent years, e-procurement systems increased in popularity and firms started to extend their adoption also to other areas—including IT purchases, with a specific focus on the partners' selection process [1]. The literature has explored how the adoption of online systems to select IT suppliers had an impact on firms' competitive advantage and cost reduction strategies. It is important to highlight that e-procurement systems are now evolving towards more integrated management and governance systems for outsourcing relationships. Digital collaboration tools are able to assist managers along all the phases of the value creation process, beyond the initial step of supplier selection.

Understanding how the adoption of such collaborative systems, which enable virtual interaction between client and suppliers, may have an impact on personal and inter-firm relations is an important and growing area of research interest [2]. With this paper, we aim to advance our knowledge of this impact by explicitly focusing on relational governance and on trust within IT outsourcing relationships supported by digital collaboration tools.

In recent decades, the literature on information technology outsourcing (ITO) has progressed significantly: scholars have examined several aspects of this phenomenon, from the motivations behind outsourcing decisions, through to their consequences and strategic implications for management and governance [3]. The governance of inter-organizational relationships has been identified, among others, as one of the main issues firms have to tackle in order to reach superior ITO outcomes [3], and it has been found that the inter-organizational relationships can make the difference between a successful versus an unprofitable ITO deal.

This paper contributes to the field by reporting on an exploratory case study that analyzes how the adoption of a digital collaboration tool influenced trust and the effectiveness of relational governance in an IT outsourcing relationship. This research was guided by two main research questions: (1) how the adoption of a digital collaboration tool affects the development of trust, as a component of relational governance, in ITO relationships, and (2) how the adoption of a digital collaboration tool and improved trust and relational governance potentially affect the achievement of performance outcomes?

The paper is organized as follows: the next section reviews the relevant literature; the third section presents the case methodology; the fourth section reports the data analysis and findings; the fifth section discusses the results, the sixth section presents limitations and future research opportunities and the last section summarizes our conclusions.

2 Theoretical Background: Relational Governance and Virtuality

The governance of inter-organizational relationships has been identified as one of the main issue firms have to tackle in order to reach superior outcomes in IT outsourcing projects [3]. The literature has traditionally identified two main approaches to ITO governance [4]: contractual and relational governance. While the concept of governance, indeed, is predominantly framed in the ITO literature within a transaction cost approach [5], studies on relational mechanisms have emerged and informed governance research in the last decade in response to more dynamic environment and business relations [6]. The concept of relational governance is reported here as "the role of the enforcement of obligations, promises, and expectations that occur through trust and social identification" [7, p. 121].

The literature is mostly aligned in stating that the two are complements rather than substitutes, and specifically that contractual governance needs to be opportunely sustained by the development of collaborative relationships between client and supplier [7–9]. Commitment, mutual dependence, trust and relational norms play a significant role in the maintenance of exchange relationships among firms, especially in the context of IT outsourcing [10]. In fact, successful management of an outsourcing relationship today requires a highly interactive, flexible relation between two organizations.

Today, this area of investigation needs to confront the fact that social processes and means of interaction, including IT outsourcing deals, are becoming more and more virtual, due to the prevalent use of digital collaboration tools. The shift from conventional to new virtual organizational forms, supported by advances in information and communication technologies such as smart mobile devices, social media, the internet of things, etc. (today labeled "digital media"), has resulted in new questions about relationships developed both within a company's boundaries and with external actors, where the concept of "virtual" implies permeable interfaces and boundaries. Global virtual team research was a useful guide for our study [7, 9].

Virtual work, decomposed into different ontological forms of companies, groups or networks, has produced more flexibility and favored temporary and fluid relationships based on explicit agreements. Virtual organizations have been shown to improve resource utilization, support better quality products and services, strengthen managerial control, and lower costs [11]. However, there are some difficulties that can inhibit the switching from conventional to virtual forms, which have been studied by the literature [12. p. 791]: "such dysfunctions as low individual commitment, role overload, role ambiguity, absenteeism, and social loafing may be exaggerated in a virtual context". Social relations, naturally, are affected by these means with an impact on mechanism of coordination and management of business relation. Trust is one of the most powerful mechanisms within the general concept of relational governance and scholars are paying more and more attention how this "tool" is affected by virtuality.

According to Handy [13], the question is whether virtual work can function effectively in the absence of frequent face-to-face interaction, given that "trust needs touch" [13, p. 46]. Also that literature shows how trust is still a critical element that characterizes successful projects. Jarvenpaa and Leidner [14] consider trust as "pivotal" in a global virtual team to reduce the high levels of uncertainty endemic to the global and technologically based environment. This problem is amplified in ITO relations often developed on the basis of opportunism. If trust is identified as fundamental for successful virtual interactions, no studies—to our knowledge—have investigated if a virtual environment may help in sustaining trust development between parties during the complex context of the partners' selection phase.

In this research, we conduct an exploratory case study on the adoption of a digital media tool to govern ITO processes, in order to contribute to the theory in this domain. In particular, through our empirical investigation, we propose an inductive study on the impact of a digital media tool on ITO relational governance, focusing on trust as the most relevant dimension for virtual environments.

3 Methodology

3.1 The Empirical Setting

Our case study is based on an ITO project developed by Infocert, the first Certification Authority in Italy, having issued and managed more than 4,500,000 qualified certificates of digital signature. Infocert, started its business in 2007, and with 30 M euros in revenues and roughly 150 employees, is a market leader for services like electronic archiving and long-term storage, registered e-mail. Infocert designs and implements IT solutions for document dematerialization. The company has clients in several industrial sectors such as: banking, insurance, pharmaceutics, manufacturing, energy, utilities, retail trade, environment, quality, security, healthcare, government, trade associations and professional associations. The core business of the company is represented by delivering projects and complex solutions on paper dematerialization, where they have at competitive advantage.

Infocert's business is largely based on technology exploitation in the collaboration with its technology suppliers. Since 2007 Infocert's technology suppliers have been quite stable.[1]

In the first semester of 2012, Infocert decided to strengthen its strategic approach to ITO, and in July set up a 6-month project with the aim of restructuring the outsourcing lifecycle. The main goals of the project were to: standardize contracting and categories of outsourced services; improve the selection and monitoring of suppliers; design a workflow for authorizations and document management; define clear criteria

---

[1] During interviews, people reported that the number of suppliers ranged from 30 to 50, and over time the rotation rate is roughly 10%. 10 suppliers are tagged as partners because are more proactive and they share business goals and priorities with Infocert: "A partner is an external company with whom I can share business intents, continuously, where everything is synchronized and fluid" (Infocert's Chief Information Officer).

for negotiation and organizational levels to be involved. Results expected from the project were a reduction of time spent in the whole process of about 30% and a cost saving of about 15%.

In fact, Infocert's ITO practices, at that time, could be characterized as follows:

- lacking a sourcing strategy;
- low use of advanced negotiation techniques;
- lacking Key Performance Indicators (KPIs) and supplier evaluation methods;
- lacking Service Level Agreements (SLAs);
- high transaction costs, due to the high effort required both to find the best supplier for specific services, and to start and manage long negotiation processes; and
- lacking a structured outsourcing workflow with clear responsibilities, roles, and goals.

Moreover, one of the main challenges faced by Infocert that motivated the decision to restructure the outsourcing process was the loss of information and transparency during the outsourcing lifecycle because 70% of the outsourcing activities occurred outside the procurement office. Infocert noticed that ITO relationships were managed mostly outside formal protocol and developed instead through informal interactions, as is prevalent in the Italian business environment, causing communication and trust problems).

The company started the outsourcing improvement project on November 2012 with the introduction of a digital collaboration tool for the management of supplier engagement, evaluation and monitoring. By means of the tool they wanted to achieve three distinct objectives:

- a more transparent process of information gathering about supplier rankings from internal and external sources (for example, decision makers and influencer communities);
- a better selection of suppliers through a self-application procedure, in order to have the best match between competences needed by Infocert and offered by the supplier;
- a strong collaborative relationship with suppliers during the early stage of service design (through a flexible definition of the Request for Proposals, namely the purpose of the bid in terms of products and services), in order to achieve superior outsourcing outcomes.

The digital collaboration tool was designed to manage the internal workflow, the process of scouting and ranking of suppliers, the supply specification and the evaluation of suppliers. The final digital collaboration solution was selected and implemented by the end of 2012: it included all functionalities of social collaboration like members' profiles (to find and discover expertise), forums, activities (to view, manage and organize tasks and tap into the professional network), files (to share documents, presentations and other files with colleagues), etc. The tool enabled the involvement of suppliers on the basis of a self-application and, for each tender, it created a new collaboration environment where suppliers and Infocert could exchange information.

Our research observation began with the first ITO project that used the new digital collaboration tool described above. The ITO project was started by Infocert to select the supplier for a data storage.

3.2 Data Collection

The consideration of process-related and contextual features and the need to explore an under-investigated area of research, and in particular the relationships between different areas of investigation, called for exploratory and inductive research by means of a case study [15, 16].

We followed Lincoln and Guba's [17] guidelines for "purposeful sampling" in choosing our informants. We initially selected interviewees from both Infocert and the competing suppliers who actively participated in the bid process, and who would be qualified to answer our main research questions concerning how the adoption of a digital media tool influenced ITO relationships and performance outcomes. We next used a snowball technique, asking each informant for his or her recommendations as to who could best explain our topics of interest.

We made 19 interviews to key participants from both the client and the supplier side (four suppliers, none of them was among Infocert's "partners", namely suppliers with a long-term relationship with the client—see footnote 1) of the relationships, in three different rounds of interviews developed across three years—2013, 2014, and 2015.

More than 20 h of interviews were carried out by the authors individually and in various combinations, involving the IT Manager, Purchasing Manager and individuals directly involved in ITO decisions on the buyer side, and the managers responsible for the tender on the supplier side. Additionally, we collected archival data regarding all ITO-project documents (initial request by the client, first offers by suppliers, modifications and updates, up until the final winning offer), and chat logs from the digital media platform (recording all the interactions between client and suppliers, and between the client-firm's members who took part in the ITO decision). We recorded and took notes during interviews, and in those instances where data was inconsistent we developed a new round of interviews.

Inconsistencies have been specifically confronted and resolved through triangulation with archival data, and in some cases, they have been considered indicative of different perspectives and used to better explain the very nature of supplier-buyer relationships.

Given our main research questions, we focused our interview structure on the governance of the relationship between Infocert and suppliers and on related ITO outcomes. We asked our informants how the relationship was managed and developed, exploring in particular the use of relational governance. We investigated how the digital tool affected trust, explicitly highlighting the differences between virtual and traditional settings, and we tried to understand if our informants perceived that the use of the digital tool also affected the ITO outcomes.

4   Analysis and Findings

In the analysis of our data we adhered closely to the guidelines of Gioia's methodology [18], recognized and accepted as a coding procedure, following a three-step process: (i) recording emergent first-order concepts; (ii) identifying second-order themes; (iii) defining aggregate dimensions. This methodology for qualitative analysis has been developed with the explicit aim of making the process of analysis more transparent and rigorous. The methodology, in fact, makes researchers present explicitly the connection between evidence (raw data) and derived theoretical constructs used for theorization processes. Thus, following the procedure:

1. We started our analysis by identifying initial concepts in the data (open coding). With the progress of data coding, we started searching for similarities in order to reduce the number of emerging categories. In this first phase we used in vivo codes in order to adhere faithfully to informant terms whenever possible, or a short descriptive phrase when an in vivo code was not available.
2. Then we started the second-order analysis, confronting our first-order codes with researcher-centric concepts, themes, and dimensions. In this second phase we assembled similar codes into several overarching dimensions, which we then compared with those from our theoretical background in order to discover whether they had adequate theoretical referents in the existing literature.
3. From this comparison, we extracted our final aggregate dimensions, which constitute the core of our results.

The final data structure [18] is illustrated in Fig. 1, which summarizes the process and highlights how we derived the final aggregate dimensions from the first-order concepts.

As presented in our data structure (Fig. 1), the results of our analysis highlight four aggregate dimensions: (1) Relational Governance, (2) Trust, (3) Collaboration, and (4) Innovation in ITO.

Relational Governance Relational governance has been described in our data-structure as composed by two second-order themes: (i) objectives alignment and (ii) social relationships. Our data highlight that the two main issues that the ITO participants had to face were (1) to align their (conflicting) goals and (2) to manage social relationships between employees from different companies in a completely different, virtual environment. The main mechanism at work to govern these two challenges was trust, as we present at the following section.

The challenge of objectives alignment was solved mainly through relational mechanisms: all suppliers, in fact, describe their interactions with the client as characterized by a relevant process of sharing goals, since client and suppliers started working together to reach the best solution, thus strongly based on cooperation and reciprocity.

We shared common business objectives. (Client—IT Manager)
Interactions were developed through dialogue. (Supplier 3—Bid Manager)

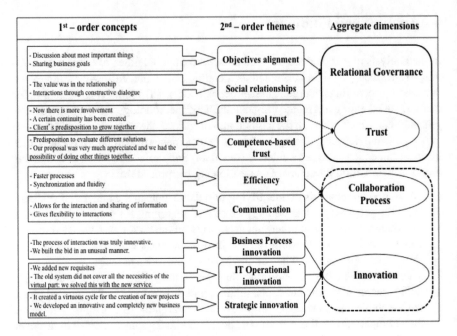

Fig. 1 Data structure—impacts of the digital tool

Even though the engagement process was developed virtually (through the digital tool), it also allowed for the building of personal ties among the employees of both the client and the suppliers. Human relationships were fostered by the initial virtual interaction, and the cooperative attitude was the trigger for developing or reinforcing valuable personal relationships.

The technical level of interactions developed through the digital tool generated also a lot of curiosity by the client, that maybe thought "these guys know the subject very well, they made a very interesting question, a good proposal, ..." and thus pushed the parties to a constructive dialogue. It gave birth to a professional, but also personal relationship. (Supplier 1—CEO)

The value was in the relationship. (Supplier 2—Bid Manager)
The relationship with the client, also from the personal point of view, has been reinforced. (Supplier 3—Bid Manager)

Trust The aggregate dimension of trust is composed by two second-order themes regarding two distinct aspects of trust already identified in the literature: (i) personal trust and (ii) competence-based trust. Weeks and Feeny [3] define personal trust as the confidence one has that another person will work for the good of the relationship based on their integrity and adherence to moral norms, whereas competence-based trust exists when one party has confidence that the other will successfully deliver their allocated tasks and responsibilities (successful completion of projects and achieve-ment of joint goals will enhance competence-based trust, while operational failures will degrade it).

As pointed out above, trust emerged as the main mechanism of relational gover-nance that was at work during the ITO process. Our results show how, during the ITO process, all persons involved developed a personal trust in client-supplier rela-tionships. Our informants talked about involvement, reciprocity, and continuity in describing the relationship created with the client. Additionally, our data demon-strates the development of competence-based trust, describing trustful relationships based on the mutual recognition of others' competences. Suppliers felt that the client was willing to evaluate different solutions, basing its evaluation only on meritocratic aspects. Cooperation in designing the IT service was sustained and in turn sustained the development of trust between client and suppliers.

As a result the client demonstrated a predisposition to grow and to avoid a monolithic approach to only one supplier. (Supplier 1—CEO)
There was a constant process of sharing information and motivations of certain choices. (Supplier 2—Bid Manager)
From the competence side, we could show that we were reliable and competent. Our image has improved, since the platform allowed to break the prejudice clients have always against new suppliers. (Supplier 3—Bid Manager)

The demand specialist and supplier managers reported that before the introduction of the digital collaboration, the relationship with suppliers was managed on the basis of personal relationships and outside formal lines of communication, a typical impediment in Italian business relationships. Affective trust was the main element through which the company based outsourcing relations with suppliers. This led to a low transparency within the company, due to the negotiation carried out "behind the scenes", and it had a detrimental effect on the level of trust among colleagues. This level of internal mistrust had one main detrimental consequence: the company preferred to look for standard IT solutions to allow no personal interest into bids, thus limiting innovation opportunities.

From the internal point of view, during the digital tender the procurement office and the top management adopted a more active role and were more committed to the demand specialists and other employees who were involved in the tender. Infocert's employees had the chance to demonstrate their competences and ideas about tech-nology innovation and IT service innovation to their managers, thus increasing their reputation. They also experienced an improvement in relational trust lowering the detrimental effect of low transparency, through the direct management of suppliers.

We need to remain unbiased but we need flexibility i.e. sometimes we need to move beyond the requirements that we have ... and this tool gave us the chance to achieve a balance between transparency and innovation (Client—Demand Manager)

After the tender, all the bid offers received by Infocert were nearly the initial price set by the client. Nevertheless, the client judged the higher price to be "reasonable." The process of interaction created competence-based trust between client and suppliers. As a result, through the interactions with suppliers, the procurement officer realized the complexity of the design process, and that the technical offers and their corresponding prices were aligned with other solutions available on the market. In July 2013 they signed a standard (template) contract, with a negligible involvement of the legal office, because of the relationship they built through the virtual platform:

> Now the relational impact with the supplier during negotiation is less difficult. We shared the entire process from the beginning and now I know the effort involved in reaching a solution. The supplier does not allow a saving just to recognize my role, as was done in the past, but we agree on the project and a future target. (Client—Purchasing manager)

Digital Collaboration Process This aggregate dimension described the impact played by the digital tool on collaboration during the ITO process and is characterized by: (i) efficiency and (ii) communication effectiveness. The first theme highlights the cost and time savings resulting from the virtualization and digitalization of ITO processes. All informants underscore the relevance of the digital collaboration tool in allowing a faster, more fluid, and less costly interaction between client and suppliers. Additionally, the digital tool was recognized to have also very important effects on transparency allowing more information sharing, and an easier and flexible way of interacting between actors of ITO processes.

> The digital collaboration tool increased interactions' transparency. (Client— Service Manager)
> Through the digital media tool, the boss can see how you carry out your job. (Client—Purchasing Manager)
> Functionalities are clear and well-documented. (Supplier 1—CEO)
> Personal dialogue is always preferable, when available. However, when there is the need for transparency, it is preferable such a solution. Questions and answers are public, and thus all competitors are on the same starting grid. (Supplier 3—Bid Manager)

The transparency fostered by the use of the digital tool played a fundamental role during the whole ITO process, both within the client company and between client and suppliers. In fact, thanks to more traceable and open communication developed through the digital collaboration tool, all the participants involved in the ITO process were able to consolidate their social relationships. The internal transparency at Infocert was based on the clarity of the process through which a "winning" supplier was selected. In particular, no doubts about the role and the legitimacy of selection decision were raised, since all information and actions were traceable, documented and justifiable. The external transparency characterized the exchange between client and suppliers in the specification of clients' requirements and expectations. In particular, all communications were traced and all requirements documents were posted.

All stakeholders had the opportunity to ask for clarifications and to receive prompt answers, thereby easing interactions and consolidating personal relationships.

The two dimensions of efficiency and sociality were highlighted during several phases of the project. The "Request for Proposals" was continuously shaped and improved by client and suppliers through interactions. Different cycles of improvement took place, during which all actors involved could observe, participate and learn. The tool facilitated a continuous evaluation process developed through the collection of feedback from the internal communities-of-practice and the external communities of decisions makers. This continuous evaluation process also continued during the delivery phase. This digitally supported process made it possible to discuss any problems or doubts in real time, thus reducing the necessity to formalize every detail in contractual agreements.

Firm Performance: Innovation Through ITO The second-order themes related to this dimension are (i) Business Process Innovation, (ii) IT Operational Innovation, and (iii) Strategic Innovation. During the interviews, we looked for potential impacts on performance outcomes. We uncovered additional and un-proposed findings from the interview data.

Analyzing and conceptualizing these data we used the three categories developed by Weeks and Feeny [3] who positioned ITO innovation "as the introduction of strategies, business processes, or technologies that are new to the relationship and are intended and expected to lead to new business outcomes". Authors define IT Operational innovations as advances that involve technology changes like new operating systems or hardware, while Business Process innovations change the working processes of the organization and, finally, Strategic innovations are those that change product/service offerings or enable the company to enter new markets.

Here **Business Process Innovation** refers to the outsourcing process itself developed through the new digital collaboration tool. Indeed, our results show how documents and informants recognized a significant process innovation in the management of outsourcing relationships through the tool. For example, the tender was conducted in a completely new way, especially in the definition of requirements. The possibility of posing questions to the client (and to see all the questions posed by the other suppliers) and receiving quick feedback on the first drafts of proposals was deemed by informants to be a significant business process innovation.

Strongly linked to the process improvement outcome was IT **Operational Innovation**. Infocert discussed with suppliers the physical segregation of two IT infrastructures—Datacenter and Certification Authority—and the types of backup and the sizing of the repository. Through continuous interactions, suppliers proposed to the client a new multi-tenant architecture, improved the security system, and the use of the service through a new "single technology platform" This innovation in architecture is able to handle heavier workloads than the previous solution and the database uses only a fraction of the server hardware capacity.

Through continuous interactions the client understood what the available solutions were. (Supplier 1—CEO)

The analysis of the initial Request for Proposals and the final service purchased by the client, as well as the informants' declarations, show how the IT service as initially designed was significantly improved. In particular, the service was re-designed in a collaborative way between the client and suppliers, and the resulting requirements were considerably different. The result, in our informants' opinion, was a more efficient and cost effective IT architecture.

> *The information exchange that took place during the evaluation phase of technical proposals had produced a final proposal of architectural modification relevant in terms of operational innovation. (Client—IT manager)*
>
> *The constructive dialogue with the supplier allowed us to introduce an incremental innovation that, without this contribution, probably would have never been implemented. (Client—Demand manager)*

As reported by our informants, this improvement resulted in several benefits for the client, including: (1) cost reduction in the long run (due the consolidation of hardware and shared database memory and files, which reduced costs for hardware, storage, availability, and labor); (2) easier and faster transfer of data and code; (3) easier management and monitoring of the physical database; (4) simpler backup strategies and disaster recovery; (5) secure separation of administrative duties; (6) easier performance tuning process; and (7) fewer database patches and upgrades.

Additionally, two years after the conclusion of the tender, another important outcome; namely, **Strategic Innovation** emerged. As a result, of the collaborative procurement process and resulting competence-based trust, the client and one of the suppliers (different from the firm winning the tender at that time) together developed an innovative new commercial product. As reported by our informants, a strategic innovation was jointly developed based on a new innovative business model. Focusing on their respective core competences, which were discovered through interaction in the virtual environment created for the tender process, the two firms discovered a potential area for collaboration, and introduced a new information product to the market. The client had the opportunity to study in depth the supplier's sets of resources and competences, thus launching a positive discussion and the emergence of new and innovative ideas.

> *Since it was necessary to be very concise and incisive with our questions, we tried to be very precise from the technical point of view. This, in turn, made the client answer in a very precise way, to give answers that were at the level of the questions posed. This generated a relationship that some time later allowed us to develop together an innovative business model, going to the market in a completely different way. We developed a common intermediation platform for managing information for our business clients: and all of this was possible because we both had the technology, and thus we were able to make our ideas real. (Supplier 3—CEO)*

Based on these findings we discuss the primary contribution of our research in the following section.

5 Discussion

The analysis and findings of Infocert case study emphasizes the positive influence of the digital collaborative media on trust as a component of relational governance and more importantly on ITO firm performance, particularly operational and strategic innovation outcomes.

In the Infocert case study the digital collaboration tool enabled relational governance during the ITO process and created a virtual environment that enhanced trust between client and suppliers. In particular, collaborative relationships have been developed on the basis of a competence-based trust, instead of an affective kind of trust as found in the literature. In this case, governance of the relationship was not focused on the level of trust between the parties. Jarvenpaa and Leidner [19], for instance, highlight how trust in virtual teams can increase or decrease over time, and then become a potential governance mechanism. In our study, the focus is on the type of trust that makes the temporal dimension less important. As our analysis shows, in fact, relational governance has been developed through a kind of trust that does not require the development of interpersonal relationships, and thus significantly reducing the necessary timeframe.

In line with Rai et al. [19] we noticed that the exchange of high quality information and the use of effective communication tools are essential facilitators for process integration and for building trustful relationships in collaboration agreements. The process of trust development, in our case, followed a quite different path with respect to ITO than found in non-digital settings. The bidding process lasted over 3 weeks and led the team of client personnel and suppliers to cooperate and have an open communication relying more on "cognitive" elements [20]. Meyerson et al. [20] noticed that people working in a temporary system deal with each other in terms of professional roles, instead of social relationships. In this context trust is conferred ex ante. This is called swift trust [19, 21].

Early in the process, suppliers started to share information and ideas within the tool to interpret the Request for Proposal and reshape its scope, i.e. the characteristics of the outsourced IT service. Client and supplier personnel perceived reciprocal professionalism and competencies and a willingness to share information in order to complete the task in the best fashion. Nevertheless, the collaborative relationship between suppliers and between client and supplier, was not based on interpersonal social relationships (personal/affective trust), as predicted by the ITO relational governance literature and by common in Italian business relationships. In this case, five (5) informants on the client side and four (4) persons from suppliers reported changes in the type of trust before, during and after the virtual RFP. Trust shifted from a pure relational base to a combination of competence and identification dimensions. In the relationship between client and suppliers during the RFP process, parties understood the problem to be solved and they supported each other. The environment in which internal employees and suppliers discussed the design of the service (leaving out the discussion of contract terms) led to a mutual understanding of the company's objectives and processes. This is defined as identification based trust [22].

Moreover, inter-organizational coordination increases managerial complexities, especially regarding aspects such as sharing information, developing a common knowledge base, aligning risks and incentives, thus making it more difficult to exploit innovation opportunities. The literature is mostly aligned in stating that it is not ITO in itself that can ensure or negate innovation but rather identifies relational governance as the main dimension that influences innovation [3]. Our empirical analysis shows that the adoption of a digital collaboration tool to manage IT outsourcing relationships, beyond the mere e-procurement system functionalities, can lead to innovation in ITO through improved relational governance.

The outcome of the virtual design and negotiation processes has been a new innovative and more effective architecture solution for the client (operational innovation). The analysis of the initial Request for Proposals and the final service purchased by the client, as well as the informants' declarations, demonstrate how the client's IT services experienced significant improvements. The opportunity to pose questions to the client (and the sharing of all questions posed by the other suppliers) and to receive quick feedback on the first drafts of proposals was deemed by informants to be a significant procurement business process and IT operational innovation.

Importantly, we discovered that, in the long run, the use of the digital tool for governing interactions between client and suppliers during the procurement process enabled the client and one of the suppliers to jointly develop a strategic innovation, introducing to the market an innovative new information intermediation service.

6 Limitations and Future Research

There are limitations to this study that should be acknowledged. Our case study focused primarily on the trust component of relational governance in an IT outsourcing project, but not on other important components such as commitment, relational norms, harmonious conflict resolution, mutual dependence [23]. Thus our research does not provide insight as far as a comprehensive model of relational governance in the ITO virtual relations in the different stages of the ITO lifecycle. A second limitation regards the lack of analysis between the use of formal governance, based on contracts, and relational governance, and the dynamic evolution between them.

Future research should further study the relationship between digital collaboration tools, trust and other relational governance dimensions and the impact on firm performance outcomes, such as operational and strategic innovations, in IT outsourcing context. Another interesting and important stream of research that could be developed by future research regards the analysis of competitive and opportunistic dynamics that can arise between suppliers, since the research here presented did not explicitly tackled this point. This study has been influenced by the Italian context where personal ties are critical to the development of business relationships, so ITO governance is influenced by these cultural frames. Other studies should analyze the dynamics of governance in virtual ITO relations within different cultural business environments.

7 Conclusions

Our findings show how digital collaboration can affect trust before and during the engagement phase of the IT outsourcing process. The digital media tool increased communication flexibility and supported temporary relationships based on explicit rather than implicit agreements. This case, therefore, highlights how the use of a digital collaboration tool can change relational governance in a short time frame as trust among client and suppliers switched swiftly from affective attitudes to a more objective relations based on competencies. Most importantly the trust and relational governance changes facilitated by digital collaboration resulted in significant operational, business process and strategic innovations. These findings contribute to our knowledge of the powerful impact that digital collaboration tools can have on building competency-based trust relationships between clients and suppliers in ITO that can produce operational and strategic innovations.

References

1. Davila, A., Gupta, M., & Palmer, R. (2003). Moving procurement systems to the internet: The adoption and use of E-procurement technology models. *European Management Journal, 21*(1), 11–23. https://doi.org/10.1016/S0263-2373(02)00155-X.
2. Ahuja, M. K., & Galvin, J. E. (2003). Socialization in virtual groups. *Journal of Management, 29*(2), 161–185. https://doi.org/10.1177/014920630302900203.
3. Weeks, M. R., & Feeny, D. (2008). Outsourcing: From cost management to innovation and business value. *California Management Review, 50*(4), 127–146.
4. Lacity, M. C., Khan, S. A., & Willcocks, L. P. (2009). A review of the IT outsourcing literature: Insights for practice. *The Journal of Strategic Information Systems, 18*(3), 130–146. https://doi.org/10.1016/j.jsis.2009.06.002.
5. Lacity, M. C., & Hirschheim, R. (1993). The information systems outsourcing Bandwagon. *Sloan Management Review, 35*(1), 73–86.
6. Lin, T., & Vaia, G. (2015). The concept of governance in IT outsourcing: A literature review. In *Proceedings of the Twenty-Third European Conference on Information Systems (ECIS)*, Münster, Germany.
7. Goo, J., Kishore, R., Rao, H. R., & Nam, K. (2009). The role of service level agreements in relational management of information technology outsourcing: An empirical study. *MIS Quarterly, 33*(1), 1–28.
8. Poppo, L., & Zenger, T. (2002). Do formal contracts and relational governance function as substitutes or complements? *Strategic Management Journal, 23*(8), 707–725. https://doi.org/10.1002/smj.249.
9. Sabherwal, R. (1999). The role of trust in outsourced IS development projects. *Communications of the ACM, 42*(2), 80–86. https://doi.org/10.1145/293411.293485.
10. Kim, Y. J., Lee, J. M., Koo, C., & Nam, K. (2013). The role of governance effectiveness in explaining IT outsourcing performance. *International Journal of Information Management, 33*(5), 850–860. https://doi.org/10.1016/j.ijinfomgt.2013.07.003.

11. Mowshowitz, A. (1997). On the theory of virtual organization. *Systems Research and Behavioral Science, 14*(6), 373–384. https://doi.org/10.1002/(SICI)1099-1743(199711/12)14:6%3c373:AID-SRES131%3e3.0.CO;2-R.
12. Jarvenpaa, S. L., Knoll, K., & Leidner, D. E. (1998). Is anybody out there? Antecedents of trust in global virtual teams. *Journal of Management Information Systems, 14*(4), 29–64. https://doi.org/10.2307/40398291.
13. Handy, C. (1995). Trust and the virtual organization. *Harvard Business Review, 73*(3), 40–50.
14. Jarvenpaa, S. L., & Leidner, D. E. (1999). Communication and trust in global virtual teams. *Journal of Computer-Mediated Communication, 3*(4), 0. https://doi.org/10.1111/j.1083-6101.1998.tb00080.x.
15. Yin, R. K. (2009). *Case study research: Design and methods* (4th ed.). Sage Publications.
16. Eisenhardt, K. M. (1989). Building theories from case study research. *The Academy of Management Review, 14*(4), 532–550.
17. Lincoln, Y., & Guba, E. (1985). *Naturalistic inquiry*. Beverly Hills, CA: Sage.
18. Gioia, D. A., Corley, K. G., & Hamilton, A. L. (2013). Seeking qualitative rigor in inductive research: Notes on the Gioia methodology. *Organizational Research Methods, 16*(1), 15–31. https://doi.org/10.1177/1094428112452151.
19. Rai, A., Patnayakuni, R., & Seth, N. (2006). Firm performance impacts of digitally enabled supply chain integration capabilities. *MIS Quarterly, 30*(2), 225–246. https://doi.org/10.2307/25148729.
20. Meyerson, D., Weick, K. E., & Kramer, R. M. (1996). Swift trust and temporary groups. In R. M. Kramer & T. R. Tyler (Eds.), *Trust in organizations: Frontiers of theory and research* (pp. 166–195). Thousand Oaks, CA: Sage Publications.
21. Gallivan, J. (2001). Striking a balance between trust and control in a virtual organization: A content analysis of open source software case studies. *Information Systems Journal, 11*, 277–304.
22. Choudhury, V., & Sabherwal, R. (2003). Portfolios of control in outsourced software development projects. *Information Systems Research, 14*(3), 291–314. https://doi.org/10.1287/isre.14.3.291.16563.
23. Goo, J., & Huang, C. D. (2008). Facilitating relational governance through service level agreements in IT outsourcing: An application of the commitment–trust theory. *Decision Support Systems, 46*(1), 216–232. https://doi.org/10.1016/j.dss.2008.06.005.

In Vino Veritas? Blockchain Preliminary Effects on Italian Wine SMEs

Roberta Cuel and Gabriella Maria Cangelosi

Abstract Transparency and traceability in the food industry have become two central themes for both consumers and companies. On the one hand, consumer awareness increases with more available in depth information, whilst food manufacturers try to mitigate food safety risks, reduce coordination costs and fraud by improving their presence on the market. In this scenario, innovative technologies and blockchain may have a major impact. The authors investigate the adoption of blockchain in the Italian wine industry and, in particular, the effects of blockchain on the complex inter-organizational supply chain systems SMEs are engaged in. A qualitative approach was chosen to preliminary analyse the motivations driving small Italian wineries to adopt blockchain technologies, and the advantages or drawbacks managers identified during pilot experiments.

Keywords Blockchain · Supply chain · Traceability · Transparency · Certification · Wine industry

1 Introduction

In recent years, large organizations such as technology companies and financial giants have invested heavily in blockchain-based technologies to radically transform business applications and get considerable benefits. Blockchain would contribute to the execution of secure business processes and the automation of transactions between companies.

Blockchain technology can also be considered a huge opportunity for small and medium organizations that do not have enough resources to invest in new technologies and are thus often left behind when a technological leap forward occurs.

R. Cuel (✉) · G. M. Cangelosi (✉)
Department of Economics and Management, University of Trento, Via Inama, 5, 38122 Trento, Italy
e-mail: roberta.cuel@unitn.it

G. M. Cangelosi
e-mail: cangelosigabriellam@gmail.com

© The Editor(s) (if applicable) and The Author(s), under exclusive license to Springer Nature Switzerland AG 2020
R. Agrifoglio et al. (eds.), *Digital Business Transformation*, Lecture Notes in Information Systems and Organisation 38, https://doi.org/10.1007/978-3-030-47355-6_20

According to some experts,[1] SMEs can innovate and build an edge with blockchain transformation by using blockchain-based services as well as creating their own apps on top of blockchain such as decentralized apps, or DApps. SMEs can already use different blockchain solutions. For instance, there are marketplaces for renting or selling properties on blockchain-based P2P marketplaces (real estate); managing claims (insurance); dealing with security (IoT), monitoring and tracking freight movement (logistics), and ensuring food safety via IBM's Food Trust Network to link distributors, retailers, producers, and regulators in the food industry [1].

In this paper, the authors focus on SMEs in the Italian wine industry. These companies represent 75–80% of the Italian production, which has a total turnover of 13 billion Euros, with 310,000 companies involved and 46,000 wine-making companies.[2] In this scenario, innovative technologies and blockchain may have a major impact that cannot be ignored: at present the impact is most evident on the complex inter-organizational supply chain that SMEs manage and deal with.

A qualitative approach has been chosen in order to preliminary analyse the motivations that drive small Italian wineries to improve their supply chain management by applying blockchain technology [2]. The authors will also focus on the advantages and drawbacks that managers identified during their pilot experiments.

2   Literature Review

The blockchain is a Distributed Ledger Technology (DLT), an unalterable database of information related to each transaction carried out and shared between a network of participants [3]. This technology is based on Disintermediation and Decentralization principles, namely that data can be recorded, stored and updated in a distributed manner by all network members [4]. This type of architecture allows actors to maintain and share records in a synchronized manner, ensuring their integrity via validation protocols based on consensus and cryptographic signatures [5]. The governance is based on a widespread and distributed system of mutual trust in which no actor can prevail and where the decision process is built on consensus [6].

---

[1] Blockchain Technology Applications for SMEs [Expert Roundup]—Written by Mindaugas on September 17, 2018 and retrieved from https://blog.invoiceberry.com/2018/09/blockchain-technology-applications-sme/.

[2] Federvini—retrieved 10/8/2019 from https://www.federvini.it/studi-e-ricerche-cat/1273-ismea,-fotografa-l-italia-del-vino-aumentano-produzione,-valore-ed-export-stabile-la-struttura.

2.1 Blockchain Based Supply Chain Principles

Blockchain is an integrative technology conceived with the aim of defragmenting the supply chain through the synchronization of data recorded along the same. It can be considered an integration of the existing information and legacy systems [7].

More specifically, each product is characterized by a processing cycle that involves several actors. Each actor has a unique digital identity (provided by an accreditation service) and the role of recording (tracking) all the key information regarding the development processes of the product (or service) and its status within the network. Each product is assigned to a digital identity using a specific tag (a barcode, RFID or QR Code). This tag is a unique digital cryptographic identifier that connects the physical good to its virtual identity on the network, enabling any actor to retrieve all or any associated information. In order to protect the process from theft and counterfeiting, blockchain involves the creation of a digital token associated with the digital identity when the product/service is made or exchanged between the actors in the supply chain [8]. The final product addressee can, therefore, authenticate the token and follow the history of the article from its beginning [9]. When the product is transferred (or sold) to another actor, both partners must sign a digital contract to authenticate the exchange [10]. Once all the actors have signed the contract, the details of the transaction will be stored. The actors' privacy can be modified according to the preferences of the subject involved: they can choose to remain anonymous, but their identity must be authenticated by the certifiers who guarantee trust [8].

Thus the founding principles of the blockchain technology are:

- *Transparency*: each participant can view all recorded content at any time. This is why blockchain is considered a reliable tool [11].
- *Open source*: the system is open to all participants as each registration can be controlled publicly and everyone can freely use the technology to implement any application [12].
- *Autonomy*: blockchain is a consensus-based system, open to all participating players; it can be modified only once all members have given their approval. Using blockchain, devices are able to interact with others without the involvement of a server [13].
- *Immutability*: blockchain ensures absolute inalterability and incorruptibility of all information. The only exception is the possession of 51% of the control of a node [14].
- *Anonymity*: both the transfer of data and the individual transaction can be anonymous, provided that the blockchain address of the person is known [12].

2.2 Governance and Blockchain Types

From a governance point of view, a blockchain can be *permissioned or unpermissioned*. The permissioned, or authorized, option is the alternative evolution to the unauthorized chain (one in which anyone can participate) [15]; examples are Bitcoin and Ethereum [14]. In this case, transparency is only towards authorized participants, which makes it difficult to process data that require some privacy [16]. Two types of subjects can be distinguished:

- *Participants* who can only use the system and
- *Validators* who can use the system and hold a copy of the updated ledger. Validators are responsible for the process of distributed consensus [17].

The unpermissioned blockchain does not require owners and allows all participants to own a copy of the updated ledger. In this case, participants may also be validators and are responsible for both the distributed consensus process and the system integrity [18].

Three types of blockchain are classified, namely *Public, Consortium* and *Private*, and affect [7]:

- *Consensus*: the consensus determination is gradual, passing from public, to consortium and finally private. Everyone, in fact, can take part in the public blockchain; in the consortium only a small group of nodes is responsible for the validation of the block; in the private, the chain is entirely controlled by a single organization that can define the final consensus. Moreover, a public blockchain is an example of an unauthorized chain; the other two cases, however, are models of permissioned blockchain [7].
- *Transparency*: blockchain transactions are entirely visible in the public, but this visibility tends to fade when changing to the consortium and then to the private.
- *Immutability*: from the point of view of immutability, in the public blockchain transactions are much more complex to manipulate since the number of participants who store the records is greater: the same information in a private or in a consortium system might be easily tampered with.

The main difference between the three blockchain types is that the public is totally decentralized, the consortium is partially decentralized and the private is completely centralized and controlled by a single node.

3 The Italian Wine Supply Chain with the Use of Blockchain

Various experiments have been conducted in Italy to introduce blockchain technologies into the agro-food industry and winery sector. Among others, the main goals of these trials are to tackle problems of wine counterfeiting, guarantee the wine origins, certify the product by providing the bottles of wine with a unique identity, track and trace the wine production along the entire supply chain, and to exploit technology innovations when conducting marketing campaigns.

3.1 Italian Wine Industry and Innovation

In a fast changing market, expectations and consumption dynamics change even when the reference industry is typically traditional as is the case of the wine sector. Diverse technologies have been introduced in various stages of the production from the cultivation of grapes (harvesting and destemming) to the vinification process (crushing, primary fermentation, cold stabilization, laboratory tests, blending and fining), bottling, marketing, and to the distribution of the final product. These technologies are being implemented to create added value without diminishing the quality that distinguishes Italian wine around the world. Research in 2017 by the Cisco and Digital Transformation Institute showed that the Italian wine industry's principle investments in innovation took place downstream of the supply chain [19]. At present, 77.3% of Italian wineries have not invested in ICT technologies nor spent up to €5000 the last five years. Of the remaining 22.7% that invested more than €5000 about half (49%) is represented by the largest companies. The technologies that are most affecting the wine sector are mainly related to management and business management (74%), traceability (57%) and the transmission of information in electronic forms (53%) [20].

3.2 Blockchain in the Wine Supply Chain: How Does It Work?

Ideally, since the wine supply chain commences with the vineyards, the winegrowers should generate the first block in the chain (Fig. 1). This block is checked by the majority number of miners in the system before the next block is created. All the

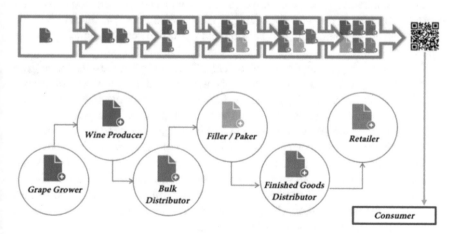

Fig. 1 Blockchain in the wine supply chain (authors' elaboration)

participants in the chain receive an identification code and a batch number indicating the quantity supplied by the wine producer. In the same way, the producer puts all his recorded information in a further block and shares it with all the other participants. Subsequently, the block is checked again and added to the chain. The procedure is repeated until the final participant. In some cases information shared could be critical and kept private, taking advantage of the cryptography keys that the technology provides [21].

One of the main features of the proposed traceability system is the possibility of tracing the origin of each individual bottle of wine. The consumer can trace the complete flow of data and related information by scanning a tag, e.g. a QR code, placed on the bottle label.

4   Hypothesis, Research Method and Sample of Analysis

The purpose of this study is to investigate the impact of blockchain technology in the Italian wine sector. Through ethnographic interviews conducted on a sample of companies, the authors explore both the benefits and limitations perceived by developers and managers in pilot experiments where blockchain technology was adopted to certify, track and trace the agro-food supply chain.

Two hypothesis are analysed:

- H1: blockchain technology allows effective and efficient control of inter-organizational business processes and the supply chain flow.
- H2: blockchain technology it is a transparency vehicle, both inside the company and in the relationship between the firm and the final consumer.

An exploratory and comparative survey was carried out by means of semi-structured qualitative interviews with eight managers who were involved in the pilot projects. In order to obtain a complete scenario, the authors also interviewed two representatives of companies that develop and resell blockchain technology in the agro-food sector.

The authors adopted the inductive "emergent" method where results derive from the observation, analysis and comparison of empirical evidence, and particular manifestations of the companies' experiences, facts and circumstances in the considered context. A research model inspired by the Grounded Theory was adopted as the main reference in the analysis of the text (coding). Through interviews focused on coding, categories and subcategories were defined, compared during the analysis of the interviews, and grouped into theme sets. The authors developed the latter through a thorough reading of the interviews and examining long pieces of the reported texts. The categories considered most important were used to explain the macro-themes and the sub-themes identified. Using NVivo software, the categories are represented by the nodes and the subcategories by the child nodes.

The sample of analysis contains SMEs operating in the Italian wine industry. The authors contacted all the companies that are presently investing in technology

Table 1 *"Sample respondents" features (personal elaboration)*

Respondent	Position	Project	Project owner
Respondent 1	Co-owner	MyStory	DNV GL
Respondent 2	Biologist	Wine blockchain EY	EY
Respondent 3	Export manager	Wine blockchain EY	EY
Respondent 4	Owner	eNology	MIPAAFT
Respondent 5	Quality manager	MyStory	DNV GL
Respondent 6	Quality manager	MyStory	DNV GL
Respondent 7	Owner	eNology	MIPAAFT
Respondent 8	Owner	eNology	MIPAAFT

and adopting a supply chain system based on blockchain, but only seven answered and were available for further contact and interviews. To obtain complete explorative information, individuals with different organizational roles were interviewed (Table 1). The companies joined three different pilot projects aimed at experimenting with blockchain technology to track, trace and certify products. Three out of the seven companies are part of DNV GL, one of the most important certification authorities in Europe in the agro-food industry. One of the companies has joined the Ernst and Young project in collaboration with the start-up technology developer, EZ lab. Three companies have been involved in the testing program supported by the Italian Ministry of Agriculture and Forestry (MIPAAFT), in collaboration with Almaviva (a developer), SIAN (National Agricultural Information System) and AGEA (Agricultural Supplies Agency).

5 Result of Analysis

From an in-depth reading of the interviews, the authors identified 11 categories and 15 sub-categories. The coded nodes emerged from the most recurrent, sometimes implicit, issues discussed during the interviews. Although a detail-oriented analysis was carried out, the degree of abstraction of the conceptualization is quite high. Using NVivo coding, macro-themes were distinguished from sub-themes (Table 2). The purpose of the aforementioned subdivision between nodes and sub-nodes is to clarify the multiple facets of each of the 12 themes that emerged. In the following sub-paragraphs, the authors comment on each of them, once grouped by identifying the boundary objects between each of them.

Table 2 Groups of macro-themes and sub-themes (authors' elaboration)

Groups	Macro-themes	Sub-themes
Group 1	1. Certification	Quality and sustainability; role of the certification body; role of the blockchain
	2. Transparency	Company—consumer relationship
	3. Traceability	Tracing
Group 2	4. Communication	Reputation and image
	5. Strategy	
	6. Processes	Supply chain management
Group 3	7. Collaboration	Complexity
	8. Safety	Trust; inalterability of the data; privacy; regulation
	9. Territorial identity	
Group 4	10. Training	Skills; required roles
	11. Dissemination	

5.1 Group 1: Certification, Transparency and Traceability

All the respondents consider essential the registration in the blockchain of only the information validated a priori by a certification body. In their opinion, being *certified* by a third body protects the company from its own responsibility but also protects the consumers.

> [...] there is an impartial entity that testifies, guaranteeing that this data is true. I pay the certification body to attest that my work meets the requirements of the standard for which I certify my work. [...] The certification body acts as my guarantor by promoting its brand. [Respondent 5].

This consideration calls into question the usefulness of blockchain technology as an autonomous and independent certification system in the agro-food supply chain. It is not clear to the interviewees what differences there are between the operation needed for traditional certification and that of the blockchain. In other words, the procedure for blockchain seems almost repetitive.

> All this, however, is already done by certification bodies that check me step by step in this process [...] So it makes no sense to do it twice also because [...] with the blockchain no one is verifying your data; you are the one who in good faith decides to load it into blockchain and then make it unchangeable. [Respondent 1].

With regard to the issue of *transparency*, two very interesting aspects emerge from the analysis: the desire to be completely frank and transparent with the consumers and win him over or allow the consumer himself to easily understand the product he/she is buying. In the first case, the blockchain is seen as a tool that can be used to enhance the reputable image of the company. In the second, the reflection shifts to the opportunity to offer consumers more information and a more interactive, engaging and aware approach in evaluating the products he/she is purchasing. One of the respondents defined this as "consumer empowerment".

> The topic is, as always, consumer empowerment. Do consumers freely choose the product? Are their choices dominated by brands, distribution channels or industries? The blockchain gives power to the consumer and we like it because consumers are able to acquire more information than other certification mechanisms. These latter are usually find on the product labels, but it is not clear what value they give the consumers. [Respondent 3].

As regard *tracing*, certifying the supply chain also means offering the consumer the instruments to go back over the supply chain, even to the raw material. Equal importance is given to both the traceability and the product certification profiles. This is because if there were a problem with the quality/composition/state of the product, it would be crucial to trace it back to its origin. For example, with blockchain, it would be easier to identify a damaged batch number, thus avoiding an enormous waste of resources on the part of the company.

> [...] the person knows where that bottle comes from, otherwise he would only know that it has been certified, namely that it satisfies the certification requirements. [Respondent 7].

5.2 Group 2: Communication, Strategy, and Processes

The internal motivations that drove managers to join the pilot experiments were codified into the following categories: *"Communication"*, *"Strategy"*, *and "Processes"*.

As for the first node, the authors returned to discuss the relationship between company and consumer, recalling the previous *"Transparency"* category. The transparency principle represents the first boundary object between the first two groups of nodes. However, due to the short term of involvement in the pilot project, the companies did not fully discern the effects of the blockchain on consumer engagements. In fact, while the information about values, history and certifications transmitted is considered a guarantee for the consumer, not all have a real usefulness.

The interviewees declared that they would like to use blockchain to improve their company's reputation or visibility on the market, or to access new markets. Visibility in the wine company arena is guaranteed by a good reputation on the market, but also by knowing how to be ahead of competitors. In particular, a higher visibility is required in new and foreign markets, where consumers, unlike the Italians, conceive wine as a luxury products and are willing to pay more. In this more demanding market, a more attentive approach to innovative technology might provide some advantages.

> [...]in my opinion it is first of all something that guarantees the consumer something extra and it can also be used from the marketing point of view ... so the origin of the vineyard, the production and all these things are data that for the consumer become a sort of warranty. [Respondent 7].

From the point of view of supply chain management, respondents stressed the fact that the control procedures have remained unchanged, without any need for reorganization.

We already have the issue of supply chain control with or without blockchain. The agriculture sector is one of the most advanced and experimental. We check all our batches of grapes, wine, and what ends up in every single bottle. These data are on paper. [...] 30 years ago we already had and published this information. [Respondent 4].

5.3   Group 3: Collaboration, Safety, and Territorial Identity

One of the results that pilot companies verified was that involved actors understood the importance of the documentation provided. The authors did not discover any internal resistance or hostility: what was reported was good team spirit and enthusiasm for the experimentation. The link between the second and third group of nodes is therefore the *"collaboration"* between the players operating in the supply chain: better supply chain management depends on the maximum cooperation between the parties involved in every stage of the production chain. However, the extra work required to retrieve precise information about a very long term process was found to be the factor of greatest hostility.

[...]Perhaps it becomes more complicated for those who have lots of actors in the supply chain and therefore when farmers, producers, transformers, bottlers and the distribution crews have to coordinate/cooperate [...]. [Respondent 8].

As regards safety, especially on the non-modifiability of the data, the debate opens about the truthfulness of the recorded data and returns, once again, to the discussion on the central role played by the certification body. When there is no certification body mediation (the self-certification case) the problem exists.

The blockchain guarantees the immutability of information, but not its truthfulness. Truthfulness lies in the common sense of the people who upload and provide real data because in this way they open themselves up. [Respondent 1].

Furthermore, the trust question relies not only on the good faith of those who are uploading data to blockchain, but also on the guarantee of the reliability of a system that, according to most experts, should protect against fraud and counterfeit products. Not all respondents saw the absence of regulation and laws as a limit possibly because they believe that the aspects of traceability and the information that the consumer can actually read from the QR Code scan have a greater weight.

[...] This thing goes beyond any type of regulatory system. [...] with the blockchain the end user is able to realize things that fail with any other certification. [Respondent 3].

A last significant child node concerns the disclosure of more confidential data and hence the management of privacy. In this case, attention is no longer paid to information that intrigues the consumer but rather to what data the company can load without incurring theft (plagiarism) from other competitors.

As regard the territorial identity, this issue is the subject of heated debate between those who support the enhancement of *Made in Italy* and those who do not entirely agree. In favour of the territoriality exaltation, the product geolocation is made visible through the inclusion of maps, satellite photographs and films showing the origin of the bottle of wine in the code on the label.

> [...]Certainly it is a very direct system that shows the consumer the related cultivation and this is very important because from there we can even get the satellite photo. [...]. Compared to what already exists about the territorial identity and the Made in Italy, the blockchain solution provides great results. [Respondent 8].

5.4 Group 4: Training and Dissemination

The collaboration discussed in the previous sub-paragraph is also influenced by the "*Training*" of those who contribute to the development of the supply chain activities. In this case the boundary objects between the third and the fourth group are the two micro-themes "*Skills*" and "*Required Figures*". For this reason, the discussion shifts to the need for trained and experienced figures in the use of advanced technologies. Since both the organization and the supply chain managerial mechanism remain unchanged, the skill required by the pilot companies was the ability to find accurate and precise information. No external staff were hired because consultants had been involved in the implementation of the solution. Many of the respondents felt the need to gain a better understanding of how the technology functions, a greater ability to disseminate the benefits of the blockchain applications to consumers, and the desire to create awareness among other companies in the wine and agro-food industry.

> It is one of those innovative and pioneering technologies. Let me explain... it is a technology that is widely known and used, but in the application of supply chain it is certainly pioneering. [...] So maybe in 10 years time all the products all over the world will come out in blockchain because it will be what the market wants. [Respondent 3].

According to the interviewees, large-scale retailers or government institutions (e.g. Ministry of Agriculture) would undoubtedly promote this new scenario.

5.5 Comparison of Wineries Versus Developers

The issues discussed with the pilot companies were undertaken with the two developer companies (Table 3).

This in-depth analysis aims to allow the technology experts to clarify some aspects neglected in the interviews with the pilot companies. It was decided to compare the two perspectives only on the issues that were defined as *boundary objects*, or the

Table 3 "*Out-of-the sample respondents*" features (authors' elaboration)

Respondent	Position	Project owner
Respondent A	Business developer	Ambrosus
Respondent B	Business analyst	Food chain

link between the four groups of categories already identified and analysed, namely *"Transparency"*, *"Management of the supply chain"* and *"Training"*.

Companies see the principal utility of blockchain in *transparency*: it is perceived as a guarantee for the consumer, the company itself and the territory. Developers, however, consider it to be secondary compared to the management benefits. Contrary to what developers expected, companies did not significantly change any process within their wine *supply chain management*. For both companies and developers, blockchain is seen as a constant traceability guarantee, thanks to the use of a management platform with a friendly-user interface.

> [...] There is a conflict of interest between what the blockchain entails and what the activity is because the blockchain [...] provides more visibility than daily activities. For example, information about the logistics process or company policy can be provided, even if not everyone is obviously willing to give this kind of data to their customers. So if an operator (let's say one in logistic) who tends to have a 1-2% error by not respecting the declared SLAs cannot deal with the blockchain because with the blockchain it becomes very difficult to manipulate this information. [Respondent A].

Training is the only contact point between the two perspectives. Both wineries and developers do not consider it necessary to employ any new IT-oriented staff because the technology is developed by third parties and company workers will have time to learn. Instead, more information on data security and privacy issues should be disclosed.

6 Discussion

The authors have identified which positive factors and limitations experts perceive during the experimentation of blockchain in the wine industry. According to the results of the analysis the two hypotheses formulated above were not proven. A gap was found between what was presented in the scientific literature and the actual state of the art in the context examined. This was further supported by the discordant points of view that emerged during the comparison between companies and developers. The pilot companies seem to have taken into account only the communication aspects linked to marketing and transparency. Empowering the final consumer or providing more in-depth information to gain entrance to new markets is their main goal.

Developers, while confirming the importance of the previous point of view, are more conscious that the real change is in the simplification and efficiency of the business processes that are the basis of the correct development of the supply chain and the improved awareness of the actors involved.

The only contact point seems to be training, which is perceived as the need for greater dissemination and consciousness of what the blockchain is and how it should be implemented. However, some considerations need to be made in favour of the analysis of the pilot companies. Since the projects were carried out on only a small group of wine producers and under a limited period of time, it is too early to observe concrete changes in all the related business processes and, consequently, a tangible evolution in the supply chain function. We do expect that the long-term adoption and spread of the blockchain technology will have a stronger impact in the whole sector.

From the point of view of the consumer no result was found but this may be as a consequence of the time factor required to launch blockchain certified products on the market and understand what the real impact on consumers is. The answers given by the pilot companies to the questions on the topic were based on expectations, hopes and forecasts to be verified, once again, only in the long term. The most evident benefit was the commitment at the organisational and supply chain level to a careful search for the information to be recorded in blockchain. The possibility of tracing the supply chain in detail has also given space to those players such as winemakers whose work seems to stop once the harvest is over.

The perception of greater transparency for consumer protection has also increased. The recording of information validated by a certification body in the first instance has imparted more protection to companies encouraged by the fact that they do not input data directly into the blockchain. A third body does it and usually is accredited and recognized at national and international level (DNV GL in the case of MyStory and Ernst and Young for Wine Blockchain EY). This reduces the autonomous nature of blockchain technology because it is private, and the companies do not have full control of the published data, resulting in the disappearance of two of the main features of the technology, namely decentralization and disintermediation.

The exploratory analysis carried out has some research limitations. Despite a group of sixteen companies participating in the three projects, only seven of them made themselves available for interviews. The small sample on which the qualitative analysis was carried out precludes the possibility of extending the results of the research beyond the boundaries of the sample itself. Finally, the main limitation was the lack of opportunity to also listen to the point of view of the companies that provided the technology in the wine sector, of the EY consulting firm and DNV GL certification body. Being aware of the perspectives of the three organizations, for example, would have provided a deeper understanding of the reasons behind the implementation of a private blockchain solution and a better analysis of the issues of data recording through appropriate platforms created ad hoc. Listening and including the point of view of all the actors involved would have opened up new research paths and other aspects of the subject matter.

References

1. Brody, P. (2017). How blockchain is revolutionizing supply chain management. *D!gitalist Magazine.* http://www.digitalistmag.com/tag/Blockchain-and-supplychain. 28/11/2018 viewed.
2. Cangelosi, G. M. (2019). *In vino veritas? La Blockchain nella filiera vitivinicola italiana* (Master research thesis). University of Trento, Trento, Italy.
3. Morabito, V. (2017). *Business innovation through blockchain: The B. perspective.* Milano: Springer. http://Blockchainstudies.org/files/Morabito.pdf. 23/2/2019 viewed.

4. Wright, A., & De Filippi, P. (2015). Decentralized blockchain technology and the rise of lex cryptographia.
5. Benos, E., Garratt, R., & Gurrola-Perez, P. (2017). *The economics of distributed ledger technology for securities settlement.* https://www.bankofengland.co.uk/-/media/boe/files/working-paper/2017/the129economics-of-distributed-ledger-technology-for-securities-settle ment.pdf. 23/2/2019 viewed.
6. Bellini, M. (2017). *Blockchain per la smart agrifood: EY presenta Wine Blockchain con EZ LAB a difesa del Vino Made in Italy.* Blockchain4innovation. https://www.blockchain4inno vation.it/mercati/agrifood/blockchain-la-smartagrifood-ey-presenta-wine-blockchain-difesa-del-vino-made-italy/. 18/11/ 2018 viewed.
7. Zheng, Z., Shaoan, X., Hongning, D., Xiangping, C., & Huaimin, W. (2017). An overview of blockchain technology: Architecture, consensus, and future trends. In *IEEE 6th International Congress on Big Data,* (pp. 557–564). IEEE, Honolulu, HI, USA.
8. Abeyratne, S. A., & Monfared, R. (2016). Blockchain ready manufacturing supply chain using distributed ledger. *International Journal of Research in Engineering and Technology, 5*(9), 1–10.
9. Francisco, K., & Swanson, D. (2018). The supply chain has no clothes: Technology adoption of blockchain for supply chain transparency. *Logistics, 2*(1), 1–13.
10. Christidis, K., & Devetsikiotis, M. (2016). Blockchains and smart contracts for the internet of things. *IEEE Access, 4,* 2292–2303.
11. Zyskind, G., & Nathan, O. (2015). Decentralizing privacy: Using blockchain to protect personal data. In *2015 IEEE Security and Privacy Workshops,* (pp. 180–184). IEEE, The Fairmont, San Jose, CA.
12. Lin, I.-C., & Liao, T.-C. (2017). A survey of blockchain security issues and challenges. *IJ Network Security, 19*(5), 653–659.
13. Reyna, A., Martín, C., Chen, J., Soler, E., & Díaz, M. (2018). On blockchain and its integration with IoT. Challenges and opportunities. *Future Generation Computer Systems, 88,* 173–190.
14. Rodrigo, M. N. N., Perera, S., Senaratne, S., & Jin, X. (2018). Blockchain for construction supply chains: A literature synthesis. In *Proceedings of the 11th International Cost Engineering Council (ICEC) World Congress & the 22nd Annual Pacific Association of Quantity Surveyors Conference,* (pp. 18–20). Sydney, Australia.
15. Vukolić, M. (2017, April). Rethinking permissioned blockchains. In *Proceedings of the ACM Workshop on Blockchain, Cryptocurrencies and Contracts,* (pp. 3–7). ACM.
16. Beck, R., & Müller-Bloch, C. (2017). Blockchain as radical innovation: a framework for engaging with distributed ledgers as incumbent organization. In *Proceedings of the 50th Hawaii International Conference on System Sciences* (pp. 5390–5399). Hilton Waikoloa Village, Hawaii.
17. Faioli, M., Petrilli, E., & Faioli, D. (2016). Blockchain, contratti e lavoro. La ri-rivoluzione del digitale nel mondo produttivo e nella PA. *Economia & lavoro, 50*(2), 139–158.
18. Atzori, M. (2015). Tecnologia Blockchain E Governance Decentralizzata: Lo Stato È Ancora Necessario? (Blockchain technology and decentralized governance: Is the state still necessary?). *Blockchain technology and decentralized governance: Is the state still necessary.*
19. EUIPO. (2016). *Il costo economico della violazione dei diritti di proprietà intellettuale nel settore degli alcolici e dei vini.* Alicante, Spagna. https://euipo.europa.eu/tunnel-web/secure/webdav/guest/document_library/observatory/resources/research-and-studies/ip_infringem ent/study8/wines_and_spirits_it.pdf. 12/5/2019 viewed.
20. Cisco. (2017). *Ricerca Cisco—Digital transformation Institute: il settore agroalimentare Italiano deve prendere il treno della digitalizzazione adesso.* Cisco. Disponibile da https://www.cisco.com/c/it_it/about/news/2017-archive/20170504.html. 20/2/2019 viewed.
21. Biswas, K., Muthukkumarasamy, V., & Lum, W. (2017). Blockchain based wine supply chain traceability system. In *Future Technologies Conference,* (pp. 1–7). Vancouver, BC, Canada.

Digital Competences for Civil Servants and Digital Ecosystems for More Effective Working Processes in Public Organizations

Nunzio Casalino, Tommaso Saso, Barbara Borin, Enrica Massella, and Flavia Lancioni

Abstract Advancements in digital transformation, artificial intelligence, cloud computing, the Internet of Things (IoT), block-chain, big data, smart-working, information systems' interoperability, etc. are changing the nature of the link between technology and employment in public sector. There is the potential that these changes could bring also benefits beyond labour substitution, including higher levels of output, better quality, and fewer errors that are achievable through automation. The increasing introduction of automation and other digital technologies in public organizations means information systems could progressively substituting traditional outdated workers in performing routine, codifiable tasks while at the same time amplifying the productivity of workers in supplying problem solving skills and adaptability. In a specific report of 2018 PwC calculated that 5.1 million jobs, or 44%, were at risk of digital disruption. A digital workplace value chain has becoming a revolutionary and dominant part of the world economy. Each stage can occur in different countries and under different regulatory conditions and be implemented wherever the necessary skills and materials are available at competitive cost and quality. Digital transformation itself should not be seen as a negative for the workforce. If adopted successfully and combined with successful organisational change and change management practices, they can help public organizations to be able to achieve and became more

N. Casalino (✉) · T. Saso
Guglielmo Marconi University, Via Plinio 44, 00193 Rome, Italy
e-mail: n.casalino@unimarconi.it

T. Saso
e-mail: t.saso@unimarconi.it

B. Borin
LUISS Guido Carli, Viale Pola 12, 00198 Rome, Italy
e-mail: bborin@luiss.it

E. Massella
AgID—Agenzia per l'Italia Digitale, Via Liszt 21, 00144 Rome, Italy
e-mail: massella@agid.gov.it

F. Lancioni
SAS Italy, Public Sector, via Darwin 20/22, 20143 Milan, Italy
e-mail: flavia.lancioni@sas.com

© The Editor(s) (if applicable) and The Author(s), under exclusive license to Springer Nature Switzerland AG 2020
R. Agrifoglio et al. (eds.), *Digital Business Transformation*, Lecture Notes in Information Systems and Organisation 38, https://doi.org/10.1007/978-3-030-47355-6_21

competitive. This article aims to describe the main goals and the preliminary results of a research that aims at analysing the digital technologies adoption rate in the European public sector, in order to assess also the motivations about the adoption as well as the no-adoption decision, the kind of technologies principally actually adopted inside public organizations and the activities of value chains where the new investments in these new technologies are focused.

Keywords Digital competencies · Digital public organizations · Civil servants · Digital ecosystems

1   Introduction

Digital transformation is becoming a key element of working procedures improvement and there is a direct relationship between technological innovations and methods for managing digital working processes and integrated digital working systems. Besides several public organizations in their value chain lack seriously the capacity to develop specific education programmes on their own. The European training curricula in the public sector need to adapt these innovative requirements in effective changes to be able to train concretely the labour force. With our DigiWork research we aim to identify the key skills required to create a qualified workforce that digital transformation demands and to allow to equip the civil servants' workforce with suitable skills and competences. The target groups of the research are the civil servants, decision-makers, policymakers involved in public organizations. The European industrial and services organizations require also the raising of awareness and transfer of know-how in order the extend the implementations of new products and services, supporting individuals in acquiring and developing specific skills and key competences. Both the OECD and the European Commission are now recommending a turning point. The digitalization government is not only a process reengineering through technology or moving services online, but an in-depth digital transformation of all workplaces, a transformation that requires the early integration of digital technologies into services and in the decision-making processes [1]. It is time to prepare in the right way people to fully adopt the operational model of the networked digital age so that it could increase efficiency and productivity, establishing new working opportunities for EU citizens and enterprises.

The main three topics addressed by the research are:

- ICT—new technologies—digital competences;
- New innovative curricula/educational methods/development of training courses;
- Open and distance learning available platforms.

So, the urgent need is to transfer to civil servants all the needed contents on digitalization and also Industry 4.0 pillars, their implementations in the services sectors, and what operational changes have to be considered. The DigiWork research is focusing on the new digital production approaches that are starting to be adopted in European market following the OECD recommendations, the EU's strategy for e-Skills in the twenty-first century and several European Commission Directives, which imply a real digital revolution in processes and competences.

Digital competencies cannot be easily defined because of the changing nature of the phenomenon [2].

Innovative digital ecosystems will impact on public ecosystems, designating a link between physical assets and online business. It will be required the integration of the ICT technologies, digitalization of workflows and innovative production systems within a network with suppliers and the application of new technologies and methods in various technical levels and systemic effects. Industry 4.0 knowledge will imply low cost, space saving, low heat producing and high safety devices, operating tools and software systems. It will also involve a network among different facilities for information and data exchange. This new concept of facilities is requiring highly qualified profiles, especially on advanced digital skills, problem solving, complex decision-making, etc. So more qualified workforce is required in public organizations at national and local level [3]. It is needed in EU a specific curriculum and, most of all, a free course to improve specific and transversal skills for civil servants. So, we are identifying a data analysis technique for our quantitative and qualitative research, discussing the interpretation of findings using multiple data sources. The research is involving several public administrations, but also other stakeholders as professionals, industrial organisations, citizens and no-profit associations. All of them will carry out surveys to assess the situation and contribute to the reporting of the research results. We are considering also the AgID—Presidenza del Consiglio dei Ministri knowledge base and specific experience analysing its recent strategic digitalization governmental guidelines (2017, 2018 and 2019 years) as the "Plan for the Digital Transformation of Italy", the "Cloud computing guidelines", "The e-payment system PagoPA", the "Italian Digital Agenda" connected to the "European Digital Agenda", etc., giving a solid contribution to support the research and define the right methodology of analysis.

2 Digital Competencies Priorities in Public Sector at National and Local Level

Digital technologies are transforming society and the economy faster and in new ways, generating outcomes that are irreversible and unstoppable; social media, wearable devices, cloud computing, blockchain, sensors, big data, artificial intelligence will change the work processes and the interaction between citizens, enterprises and institutions. Professionals, enterprises and citizens require sophisticated, personalized, on-demand services, easy to use and accessible. As pointed out by OECD (Organization for Economic Cooperation and Development), the EU eGovernment Action Plan 2016–2020, several EU Directives and Regulations, the on-demand digital economy represents a challenge for private and public organizations. Digital transformation is crucial to the growth, the development and the competitiveness of the EU and its market. This implies a more and more urgent need of cross-sectorial advanced competencies that will enable people and enterprises to compete at a satisfactory level [4]. In particular, digital transformation involves the public sector bringing about deep changes in the strategies, processes, and practices of production and at the workplace. The DigiWork research is focusing on the new digital production approaches and online services delivering that are starting to be adopted in European market following the European Digital Agenda recommendations and the Industry 4.0 pillars, which imply a real digital revolution in processes and operative working competencies. The term Industry 4.0 implies concretely new production concepts in an innovative digital ecosystem, which involves the use of digital technologies, designating a link between physical assets and a "virtual" enterprise. Digital transformation requires the integration of the ICT technologies, the fully digitalization of workflows and innovative production systems within a network of suppliers together the application of new technologies and methods in various technical levels and systemic effects. The working and production systems will imply low cost, space saving, low heat producing and high safety devices, operational tools and smart software systems. It will also involve a network among different facilities for information and data exchange. This new concept of digital facilities will require profiles of highly qualified personnel, especially in ICT but also in interdisciplinary activities, problem solving, complex decision-making skills, etc. Taking in account also the DigCompOrg framework (see Fig. 1) that includes seven key macro elements and fifteen sub-elements that are common to all education sectors, the research is evidencing that it is needed in public sector a specific curriculum and, most of all, to improve specific and transversal skills on digitalization of working processes and information systems.

Collecting the acquired feedbacks and including all specific analysis, DigiWork research is identifying innovative training modules on the following topics: disruptive technologies enabling digitization of the public organizations; managing digitalization; digital integration with physical production assets; rethinking the design of classical production systems; manage, integrate, and analyse data inside and between organizations; business data evaluation and big data management; Internet of Things; document management systems and digitization of workflows; human machine interaction, touch interfaces and accessible GUIs; virtual and augmented reality; environmental impact of production systems; smart factories. The training curricula in the public context need to adapt these innovative requirements in effective digital skills [5] to be able to train concretely the labour force. With DigiWork the determination of key competences required to create the qualified workforce that the digital transformation demands and concretely contributing to train the workforce equipped with suitable skills and competences is being targeted. The European public organizations are requiring also the raising of awareness and transfer of know-how [6] in order the extend the implementations in a wider way. Digitalization influences mission-critical applications in B2G and B2B processes and it is expected a transformation also in companies long investment cycles, giving to EU people new employability opportunities. So DigiWork research is giving an advanced contribution by researches, reports,

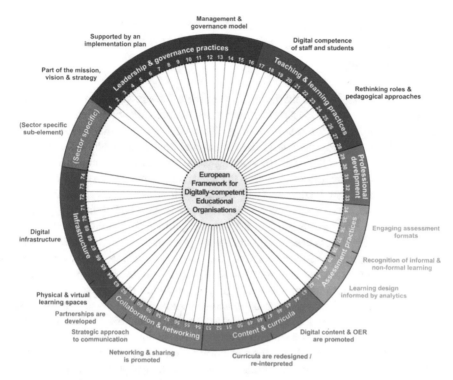

Fig. 1 The European framework for digitally competent organizations, DigCompOrg, JRC Science Hub, European Commission, 2015

sharing good practices, making sectoral analysis and defining the most innovative educational digital needs, working in close cooperation with the main institutions and associations. Digital economy will be central for the growth, the development and the competitiveness of Europe and its economy. It generates turnover of more than 7 billion, accounts for 15.5% of the total Added Value, purchases more than €5400 billion in goods and services each year, and still employs 14.2% of the total workforce. Likewise, public sector has a significant weight in EU economy with a 49.4% share and a total of more than 340 billion of euro. For this reason, Digi-Work research could create an international synergy to integrate the actual European limited open knowledge and experiences, sharing them and creating effective models that will give benefits for the employability of thousands and thousands of people in Europe. It could have a concrete impact at European level to contribute to the development of the economy and the job market, by sharing the most innovative training contents and preparing the European public workforce to the opportunities of the digital change.

3 New Digital Work-Based Skills for Operational Workflows, Administrative Processes and Integrated Ecosystems

In the recent years, EU job market is undergoing a transformation that concerns a full digitalization of working processes. Smart technologies, blockchain, big data and cloud-computing, Internet of Things (IoT), augmented reality are some new technologies are driving the rise of the new digital industrial revolution, known as Industry 4.0. A greater flexibility of working processes and a greater attention to the customers/citizens are necessary to face the increasing complexity. Recent literature [7, 8] shows that new technologies of Industry 4.0 allow organizations reaching such results and, specifically, achieving higher efficiency and productivity rates, quickly customized products and time to market responses. To support the new digital challenges, policymakers in several countries are planning a research and technology agenda as also provided in a well know study made by OECD—Organisation for Economic Cooperation and Development regarding the civil servants (see Fig. 2).

In business operational processes, digitalization refers to enabling, improving and/or transforming business operations and/or business functions and/or business models/processes and/or activities, by leveraging digital technologies and a broader use and context of digitized data, turned into actionable, knowledge, with a specific benefit in mind. It requires digitization of information, but it means more and at the very center of it is data. While digitization is more about systems of record and, increasingly systems of engagement, digitalization is about systems of engagement and systems of insight, leveraging digitized data and processes.

The research is based on a needs' assessment, baseline surveys and situational analyses, collecting qualitative and quantitative data by the evidence-based decision-making and programmatic learning methodologies. It is also evaluating the role of public development policies at EU level in supporting Member States as regards the transformation required to connect digital technologies with products and services [9]. Then it is looking into the details of relevant digital transformation and Industry 4.0 aspects, considering three key dimensions of change that we are exploring: technological, social and the business paradigm.

Finally, the policy implications will be outlined and effective recommendations for public decisions making will be also made. An analysis of the main kinds of production establishments (for example the concrete adoption of lean methods for traditional or online services) will permit to evidence how it is possible to increase efficiency by up to 50%. If public bodies will adopt digitization processes, there is a further margin gain of up to 30%. The research is demonstrating how digitalization can be the way to detect and measure processes data, providing information and allowing to direct events on the production line in real time. It is demonstrating that expected big investments are not needed, but the organization [10] and mentality of civil servants must be changed.

A scientific methodological analysis has been held to analyse and discuss the more updated training gaps and determine how to carry out them, obtaining the best

Fig. 2 Skills for high performing civil services, OECD—organisation for economic cooperation and development public governance review, 2016

impact and taking un account the national regulations in each country. After that the research is determining and will propose the key and transversal competences, the requirements for adaptation in training programs, the required sources and the new training needs. The research is identifying the new digital work-based training for operational workflows, administrative processes and integrated ecosystems, together the determination of key competences (including vocational competences). Will be also considered transversal competences for various vocational qualifications and levels, and that will have an impact on the training programmes, arrangement and procurement of the required equipment infrastructure or human resources.

4   Skills Gaps Analysis and Curriculum Design

The adopted methodology for curriculum development is giving several information takings in account an innovative focused user-oriented approach [11] respecting the following teaching primary principles:

1. to customize the training process, allowing learning to be adapted to the emergent opportunities, characteristics and interests of each individual, so that the learner himself become the manager of the learning process, thanks to a modular structure of the training tools;
2. to enrich the training program with any valuable contribution from the single Partners;
3. to promote the ability to apply the proposed contents, so that learners involved in the training process can achieve immediate results in their practice;
4. to carry out a critical analysis to respond to emerging needs. It will include also the results of the preliminary mapping of the existing knowledge in the public field (articles, existing learning contents, scientific studies, economic and social analysis, main implementation models, sector's studies, previous projects, statistics, etc.) and of models, etc.

It is including the relevant networks and stakeholders linked to the DigiWork research target groups. The adopted methodology is including several fields and the most relevant are:

- the state of the art of digitalization and innovative automation practices;
- a context analysis of the innovation in digitalization practices;
- an adaptation of the requirements to the research target groups features and needs;
- the best practices individuation, recognizing almost 5 successfully technology cases and related digitalization practices in public organizations.

The actual educational profile for a typical digital transformation expert or worker still needs to be developed and updated. Digitalization requires substantially not only operational capabilities, but also must encompass ICT and managerial capabilities being able to see the organization as a whole, understand industry, and how different industries interrelate in terms of value chains and other processes, communication skills and customer skills. It is not just a question of training a digital civil servant.

We also identified some auxiliary components to improve the needed training activities. In particular:

- Multimedia tutorial, that will introduce the participants to the training activities;
- Data and report about context analysis and needs;
- Map of the transversal and distinctive competencies (attitudes, comportments, skills, abilities and knowledge) related the fields of digitalization, innovation trends, lean processes and managerial practices to develop the right change management;
- Skills assessment tools to evaluate the initial know-how of the civil servants and the knowledge acquired;

- Case studies and best practices;
- Skills assessments to evaluate the know-how or gaps of the civil servants.

All of them include all feedbacks from the previous analysis by a participative design approach [12] with all stakeholders.

A data base of questions has been set considering the main trend of conceptual, applied and operational aspects available in workplace digitalization, workflow management, transparency of processes [13, 14], innovative online service delivering.

Taking in account the preliminary collected feedbacks we identified several learning topics and decided to evidence 18 of them. In detail:

1. Disruptive technologies enabling digitization in operational processes. The general analysis of innovation and disruption paradigms in operational processes is a cornerstone of digital transformation.
2. Governance of the digitalization in the public sector. The digital transformation is a complex, multi-faceted process that involves every sector-specific knowledge field, and thus requires a strong commitment in governance and management.
3. Digital integration for production assets and online services. Consolidation of physical assets through digital assets and smart contract allows automatic asset management.
4. Document management systems and digitization of workflow. Integration of traditional workflows in novel digital paradigms allows a gradual introduction of disruptive technologies whilst safeguarding foregoing investments.
5. Rethinking the design of classical information systems. Information architectures are moving toward a more and more decentralized configuration: cloud computing, edge computing, distributed ledger technologies.
6. Managing, integrating, and analysing data inside and between organizations. The analysis of data, both those produced by an organization and those produced by its environment, is vital in order to gain a proper knowledge of a world that is becoming more and more complex.
7. Business data evaluation and big data management. The sheer volume of data produced by mankind is exponentially increasing, in each of 5 basic dimensions: volume, velocity, variety, variability, and value. A successful approach to big data requires good processes and adequate investments.
8. Internet of Things. IoT is the extension of internet connectivity to physical devices and everyday objects. In combination with advanced connectivity (5G) and smart computing technologies (AI, DLT), IoT is vital in building a fully digital-enabled environment.
9. Human machine interaction, touch interfaces and accessible GUIs. Human machine interaction and advanced interfaces are essential to improve accessibility and usability of digital devices.
10. Virtual and augmented reality. Virtual reality and augmented reality (which is a way of "enriching" reality by superimposing to it computer-generated imagery) allow for advanced interaction with machines and products, allowing e.g. remote operation in dangerous or small-scale production environments.

11. Additive manufacturing. Additive manufacturing describes technologies that build 3D objects by adding layer-upon-layer of material (useful especially for hospitals and other health organizations). In particular, it encompasses technologies including subsets as 3D Printing, Rapid Prototyping (RP), Direct Digital Manufacturing (DDM), layered manufacturing and additive fabrication.

12. Advanced robotics and human-robot collaboration. New models of human-machine interaction are essential to increase efficiency and quality of information systems.

13. Energy savings and environmental impact of production systems. Measuring environmental impact of digital system is essential in everyday operations and performance evaluation.

14. Digital inefficiencies and risks in professionals' environments. Risk mitigation and reduction of inefficiencies must be included from day zero in digital integration projects.

15. Automation systems integration and smart factories. Through the identification of main smart approaches, integrators can now show how solutions directly impact the bottom line to help civil servants to achieve business goals—especially those related to safety, profitability, security, reliability, and productivity.

16. Data protection and privacy in public organizations. EU data protection rules (such as also GDPR) guarantee the protection of personal data whenever they are collected and apply to both companies and organizations in the EU and those based outside the EU who offer goods or services in the EU. It is vital to implement privacy by design in all digital processes and products, bearing in mind that rules can be not only a constraint, but also an opportunity.

17. Artificial intelligence and expert systems. AI and expert systems are more and more crucial in coping with advanced needs from customers and from the market itself. AI is becoming the dominant digital technology through its extreme flexibility.

18. Supply chain certification and automatic process verification/accountability. Distributed ledger technologies and smart contracts make it possible to implement traceability, certification and accountability throughout a supply or production chain.

5 Conclusions

Digital transformation and Industry 4.0 pillars are a new phenomenon aimed at changing operational rules especially for the public. The peculiar feature of this revolution is its higher degree of complexity compared to the previous ones. Essentially, digital transformation considers the usage of new technologies with the aim to integrate workers and machines across organizational boundaries to form a new type of networked value chain. Organizations implement three-types of integrations: horizontal, vertical and end-to-end integration, which allow them to improve the efficiency of production processes and maximize the customization of services. The EU's eGovernment Action Plan 2016–2020 "Accelerating the digital transformation of government" and "EU's strategy for e-Skills in the twenty-first century" set an ambitious target for all Member States. By 2020, public institutions and private organizations should be efficient and inclusive, providing borderless, transparent, personalized, user-friendly digital services [15]. But real innovative skills need to be acquired by workers of public sector, applying them to design products and deliver better services for the EU citizens, professionals and entrepreneurs. The DigiWork research is making an in depth analysis on the main pillars and grounds of the mix of digitalization and business processes (e.g. lean production, Internet of Things, Internet of Services, blockchain, smart factories, smart-working, coding, information systems integration, interoperability, etc.) and newly emerging requirements especially for different public organizations such as digital work-flow technologies.

The DigiWork research is focusing on the new digital working approaches that will be more and more needed in Europe and that imply a real digital revolution in processes management and competences. Digitalization implies also new working concepts based on the adoption of innovative digital ecosystems which will involve all the most recent digital factors and expertise. The real and the virtual business contexts will be seamlessly connected giving rise to what are known as digital integrated systems. It will be required the integration of devices and online working tools, the digitalization of workflows and several innovative production systems within a network of suppliers together the application of new operational activities and methods in various technical levels. Digitalization will also consider the strong relations among different facilities for information and data valorisation. This new concept of advanced organization will require highly qualified profiles and more qualified workforce to cover the requirements of new digital jobs. Digitisation, archiving and electronic management of documents are having also a deep impact on business practices in companies and public institutions. In this sense, digital transformation and the consequent reorganisation of business work is certainly a central point. So, there is the need in EU of a specific open curriculum to improve specific and transversal skills for civil servants. The training curricula needs to adapt these requirements in effective changes to be able to train concretely the labour force. With DigiWork the determination of key competences required to create the qualified workforce that the digitalization demands in the advanced business process and concretely contributing to train the workforce, with suitable skills and competences, is being targeted. DigiWork could give a contribution in researches, reports, sharing good practices, making sectoral analysis and defining the most innovative educational digital needs, working in close cooperation with the main institutions and associations. The urgent need is to learn more about the concepts of digitalization, its implementations in public sector, and what changes this will bring for the future. So DigiWork could create an international synergy to integrate the actual EU limited open knowledge and experience, sharing it and creating effective results that will give a benefit for the employability of thousands and thousands of people in Europe. It is expected to create an impact on EU level to contribute to the labour force development of EU by sharing the outputs and each time adding on the previous studies to prepare the future changes [16]. The European public sector is requiring the raising of awareness and transfer of know-how in order the extend its effectiveness. Digitalization influences mission-critical applications in B2G and B2B processes and citizens are waiting and need of a public organizations real transformation to receive effective public services.

References

1. Hague, C., & Williamson, B. (2009). *Digital participation, digital literacy, and school subjects: A review of the policies, literature and evidence.* Futurelab.
2. Dawes, S. (2009). Governance in the digital age: A research and action framework for an uncertain future. *Government Information Quarterly, 26*(2), 257–264.
3. Parks, W. (1957). The open government principle: Applying the right to know under the constitution. *The George Washington Law Review, 26*(1), 1–22.
4. Rose-Ackerman, S. (2008). Corruption and government. *International Peacekeeping, 15*(3), 328–343.
5. Ciborra, C. (2005). Interpreting e-government and development: Efficiency, transparency or governance at a distance? *Information Technology & People, 8*(3), 260–279.
6. Lee, G., & Kwak, Y. H. (2011). *An open government implementation model, using technology series.* Washington.
7. Chun, S. A., Shulman, S., Sandoval, R., & Hovy, E. (2010). Government 2.0: Making connections between citizens, data and government, *Information Polity, 15*, 1–9.
8. Dawes, S. S. (2010). Stewardship and usefulness: Policy principles for information-based transparency. *Government Information Quarterly, 27*(4), 377–383.
9. Casalino, N., Armenia, S., Medaglia, C., & Rori, S. (2010). *A new system dynamics model to improve internal and external efficiency in the paper digitization of Italian Public Administrations.* Roma: European Academy of Management, EURAM 2010.
10. Yin, R. K. (2003). *Case study research: Design and methods.* California: Sage Publications.
11. Casalino, N., Capriglione, A., & Mauro, D. (2012). A knowledge management system to promote and support open government. WOA 2012, Verona University.
12. Darbishire, H.: *Proactive transparency: The future of the right to information? A review of standards, challenges, and opportunities* (pp. 1–60). Washington, MA: WBI.
13. Winner, M. A. (2002). Integrated service modelling for online one-stop government, *12*(3), 149–156.
14. Casalino, N. (2008). *Gestione del cambiamento e produttività nelle aziende pubbliche.* Cacucci, Bari: Metodi e strumenti innovativi.
15. Fukuyama, F. (2005). Global corruption report: Corruption in construction and post-conflict reconstruction, transparency international. Auflage.
16. Sorrentino, M., & De Marco, M. (2010). Evaluating E-government implementation. Opening the interdisciplinary door. In H. J. Scholl (Ed.), *E-Government: Information, technology, and transformation* (Vol. 17, pp. 72–88). Armonk, NY: M.E. Sharpe.

Author Index

Printed in the United States
By Bookmasters